Native Apostles

NATIVE APOSTLES

*Black and Indian Missionaries in the
British Atlantic World*

EDWARD E. ANDREWS

Harvard University Press
Cambridge, Massachusetts, and London, England
2013

Library of Congress Cataloging-in-Publication Data

Andrews, Edward E., 1979–
  Native apostles : Black and Indian missionaries in the British Atlantic world /
Edward E. Andrews.
    p. cm.
  Includes bibliographical references (p.   ) and index.
  ISBN 978-0-674-07246-6
  1. Missions—History. 2. Indigenous peoples. 3.Missionaries. 4. African
American missionaries. 5. British—Atlantic Ocean Region—History. 6. United
States—History—Colonial period, ca. 1600–1775. 7. Great Britain—Colonies—
America—History. I. Title.
  BV2120.A53 2013
  266.0089'960171241—dc23   2012034736

For Mary

Contents

Illustrations

Introduction

ON THE ELEVENTH DAY of March in 1779, a former slave who became a converted Christian petitioned the Bishop of London to ordain him as an Anglican missionary. The applicant hoped to return to Africa to spread the gospel, as he said, "amongst my countrymen." His letter outlined his missionary credentials carefully, asserting that he was a faithful adherent to the Anglican Church and vowing that his only motive for requesting this post was so that he "may be a means, under God, of reforming his countrymen and persuading them to embrace the Christian religion." He explained that he was moved not only by a sincere Christian zeal, but also by the gains that other nations, especially the Portuguese and the Dutch, had made after training native Africans for missionary work. Both of those nations encouraged the rise of a black evangelical corps in West Africa and, as the applicant noted, the new evangelists were clearly "more proper than European clergymen," who were "unacquainted with the language and customs of the country."[1]

Matthias MacNamara, the man's employer and one who persuaded him to request Anglican ordination, drew upon seven years of experience as governor in West Africa to draft a supporting letter. MacNamara suggested that the Anglicans' own history of using black ministers should convince the Bishop of London to ordain this son of Africa. He boasted that he was personally acquainted with Philip Quaque, an African Anglican missionary stationed at Cape Coast Castle, whom he described as a "very respectable character." MacNamara, like the black applicant, said all the right things. He emphasized evangelical competition with rival powers, appealed to the successes that those powers had in training African missionaries, invoked Philip Quaque's missionary efforts on the Cape Coast, and outlined the linguistic and cultural advantages of African preachers over European ones. And yet, the Bishop of London coolly responded that he and other Anglican Bishops were "not of opinion of sending a new missionary to Africa."[2]

The disappointed applicant's name was Olaudah Equiano. A "self-made man" who gained renown as a slave, sailor, transatlantic traveler, famous autobiographer, and celebrated abolitionist, Equiano was also an aspiring native missionary.[3] His rejection might suggest that the Bishop of London had simply denied the petition because of the applicant's race. Equiano's identity might have played a role, but his rejection was more likely the result of Equiano's lack of formal Anglican training, the ongoing tumult of the American Revolution, and the fact that MacNamara had recently been dismissed from his position in Africa due to illegal trading and illicit activities. While the comparison with Philip Quaque might have seemed apt, Quaque spent a decade of his most formative years under Anglican tutorship in England. One could not simply ask for ordination and receive it. Anglicans believed that ordination, like conversion, was a long process, one that took years of training, biblical study, contemplation, and preparation. Furthermore, Philip Quaque's mission to West Africa had been far from a glorious success, so if Equiano and MacNamara were looking for a positive black role model, they probably chose the wrong one.

The Bishop's rejection of Equiano's application was, in some ways, also a rejection of generations of missionary experience in the British Atlantic world. As a person of African descent aspiring to preach among Africans, Equiano was certainly not alone. He was but one of the hundreds of African, Afro-American, and Native American missionaries who sought to evangelize blacks and Indians throughout the British Atlantic world during the seventeenth and eighteenth centuries. These "native" missionaries were not necessarily native to the land, but rather they generally came from the same population as their potential converts. In spite of their ubiquity, they have remained barely visible, and we know very little about them. We do know that, by the nineteenth century, as many as 85% of the people working in British missions were not actually British.[4] In the Travancore state of southern India during the turn of the twentieth century, for example, fifty European missionaries were stationed among 882 native ones. The Church Missionary Society recorded that it employed about 360 native teachers in their North Pacific Island missions in the last few decades of the nineteenth century, and the

Methodists listed about 635 native preachers at the same place and time. Nearly 900 native missionaries left Fiji, Somoa, the Cook Islands, the Solomon Islands, and Tonga to act as evangelists on other Pacific Islands in the late nineteenth and early twentieth centuries. Historians of later missions have recognized the importance of native preachers to the development of Christian evangelical enterprises in America's Great Plains, Africa, Asia, and elsewhere.[5] Historians of the early modern

Olaudah Equiano. (Image courtesy of the John Carter Brown Library at Brown University.)

Atlantic, however, have not followed suit. Although we have a handful of studies of some of the most celebrated indigenous missionaries, such as the famous Mohegan Indian Samson Occom, no one has explained how native Christian preachers as a whole fit into the larger debate over race and the future of Indians and Africans in Western Christendom.[6] Perhaps most importantly, no one has yet applied a transatlantic approach to these missionaries. Native preachers, who could be found from New England to the Caribbean, the Carolinas to Africa, and even Iroquoia to India, became vital participants in an increasingly expansive Protestant missionary effort.

Equiano's attempt to evangelize West Africa was part of a larger story of Native Americans, blacks, and Africans attempting to Christianize their communities. During a period characterized by Native American dispossession, the expansion of the transatlantic slave trade, the institutionalization of racial slavery, and the creation of a scientific understanding of race itself, Anglo-American missionary groups invested a tremendous amount of time, effort, money, and spiritual authority into hundreds of Indians and blacks in the hope that they would be the means whereby the Atlantic world would be converted to Christianity. Why they did this and what these native preachers meant for the development of indigenous Christianities and for the relationships between such diverse peoples is an untold story that helps explain how colonized peoples responded to, rejected, shaped, and appropriated Christianity. Native missionaries, in other words, were at the very core of these cultural exchanges.

The seventeenth and eighteenth centuries represented a decisive period for the development of English and, later, British missions. The Columbian "discovery" of the New World tied Europe, the Americas, and Africa into a tighter economic and imperial integration, but every European power also wrestled with the religious questions that European expansion exposed. The Spanish, for example, witnessed a heated debate in the middle of the sixteenth century which pitted those who argued for more benevolent treatment of potential Indian converts against those who contended that Indians were natural slaves who were born to be imperial subjects. Many Europeans saw economic and political opportunity in European expansion, but missionaries viewed it as a chance to convert the world and unite it under one banner of Christianity. They agreed on the totalizing and homogenizing effects of Christian conversion even as the diversity of Christianity itself undermined that ideal.

At the same time, Africans and indigenous Americans were forced to confront both the challenges and potential benefits of evangelization, and recent studies have creatively explored how both blacks and Indians approached Christian missionaries. Naturally, their responses were as diverse as the peoples themselves. Some rejected Christianity wholesale, others "converted" (certainly a loaded term, since people then and since have defined it differently) to gain political favor with the colonizers, and still others fused Christianity with their existing spiritual ideas, traditions, and rituals.[7] So, the religious encounters between Europeans, Africans, and Native Americans in the early modern British Atlantic offered *both* budding opportunities *and* unprecedented challenges for all groups involved. This complexity underscores the point that missionaries, especially native ones, cannot simply be lumped into the binary categories of compassionate martyr versus avaricious imperialist. Missionaries represented a panoply of reactions to these religious exchanges, and black and Indian evangelists did what they did for different reasons, at different times, and in different ways. The result was a complex spiritual pastiche, an early modern babble of tongues that spoke to the problems of racial and religious encounter during a period of vigorous colonization.

Indigenous evangelists believed they had access to spiritual power, but their roles as native preachers often left them abysmally poor, socially ostracized, psychologically depressed, and spiritually anxious. Many lived, worked, and died in social isolation, and the letters we have from them reflect a genuine concern for the souls of the people they were trying to save as well as their own. At the same time, their position as cultural intermediaries gave them unique opportunities to challenge colonialism, situate indigenous peoples into a longer history of Christianity, and harness scripture as a rhetorical weapon to secure a place for themselves and their people.

Not all indigenous evangelists were hired by Anglo-American missionary organizations. Although we can only trace the indigenous preachers that left behind some sort of documentary trail, there were probably dozens, if not hundreds, of other Native Americans and Afro-Americans who preached on their own. A fair percentage of these spiritual leaders, in fact, may have been women. Their actions as evangelists were rejected by white missionaries who denied women the authority to preach in their own congregations. Protestant missionaries understood women's roles to be domestic and exemplary. They were to raise good Christian children and, through that act, serve as paragons of Christian virtue for other women. Exhortation, in other words, was not intended to be their lot, at least not until British missionary societies started actively employing them in the nineteenth and twentieth centuries. And yet, women often had important spiritual roles in both indigenous American and African societies, and have historically been vital to the development of Christianity among non-Europeans. Even though they are largely absent in most of the surviving documentation, women were likely to be more important than the historical record reveals.

In spite of these challenges, the evidence for most native preachers is more robust than we might expect. Theologians, ministers, and missionaries (white as well as black and Indian) were among the most literate and conversant of all Atlantic world characters. Missionaries left an enormous documentary trail of both published and manuscript sources that chart the role that native evangelists played in the cultural exchanges between Europeans, Africans, and indigenous Americans. Because most Anglo-American missionary history has often sought to elevate or vilify white missionaries, the role of indigenous peoples has usually been relegated to the background. But it was rarely erased. Instead, the stories, choices, and experiences of native evangelists are often deeply embedded in the manuscript and printed texts that were left behind. Although missionary sources are mediated, formulaic, and problematic, they still—when used cautiously and when cross-referenced with other sources—provide a wealth of information about religious exchange in the early modern era.

At the same time, there is a surprising body of material on native Christians produced by their own hands. One could even make the argument that Christianized Indians and blacks were the most literate individuals from their respective groups, thus giving us precious opportunities to understand them more thoroughly. Philip Quaque, an Anglican African missionary, as mentioned previously, wrote several dozen letters—totaling nearly 200 pages—that record his mission to West Africans for over half a century. Algonquian Indian missionaries wrote hundreds of letters, sermons, and diary entries, and their mission to the Oneidas alone produced nearly 100 personal letters that detail their work among the Iroquois, their relationship with their hosts, and the conflicts that their evangelism engendered. Native preachers thus left a surprisingly rich trail of manuscript and published material to track their movements, ideas, challenges, and strategies for converting indigenous peoples.

These letters, sermons, songs, and even the scriptures they invoke might best be understood as autoethnographic texts. While we have often viewed the adoption of Christianity—in its myriad forms—as passive subjugation to imperial and colonial authority, native preachers would have thought otherwise. Indeed, they used their sermons, letters, writings, and even identities as fulcrums against colonization, dispossession, and racial slavery, and they employed Christianity as spiritual and rhetorical weapons to fight those battles. These autoethnographic texts were therefore opportunities for native preachers to use the colonizers' terms, ideas, and idioms to frame their own identities. Evangelical Christianity was certainly culturally imperialistic, but it could also provide the ideas, language, and rhetoric of resistance, liberation, and egalitarianism. Listening to these narratives while using them in conjunction with other materials offers an amazing opportunity to grasp how native preachers understood Christianity, carved out a space for indigenous peoples within a larger Christian history, employed their spiritual authority to lobby for rights and protection, and fabricated their unique identities as non-European Christians during a period of encounter and conflict.[8]

To understand the role that native preachers played in the development of transatlantic missions, we must first rethink missionaries from the inside out. There has been a tendency to assume that Christian missionaries were Euro-Americans who entered into what they considered an exotic, unfamiliar world when they began missionary work. On the most basic level, we assume that Christian missionaries were white. And yet, indigenous evangelists have always been an essential component of Christian missionary activity. Writing about the rise of native clergy in the Philippines, Jesuit scholar Horacio De La Costa noted that "one of the most important tasks of the missionary, if not the principal one, is the formation of native priests who can eventually receive from his hands the administration and propagation of the Catholic Church in their own country." De La Costa went on to quote from French scholar Pierre Charles to assert that "the native clergy, therefore, is not the coping stone of the missionary edifice; it is the foundation stone. The truth is, that as long as it does not yet exist, the mission itself does not exist either."[9] While De La Costa was writing about Catholic missions, the same could be said for Protestant ones. Despite the overwhelming emphasis on white missionaries, native preachers often outnumbered the white ones working beside them.

Black and Native American missionaries had several advantages over white, Euro-American ones. Most importantly, they had language. Native preachers could act as literal and cultural translators between evangelical leaders and indigenous audiences. In spite of the best efforts by divines like John Eliot, John Cotton, and Roger Williams to understand and publish texts in indigenous languages, native missionaries' ability to speak local dialects gave them an advantage that few English preachers had. One commentator noted as early as 1642 that, if Puritans were to instruct Indians, it "must be in their *owne* language, not *English*."[10] Puritan missionary John Eliot even juxtaposed the useless effect of English preaching with the efficacy of Indian preaching by invoking native linguistic skill: "An *English* young man raw in that language, coming to teach among our Christian-*Indians*, would be much to their loss; there be of themselves such as be more able, especially being advantaged that they speaketh his own language, and knoweth their manners."[11] Eliot even admitted that, "as for my preaching . . . I see that it is not so taking, and effectuall to strangers, as their own expressions be, who naturally speak unto them in their own tongue."[12] One divine assumed that any Indian who knew his own could easily pick up as many as twenty different languages in a few years and be serviceable to as many as forty different Indian nations.[13] The importance of indigenous languages is best demonstrated by Philip Quaque's eventual loss of African dialect and the concern his Anglican sponsors expressed when they discovered that the African preacher could no longer speak to his own people in their language. When they heard this news, they brusquely insisted that he "recover his own language."[14] Quaque lost his native tongue as a result of over a decade of training in England, but this threatened to take away one of the very reasons why he was sent there: to communicate with Africans on their own terms. White missionaries could, of course, learn other languages, but not with the grace and ease of local, native evangelists.

Another major advantage that indigenous missionaries had over English ones was the ability to tap into existing networks of kinship, trade, and friendship. Many Anglo-American missionaries assumed that conversion would spread much more speedily if it were hastened by friends, neighbors, and kin. This seems simple enough, but it also brought to the surface several problematic issues for peoples whose societies were rooted in kinship networks. New England Indians, for example, sometimes asked whether they should abandon kinship ties if they were Christian and their relatives were not. John Eliot asked a group of Indians about this problem in 1649, and they replied, much to Eliot's satisfaction, that "when a strange Indian comes among us whom we never saw before . . . *if he pray unto God, we do exceedingly love him: But if my own Brother, dwelling in a great way off, come unto us, he not praying to God, though we love him, yet nothing so as we love that other stranger, who doth pray unto God*."[15] New Christian identities might have challenged existing kinship ties, but it would be foolish to assume that this was universally the case. In fact, many Indians had questions about how they could fuse an understanding of their new relationship to their preacher with traditional ideas about native kinship. One group asked, if a wise Indian who teaches "good things" came among them, whether that Indian was to be "as a father or brother unto such Indians he so teacheth?"[16] Some missionaries initially embraced Christianity only because their kin did so. When Anthony, a Christian minister at Natick, Massachusetts, gave a confession of Christian faith, he told of how his brothers "prayed morning and evening; and when they eat, and on Sabbath dayes . . . then I thought I would do so: but it was not for love of God, or fear of God, but because I loved my brothers."[17] Black and Indian evangelists could take advantage of existing loyalties and kinship networks, shoehorn native missionary work into traditional ideas of kinship, and sometimes fashion new forms of identity based upon a sense of Christian community. Compared to English missionaries, with whom Indians and Afro-Americans had no such connection, this was a very attractive benefit.

Native preachers were also more cost-effective than English ones. Ordained Anglican preachers usually demanded anywhere between forty and 100 pounds English sterling per year, depending on the circumstances. By contrast, Petrus Paulus, a Mohawk Indian who catechized, read prayers, and directed religious services at New York's Fort Hunter when Anglican preachers were absent, only cost about seven pounds annually, even though he did most of the mission's heavy lifting.[18] Native preachers who left their homes to be educated in English schools were significantly more expensive than local catechists like Paulus, but they were still more cost-effective. One Presbyterian group ran the numbers in 1767 and found that it would cost about 120 pounds to give a native preacher seven years of education among the English. It would then cost another fifty pounds annually (twenty for salary, thirty for maintenance) to support that native preacher in his mission. The Presbyterians anticipated that an English missionary would cost about 100 pounds for one year, while an interpreter would charge about fifty pounds. These calculations show that English preachers were cheaper in the short run, but native ones were much more cost-effective down the stretch, especially when contrasted with white missionaries who relied upon interpreters.[19] Therefore, and in spite of the time and money spent on his education and re-introduction among native peoples, a native preacher could provide a financial return on a missionary organization's investment after just one year of service. This was an attractive proposition for Protestant missionaries, and it helps explain why Protestants kept trying to cultivate native evangelists, even when dozens of them left their schools, turned "apostate," or created their own religious splinter groups. Missionary frugality, along with a general propensity among English clergy to "decline the Difficulties and Dangers" of missions to Indians and Africans, only made native preachers all the more indispensable.[20]

Protestant ministers generally agreed that both Amerindians and Africans could be characterized by spiritual poverty and savage barbarism. And yet, these very qualities constituted the final pragmatic reason why native peoples seemed ideal for missionary work. Few English ministers could learn Indian languages, but fewer still would bear "going native," moving out to the frontier, and living with the same Indians they hoped to save. "Experience has taught us," Eleazar Wheelock proclaimed in 1763, "that such a change of Diet, and manner of Living as Missionaries generally come into, will not consist with the Health of many *Englishmen*."[21] John Eliot, writing several generations before Wheelock, noted that missionary work in New England was difficult, "not only in respect of the language, but also in respect of their barbarous course of life and poverty; there is not so much as meat, drink or lodging for them that go unto them to preach among them, but we must carry all things with us."[22] Eliot believed that this Native American depravity rationalized his preference for native missionaries over English ones. He admitted that it was "hopeless to expect *English* Officers in our *Indian* Churches; the work is full of hardship, hard labour."[23] It seemed pointless to expect an army of English missionaries to volunteer their efforts when the challenges of eking out a living and providing for their own families demanded nearly all their energies. A missionary's life, Eliot claimed, was "Nothing but poverty and hardships, unsupportable in a constant way by our cloathed and housed nations." Indians, on the other hand, were members of "their own nation" who had been reared in the rigors of Indian lifeways and cultures. They were used to the environment and hard living, and therefore they would be "the most likely instruments to carry on this work."[24] Unlike white ministers, who would find the uncultivated climates of the American frontier harmful to their delicate constitutions, native preachers would simply "return to what they were used to from their Mother's Womb."[25] The reality of native preachers succumbing to devastating waves of epidemics often disproved this assumption of corporeal hardiness. Nevertheless, Protestants still expected that native missionaries would gladly take the burdensome and demanding evangelical jobs that English missionaries shunned. After all, their rough upbringings and brawny bodies seemed particularly well suited to do so.

A similar kind of logic was at work when missionaries considered employing African preachers in Africa and the Americas. They believed that African bodies made Africans particularly functional for the hard work of traversing the West African, Caribbean, and Carolina landscapes, but in unique and distinct ways from Native American bodies. Not only were African bodies understood to be more physically adept at surviving in the challenging climates of those places, they were also perceived as more resistant to the epidemiological havoc that tropical diseases could wreak on English bodies. In fact, the very attributes that many English commentators perceived as cultural liabilities and which painted Africans and Indians as barbaric savages—their native languages, arduous lifeways, geographic mobility, and strong bodies— ironically created opportunities for native evangelists to amass and exercise a tremendous amount of spiritual authority as preachers. The same physiological and cultural characteristics that often served to justify transatlantic slavery and Indian dispossession generated openings for Indians and Africans to perform as native preachers. Because of their linguistic skills, access to kinship networks, cost-effectiveness, and presumed durable bodies, native preachers would eventually become vital components of the early modern Protestant missionary enterprise.

There was more than mere pragmatism at work here, for Protestants also invoked scriptural and theological justifications for using indigenous preachers. They often looked back to early Christian history, not only with a sense of reverential nostalgia, but also with a belief that Christianity's first years provided an ideal model for successful evangelization. They analogized their contemporary efforts in the early modern Atlantic to those of the first apostles throughout the Mediterranean. This phenomenon can be called "sacred genealogy," that is, the ways in which Protestant neophytes were cast—and cast themselves—as part of a larger Christian lineage that was both spatially expansive (part of a global church) as well as temporally far-reaching (stretching back to the early days of Christianity and looking forward to the conversion of the entire world).[26] This is more than just repackaged millennialism. While Christian millennialism assumes that the world's gentiles would be *recipients* of the gospel, "sacred genealogy" is more concerned with how indigenous peoples became vital *participants* in a much longer tradition of Christian missionary efforts. These understandings of scripture and early Christian history created a space for Native Americans and Africans to gain access to Christian spiritual authority as preachers. At the same time, native preachers participated in the process of narrating themselves and their congregations into the history of Christianity, finding ways to detach Christianity from its Western moorings and giving it a uniquely syncretic identity that sometimes challenged traditional notions of what it meant to be a Christian.

The employment of scripture in missionary discourse goes much deeper than citing the book of Matthew to remind Christians to go "teach all nations," or using the Acts of the Apostles, which said "come over and help us," to justify English missionary work among the Indians.[27] In fact, Protestant understanding of scripture and the early history of Christian expansion in the first century both underwrote and explained why native missionaries would not only be common but ubiquitous in their missions throughout the Atlantic world. Early modern ministers understood the colonization of the New World as "a *second* remarkable period in the Gospel-progress."[28] The first was when preachers like Paul and Barnabas traveled through and evangelized the Mediterranean in the years after Christ's death. They assumed that what had worked well during the initial spread of Christianity would also work well in this newer age of transatlantic expansion. Although language was a pragmatic advantage that native preachers naturally possessed, Protestant divines still called upon scripture and their understanding of early Christian history to explain why native languages were a central component of missionary work. One missionary compared the spread of Christianity in the first century to native evangelical missions in Massachusetts, noting that "God is wont ordinarily to convert Nations and peoples by some of their owne countrymen who are nearest to them, and can best speake, and most of all pity their brethren and countrimen."[29] For missionary organizers, the cultivation of native preachers was part of God's divine plan.

This position derived partially from Protestants' perception of their place in sacred history. They often referred to the first days of the Christian church as the "age of miracles," a period when God participated directly in the evangelizing process by giving the first apostles access to spiritual powers that were unavailable to everyone else. These included not only the gift of healing, but also the gift of tongues, or the ability to speak in any language extemporaneously. Yet most early modern Protestants lamented the fact that, due to the corruption of the churches that evolved from the purer, primitive churches, the age of miracles had passed.[30] Human means were now necessary to accomplish the "gospelization" of the world. One Anglican divine suggested that, since the gift of tongues was absent and the age of miracles over, Anglicans should focus their energies on creating native teaching colleges to "improve further the Natives so initiated, and such as may be judged most capable of being useful in the Work of the Ministry."[31] Because of their linguistic skills, native preachers were expected to perform the same functions that God's miracles did in ages before.

Sacred genealogy implied spiritual equality, even as missionaries described indigenous peoples as savage and barbarous. One Anglican divine invoked sacred genealogy when he noted that all peoples who participated in the advancement of Christ's kingdom were "*Fellow-heirs*" to Christ's legacy. "The Gentiles," he observed, "are now by the Gospel capable of the same Privileges and the same Title to Salvation as the Jews, without any Difference." As spiritual descendents of Christ himself, each member was a congregant in a universal church where national distinction and even ethnicity did not matter. He concluded that "The church or mystical Body of Christ is but one, made up of the Faithful of all Nations, Jews and Gentiles, of which Christ is the Head, and all true Christians are members."[32] Experience Mayhew, who hailed from a prominent family of missionaries on Martha's Vineyard, also made this point when he cited chapters 34 and 35 from the Acts of the Apostles to remind his readers that, in spite of the lurid tales of Indian barbarity that emanated from Boston's printing presses in the wake of King Philip's War, Indians were nevertheless part of a larger Christian family. He noted that God was "no Respecter of Persons," for he had made each human equally. As equal products of God's divine will, "all nations stand on one common Level before God, both in the Duty and the Privilege of Sanctification: Where there is neither Greek nor Jew, Barbarian, Scythian, Bond nor Free."[33] Anglican William Fleetwood argued in 1711 that Indians, Africans, and Europeans were "equally the Workmanship of God, with themselves; endued with the same Faculties, and intellectual Powers; Bodies of the same Flesh and Blood, and Souls as certainly Immortal. . . . They were bought with the same Price, purchased with the same Blood of Christ, their common Saviour and Redeemer."[34]

The egalitarianism found in evangelical rhetoric was fundamentally predicated upon missionaries' sense of sacred history. One Anglican minister named John Egerton offered a sermon to a missionary society in which he claimed that, although Native Americans might seem barbaric to their eyes, they must remember that the English were formerly as barbaric and savage before they were exposed to Christianity. Any man who took stock of Indian barbarity must, Egerton concluded, "lead him to think with humility on the former condition of his own country."[35] Access to Christ was not solely based upon a national, ethnic, or even racial identity. God could bestow his grace upon anyone he chose. Native missionaries might not have been perceived as "civilized" by their English counterparts, but the fundamental belief in universal spiritual equality by virtue of God's creation (as well as their equality under sin) gave them access to membership in a larger Christian church, even as the social realities of racial animosities problematized this relationship.

According to Protestant writers, God's omniscience and omnipotence helped explain the use of native agents in Protestant missions. One metaphor that was frequently used in missionary discourse was that of the instrument. Protestants agreed that humans were vessels of God's will, even if they could not understand their place in God's divine plan at that time. They believed that God's knowledge and power could create suitable instruments as God saw fit, even when such an act seemed irrational or illogical to human eyes. "One single Savage," an Anglican divine proclaimed in 1760, "may perhaps, thro' the power of the living God . . . be rendered an Apostle to the rest, and an instrument of turning thousands from the ways of Darkness."[36] When Ezra Stiles, a minister from Newport, Rhode Island and Charles Chauncy, a minister from Boston, Massachusetts squabbled over the efficacy of sending former slaves as missionaries to West Africa in the 1770s, Stiles reminded his colleague that God can make use of whatever instruments he desired. He noted that God could "endow those whom he intends for Singular usefulness in the world especially those whom he designs for propagating the Gospel among the benighted Heathen & enlarging & building up the Kingdom of the blessed Emmanuel." "From small beginnings and seemingly despicable Instruments," Stiles concluded, "God has often accomplished great things though often undertaken in *spem contra spem* [hope against hope]."[37] In spite of contemporaries' reservations about the innate "capacity" of Indians and Africans, many missionaries still suggested that God could fashion a native ministerial elite if he ultimately saw fit. Protestant divines believed that this was how the gospel was spread in the earliest days of Christianity, and they applied the same evangelical model to their own history as well.

The symbolic process of ordination was one way in which sacred genealogy connected indigenous preachers not only to the early days of the Christian church, but also to Christ himself. During a typical ordination ceremony, the clergy would participate in the practice of laying their hands on the new minister. Although this might seem like an arcane ecclesiastical formality, the act of putting one minister's hand on the future preacher signified a transfer of spiritual authority. Two Wampanoags from Martha's Vineyard participated in this ceremony, with John Cotton, Jr., and John Eliot being the hand-givers. When one of them (Japhet Hannit) used his newfound spiritual authority to secure William Simmons' position as Dartmouth's Indian preacher, he did the

same. The ritual solidified in the minds of the new preacher, the ministers, and the congregation that Simmons (like Hannit before him) had
been initiated into a global community of preachers; a community that
traced its spiritual lineage back to Christ through the ceremony of laying
on of hands.[38] This practice was repeated in 1759, when Samuel Buell
ordained a Mohegan Indian named Samson Occom. After praising
Occom's piety, modesty, and Christian conversion, Buell placed his hand
on Occom and urged the new minister to "Go in the Spirit of an Apostle,
go do the Work of an Evangelist; Go lift up your voice in the Huts of
Savages, and cry aloud to the People that dwell in the gloomy Shades of
Death!" As a newly ordained minister, Occom had been accepted into a
sacred community that traced its lineage back to the apostles. In fact, by
virtue of his ordination, Occom had become one of them.[39]

Native preachers did not necessarily need this official process of ecclesiastical ordination to act as Christian missionaries. Protestants agreed
that the church-based congregation was the backbone of the Christian
community, but they also understood that evangelism could not happen
without a certain degree of itinerancy. Some even noted that itinerant
preachers who took to the roads to gain new converts, rather than settled
ministers, could more accurately be called heirs to Christ's calling. One
Puritan minister claimed that "Evangelists, or Preachers of the Gospel
and Gatherers of Churches among the *Heathen,* are *much more properly
and strictly,* the Successors of the Apostles, than the *stated Bishops* or
Elders of particular Churches: the Office of the *former* much more
resembling that of the Apostles, than the Office of the *latter.*"[40] Indians
who set out on the road to preach to other Indians—such as Japhit
Hannit, Samson Occom, and even unordained teachers and preachers—
were therefore acting as latter day apostles. Some Indians and black religious leaders broke away from white churches and formed their own
separatist congregations, a process that was even more common later in
the eighteenth century. Even as missionary writings provided the rhetorical ammunition for dispossession, enslavement, religious violence,
and the creation of imperial identities, there were a few unique ways in
which missionary discourses opened a window for native preachers to
gain access to spiritual authority, as most missionary minds looked to
the early days of Christianity to explain how the gospel could be spread
through the rapidly expanding Atlantic world.[41]

Just as Protestant ministers looked to early Christianity's first apostles
as a model for how indigenous evangelization might unfold in their
own world, they were also enormously interested in how other groups,

particularly the Catholic nations and the Dutch, tried to cultivate a native pastorate. The Catholic Church officially backed the advancement of indigenous religious leadership. This received its most earnest expression when the papacy founded a seminary, known as the Propaganda Fide, for the training of both European and native missionaries in the 1620s. The secretary of this institution argued that because all men could understand religion, there must be some among the world's indigenous peoples "who are apt to be promoted to priesthood."[42] The Propaganda Fide and the handful of other seminaries that developed around it were designed to serve as the hub of an international, intercontinental missionary thrust from which native preachers would commence converting the world. The college's multilingual printing press churned out sacred texts in a panoply of languages, and during the Epiphany one could hear orations being delivered in the common European languages alongside those given in Persian, Hebrew, Chinese, Japanese, a range of Indian dialects, Armenian, and Arabic tongues.[43]

Although Rome would encourage Catholic nations to cultivate a native pastorate, the Iberian powers that led the way in colonization expressed ambivalent attitudes and practiced inconsistent policies regarding indigenous preachers. By the middle of the seventeenth century, one cleric reported that Portugal's Cape Verde Islands had "clergy and canons as black as jet, but so well bred, so authoritative, so learned, such great musicians, so discreet and so accomplished, that they may be envied by those in our own cathedrals at home."[44] Seminaries were formed for the education of a native pastorate in Cape Verde, São Tomé, Principe, Angola, and Mozambique in the seventeenth and eighteenth centuries. The Franciscans opened a school solely for the training of non-European evangelists in India in 1541. And yet, some Portuguese officials questioned whether a fully ordained native pastorate was effective or necessary. Some had alleged that Portuguese colonists would never attend religious services if they were conducted by someone other than a purebred Portuguese. The Jesuits responded to similar pressures in 1579 by banning native clergy in India, though they made a few exceptions for clergy in Japan, Korea, Vietnam, and China. Some indigenous Christians rejected this racial reasoning and ardently sought acknowledgement of their potential as evangelists. A Christian Brahmin named Matheus de Castro, for example, was refused ordination by the Archbishop in Goa, India. Seeing no other alternative, he trekked overland from India to Rome in 1625, finished his theological studies, was ordained a priest, and then was consecrated Bishop of Chrysopolis and appointed Vice-Vicar of Bijapur. When he proudly returned to India, the Jesuits accused him of forging his ecclesiastical documents and refused to accept him. Years later, an East African convert to the Dominican order traveled to Goa to receive further religious instruction and ordination. One Italian missionary reported that, although this African Dominican was a "model priest," he still faced intense discrimination. As the Italian sadly reported, "not even the habit which he wears secures him any consideration whatever in these places, just because he has a black face. If I had not seen it, I would not have believed it."[45] The Portuguese empire began their missionary drive by embracing native pastors, but intense racism had ensured that only a few indigenous peoples in their empire would be ordained. By the middle of the eighteenth century, however, the Portuguese returned to their original policy of allowing indigenous ordination. The result was that of the 200 Catholic missionaries operating in India in 1835, only sixteen were European. By 1939 over 2,000 Chinese priests were attempting to spread Roman Catholicism throughout the world's most populous nation.[46]

Clerics in Spanish America expressed a similar ambivalence about the propriety of employing native missionaries. Colonized Americans often served as translators for sacred texts and interpreters for missionaries. One Spanish missionary even argued that a single native preacher would be "of greater profit in attracting others to the Faith than will fifty [European] Christians."[47] Another recalled that native interpreters would preach to Mexican audiences "with so much authority, energy, exclamations, and spirit, that it made me very envious of the grace that God had communicated to them." "It was they," the missionary conceded, "who carried the voice and sound of the word of God."[48] These attitudes helped catalyze the opening of a college for indigenous elites in Mexico City during the 1530s. The College of Santiago Tlatelolco annually had about sixty to seventy indigenous students taking classes in grammar, music, rhetoric, logic, philosophy, and even "Indian Medicine." They lived a monastic life, reciting the prayers of the Virgin Mary, attending Mass, and gaining enough fluency in Latin to speak it "with the elegance of Cicero," as one commentator put it.[49]

Although the school had the nominal support of some of New Spain's ministers, it was constantly under fire by settlers, government officials, and even Catholic clerics from the moment it opened its doors. Hardening racial ideologies and a corresponding concern that indigenous peoples would spread religious heresy conspired to close opportunities for indigenous preachers just as they seemed to be opening up. One contemporary concluded that Indians "cannot and should not be ordained, because of their incapacity." Others opined that it was "an error fraught with dangers" to teach Indians and "put the Bible and all the Holy Scriptures into their hands to be read and interpreted as they pleased." At the First Council of Mexico in 1555, Catholic leaders concluded that Indians, Africans, or any mixed-race peoples could never be fully ordained in the Catholic Church. Although this would be tempered somewhat by later councils and royal decrees, the point was clear: the Spanish had briefly experimented with a native priesthood, and the experiment had apparently gone terribly wrong. A few Indian preachers still operated in the countryside in the seventeenth century, but they were rarely ordained and were often relegated to the "inferior posts" and "thankless work" of preaching to poor mission villagers. In spite of these problems, indigenous Americans still worked to create a syncretic form of Christianity that blended American cosmologies, rituals, and ideas with Catholic ones. Throughout New Spain this produced both cultural accommodation and physical violence, but, in all cases, indigenous peoples played a key role in how Christianity was understood, interpreted, and contested.[50]

Like their Catholic counterparts to the south, the French missionaries who arrived on the shores of New France also used native catechists regularly to help Indians learn the fundamentals of Catholic theology. Claude Chauchetiére recalled how, after Jesuits had given some Indian catechists a picture book that summarized Catholic history and practice, the neophytes not only read them "with pleasure and profit" but also "preache[d] long sermons" from the work.[51] The Jesuits were particularly concerned with educating indigenous women and portraying them as model Christians. The most notable of these was the famous Catherine Tekakwitha, a Mohawk who converted to Catholicism and later had her life celebrated as one of ideal Christian virtue in the face of human suffering. And yet, French training of native Christians produced its own problems. Several high profile converts turned "apostate" and rejected the French missionaries that had trained them. The large number of Catholic missionaries in New France also might have had a paradoxical effect by limiting the development of native preachers. In fact, the Jesuits became more flexible in their approach to missionary activity after 1640, allowing more indigenous rituals and customs to penetrate into native Christianity and attempting to find common ground between native religions and their own. Ironically, this flexibility did not translate into a recruitment of native preachers. As late as 1832, when two Ottawas were sent to Rome to become Catholic missionaries, there were still no native priests in Canada. Whatever the reasons, not a single North American Indian was promoted to the Catholic priesthood by the French during the first few centuries of cultural encounter in the Americas.[52]

Anglo-American Protestants certainly knew of Catholic missionary efforts in these places, but they also watched out for their own Protestant competitors. The Dutch proved to have the biggest influence on English attempts to use indigenous missionaries in the Americas, as Anglo-American evangelists frequently invoked missionary work in the Dutch East Indies when considering their own progress as Christian evangelists. Many of the reports that emanated from these mission fields contained not only astronomical numbers of Christian conversions, but also compelling stories of Asians becoming missionaries to their own people.[53] Missionary texts underscored the fact that newly converted Asians taught their friends and neighbors the rituals of Christian life, including "The *Lords Prayer,* the *Creed,* the *Ten Commandments,* a *Morning Prayer,* an *Evening Prayer,* a *Blessing* before Meat, and *another* after."[54] All missionaries understood that the calculations of conversions and narratives of native evangelism could be hyper-inflated. Nevertheless, Anglo-American Protestants in the Atlantic world still looked to the missionary successes of other groups with a mix of disgust, envy, and admiration, and they often invoked the gains made in other places when trying to drum up support for their own evangelical enterprises.

The Anglo-American and native evangelists who comprise this history were never isolated from other evangelical efforts in other places, for their leading divines were quite aware of the missionary histories of other sites. Transatlantic networks of printing and correspondence ensured that they would always be tied into larger developments happening in other regions throughout the Atlantic world and beyond. When Protestants began to consider missionary work among Africans and Indians in the British Atlantic, they looked to scriptural history as well as to other missionary enterprises throughout the world as models from which to guide their efforts. Practical considerations, an understanding of early Christian history, and an acute awareness of what their competitors were doing all led Protestant missionaries to the conclusion that native preachers would be vital to any evangelical enterprise they undertook. The ensuing development of black and Indian missionaries fundamentally shaped cultural interactions between Europeans, Africans, and Native Americans during the most formative period of those encounters.

CHAPTER ONE

Apostles to the Indians

THE SERMONS DELIVERED to a small Massachusetts congregation in November of 1658 were part of a longer period of fasting and prayer that was organized "because of the great raine, and great floods, and unseasonable weather, whereby the Lord spoileth our labours."[1] Ruined crops, cattle on the brink of death, and rampant disease had ravaged the community. These were dark times. God clearly seemed furious with the congregation, and the first sermons of the morning made it all too evident that they had to repent for the sins which brought this terrible fate upon them. One preacher, described elsewhere as "bashful," appeared none too bashful when he chastised the praying community for their lackluster piety.[2] He drew from the twenty-second chapter of the Book of Genesis to explain how Noah, like his own congregation, had to make sacrifices to God in order to be preserved. The comparison with Noah made sense, for the torrential downpours they experienced that autumn drew obvious parallels to the flood that Noah survived. This preacher exclaimed, "God has chastised us of late, as if he would utterly *Drown* us; and he has *Drowned* and Spoiled and Ruin'd a great deal of our hay, and threatens, to kill our Cattel. 'Tis for this that we *Fast* and *Pray* this Day." "We must by repentance purge our selves," he continued, "and cleanse our hearts from all sin." If they were sufficiently penitent, the preacher claimed, God would "with-hold the *Rain*, and Bless us with such *Fruitful Seasons* as we are desiring of him." The message of repentance during a time of trial was a classic Puritan jeremiad: repent for your sins lest your soul (and your society) descend into an infinite pit of hellfire.[3]

In spite of the similarities with typical Puritan sermons, these were not "typical" Puritans. Instead, the audience was a group of Massachuset Indians. Most importantly, their preachers were also Indians. That Nishokon, the "bashful" Indian evangelist who implored his audience to repent for their sins, chose the story of Noah is no coincidence. Although the parallel with the torrential downpours was obvious, Nishokon may have had another agenda in mind. In fact, his sermon can be read against the many debates and tensions inherent in the effort to bring the Christian gospel to Native Americans. Nishokon preached from Noah's story because he was situating Native American trials and experiences into a larger, sacred history of Christianity. The Old Testament claims that, after the famous flood, Noah's three sons populated the earth. Japhet went to Europe, Shem to Asia, and Ham (the one who failed to cover up his father's nakedness in a tent) went to Africa. Nishokon thus established a connection between Old Testament history and Native American Christianity by employing a biblical story that offered no place for Native Americans in the sacred geography of the world.[4]

Nishokon's sermon was an attempt to use Christianity as a rhetorical device through which the Indian preacher could establish his congregation as legitimate heirs to Christ's salvation. By analogizing Indian trials with those of Noah, he carved out a space for indigenous Christians within a larger community of believers. Yet, the sermon was more than a text, for its deliverance could be identified as an act of sacred performance. The very *act* of having an Indian preach the gospel meant that Nishokon, like other native preachers, became an active participant in the process of reinventing and translating the meaning of the gospel message. In placing Indians within a sacred genealogy that connected them not only to Christ but also to the ancient patriarchs of the Old Testament, Nishokon assured his listeners that Native Americans did have a place, and a central one, in the history and future of Western Christianity.[5]

Explorers, philosophers, and missionaries all wondered how Indians came to inhabit the Americas, and many searched for biblical evidence of their origination. The result of these searches, more often than not, was the assertion that "these are the children of *Shem* as we of *Japhet* . . . yea it seemeth to me probably that these people are Hebrews, of Eber, whose sonnes the Scripture sends farthest East . . . certainly this country was peopled Eastward from the place of the *Arks* Resting."[6] Several commentators wrote extensive tracts, including the cleverly titled *Jews in America*, to contend that Native Americans were one of the lost tribes of Israel.[7] If this was true, of course, the significance for Indian and English preachers could not be overstated. Missionaries believed that the

rediscovery and conversion of the Jews would lead to the eventual conversion of the entire world, bringing forth the final days of judgment and
revealing the truths of God's glory to all humankind. The stakes were
high. Protestant ministers believed that the creation of American missions would be a seminal moment in the sacred history of Christianity,
rivaling that of Christianity's rapid expansion in the first century. Native
preachers would be as central to the expansion of Christianity in the
early modern Atlantic as they were when the first apostles set out from
Jerusalem. And yet, in spite of their centrality to the aspirations of ministers and the daily practice of native Christian communities, indigenous
evangelists have remained overlooked in seventeenth century Puritan
New England. Indeed, if we understand missions less as sites of western
imperial oppression and more as a middle ground, a physically and met-
aphorically contested space where indigenous peoples and colonists had
to negotiate with one another instead of destroying each other, then the
role of native preachers to these missions becomes all the more vital.[8]
John Eliot, the celebrated Puritan who helped pioneer these missions,
has been dubbed the "apostle to the Indians." What we have forgotten,
however, is that he was not alone.

The first English effort to employ indigenous missionaries in the Anglo-
American colonies was in tidewater Virginia, not Puritan Massachusetts.
The first charter of Virginia in 1606 claimed that one of the colonists'
motivations was to spread Christianity "to such People, as yet live in
Darkness and miserable Ignorance of the true Knowledge and Worship
of God."[9] In fact, one of Pocahontas's kin was a Powhatan Indian named
Nanamack, who was sent to England purportedly for missionary
training. He lived there for a year or two but died prematurely, before he
could even be baptized and sent back to his people as a missionary. Since
the English had little success bringing Indians across the Atlantic to an
English college, they decided to build an English college for them in
Virginia instead. This was precisely Sir Thomas Dale's plan for a settlement at Henrico, only a few miles upriver from Jamestown. By the 1610s
Dale was trying to establish the settlement as a protection against foreign invasion and a springboard for cultural diplomacy with Native
Americans. He dreamed that the more scholarly of the Indian students
would transform into "fitt Instruments to assist afterwards in the more
generall Conversion of the Heathen people."[10] Dale's ambitious plan had
major flaws. Although he intended to pay ministers forty pounds a
year—plus room and board—he had trouble securing them. Colonists
who were recruited early to settle there were irate at the lack of urgency

in constructing the settlement, as Indians shot at unsuspecting settlers from behind the forest's trees. No indigenous peoples seemed willing to part with their children and place them in Dale's English school. Thus, he had neither teachers nor students, so it was no surprise that, by 1622, the college had yet to be built. In that year a violent uprising against the Virginia settlers, orchestrated by a new Indian leader named Opechang-anough, effectively destroyed Dale's utopian scheme just as swiftly as Indians and English destroyed one another on Virginia's riverbanks.

The missions established by Puritan evangelists in New England in later years would be more successful, and have a more enduring legacy, than their Virginia counterparts. With the volume of biblical texts he translated into indigenous languages as well as his creation of an ambitious network of Indian praying towns, John Eliot was certainly a key figure, but there were a handful of other English missionaries operating in early New England, including Richard Bourne, Thomas Mayhew, and John Cotton, Jr. There were also Indian preachers. In fact, the Indian evangelists outnumbered the English ones. From about 1640 to 1700, New England held twenty-four ordained Indian ministers and many more native teachers, deacons, and informal missionaries. By the time of the American Revolution, over 130 indigenous preachers had worked as evangelists to other Native Americans in the American colonies. As important as he was, Eliot was just one actor in a long drama of Christian missionary activity among New England Indians.[11]

New England Puritans expressed a complex range of impressions about Indian religion. Many agreed with the convention that the region's indigenous peoples were, as Cotton Mather put it, "infinitely barbarous."[12] Indians were often characterized as "Forlorn and wretched *heathen*," and "wild creatures, multitudes of them being under the power of Satan, and going up and downe with the chains of darkness rattling at their Heels."[13] However, for all of their rhetoric about the barbarity of Indians, Puritan ministers from John Eliot to Jonathan Edwards still believed that Indians were ultimately redeemable. Although there were major religious differences between Indian and Puritan spiritualities— the Calvinist emphasis on original sin and literacy were novelties to New England Indians—there were some general similarities. Both Puritans and indigenous New Englanders believed that God (or multiple forces) and Satan (or an evil counterforce) were active in peoples' everyday lives. Daniel Gookin remarked in 1674 that indigenous religion was akin to that of the primitive Christian churches. Native Americans had some nascent ideas of God and Satan. "Generally they acknowledge one great supreme doer of good," Gookin explained, "and him they call Woonand, or Maunitt: another that is the great doer of evil or mischief; and him they call Maupand, which is the devil; and him they dread and fear, more than they love and honour the former."[14] Unlike Gookin, John Eliot painted Indian religion as nonexistent, as a *tabula rasa* that Puritan theology would inscribe with its own meaning. He claimed that New England Indians had no religious principles at all, thus they "most readily yield to any direction from the Lord, so that there will be no such opposition against the rising Kingdome of Jesus Christ among them."[15] Nevertheless, Eliot, Gookin, and other Puritan ministers agreed that Indians were savage but salvageable, riddled with barbarity but ultimately redeemable.

Indian redemption was allegedly one of the driving forces behind Puritan colonization in the first place. The first charter of Massachusetts, drafted in 1629, contended that one of the primary motives of colonization was that Puritans "maie wynn and incite the Natives of Country, to the Knowledg and Obedience of the onlie true God and Savior of Mankinde, and the Christian Fayth." This, it proclaimed, was "our Royall Intencon" and "the principall Ende of this Plantacion." The Massachusetts Bay Colony's official seal even had a Massachuset Indian at its centerpiece, invoking the 16th chapter from the Acts of the Apostles and imploring English Christians to "Come Over and Help Us."[16]

By the 1640s, however, little had been done in the way of missionary activity, a point that Thomas Lechford noted in his notorious tract, *Plain Dealing*. Lechford assaulted Puritan leaders for not going out and preaching in Indian country, exclaiming, "They have nothing to excuse themselves in this point of not labouring with the Indians to instruct them, but their want of a staple trade, and other business taking them up."[17] Lechford's criticisms highlighted English laxity in preaching to the natives and criticized colonists for being concerned only with the commercial, rather than spiritual, gains that the English might make in Indian country. But, while English settlers spent the first decades of their colony ignoring Christian evangelization, some Indians were already participating in it. In fact, the first Christian missionary to Indians in Massachusetts was not John Eliot, but rather a Massachusett native who traveled to a minister's house in Salem, heard stories from the Bible, and then "went out amongst the Indians, and called upon them to put away all their wives save one, because it was a sinne."[18] Indian evangelists began the work of Christian evangelization while Puritan ministers dragged their feet.

Even John Eliot, the most famous apostle to the Indians, did not express interest in missionary activity until the 1640s, and he had been in

Massachusetts since 1631. Exactly why he took up the call to preach to Indians is still heavily debated, but we do know that he began learning indigenous languages in 1643, most likely from an Indian who was taken captive during the Pequot War, a violent conflict that pitted English and Narragansett Indians against Pequot Indians living in coastal Connecticut. Eliot felt that by 1646 he knew enough Massachuset to try to convert some Indians, so he organized a series of camp meetings in the fall and early winter of that year. They took place in the hut of an Indian named Waban, a man who previously held no office or position of honor in indigenous society. English missionaries often tried to cultivate an indigenous spiritual leadership among existing native political leaders to graft a new, Christian hierarchy onto what they perceived as an already well-established indigenous one. When they failed to do so, they simply worked with whoever was willing to work with them, as was the case with Waban. The meetings that Waban and Eliot established were informal gatherings, but Eliot used them as opportunities to ask Indians questions concerning religion, deliver a series of lectures (one of the main themes was the

Seal of the Massachusetts Bay Colony. (Image courtesy of the Secretary of the Commonwealth of Massachusetts.)

scattering of peoples after Noah's flood), and even draw support for a praying town in Noonatomen, near present day Watertown. Waban was installed as a kind of Justice of the Peace there.[19] This new settlement was not just an experiment in "civilizing" Indians, but also a base for future evangelical work among them. Waban began using his newfound spiritual authority to set out on his own and preach among Indians near Concord, Merrimack, and other destinations north and west of Boston. His most important accomplishment, according to English officials, was to encourage others to take up the mantle of spreading the gospel. One Puritan divine even recalled that Waban produced a veritable cadre of skillful indigenous evangelists, as there were "now many others whom he first breathed encouragement into that do farre exceed him in the light and life of the things of God." As Waban and other native preachers began the work of evangelizing other Indians, Puritan commentators began to boast of the progress of Christian evangelism in their own "city upon a hill", a model for the rest of the world to follow. Thomas Shepard, the popular Puritan divine and Eliot's personal friend, even proclaimed that the early evangelical triumphs of Eliot and Waban should "move bowels, and awaken *English* hearts to be thankfull."[20]

The centerpiece of the Puritans' evangelical plan was the praying town. Praying towns were similar to the famous *reducciones* of the Spanish and Portuguese empires, though they were much smaller and did not initially involve forced migration. In these towns Indians were supposed to build English style homes, cut their hair European-style, practice monogamous marriage, establish permanent farms, and generally subscribe to English ideas of civilization and Puritan ideas of religion. They were also to follow a series of behavioral codes that included avoiding alcohol, shunning local shamans, and refusing to "lie with a beast" upon penalty of death.[21] And yet, a remarkable degree of autonomy was characteristic of many growing Christian Indian communities. Although Eliot was the central figure in their creation, the offices of church leadership were almost always filled with Native Americans, and usually along familial lines. The ascension of Native Americans into positions of secular and spiritual authority meant that the quotidian operations of Puritan missions were left to the Indians themselves. In transferring that spiritual authority to Indians, Puritan missionaries created opportunities through which native preachers could exercise some degree of cultural and spiritual autonomy.[22]

The most famous Massachusetts praying town was Natick, founded in 1651 and based upon a Mosaic system of civil rulers, spiritual pastors, and teachers. But, if Natick was the most celebrated Indian town, it was also the most atypical, as it was large, close to English settlements, and frequently visited by English officials. Natick's Puritan supporters believed that it was "absolutely necessary" for their Indian charges to "carry on civility with Religion."[23] However, Natick's status as an Indian "city upon a hill" made it just as much a point of departure for native missionaries as it was a destination. Just as Waban set out from Noonatomen, praying Indians who lived in Natick and other towns also traversed the Indian frontier, using the towns as bases of operations. Cutshamoquin, for example, traveled all the way from Natick to Rhode Island to try to convert the Narragansett Indians. When Daniel Gookin and Eliot began establishing a second wave of praying towns in 1673 and 1674, they usually installed native preachers who had lived, learned, and prayed in Natick as teachers and preachers in the new towns. Eliot bragged in 1673 that many of these missionaries could "read, some write, sundry able to exercise in publick," and that many of them offered several religious lectures a day when they were in Natick.[24] In other words, the praying towns, especially Natick, were designed to serve as hubs in an integrated indigenous missionary network that stretched to southern New Hampshire, Cape Cod, Rhode Island, Connecticut, and even Long Island. When Indians set out on these evangelical journeys, they were usually alone.

If this mobility created tensions in the Protestant missionary model, Eliot never mentioned it. For Puritan and other Protestant theologians, the parish-based community was the locus of religious activity, and bands of wandering Indians could potentially challenge that model of Christian community. Nevertheless, Puritan divines realized that Indians had to hit the trails as itinerant preachers if they were to pull other Indian tribes into the orbit of Christianity. Puritans paradoxically believed that it took a wandering Indian to keep other Indians from wandering and persisting in lives of darkness, mobility, and savagery.

Each of the seven praying towns established by 1670 had their own indigenous ministers, church officers, deacons, and teachers. Hassanamesitt, near present day Grafton, had a teacher named Joseph Tuckapawillin, whose father had previously been a deacon of the church there. Okommakamesit, near Marlborough, employed a hard-drinking teacher before Solomon, a "serious and sound Christian," took over and restored order.[25] There were also Indian preachers at Nashope (near Littleton), Wamesit (Tewksbury), Magunkukquok (Hopkinton), Panatuket, and Punkapoag (Stoughton). Samuel Danforth noted that, even in Little Compton (in present-day Rhode Island), "They have pastors and elders of their own, ordained sometimes by the hands of English Ministers, and sometimes by the hands of Indian Ministers in the presence of the English."[26] By 1674 there was only one English missionary working in Cape Cod among a handful of Indian ones. The New England Puritan missionaries who traversed the frontiers, supervised the praying towns, and connected thousands of praying Indians through an interlocking web of native relations were themselves Native Americans, not English colonists. The praying towns were thus not the most important or effective aspect of Puritan missions: the native evangelists who administered them were.

If the missionary effort on the mainland was fundamentally dependent upon indigenous agents, evangelical efforts on the island of Martha's Vineyard, which the Wampanoags who lived there called Nope, were even more so. In fact, while John Eliot was learning the local language and preparing to preach in the early to mid 1640s, a nascent Indian Christian community was being formed around a handful of charismatic Wampanoag spiritual leaders. When Thomas Mayhew, Sr. settled on the island around 1642, he and his son began to learn the Wampanoag dialect and peripatetically instruct Indians in Christian literacy. Although the younger Thomas would die tragically in a mysterious shipwreck in 1657, by that time the mission was in the hands of the native preachers whom he and his father had trained. The Mayhews, as well as another missionary named John Cotton, were merely catalysts. The Vineyard's indigenous preachers were the backbone of Christian missionary work there.[27]

The first of these was Hiacoomes, a man who became perhaps the island's most celebrated Christian Indian. About 23 or 24 years old by the time the Mayhews arrived, Hiacoomes was described as a "sad and sober spirit" who had few friends and even less to say in his community.[28] Writing in the 1720s, Experience Mayhew (grandson of Thomas Mayhew, Sr.) recalled that Hiacoomes' "Descent was but mean, his Speech but slow, and his Countenance not very promising." Chiefs and other local men of import thought him "scarce worthy of their Notice or Regard."[29] Faced with disrespect from fellow Wampanoags, Hiacoomes probably viewed the arrival of the Mayhew family as an opportunity to recast his identity. He approached the English family, befriended them, asked for Christian instruction, and began fashioning a new reputation for himself as a Christian Indian. From 1643 to 1646, Hiacoomes studied scripture with the Mayhews, coming to understand his own sinfulness, the love and wrath of God, the inner depravity of man, and other Calvinist doctrines. Yet it was not until a devastating epidemic hit that Hiacoomes emerged as a legitimate spiritual leader.

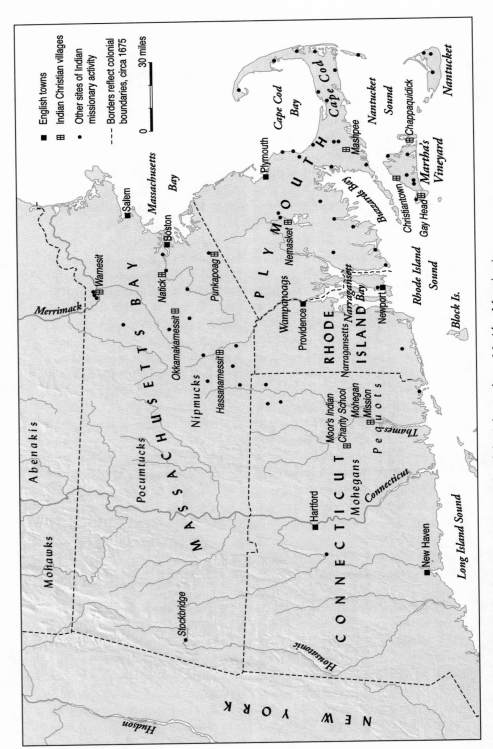

Map of early New England native missions. (Map by Philip Schwartzberg, Meriden Mapping.)

Disease, which not only wrought havoc on native communities but also proved to be a major disadvantage to indigenous missionary activity in other places, helped native missionaries gain adherents on the island. The Vineyard Indians had experienced periodic illnesses, but few were worse than the series of epidemics that swept the island from 1643 to 1645. Seemingly miraculously, the small band of converts who were beginning to listen to Hiacoomes' preaching were hit less hard than the rest of the population by this wave of diseases, and Hiacoomes and his family suffered not at all. Hiacoomes seized this moment to rail against indigenous customs, especially the use of medicine men and shamans (also called pawwaws) to cure sickness. When his neighbors inquired about his apparent immunity to diseases, he replied that he no longer needed medicine men or the spirits with which they tried to court favor. Puritans recorded that Hiacoomes explained, "I have throwne away all these, and a great many more some years ago, yet am preserved as you see this day."[30] He openly declared his faith in Christianity, doing so with excessive "Zeal and Boldness," attacking the pawwaw system, and exhorting his neighbors to repent for their sins lest another epidemic wipe them off the face of the island.[31] Hiacoomes' charismatic preaching and alleged immunity to English diseases helped him to cultivate a size-able following, even as other Christian Indians emerged as new spiritual leaders to challenge the traditional religious authority of local shamans. It is clear that many Indians who followed Hiacoomes and other Christian leaders expected that, at the very least, identifying as Christians would help preserve them from the waves of epidemics that had devastated Indian communities since the arrival of Europeans.

Of course, disease brought death, which also provided missionaries— native and Anglo-American—a chance to articulate their ideas about proper funerary rituals, the path to salvation, and the manner of a good Christian death. When one of his own children later died from disease, Hiacoomes apparently used the heartrending event as an opportunity to try to extirpate Wampanoag funerary practices and embrace Puritan ones. As Experience Mayhew recalled, "at the Funeral there were no black Faces or Goods buried, or howling over the dead, as the manner of the *Indians* in those Times was, but instead thereof a patient Resignation of the child to him that gave it."[32] Not all funerary rituals followed this pattern, and there were certainly examples of "unorthodox" deathbed scenes that included visions, expressions of either excessive confidence or fear about the future, the presence of traditional shamans, the ritual use of tobacco, and other indigenous practices. When an Indian child from Noonatomen passed away, the Indians participated in the customary

Puritan rituals of solemnly placing the child in a casket and lowering it into the earth. Afterwards, however, the Indian mourners went into the forest, congregated around a tree, and heard Totherswamp, an up and coming Christian leader, offer some prayers for the dead child. The very act of meeting together and praying for the child was a traditional indigenous practice, one that Puritans avoided because of their belief in predestination. Indians fashioned an eclectic palette of practices and rituals around death, and these moments were opportunities for native preachers like Hiacoomes and Totherswamp to articulate what they thought Indian Christianity meant.[33]

Although Hiacoomes remained a student of the Mayhews, who still instructed him and offered weekly advice on how to deliver compelling sermons to the Island Indians, by the 1650s he had become a leader of impressive standing in his own right. One Puritan who traveled to the island in 1651 met Hiacoomes and later declared him to be "a man of prompt understanding, of a sober and moderate spirit, and a man well reported of for his conversation both by English and Indians."[34] Christian teaching offered Hiacoomes a chance to shake off a life of isolation and inconsequence to begin a new one characterized by leadership, social importance, and spiritual power. By the 1660s, his sacred transformation seemed complete. Experience Mayhew summed up Hiacoomes' spiritual and social journey eloquently when he noted that, although Hiacoomes was once "harmless," "unaccounted of," and speechless in meetings, now he was "Teacher of them all."[35] When Hiacoomes attended a service in Boston during one of his missionary trips to the mainland, the Puritan congregation politely offered to "receive that good *Indian* into one of their pewes," not an insignificant gesture considering the rigid hierarchy with which Puritans ordered their seating.[36] A formerly forsaken Indian, Hiacoomes now found himself rubbing elbows with Boston's Puritan elite.

It was propitious timing for the indigenous missionary movement on Martha's Vineyard. Disease compelled the residents to explore alternative explanations for their trials while Hiacoomes' sudden transformation from quiet outcast to respected leader provided a model and catalyst for future Christian indigenous leaders. They came in droves. Mittark, a sachem at Gay Head, embraced Christianity in 1663 but was shunned by his own people for doing so. He migrated to the other side of the island for a while but eventually returned to his own people as a preacher. Cotton Mather even gave Mittark sole credit for making the Gay Head Indians "all Christians by profession."[37] John Tackanash, a more scholarly Indian missionary, was "reckoned to exceed the said *Hiacoomes,* both in his natural and acquired Abilities." He preached with Hiacoomes at Edgartown, but when the church became too big, it split into two congregations, Hiacoomes taking the small island of Chappaquidick and Tackanash heading the one at Edgartown.[38] Japhet Hannit, another celebrated Indian preacher on the island, seemed destined for greatness since his birth. His mother had experienced several failed pregnancies before finally forsaking her pawwaws. One day, when she was pregnant with Japhet, she slipped off into a field and had an epiphany that there was only one true God, the God of the Englishmen. Her child was miraculously delivered without complications and ended up becoming a Christian preacher "who not only is pastor to an Indian church on Martha's Vineyard, consisting of some scores of regenerate souls, but also has taken pains to carry the gospel unto other Indians on the main land with a notable effect thereof."[39] In addition to these major leaders, there were dozens of other preachers, deacons, and ministers in Wampanoag churches on the Vineyard. These included Momonequenm, John Nahnosoo, Wunnanauhkomun, William Lay, Janawannit, Paul (or Mashquattuhkooit), Joshua Momatchegin, and nearly fifty others. Like their counterparts on the mainland, native preachers were the foundation for Christian missionary activity on Martha's Vineyard.

The island's women also played a central role in Wampanoag translation of Christianity. Women, of course, were not allowed to be ordained in Puritan churches as ministers or exhorters, and public leadership roles were restricted to men. Nevertheless, Puritan Christianity still gave women important roles as wives, mothers, and exemplary figures who could serve as models of Christian piety. In a kind of evangelical twist on the later concept of republican motherhood, Wampanoag women contributed to the community publicly by raising their children as devout Christians. Experience Mayhew offered multiple accolades for Sarah Hannit (Japhet's wife), who "was careful to bring up her Children in the Nurture and Admonition of the Lord, frequently gave them good Instruction, and would faithfully reprove them when they did amiss; and did also frequently exhort them to the great Duties of Religion, and particularly of that of secret Prayer to God."[40] Even though they never performed as official preachers, women still acted as agents in the adoption of at least some elements of Puritan Christianity among New England's native population.

By the mid-1670s Martha's Vineyard had become an important centerpiece in Indian Christianity. As on the mainland, positions of Christian Indian authority descended through genealogical lines. Of the thirty native church officials operating in Massachusetts by the end of the

seventeenth century, well over half of them came from the families of
chiefs, elders, or other elite lineages.⁴¹ These native Christian leaders
also merged secular positions and spiritual offices. Japhet Hannit was a
magistrate before he became a minister, and William Lay used both religious authority and civil power to punish transgressors. Experience
Mayhew recalled that Lay's technique was "first to apply himself to them
as a Minister of Religion, or of the Word of God, of which he was a
Preacher, and endeavour to convince their Consciences of the Sins of
which they were guilty, and then bring them to a humble Sense and
Confession of their Faults." If gentle Christian persuasion did not work,
Lay would change his tune and "severely chastise them for their Offences,
making them know what *Stripes for the Backs of Fools* do intend."⁴²
Through their identity as Christian leaders, their apparent immunity to
devastating diseases, and even through physical force, Lay, Hannit,
Hiacoomes, and other native preachers embraced their authority as spir-
itual and social leaders as they sought to carve out a space for native
Christians in a colonial world.

The narratives of Indian conversion that John Eliot and other English
missionaries recorded offer a sense of why some native preachers found
Christianity appealing and compelling. Far from being forced into
embracing Christianity, native preachers became evangelists for multiple
reasons, and many understood their value as cultural mediators between
Euro-American missionaries and potential converts. For many indigenous peoples, Christianity helped to provide explanations for unprecedented problems: diseases, dislocation, warfare, changing political
dynamics, and other novel historical issues that European colonialism
created or exacerbated. Christianity became one of several systems of
meaning that native evangelists could draw from to explain their past
and provide hope for their future. And, in most cases, Indians accepted
the tenets, rituals, and ideas that made sense to them while discarding
the rest.⁴³

On the micro level, the conversion narratives produced by Indian
preachers and recorded by English observers run the gamut from the
compelling and sincere to the bizarre and likely apocryphal. John Speen,
a preacher at the famous praying town of Natick, claimed that he knew
little of, and cared less for, Puritan doctrines of sin and the afterlife
when he had first learned about Christianity. In a confession taken down
in the 1650s, Speen admitted that "When I first prayed to God, I did not
pray for my soul but only I did as my friends did, because I loved them;
and though I prayed to God, yet I did not fear sin, nor was I troubled at

it. I heard that when good men die, their souls go to God, and are there happy, but I cannot say that I believed it."⁴⁴ John's brother, Anthony, who began praying because his brothers prayed, never expressed a belief in the Christian gospel until one day, as he was building a house, a hefty piece of lumber fell from above and crashed directly on his skull, splitting it open. Anthony survived, but he always remembered the winter that "God broke my head" as a seminal moment in his spiritual transformation, for he believed that this incident was a sign that he needed to undergo a dramatic spiritual transformation to survive in this new cultural landscape. Nishokon, the supposedly bashful man who gave that emotional sermon on Noah's flood, admitted that at first he only did what was fashionable in order to increase his chances with the ladies. Cutting one's hair was essential to living in a Christian community (it was illegal to keep one's hair long), but Nishokon said, "If I cut my hair, it was with respect to lust, to please women; if I had long hair, it was with respect to lust, and all I did was with respect to lust and women."⁴⁵ Nishokon's first exposure to Christianity and English civility, then, was not predicated upon a profound spiritual longing, but rather an attempt to fulfill more basic needs. A few native ministers probably became Christians in name only and began preaching just for the money. It is impossible to determine how often this happened, but being a preacher certainly had its temporal rewards. By 1671 Hiacoomes was paid ten pounds a year (half as much as an English minister), John Tackanash made five, and Mittark made three.⁴⁶ There is little doubt that some New England Indians became preachers simply to earn a living.

Other native missionaries might have had more lofty motives. For Monequassum, his acceptance of Christianity was rooted in his sense of place. He confessed that he initially rebuked the Christian message he heard in his town at Cohannet. As the town became Christianized he even considered running away. Yet he eventually agreed to become a Christian because, "I loved to dwell at that place, I would not leave the place, and therefore I thought I will pray to God, because I would still stay at that place, therefore I prayed not for the love of God, but for love of the place I lived in."⁴⁷ Love of place, rather than love of Christ, motivated many would-be missionaries who saw their communities and neighbors turning to Christianity and wanted to belong with them. Other confessions taken down by John Eliot and his son suggest other reasons, including an anxiety about sins and wrongdoings against other people (rather than God), a desire to gain the upper hand against Indian enemies, or even an effort to protect oneself from the wrath of English military forces. One Indian named Wequash became a preacher out of fear. A captain during the Pequot War, Wequash witnessed an English slaughter of the Pequots, "where divers hundreds of them were slaine in an houre." When he went out to preach in Connecticut, Wequash warned Indians of the apparent power that Englishmen had by virtue of their relationship with God, telling of their successes in war and admonishing his neighbors to cast off their sin, lest they share the same fate as their Pequot neighbors.[48]

Indigenous Christianity was also a matter of power. Many peoples began to believe that traditional religious beliefs and rituals alone no longer served as efficient responses to the novel conditions of disease, colonization, and war that the English presence had wrought. Accepting elements of English religion was not a marker of complete and total subservience, but rather a way to appropriate Christian power, command it, and use it to guide future Indian affairs. Indians were seeking *manitou,* or supernatural power, and they saw Christianity as a wellspring of spiritual power. Hiacoomes was an example of this phenomenon. He who appeared completely powerless suddenly had access to great reserves of *manitou* that even the traditional pawwaws could not break. He and his family—notwithstanding his daughter—were generally immune to diseases, and he was now a person of great repute. Pawwaws who tried to harm him were ineffectual. Hiacoomes, some Indians now believed, clearly had access to new forms of spiritual authority and protection by virtue of his covenant with the English God. Many native preachers became Christian evangelists because they were placing themselves under the guardianship of a spiritual power that would rejuvenate their culture and protect their people.[49]

At the same time, indigenous preachers expressed varying levels of Christian commitment. They appropriated and translated different elements of Puritan theology and fused Christian beliefs and practices with native ones. Some Indians saw Christianity as a kind of native revitalization movement, or a rebirth of spiritual knowledge that the ancestors possessed but had long been forgotten by later generations. An oral tradition taken down in the seventeenth century reminded audiences that, far from introducing novel concepts and cosmologies, Christian missionaries were simply picking up where the ancients had left off. The folk tradition suggests that the central tenets of the Christian message dealing with "the Commandments of God, and concerning God, and the making of the world by one God" were part of the Indian corpus of spiritual beliefs. In fact, the older Indians had apparently "heard some old men who were now dead, to say the same things, since whose death there hath been no remembrance or knowledge of them among the Indians until now they heare of them againe." Christianity was, according to this narrative, an ancestral Indian religion that needed to be revitalized. Native preachers didn't always see their adoption of Christianity as a paradigm shift in their spiritual lives. Instead, they believed many were incorporating Christian beliefs into existing Indian cosmologies and spiritual traditions. And, rather than producing a single, monolithic culture, this spiritual encounter and adaptation resulted in innumerable, complex fusions and multivalent answers for what it meant to be a Christian Indian in New England.[50]

It was one thing to nominally embrace elements of Christianity, but quite another to prepare for the rigors of missionary activity that Puritan officials demanded from native evangelists. Although indigenous missionaries possessed countless advantages over English ones, including language proficiency, access to kinship networks, and the ability to survive in the difficult terrain of the frontier, not everyone could take on the task, for being a missionary meant being invested with an incredible amount of authority and responsibility. The New England Company for the Propagation of the Gospel, founded in 1649, even rejected English applicants who appeared to have some intellectual skills, but were not so "Godly & soe qualified for the spirtuall parte of this worke."[51] For a few native missionaries, their newfound roles as spiritual leaders produced in them a crisis in confidence. One such preacher doubted his abilities and feared that "I am one blind, and when I teach other Indians I shall cause them to fall into the ditch."[52] Indian missionaries needed to be well prepared for the onslaught of questions and criticisms they expected to face in the field. Puritan divines often commented on the number and difficulty of such questions, and they interpreted Indian criticisms as both a demonstration of sincere interest in Christianity as well as a real challenge for missionaries who were just learning Christian doctrine. Since such criticisms and complex theological questions made preaching to Indians all the more difficult, a missionary had to be familiar with theological argument and rhetoric. As John Wilson noted, "there is need of learning in Ministers who preach to Indians, much more to English men and gracious Christians, for these had sundry philosophicall questions, which some knowledge of the arts must helpe to give answer to; and without which these would not have been satisfied."[53] Although many contemporaries likely doubted the ability of America's indigenous peoples to understand the intricacies of Calvinist theology, English missionaries still believed that natives would be central to conversion. If critics ever expressed doubts about Indian aptitude, Puritan clerics could simply invoke the infinite and mysterious power of God to advance his kingdom and claim that God "can make use of what Instruments hee pleaseth for this work."[54]

Because Indians were perceived as an essential component of God's plan for the salvation for the world, their training and education would be central to how the rest of sacred Christian history would unfold. "Seeing they must have Teachers amongst themselves," John Eliot summarized, "they must also be taught to be teachers."[55] It was in this spirit that indigenous missionaries underwent two main types of training. The first was in-school training, and there was no better place to build an "Indian Oxford" than at Harvard College. By 1656, the New England Company had amassed enough funds to construct a basic structure on campus. One Indian student who graduated from Harvard even before this "Indian College" was built was John Sassamon. He had served as a preacher at Natick, attended Harvard, and eventually became an advisor to the famous Indian leader King Philip.[56]

Two other students were personally educated by college President Charles Chauncy in the late 50s and early 60s. One was Joel, the son of Hiacoomes, and the other was a promising student named Caleb. Chauncy publicly examined the Indian candidates at Harvard's spring commencements in subjects they had learned that academic year, especially Latin. If they followed the traditional Harvard regimen, the future preachers would have also dabbled in logic, medicine, ethics, politics, arithmetic, geometry, and even astronomy, not to mention Greek, grammar, and etymology. The best students would undergo some training in Hebrew and other languages in order to access and understand ancient sacred texts. By 1664, Chauncy proudly boasted that he had "trained up two of the Indians and instructed them in Arts and languages until that nowe they are in some good measure fit to preach to the Indians and doe it w(ith) hope of comfortable success."[57] Sadly, Joel and Caleb's futures were not as bright as their successes at Harvard. Joel died when his boat was shipwrecked during a return trip from visiting his family on the Vineyard in 1665. Caleb, who graduated from Harvard that same year, died the following winter from tuberculosis. Proximity to English instruction also entailed proximity to English diseases, to which Indian students were extremely vulnerable. Eleazar, another promising young Indian student, died just before his own graduation. Benjamin Larnel, of the class of 1716 did the same. Harvard had a handful of capable young Indian students, but they frequently died from disease, perennially putting the indigenous missionary effort back at square one. Native preachers who went to Harvard or received an education from white ministers often died in droves. The problem of Indian death became so acute that Harvard eventually abandoned the Indian

College and their native missionary project. Only a few years after the Indian College opened, it was transformed into a printing office. By 1698 the building was unceremoniously torn down to make room for other college offices.

The second form of training was field training, and English missionaries believed that written texts would be essential to this training. Perhaps not coincidentally, the printing press stored at the Indian College was the same press that began printing thousands of pages of biblical texts in Algonquian in the 1660s and 1670s. John Eliot had previously published a catechism in 1653, but in the 1660s he published an entire bible, an Indian grammar, and an Indian primer. He also had printed Lewis Bayly's *Practice of Piety* and Richard Baxter's *A Call to the Unconverted,* two texts which emphasized repenting for sin while embracing inward piety. As early as 1650, when there was dim hope he would have anything printed at all, Eliot asserted, "my chief care is to communicate as much of the Scriptures as I can by writing: and further, my scope [is] to train up both men and youths; that when they be in some measure instructed themselves, they may be sent forth to other parts of the Countrey, to train up and instruct others, even as they themselves have been trained up and instructed."[58] The creation of Eliot's library in the Indian language was therefore not only intended to create converts, but also to train native preachers. The centerpiece of this scheme was Eliot's *Indian Dialogues,* published in 1671.

Designed to help English and English-speaking Indian evangelists in the missionary field, *Indian Dialogues* consisted of a series of three prolonged, imaginary conversations between indigenous missionaries and audiences who questioned them. As Eliot readily admitted, the line between fact and fiction in these conversations was not very clear. In the preface he conceded that "These dialogues are partly historical, of some things that were done and said, and partly instructive, to show what might or should have been said."[59] While the second dialogue discussed the theological intricacies of Puritan doctrine, the third was an imaginary conversation between King Philip and other indigenous missionaries, with King Philip eventually happily converting to Christianity, of course. The first dialogue, however, represented what Eliot and other English missionaries assumed, or even hoped, a typical meeting between an indigenous missionary and a non-Christian Indian would be like.

In this first dialogue, Piumbukhou, an Indian preacher, visits Kinsman, his long-lost relative. They begin with a cordial salutation and Kinsman wishes to hear more of the new religion that Piumbukhou was proselytizing. After only a few minutes, however, Kinsman quickly accuses Piumbukhou of leaving his home, abandoning his identity, and forgetting his old ways. Piumbukhou readily responds that his new religion, his new identity, was forged in the light, whereas his former self lived in perpetual darkness. The debate rises in intensity after Piumbukhou is invited into Kinsman's home to stay the night. Once inside, Kinsman asks the obvious question that most Indians wanted to know: what were the material advantages of conversion, and will "your praying to God exempt you from sickness, poverty, nakedness? Will praying to God fill you with food, gladness, and garments?" Piumbukhou immediately notes that all Christian Indians, at least at Natick, were healthy, well-fed, and happy. Yet even as the native missionary answers in the affirmative to these questions, he also contends that material advantages were not the main reason for his own adoption of Christianity: "If praying to God did bring with it outward plenty and worldly prosperity, then a carnal people would pray to God, not because they love God, or praying to God, but because they love themselves." Kinsman seems satisfied with the answer—he was, all the while, a fairly easy sell—but his wife and family are less convinced.[60]

Piumbukhou then ups the ante, comparing indigenous religious practices to living like dogs and even invoking the fire and brimstone rhetoric that was central to Puritan sermonizing. Piumbukhou warns his audience to repent, for there were more than lifestyle changes at stake: "Your souls feed upon nothing but lust, and lying, and stealing, and killing, and Sabbath-breaking, and pauwauing. And all these sins are sins which poison, starve, and kill your souls, and expose them to God's wrath that they may be tormented among devils and wicked men in hell fire forever." Predictably, and in spite of their initial reservations and doubts, Kinsman and his kin come around, eventually acknowledging the superiority and ultimate truthfulness of Christianity. Although this was a fictional exchange between a neophyte and a potential convert, the lessons that native missionaries in training could take from it were quite tangible: kinship networks could be vehicles for conversion, Christianity did indeed imply some material advantages, traditional Indian religion should be analogized to a primitive life of carnal sin, and different sectors of Indian society would respond differently to native missionaries.[61]

Although it is impossible to assess the success of *Indian Dialogues* in training native missionaries for their work—it was limited to those who could read English, or have someone who could read it to them—the text does shed light on the centrality of indigenous actors to debates about missionary work and exposes the kinds of opportunities and challenges they might have encountered. Eliot was only occasionally at Natick, his flagship praying town, and he was certainly less active in the handful of other towns that employed Christian evangelists. In fact, Natick was rather exceptional, which probably explains why Eliot invoked it so frequently in publications and letters to friends, donors, and colleagues. Even Eliot's textual translations were problematic. Cotton Mather, for all of his later effusive hagiography of Eliot, noted that the apostle's translations were flawed, to say the least. Mather suggested that "There are many words of Mr. Eliot's forming which [Indians] never understood. This they say is a grief to them. Such a knowledge in their Bibles as our English ordinarily have in ours, they seldom any of them have; and there seems to be as much difficulty to bring them unto a competent knowledge of the Scriptures, as it would be to get a sensible acquaintance with the English tongue."[62] Because Eliot was very rarely in the praying towns he established, and because his Algonquian texts were poorly translated, the connection between Eliot and the scores of Indians he tried to convert was relatively weak. Eliot *began* the mission, but he *was not* the mission. In fact, Eliot's absences and shortcomings put more responsibility into the hands of native missionaries even as his rare visits created spaces in which they could operate. Native preachers, not John Eliot, were the ones responsible for spreading Christianity to New England Indians in the first stages of cultural encounter.

Although native preachers became indispensable to Christian missionary work by the middle of the seventeenth century, the role of these indigenous missionaries was fraught with ambiguity, tension, and contradiction. Missionaries faced many challenges in their new identities as apostles to Indians, and they were caught between two societies that regarded them suspiciously. As one native missionary said, "because wee pray to God, other *Indians* abroad in the countrey hate us and oppose us, the English on the other side suspect us, and feare us to be still such as doe not pray at all."[63] It was difficult for indigenous missionaries to befriend Indians if the latter felt that they were being victimized by imperialistic and land-hungry English, to whom native missionaries seemed allied. Many missionaries also forsook their Christian religion and training, using the cultural negotiation skills they learned while at school to try to make a more lucrative living. Daniel Gookin recalled in 1674 that some well-trained evangelists had "entered upon other callings: as one is a mariner; another, a carpenter; another went for England with a gentleman."[64] And then, there was the issue of institutional and financial support. Eliot often complained that the New England Company rarely paid its missionaries enough (or at all). He quipped in 1671 that "messengers & instruments looke for theire pay. & if y[t] faile the wheele moves very heavyly, & will quick stand still. . . . if instruments faile, the work will fall."[65] Native missionaries had to worry about challenges from competing religious groups as well, including Jesuits, Quakers, Baptists, and Anabaptists. The biggest challenges, however, came from three sources: the struggle of enforcing religious orthodoxy, the resistance of the pawwaws, and the affliction of disease.

No moment better exemplified the tension inherent in native missionaries' position than the Sabbath Day. Every week Indian preachers were supposed to gather their congregations at the beating of a drum, and the services would include prayer, singing of psalms, reading from scripture, and, of course, sermons. Indians sometimes asked for assistance from English ministers on their sermons, but they often performed them on their own. Cotton Mather described these Indian sermons as rather formulaic and consisting of several parts: "you may have in their sermons, a, *Kukkootamwehteaonk*, that is, a *Doctrine, Nahrootomtoehceaonk*, or, an Answer, a *Witcheayeuonk*, or, a Reason, with an *Ouworeank*, or an, Use for the close of all."[66] It was a perpetual challenge to gather an audience in the first place, for many Indians naturally opted to spend their Sundays in other ways. When one Indian woman went out on a Sunday morning to get some water, she met a friend and began to discuss "worldly matters." The local native preacher discovered the exchange and took this opportunity to organize his entire sermon around respect for the Sabbath and observing exclusively spiritual matters, pointing her out and chastising her while confirming Sabbath-breaking as a sin.[67] Native preachers employed cautionary tales about breaking the Sabbath. One local chief, for example, tried to stop his men from killing pigeons on a Sabbath day. When they ignored him and climbed high into a tree to hunt a pigeon, "one of them fell down from off the tree and brake his neck, and another fell down and brake some of his limbs."[68] Native missionaries could exploit these cautionary tales, apocryphal or not, to emphasize that Sabbath-breaking was not only sinful, but worthy of God's quick and decisive punishment. And yet, while native preachers could use these examples as teaching moments for their Christian Indian congregations, they also ran the risk of humiliating and alienating the very people to whom they were trying to appeal.

Indigenous missionaries were not always as orthodox as Puritan clergymen probably hoped. Indeed, there was a great deal of syncretism, or cultural mixing, between Puritan theology and indigenous religious thinking and practice. When Indians placed English material objects into the graves of their loved ones, for example, they injected the spiritual power of Christianity into traditional funerary rituals.[69] Puritans

rarely used images, dance, or other rituals to proselytize, but native missionaries made fairly effective use of song. It was in biblical psalms that
native missionaries found common ground with indigenous traditions of
singing and chanting. Eliot noted that many native evangelists and their
congregations expressed their religious devotion by becoming "*skilful*
and *graceful* Singers."[70] John Endecott, the Governor of Massachusetts
Bay Colony, visited Natick in 1651 and heard both the sermons and
singing there. He recalled that praying Indians sang the psalms "with
such reverence, zeale, good affection, and distinct utterance, that I could
not but admire it" and was so satisfied with the religious expression that
he claimed that his trip to the praying village was "one of the best journeys I made these many years."[71] If the Sabbath was a point of contention, song was a point of accommodation. English audiences viewed
Indian singing as outward expressions of Christian piety while Indian
congregations easily incorporated psalm-singing into their religious cosmology because orality and singing were already central to their own
religious practices and rituals.

Native missionaries also faced fierce resistance from Indians who felt
challenged by the new authority they wielded. These included both
sachems and pawwaws. According to the Puritan narratives that made
their way into print, conflicts between native preachers and traditional
Indian spiritual leaders universally ended poorly for the non-Christians.
For example, Hiacoomes had a heated rivalry with Pakeponesso, a
sachem on Martha's Vineyard. Pakeponesso invited Hiacoomes to his
home, ridiculed him, and even slapped him across the face. Later on,
after Pakeponesso ridiculed him again, a bolt of lightning surged through
his wigwam and struck him down. As he lay unconscious, his leg
remained burning in the fire. He survived, however, and eventually (and
predictably) converted to Christianity.[72] Others who resisted God's word
were not as lucky. Japhet, another Martha's Vineyard missionary, took a
trip to the mainland and supposedly converted a large group of Indians
there. Yet as soon as Japhet left, one of them mocked the missionary and
vowed not to worship God. Coming home from a long journey only a
few days later, the man discovered that "His house was consum'd by fire;
and his three children, where were all he had, consum'd in it." He, like
Pakeponesso, predictably offered a sincere conversion to Christianity
after his affliction. Tragedy stalked the natives and missionaries often
benefited from it.[73]

Unlike sachems and skeptics, pawwaws attacked native missionaries
because they represented a direct assault on their traditional religious
authority. Daniel Gookin described pawwaws as "partly wizards and

witches, holding familiarity with Satan, that evil one; and partly are physicians, and make use, at least in show, of herbs and roots, for curing the sick and diseased."[74] Because many Puritans believed in the power of witchcraft, the occult, and superstition, a pawwaw's authority was not to be taken lightly, and it was assumed that they were in league with the devil. Praying villages even had explicit rules against "pawwawing," and shamans were accused of sending spies to infiltrate Christian communities and even killing native Christians. However, the fundamental tension between pawwaws and indigenous missionaries was less a matter of religious incompatibility and more an issue of competition: both groups demanded obedience, provided explanations for historical and spiritual forces, and both called on spiritual authorities that could never be proven to exist. Just as Hiacoomes had a showdown with a sachem, he also took on the pawwaws, producing a confrontation which eventually gave him even more legitimacy on the Vineyard. One of the pawwaws there tried to conjure up a snake to kill Hiacoomes, but that was ineffectual. Others claimed that they could kill him in an instant, but he publicly called their bluff and exclaimed, "*Let all the powawes in the island come together, I'll venture my self in the midst of them; let them use all their witchcrafts; with the help of God, I'll tread upon them all.*" Some pawwaws even showed up after Hiacoomes had finished preaching on a Sunday and threatened to kill him. Hiacoomes casually replied that they could do nothing, pointing to his heel and saying that he would crush them underneath it. Hiacoomes thus not only tried to derail the pawwaws' power, but also endeavored to publicly humiliate and intimidate them.[75] Hiacoomes was not alone in attacking the pawwaws. When one Christian Indian name George got sick, he consulted a pawwaw. But his neighbors suspected that the pawwaw had made George sick in the first place, so they grabbed the pawwaw and threatened to throw him in a fire. As soon as he felt the heat, the curse was lifted and George felt fine again.[76] These victories over pawwaws, of course, were surely not as lopsided as Puritan commentators assumed them to be. Yet this challenge from the pawwaws was both a problem for indigenous missionaries and an opportunity for them to demonstrate their own authority as new spiritual leaders of indigenous communities.

Disease, however, proved to be as capricious as ever. Just as disease helped native missionaries gain adherents on Martha's Vineyard by preserving Hiacoomes and quieting the pawwaws, it almost destroyed the indigenous missionary movement on the mainland. In 1652, several praying towns experienced a flux that killed off many missionaries, as well as their kin, and cast doubt on their newfound status as God's chosen people. Some tried to capitalize on disease by using its transmission as an opportunity to highlight those who had become model Christians and admonish those who had not. John Eliot, for example, published a tract called *The Dying Speeches of Several Indians,* which emphasized that disease, for all its temporal pain, ultimately brought victims to the light of the gospel. One dying victim even rejoiced, "By this sickness God calleth me to repent all my sins, and to believe in Christ. Now I confess myselfe a great sinner, Oh pardon me and helpe me for Christ his sake."[77] The famous Waban gave a sermon in 1659 that equated bodily sickness with a lack of faith, which he called "sicknesse in our soul." In Waban's view, Christ was not only a spiritual power but also a physician, supplanting the responsibilities of the traditional pawwaws and offering an alternative method for dealing with the demographic and epidemiological implications of European colonization.[78]

For all of these attempts, Puritan ministers could not help but notice that their best missionaries were dying all around them. A group of ministers complained, "It hath pleased the Lord to frown upon our endeavours in this kind; taking away by death, at sundry times, six youths or more, upon whom considerable cost had been expended for their education."[79] Puritan divines felt "great discouragement" at losing so many "pretious instruments" and "hopefull buds" for the missionary enterprise.[80] In 1669, John Eliot regretted that, in Natick, "many of our choyce instruments of this place are dead."[81] Martha's Vineyard, which had experienced periodic epidemics from the 1640s to 1690, felt the pain of disease more acutely by the end of the century. One English missionary lamented that, "of the number of more than one hundred Adult Persons that dyed, not less than *three fourths,* were of the *Sober Religious Professors.*"[82] Intimate access to English culture had, of course, meant exposure to English diseases. The very people who claimed to be under God's protection were sometimes the ones hardest hit by God's wrath.

Of all the impediments that native preachers faced, few were more challenging than King Philip's War, a conflict that erupted in New England in the middle of the 1670s. The decade had begun fairly well for the indigenous missionary effort. John Eliot and John Cotton had recognized an official indigenous church on Martha's Vineyard in 1670. Eliot had published his *Indian Dialogues,* which he expected would serve as a missionary training manual for future evangelists. In the meantime, he and Daniel Gookin had taken up the task of traveling even further west and south to establish new praying towns. A fundamental component of that work would be, in Gookin's words, "to settle teachers in every town."

Many of those new teachers and preachers were trained and educated in Natick, confirming that town's status as a nucleus for indigenous evangelical activity. At Manchage, or Oxford, they installed a preacher named Waabesktamin. Joseph, who was a member of the Hassanamesitt (Grafton) church, became the teacher at Chabanakongkomun, or Dudley. In fact, Joseph had established this praying village and had been preaching to the inhabitants there well before Eliot and Gookin made him official. An Indian named Jethro became a preacher at Nashaway, near Lancaster. James Speen was from one of Natick's most prominent Christian families, and he was installed at Pekachoog, near Worcester. Woodstock, Connecticut also became a veritable outpost of praying Indians, as it had several villages with native ministers there, including Daniel and Sampson. The latter was a former alcoholic who had recently abandoned his drinking, patched things up with his alienated wife, and began a life of Christian exhortation. When John Moqua was presented as preacher to the village of Maanexit in Woodstock, his first act was to set and sing a psalm, which he concluded with a prayer. These new praying towns reportedly had sober, well-established, and active native ministers who were willing to expand the kingdom of Christ. The 1670s thus began auspiciously for native missionary enterprises in New England.[83]

The rest of the decade would be quite different, and there is no better evidence that native missionaries were central to the relationship between English and Indians than the fact that the man who sparked King Philip's War was one of them. English territorial expansion, competition over trade, and other troubles were the root causes of the conflict between Indians and English, but John Sassamon's murder was the catalyst. A Christian minister who had been educated at Harvard and taught Indians at Natick, Nemasket, Assawompsett, and Titicut, Sassamon became a personal advisor to Wampanoag chief King Philip just before war broke out. Through Sassamon, Philip gained access to not only a skilled interpreter, but also a powerful cultural negotiator who could provide some leverage against the English while ostensibly gaining the support of Christian Indians. For Sassamon, his position as both a Christian evangelist and personal advisor to a sachem who maintained a notorious aversion to Christianity put him in an awkward position. Perhaps Sassamon thought he could strengthen his own hand by acting as Philip's advisor. Perhaps he thought he could be the native preacher to convert Philip, as forecasted in Eliot's *Indian Dialogues*. He would do neither. When Sassamon overheard a plan for Philip to attack English settlements, he informed the English of Philip's scheme. Shortly thereafter, he was mysteriously murdered. After the war, Increase Mather would argue that Sassamon was murdered "out of hatred against him for his Religion, for . . . he was a Preacher amongst Indians."[84] Although his status as a preacher may not have necessarily sealed his fate, it nevertheless granted Sassamon access to the kinds of abilities and skills that cultural brokers needed to negotiate between the two worlds. Unfortunately for Sassamon, when these negotiations broke down, the brokers were often the ones caught in the middle. When three of Philip's Wampanoag subjects were caught and quickly executed for Sassamon's murder, the war officially began.

On the eve of King Philip's War there was a handful of praying towns led and operated by dozens of native evangelists. In total, there were as many as 1100 praying Indians in the praying towns and perhaps thousands more on the Cape and Islands. The war put these Christian Indians and the preachers that led them in an untenable position. In spite of the professed allegiance between Christian Indians and English authorities, many English could not distinguish between a friendly Indian and an enemy one. For example, in 1675 Massachusetts passed a law making it legal for any person to "kill and destroy" any Indian caught walking or "skulking" in any English towns or woods.[85] This law must have been problematic for Indians who were on the move. Even as English authorities fantasized about keeping Indians stationary during the war, the conflict catalyzed a horrific cycle of displacement. Preachers and their congregations fled Natick and other praying towns in droves, coalescing in towns like Marlborough and Concord, migrating to Connecticut and New Hampshire, or even seeking refuge in the woods. Eventually, the English would send hundreds of Christian Indians to Boston's Deer Island, a "bleake Iland" that was barren, cold, and windswept.[86] There they were greeted with meager food supplies, scant provisions, and little shelter or fuel to protect them from the harsh Atlantic winds that pounded this veritable concentration camp in the winter.

Indian missionaries suffered horribly during the war. John Sassamon's untimely death was only the most prominent example of a native evangelist being murdered, but there were other preachers and teachers who suffered similar fates. Jethro, the teacher who had been installed at Nashaway, was accused of helping to cause the conflict and was summarily executed by English settlers. His son was killed with him. Natick's Anthony Speen dealt with his feelings of horror and loss by drinking himself into oblivion and forfeiting his prestigious position as the town's teacher. Joseph Tuckapawillin, the preacher at Hassanamesit (Grafton), feared the English would raid his praying town and kill the women and children, so he sent his family into the woods to fend for themselves.

When Eliot met with Tuckapawillin during the middle of the war, Eliot recorded what the Indian preacher said to him:

> I am greatly distressed this day on every side: the English have taken away some of my estate, my corn, my cattle, my plough, cart, chain, and other goods. The enemy Indians have also taken a part of what I had; and the wicked Indians mock and scoff at me, saying, 'Now what is become of your praying to God?' The English also censure me, and say I am a hypocrite. In this distress I have no where to look, but up to God in heaven to help me; now my dear wife and eldest son are (through English threatenings) run away, and I fear will perish in the woods for want of food; also my aged mother is lost; and all this doth greatly aggravate my grief. But yet I desire to look up to God in Christ Jesus, in whom alone is my help.[87]

Tuckapawillin's complaints demonstrate the fragile position that native evangelists occupied during a period of conflict and displacement. Caught between the English who distrusted them and the Indians who despised them, native missionaries often had to find their own solutions to their problems. Tuckapawillin had good reason to complain to Eliot, and he certainly had reason to fear. Although his family would eventually return to him, his son would die of starvation by the winter of 1676.

Tuckapawillin eventually became one of many native evangelists who enlisted on the side of the English during King Philip's War (he was captured by enemy Indians soon into his mission). Although most colonists were vehemently opposed to employing natives as military allies, their skills as scouts, spies, messengers, and warriors eventually became a key factor in the English victory. The very treacherous and deceitful attributes that commentators on the war would ascribe to inherent Indian character apparently made Indians uncommonly adept at spying and scouting. For their own part, native ministers enlisted with the English not only to demonstrate their loyalty (which the English often assumed was the paramount motivation), but to help their families navigate the troubled waters of war. Job Kattenanit, for example, was a minister of "piety and ability" who had been preaching at Magunkog (Ashland) prior to the war. When he enlisted as a spy, he used the opportunity to spearhead a dangerous rescue mission to help secure the release of his children, who had been taken prisoner by hostile Nipmuck Indians. Paid five pounds and given a pass from the Superintendent of Indian Affairs, Kattenanit went off to spy with James Quannapohit, a relative of Natick's most prominent Christian Indians. Once among the Nipmucks, they encountered Joseph Tuckapawillin, the Grafton preacher who had been captured during his own scouting mission. Tuckapawillin relayed that, given Quannapohit's pedigree, it was too dangerous for him to stay. Kattenanit, on the other hand, waited to secure the release of his children. Relying upon a network of native evangelists, Kattenanit organized a rescue mission involving himself, Joseph Tuckapawillin, and Tuckapawillin's father, Naoas, who also happened to be a deacon at Tuckapawillin's church. His children apparently made it to safety, though Job's own retreat from the enemy Indians was much more tenuous. When he finally returned to the English, and in spite of the fact that he carried a pass from Daniel Gookin and warned the English of an impending attack on Lancaster, he was suspected of being a hostile Indian, shuffled off to the army captain, sent to Boston, and transported to Deer Island. He was only able to leave the miserable island when Thomas Savage began organizing an expedition consisting of native scouts. Of the six Indians Savage chose for his mission, three of them were native preachers. Kattenanit was one of them. His experiences during the war demonstrate that native missionaries enlisted on the side of the English colonists not just to express their loyalty, but to secure their families, aid other ministers and praying Indians, and flee English military camps. When Indian preachers fought for the English, they did so on their own terms.[88]

Some praying Indians chose to fight against the English during the war. Although the older praying towns had long-established communities of Christian Indians, the new towns that Gookin and Eliot organized in the 1670s seemed much more ambivalent about their allegiances. Gookin recalled that the new praying Indians, "being but raw and lately initiated into the Christian profession . . . fell off from the English and joined the enemy in war."[89] In fact, the number of Christian Indians fighting against the English grew quickly as the war dragged on. The most notorious of all the Christian rebels must have been James Printer. The aptly named Printer was best known for setting the type for the famous Indian press but he was also a native missionary. He lived at Hassanamesit with several other Indian preachers and was assigned to teach at Waeuntug (Uxbridge) from 1669 to 1674, only a few miles off. In fact, his father was Naoas, the deacon in the Hassanamesit Church, and his brother was the same Joseph Tuckapawillin who helped James Quannapohit and Job Kattenanit in their spying missions during the war. In spite of, or perhaps because of, his family ties, long history as a Christian minister, and prominent position as a typesetter, Printer chose to side with the Nipmucks when the war began. Remarkably, after fighting on the side of the enemy Indians, Printer was able to get his old jobs back after the war. He returned to Natick for several years and eventually returned to his hometown of Hassanamesit, where he remained a teacher from 1698 to 1717. He even took up his old job of typesetting, this time contributing to the expanding market for captivity narratives by printing Mary Rowlandson's *The Sovereignty and Goodness of God.* James Printer's story, as well as the conscious decisions he made during the war, show that Christian Indian identity did not necessarily entail a passive subjugation to English authority. Instead, Christianity could be empowering for some Indians in ways that allowed them to choose sides based upon their own sensibilities and not upon an allegiance to a nominally Christian people.[90]

When faced with such a harrowing decision as choosing between the untrustworthy English or the hostile Indians, some native missionaries opted to remain neutral, leading their congregations out of their towns and into the relative protection of the forest. The praying Indians at Wamesit (Lowell) fled their town out of fear of both Indians and English. The Nipmucks burned their wigwams with the elderly inside while the English executed other residents as traitors or shipped them off as slaves to the West Indies. Mystic George, one of their Christian teachers, was struck down by disease and could not retreat with his people into the forest. When the Wamesit Indians wrote to English officials to explain their plight, they raised the specter of Indian defection to the French by blaming their diaspora on the English themselves. They then proclaimed that they were not sorry for leaving, but did regret that "the English have driven us from our praying to God and from our Teacher. We did begin to understand a little of praying to God."[91] Although Mystic George was dead, Simon Beckom led the remaining Wamesit refugees north and into the woods, hoping to find either French or friendly Indians to take them in.

During the three weeks that the Wamesit Indians were marooned in the forest, Beckom led three separate Sabbath-day meetings. He later told Daniel Gookin that he "read and taught the people out of Psalm 35, the second Sabbath from Psalm 46, the third Sabbath out of Psalm 118."[92] The use of psalms as the scriptural basis for Beckom's meetings is notable. The psalms were often the first pieces of scripture taught to indigenous converts. Missionaries could use psalms because they reflected a direct relationship with God, were relatively easy to remember, and their presentation as songs made them particularly effective in an oral, auditory culture. Beckom did not choose these psalms randomly. Instead, the psalms spoke to the unique experiences of a people who were torn asunder, forced into exile, and wondering how to understand their identity as Christian Indians during a war between mostly Christians and mostly Indians.

The first week Beckom taught from Psalm 35, which explains that "I behaved myself as though he had been my friend or brother: I bowed down heavily, as one that mourneth for his mother. But in mine adversity they rejoiced, and gathered themselves together: yea, the abjects gathered themselves together against me, and I knew it not . . . for they seek not peace: but they devise deceitful matters against them that are quiet in the land." While Psalm 35 speaks to the terrors befalling a peaceful people caught in a cycle of deceit and revenge, the next week Beckom turned away from the theme of betrayal to focus on God's protection during a time of severe trial. Psalm 46 states that "God is our refuge and strength, a very present help in trouble . . . He maketh wars to cease unto the end of the earth; he breaketh the bow, and cutteth the spear in sunder . . . Be still, and know that I am God: I will be exalted among the heathen, I will be exalted in the earth. The Lord of hosts is with us; the God of Jacob is our refuge." Transitioning from God's power to emphasize God's mercy, Beckom's third and final Psalm—118—assured his congregation that, in spite of the war waging around them, they still had to remain faithful to God, for God had remained faithful to them. Beckom told his listeners that God's mercy endures forever, and that "It is better to trust in the Lord than to put confidence in man. It is better to trust in the Lord than to put confidence in princes." "All nations compassed me about," the Psalm proclaims, "but in the name of the Lord will I destroy them." If he read or sang the psalm in its entirety, he would have concluded by proclaiming that "The stone which the builders refused is become the head stone of the corner. This is the Lord's doing; it is marvelous in our eyes." Interestingly, while the first two weeks of psalms speak to the problems faced by Christian Indians in the midst of war, the final one looks to the future. Indeed, native evangelists might have believed that the war was a scourge to cleanse the world of evil, redeem the faithful, and establish a new church built on the back of a truly Christian congregation. Given his invocation of Psalm 118, Beckom probably foresaw his congregation, and perhaps even himself, playing a central part in the construction of this new, post-war Christian order.

If Simon Beckom's final Sabbath day meeting revealed some measure of optimism about indigenous Christianity in the postwar world, the reality would be very different. Even John Eliot naively hoped that the war would not bring a cessation to native missionary activities, but an intensifying of them. Yet it was very clear that King Philip's War had devastated and nearly destroyed the Puritan missionary project. The generation that witnessed this disaster recognized the havoc that it wreaked on Indian populations. As disease and warfare ravaged native communities, produced multiple diasporas, created thousands of refugees, engendered persistent poverty and starvation, and soured the already uneasy relationship between English and Indians, several generations of Puritan writers commented in eerily similar ways about the disintegration of native Christian populations. Increase Mather stated that the destruction of native communities represented a "signal blast of heaven," while his son, Cotton, agreed that there appeared to be a "strange Blast from Heaven consuming them." Indians, as well as the missions they operated, seemed to be dying all around them.[93]

In no place was this more evident than Natick, formerly the most important of all the praying towns. As a site where generations of native preachers taught dozens of Indian families, as an Indian town that had embraced several aspects of English-style civilization, and as one of only four praying towns rebuilt after the war, Natick was both literally and symbolically significant. The decades after King Philip's War, however, exposed the challenges of maintaining an indigenous Christian community on a frontier wracked by war. Land was certainly at the center of the conflict, and the constant incursion of English settlers into Natick after the war created social and generational tensions that put the community on edge. Language and the employment of English ministers, however, proved to be just as problematic for the Christian Indian community. Although they had always thought of John Eliot as a "spiritual father," Natick Indians were irate when Englishman Daniel Gookin took over the pulpit after the war. Gookin believed that native languages perpetuated a kind of savage barbarism among Indians, so he preached to his new Indian congregation entirely in English. The Indians wisely petitioned the New England Commissioners in charge of the mission and urged Gookin to do his utmost to learn their language. They even praised Gookin's interpreter and invoked Paul's first letter to the Corinthians to explain that the use of an interpreter and the continuance of native languages had biblical sanction.[94]

By 1687 the Natick Indians got their wish; an Indian named Daniel Takawombpait, whom John Eliot had personally groomed for the pastorate, became Natick's preacher. Although he could speak the native tongue and exhibited some scriptural knowledge, Puritan divines complained about his theological "errata"—though the records fail to indicate exactly what this constituted—and considered replacing him before realizing that they could not find anyone suitable to take his place.[95] By the 1710s the Commissioners launched an inquiry into the temporal and spiritual state of Natick, found it to be "languishing and withered," and blamed its degeneration into "a very lax Procedure" on Takawombpait himself.[96] Even if the Commissioners considered dismissing Daniel, they did not have to make that decision. He died in 1716, and John Neesnumin, an Indian preacher from Sandwich, was chosen to replace him. Neesnumin himself died only a few years later, and Thomas Waban of Natick replaced him. By 1721 an English minister named Oliver Peabody became the first-ever minister in Natick who knew absolutely nothing of Indian languages. Not surprisingly, it was around this time that land deeds were being drafted in English more frequently, a new generation of Indian schoolchildren was more comfortable with the English language, and more English settlers began traveling to Natick for religious services. With the slow displacement of indigenous languages from the experience of Christian Indian spirituality, the need for native ministers decreased. The era of Indian spiritual leadership in Natick had come and gone.[97]

A more nuanced and sophisticated understanding of the "Eliot missions" demands that we take celebrated missionary John Eliot out of the picture. Heralded as the "apostle to the Indians," Eliot only traveled from his Roxbury pulpit to Natick about every two weeks. He had the same arrangement with the praying town of Punkapoag, near present day Canton. By the end of his life, Eliot was going to these villages only a few times every year, depending upon his health. Indeed, the Puritan missionary enterprise was not organized and operated solely by English missionaries, let alone John Eliot. Instead, native evangelists were usually on their own. Indian preachers and teachers appropriated Christianity for multiple reasons, and their translations of Christianity and newfound roles as Christian evangelists did not necessarily involve a complete break with their past or a rejection of their people. Instead, Christianity offered an alternative system of spiritual meaning that some Native Americans embraced during this period of tumultuous change. As apostles to other Indians, these New England preachers would become the benchmark by which later indigenous missionaries were judged. In their translation of Christianity and in their ascension to positions of spiritual leadership within a rapidly changing cultural landscape, Indian preachers played a central role in relations and interactions between English and Indians. King Philip's War disrupted this practice in many ways and, facing west from Natick, the war-torn missionary effort appeared to be in steep decline. Yet the Christian Indian communities in southeastern New England, Martha's Vineyard, Nantucket, and Cape Cod emerged from the war shaken but not destroyed. A growing cadre of native preachers there would attempt to redefine Native American identity while securing for Christian Indians a place in the postwar colonial world.

CHAPTER TWO

The Expansion of the Indigenous Missionary Enterprise

I T WAS A HISTORIC MEETING between the two men. Both were named George, both were royal representatives from their respective nations, and neither spoke English very well. Missionary history, however, would tie these men together, at least for their brief meeting in 1715. One of the Georges was the King of England; the other a "Prince" from the Yamassee Indian nation of the Carolinas. The first was a product of the Hanoverian succession, and as such was much more comfortable with German language and culture than English. The second was the son of a powerful Yamassee chief, and was sent by the Society for the Propagation of the Gospel in Foreign Parts (SPG) to England for a missionary education. In spite of the obvious cultural divides that separated George I from Prince George of the Yamassees, their meeting was collegial and the King of England received the Indian prince "very graciously."[1] Indeed, it was hoped that, when finished with the baptism, conversion, and evangelical training he was receiving in England, the Indian Prince would become an invaluable addition to the missionary effort among Indians in the southern colonies. As such, these two royal Georges represented the future of evangelical efforts in the British Atlantic world. While the members of the SPG expected moral and institutional support from King George I, they also anticipated that, with native royalty like Prince George, the Yamassee would flock to their ranks to serve as preachers to their kinsmen and communities. These assumptions expose one of the most striking ironies of the early modern Protestant missionary enterprise: the nature of Atlantic world encounters forced English missionaries to rely upon non-English people for the creation and development of Christian missions.[2]

Puritans certainly did not have a monopoly on missionary work, and Anglicans—members of the Church of England—became increasingly active in transatlantic evangelism at the turn of the eighteenth century. Like the Puritans before them, Anglicans attempted to use native preachers. However, several factors related to the organization, goals, and institutional culture of Anglican missions circumscribed how effective indigenous preachers would be. The Anglicans became fixated on native royalty as potential preachers, which ensured that their numbers were relatively few. Imperial wars put these potential preachers in harm's way, forcing them to decide between English Christianity and the indigenous peoples from which they originated. They almost always chose the latter. Anglicans, like other groups, also struggled with the question of how to navigate the relationship between evangelism and slavery. Could they make preachers out of slaves, and what impact would that have on the social and religious climates of the slave societies they were trying to convert? Such challenges made Anglican efforts to use black and Indian preachers difficult and slow to get started, even as the native missions in New England were regrouping after King Philip's War.

As destructive as King Philip's War was to Indian preachers and some of the communities they resided in, the battle of printed words remembering the war, and the role of Christian Indians in it, was equally important to indigenous missionaries. The postwar New England book market became glutted with as many as 15,000 copies of accounts of the war, most of them describing Native Americans as barbarous savages. Daniel Gookin tried to combat this trend by highlighting the contributions made by Christian Indians to the war while John Eliot desperately did the same to try to rebuild his prized praying towns. Nevertheless, accounts by military leaders and other Puritan clergy emphasized Indian ferocity and brutality while simultaneously blaming Indians for starting the conflict. Wildly popular captivity narratives like Mary Rowlandson's *The Sovereignty and Goodness of God*, first published in 1682, crystallized the negative stereotypes of Indians as barbarians and irredeemable savages that common New Englanders suspected all along. Although she despised her hostile captors, Rowlandson saved her harshest words for the praying Indians, describing them as treacherous, deceitful, and wicked. Rowlandson blamed them for failing to save English captives and even described one of them as "so wicked and cruel, as to wear a string about his neck, strung with *Christians* fingers."[3] As these popular texts were printed, sold, read, and reprinted, the image of Native Americans as irredeemable savages began to contradict the great power and authority that Puritan leaders had invested in native preachers in seasons prior. The war had done its damage, but books about the war sustained it.[4]

The battle over the memory of the war and Christian Indians' role in it generated a major debate about the propriety and efficacy of native ministers in the ensuing years. The New England Commissioners had already tried to install English preachers at Natick, which Natick Indians resisted until the 1720s. But the postwar period was also characterized by a flurry of proposals to extend the Christian missionary enterprise through means other than the employment of native evangelists. Immediately after King Philip's War, Daniel Gookin proposed a chain of English-speaking free schools around Marlborough, Massachusetts, where Indians would learn firsthand the benefits of agriculture, civilization, and, of course, the English language. He hoped to supplement the school with an expansive apprenticeship program that placed Indian children with colonial families in the hopes of introducing them to "civility" and thus alleviating the threat of another war. Importantly, there was no place for native missionaries in Gookin's scheme. He complained that their training had been too costly and ultimately "ineffectual to the ends proposed." Instead, he argued that native preachers be replaced with English ones, for they were "better to instruct them in substantial and orthodox divinity, than teachers of their own nation, who cannot in reason be imagined to be so sufficient, as if they were learned men."[5] Gookin's racial reasoning led him to the conclusion that Indian character, rather than any other factor, was the main reason why native preachers were ineffective. It wasn't because they *chose* to be poor Indians, it was simply that they were incapable of doing anything else.

While Gookin and others believed that eradicating Indian language and employing English ministers would be the most sensible approach to postwar missionary work, other divines still looked to native tongues as instruments of gospelization. Cotton Mather, for example, printed a Christian dialogue in English, Dutch, French, and Iroquois for use among the Indians west of the Connecticut River. Mather also urged the New England mission's backers to publish another Indian bible in the 1710s, arguing that the propagation of Christianity through indigenous languages was much more important and feasible than the imposition of a full-scale plan to convert Indians into Englishmen.[6] The Mayhew family, which had been serving as missionaries to the Wampanoags on Martha's Vineyard since the middle of the seventeenth century, emphasized that native preachers would be vital to rebuilding Christian Indian communities after the devastating war. In the postwar period the Mayhews printed not only accounts of successful Indian conversions and tales of prominent native preachers, but also Indian Psalters to be used by native evangelists. From their perspective on the Vineyard, which had fostered several sustained Christian Indian communities that generally avoided the horrors of the war on the mainland, it was almost impossible to imagine the conversion of New England's Indians without the help of those same Indians.[7]

It is often assumed that King Philip's War not only pushed New England's Indians west, but also occasioned the end of Eliot's missionary plan. Although there was a dramatic diaspora of Indians to the north, south, and west, there were thousands of Indians who remained "behind the frontier," eking out a living and trying to raise their children, protect their lands, and survive in the wake of war. These communities retained a remarkable degree of autonomy in spite of their newborn status as *de facto* reservations. Only a few thrived, but many survived. While original praying towns like Natick seemed to be falling apart, a new generation of native preachers took the helm of Christian Indian leadership in southeastern New England.[8]

A quick survey of their communities reveals the extent to which native evangelists were not only prevalent but ubiquitous in Indian villages after King Philip's War. Cape Cod and southeastern Massachusetts held twenty-three Indian villages that hosted over fifty Indian preachers. Mashpee, an Indian town on Cape Cod, was dominated by two evangelical Indian families: the Briants and the Popmonits. Nantucket and the Elizabeth Islands had five congregations led by about eighteen Indian evangelists. Martha's Vineyard, as it had in prior generations, became the most illustrious model of Native American Christian leadership, having twelve separate Indian congregations and over fifty Wampanoag preachers. Even on the mainland, where praying communities like Natick were struggling, there were still dozens of Indian preachers and teachers. Furthermore, women became active participants in these evangelical communities, serving not only as examples of Christian piety, but also as teachers and schoolmistresses.[9] At Manomet Ponds in the early eighteenth century, two women named Rebecca and Esther led a school for local Indian children, just as members of their families became preachers, schoolteachers, and civic leaders in their communities. In all of these Indian villages, native preachers, called *nohtompeantog* in Massachusett, began to restructure Indian communities, furnish examples of indigenous leadership, and articulate a sense of Indian identity as both Indian *and* Christian. The war had devastated evangelical efforts among Indians, but it did not annihilate them, for native peoples were the ones to reenergize, restructure, and reinvigorate Christian missions after the war.[10]

Just as Natick became a symbol for the apparent dissolution of the native missionary effort, Martha's Vineyard became an icon of its success. In fact, the small island off the southern coast of Massachusetts had several advantages that Natick did not: the atrocities of war never came home to the island's residents, there was a comparatively small number of English settlers there until well into the eighteenth century, and the Islanders quietly enjoyed a tradition of autonomy and independence among Indian churches that dated back to the days of Mittark, Hiacoomes, and other native leaders. By 1687 Puritan divines could boast that there were twenty-four Indian preachers on the island. By the 1720s the island churches were still *"under the teaching of some* English *and more* Indian Ministers."[11] These native preachers also reached out to the mainland and even installed Christian preachers on the island of Nantucket. Martha's Vineyard, not Natick, would eventually become the new "city upon a hill" for indigenous Christianity. As such, the Vineyard became vital for providing native Christian leadership and acting as a hub for indigenous itinerant preaching throughout New England.[12]

English missionaries hired Indian preachers to return to the trails in an effort to convert the distant Indians in southeastern New England. At the same time, Indians in southeastern Massachusetts cultivated an independent practice of itinerancy, with preaching Indians crisscrossing southeastern Massachusetts, Cape Cod, Nantucket, Martha's Vineyard, and even parts of Rhode Island. This was not necessarily unique to evangelical itinerancy, for Eastern Woodland Indians often traveled from village to village to share news.[13] What was distinctive about the preaching Indians was their effort to foster a sense of shared Christian Indian identity. Martha's Vineyard's Indians were particularly active in this itinerant missionary work. John Coomes (the son of the famous Hiacoomes) left the island to take over the preaching duties at Assawompsett, near present-day Lakeville. Jonathan Amos moved from the Vineyard to Dartmouth, Zachary Hossueit often traveled from the island to preach at Mashpee, John Neesnumin went from Sandwich to Natick, and Japhet Hannit set out from the Vineyard to traverse the southern coast of Massachusetts and even attempt to convert the Narragansetts of Rhode Island. Hannit traveled from village to village, ordaining native preachers who themselves could establish new churches and promote indigenous Christian spiritual authority.[14]

One of Hannit's protégés was William Simmons, a Dartmouth Indian whom Hannit ordained in 1695. When Simmons accompanied Experience Mayhew through Rhode Island, he opted not to continue the journey to the Connecticut Indians, as Mayhew originally planned. Instead, Simmons traveled north, on his own, "to a Town of Indians," where he would ostensibly do the same thing that Hannit had done for him: prepare an individual for the responsibility of establishing and leading a Christian congregation.[15] The real legwork of reestablishing connections within and between Christian Indian communities was done by Indians themselves, most of them hailing from the Vineyard. Matthew Mayhew even admitted that "by the alone Ministry of the *Martha's Vineyard-Indians,* was the Civilizing and Conversion of the *Indians* on the *Maine land,* at a place called *Succonet,* and parts Adjacent: who as they were Converted by the Ministry, sent from the church of *Martha's Vineyard,* to the Officers were by them (as likewise were those of *Nantucket*) Ordained." Indian preachers were not only preaching to their own congregations. They were actively forming new ones.[16]

Native ministers were the threads that knit many of these postwar communities together. As such, their personal relationships with one another reflected some of the obstacles that indigenous preachers faced. Perhaps most importantly, native ministers were not always friendly with one another. Zachary Hossueit apparently made some kind of "offense" after accepting Solomon Briant's invitation to preach on a Sabbath day in Mashpee. Trying to heal the rift between the two ministers, Hossueit wrote to Briant and his congregation, assuring them that "I have love for all of you in the name of our God Jehovah and the Lord Jesus Christ. And also I desire that you should be very diligent to pray to our saviour, the Lord Jesus Christ . . . And I desire to protect ('for them') true religion before God and the Lord Jesus Christ as long as I live, always." Hossueit concluded by addressing Briant personally and imploring, "I . . . your loving brother, I shrink from (?) offending in any teaching or in anything against you." The initial reasons for the conflict are unclear, but Hossueit was wise to maintain diplomatic ties with Briant, for they had collaborated on several important projects together and each represented an important ally to the other. When Briant's personal debt forced him to ask the New England Commissioners to pay it for him (so he would not have to abandon his post as a native preacher), Zachary Hossueit helped him draft his petition. Native ministers needed each other just as much as their congregations needed them.[17]

Hossueit and other Indian preachers also utilized their linguistic skills to protect, transfer, and prove ownership of Indian lands. Part of this might have been motivated by blatant self interest, for native preachers like Abraham Speen, Thomas Waban, Job Nesutan, John Thomas, Sr., Daniel Takawombpait, and a handful of others owned significant tracts of land in their own communities. When Mashpee Indians' lands were reorganized under a guardianship system imposed by the colonists, a special clause protected Indian preacher Solomon Briant's personal property. Being a native minister definitely had temporal rewards. Yet native preachers were also actively involved in land transfers and debates over land among Indians themselves. They were sometimes called to act as witnesses when wills were executed, a few of them drafted wills for friends or members of their congregation, they served on juries that debated who maintained proper title to land, and at least one of them even surveyed land under dispute. Native preachers even helped other native preachers secure their property, as when James Spotso traveled from Natick to Nantucket to ensure that James Momog kept title of the two commons he allegedly owned. Native ministers were therefore not only landowners, but active participants in the process of selling, transferring, and surveying property.[18]

Not surprisingly, indigenous preachers tried to protect native lands from colonial greed. In 1746, Massachusetts passed a law that hired white agents to act as "guardians" over Indian lands. Decisions about Indian land use would rest in the hands of these white guardians. Indians rejected this guardianship system because of its questionable legality as well as the myriad ways in which the guardians wantonly abused their privileges. When Martha's Vineyard Indians drafted a petition to resist, the signatories' names were Ponue, Hossueit, Abram, Sowamog, and Paul—all names of either active native ministers or direct descendents of people who had been.[19] Native missionaries also marshaled scripture to attack English land greed while simultaneously casting themselves as pious Christians who truly deserved to remain on their property. When Massachusetts assigned Elisha Amos to be the guardian at Gayhead on Martha's Vineyard, local ministers drafted a petition to resist the appointment. They urged the Commissioners to rethink their decision, "lest if he should do this work we would be much more miserable because of this Elisha Amos, just as the word of God says in Job 34:30." Invoking a passage from scripture that urges its readers "to keep a godless man from ruling, from laying snares for the people," the island's Indians tried to position themselves as legitimate descendents of Christ's word who were being taken advantage of by rapacious and ungodly settlers. In many of these cases, Indian conceptions of land and property were informed by their identities as Christians.[20] In 1734, a group of Indians in Lyme, Connecticut sent a petition to that colony's authorities indicating that they would accept no Christian minister unless they had "the Bounds of their Land Settled between them & some of the English, neighbouring upon them."[21] When James Ned had a land deed drafted in 1754 to sell some of his property in Plymouth, he opened the document with the phrase, "To all Christian people to whom these presents shall come."[22]

Native preachers protected their ecclesiastical autonomy just as jealously as they guarded their lands. On two separate occasions New England authorities attempted to install Experience Mayhew as the Indians' preacher at one of the Vineyard congregations. Although Mayhew came from a well-established and friendly missionary family, the Indians chose Sowamog the first time and Joash Panu the second.[23] A few white preachers administered to southeastern New England Indians in later years—such as Joseph Bourne, John Cotton, Jr., Josiah Cotton, and Gideon Hawley—but Native Americans usually preferred their own preachers. This preference sometimes occasioned institutional schisms in Indian churches, as Indians could move to and from congregations. Such a schism happened on the Vineyard around 1700, when some Wampanoags left their Congregational churches and began attending Baptist ones instead. Although Puritan divines tried to chalk this shift up to Indians being "seduced" by Baptists, it was usually a conscious decision made because of the popularity of the preachers, the influence of other kinship members on their decision, or because they were attracted to Baptist styles of preaching and rituals. Indeed, dozens of Mashpee Indians expressed their rage at the guardianship system by gathering themselves into a new church under indigenous Baptist preachers.[24]

Language was at the root of this anxiety about cultural and ecclesiastical autonomy. Although some Puritan divines had argued that urging Indians to learn at least some English was a priority, Christian Indians still strongly preferred preachers that could speak to them in their own terms and using their own idioms. As Samuel Sewall noted in 1724, the Indians at Mashpee were "very fond of their own nation, and their own Language; Insomuch that Mr. Joseph Bourn [a colonist] who succeeds Simon Papmonnit [an Indian] . . . can't prevail with the Indians to assemble on the Lord's Day, unless he will preach to them in their own Language."[25] Part of this obsession with language was the concern over its slow demise. There were no sacred texts printed in Massachusett after 1720, and in some places the spoken language itself was falling into disuse by the middle of the eighteenth century. Paradoxically, Indian congregations might have embraced native missionaries as defenders of traditional indigenous culture. These preachers would not only protect the lands and physical property of Indians, but they might also guard native culture by preserving Indians' sense of linguistic and cultural autonomy and re-channeling it through Christianity.

Native preachers were in constant correspondence with other native missionaries, and they often collaborated on social and political projects, such as writing petitions, surveying land, or preaching at one another's congregations. But they also cooperated with English ministers. Cotton Mather assured his readers that Indian preachers "very frequently apply themselves to these *English* ones, for their Advice, about Instructing their Flocks under their Charge."[26] Samuel Treat, an English minister at Eastham, reported that Indian preachers came to his home about once a week for instruction. Although Treat held his position for over forty-five years, he admitted that he preached to Indians only about once a month. In the meantime, "the more *sober, well-affected* and *understanding* persons among them . . . duly preach to them, when I am not with them."[27] It was probably in English ministers' best interest to emphasize their active participation in native Christianity. Such posturing might help curb any lingering doubts about the indigenization of Christianity while simultaneously bringing admiration to their own reputations. Some English ministers, like the Mathers and the Mayhews, might have fancied themselves barons overseeing an empire of native Christians. Nevertheless, and in spite of their cooperation with white missionaries, native leaders were the ones running the quotidian functions and spiritual rituals in these Christian communities.

Most of these native-led religious practices reportedly followed a fairly formulaic pattern. Indians would begin with a prayer. Then an Indian minister would conduct a sermon, followed by a psalm. English missionaries noted not only the gravity with which the psalms were sung, but also the melodious tones emanating from Indian congregations. One witness observed that Indian singing was "Grave," "Serious," and "Attentive," and that it displayed a "ravishing Melody" and even had a reputation for "outdoing many of the English."[28] Psalms, however, were not simply an opportunity for showing off the vocal chords. As Simon Beckom's Sabbath Day meetings during King Philip's War remind us, the singing of the psalms represented an important moment for the Christian Indian community to reflect upon their shared problems of disease, population loss, displacement, and cultural change. Just before Isaac Ompany concluded an Indian service with his own prayer, the congregation sang the third psalm, which begins: "O Lord, how many are my foes! Many are rising against me; many are saying to me, 'There is no help for you in God.' Selah. But you, O Lord, are a shield around me, my glory, and the one who lifts up my head. I cry aloud to the Lord, and he answers me from his holy hill."[29] More than a melodic distraction or ecclesiastical formality, psalms provided a mechanism through which native preachers could utilize scripture to foster a sense of Christian Indian identity during a time of tumultuous change. These rituals did not represent a wholesale surrender of indigenous religious practices and beliefs, but rather a selective amalgamation of native spiritual traditions and Christian ones. These services were still conducted in Algonquian dialects and many Indians incorporated traditional indigenous rituals into new, Christian ones. Tobacco, for example, was frequently used in native spiritual practices as a way to communicate with powerful natural forces.[30] Many Christian Indians engaged in this ritual after Christian services. It is possible that, even after they began incorporating Christian rituals, Indian spiritual leaders still may have used tobacco to mediate between themselves and the powerful spirits actively involved in their daily lives.

Because English witnesses rarely attended Indian religious services, and because Indians left few written records, it is difficult to know what an Indian sermon would entail. According to one English minister, Japhet Hannit's sermons were "not very accurate." Yet Hannit made up for his gaffs because his preaching was "very serious," and his sermons contained "a great deal of good Matter in them." Hannit even seemed to give his best sermons "when he did not try to oblige himself to any strict Method in them." While English ministers employed pre-written sermons prepared for nearly every occasion, Indian preaching was much more self-reflective, personal, and extemporaneous than English preaching. Elisha Paaonut was a preacher at Gay Head from 1683 to 1714 who had a famously superior memory (in spite of his earlier addiction to strong drink). Experience Mayhew recalled that Paaonut, like Hannit, "used no Notes in preaching, nor did he seem to need any." This extemporaneous style did not always mean that Indian ministers were wholly unfamiliar with scripture. Paaonut, for example, was well versed in sacred texts. Mayhew recalled that he "seemed to be the best acquainted with the Scriptures of any Indian that I ever met withal, could most readily turn to almost any Text that one could mention to him, if a Word or two of it were but named." Only the most accomplished Puritan divines shared Paaonut's extraordinary ability to cite scripture so effortlessly.[31]

While colonial commentators offered a sense of native missionaries' preaching styles, the marginalia that indigenous ministers left in their Indian bibles also reveal hints about their own spirituality as well as the content of their public sermons. Because no sacred books appeared in Massachusett after 1720, the thousands of Indian primers, catechisms, and bibles that were still in the hands of native preachers were literally read to shreds. Taken together, the writings that Indians left in the margins of these texts reveal a few key components of native preaching. The first is the emphasis on spiritual poverty and sinfulness. Perhaps the most pressing problem for missionaries from Canada to the Carolinas was that Native Americans had no concept of, or word for, original sin. The Jesuits tried to use words that meant anything from an offense to the Great Spirit to sexual indiscretion. Native preachers instead used the metaphors of pity and poverty to describe sinfulness as a state of pitiable, spiritual want. One owner of an Eliot bible wrote, "we are pitiful, because of our sin," and then admitted that "Oh I am a pitiful man. Who will save me from my death's body [sic]?" One of the Eliot bibles owned by Simon or Joseph Papenau (or both) also reveals some of these spiritual anxieties. Joseph was a deacon in Solomon Briant's Mashpee church, and like the notes left by other Indians, his marginalia reflect a dire concern with sin and a harrowing sense of self-pity. "Pitiful people (are) we," he recorded. "It is not good. Always falsehood is heard among us." The writer later admitted that "I am forever a pitiful person in the world" who was "not able to defend myself from the happenings in the world." Papenau's anxieties about sinfulness, spiritual depravity, and poverty were themes that certainly would have emerged in his, and other native missionaries', sermons. This bible eventually left the hands of the Papenaus and found its way into the study—and probably the pulpit—of another native missionary: Martha's Vineyard's Zachary Hossueit. When Hossueit read that Indian bible, he was sure to read Papenau's Mashpee marginalia included in it. These themes of self-reflective pity, spiritual fragility, and sin as poverty surely made their way into the sermons and prayers that Indian ministers led in early New England.[32]

In spite of native preachers' intense focus on spiritual depravity and sinfulness—classic Puritan tropes—the marginalia in these bibles also reflect some degree of optimism. Much of this has to do with native preachers' relationship with the bible as text. Many native preachers wrote not only about their own sense of sinfulness, but also the ways in which they believed that reading, studying, and learning from the bible could be a pathway to spiritual deliverance. Joseph Papenau, for example, clearly connected his reading of the bible to his own salvation when he wrote a note to himself in the margins: "This is your book, you Papenau. Read it with c[oncentr]ation (?). Your God will bless you." Native ministers probably urged their congregations to read whatever primers, catechisms, and bibles they possessed as a tried and true avenue to divine protection. In spite of the declining availability of texts in Massachusett after 1720, literacy rates in praying Indian towns were remarkably high. One visitor to an Indian village on Cape Cod even noted that almost every head of family in the praying village he visited was capable of reading scripture. Joseph Papenau thus recorded in his own bible, possibly with some delight, that "Many have read this book. I saw it." Just as the trope of the "talking book"—a text which could reveal the secrets of God's creation and offer its reader immense spiritual power—was a prominent theme in later Black Atlantic writings, so too did native ministers emphasize the centrality of engaging the biblical texts as an indispensable spiritual exercise.[33]

Native missionaries and the congregations they led did not disappear into the sunset after King Philip's War. Indeed, the ones who remained behind the frontier maintained a remarkable degree of autonomy in spite of demographic loss, colonial land greed, and laws designed to restrict their physical and economic mobility. Native Christians continued to cross-stitch traditional indigenous rituals, practices, and ideas with those of Christianity. New England's indigenous ministers were crucial to rebuilding these native churches after the war, as they knit communities of praying Indians together, fought against colonists eager to take native lands, and formulated an indigenous Christian spirituality that was Indian *and* Christian in nature. In their relationships with one another, in their itinerancy, in their sermons, and even in the marginalia they recorded in their Indian bibles, native missionaries actively fashioned a Christian Indian identity, hoping to secure a place for themselves and their congregations in the postwar world.[34]

Puritans had never been alone in their dependence upon native evangelists. Portuguese, Spanish, Dutch, and French missionaries had all employed indigenous agents to varying degrees, and the Catholic Church had long made the creation of a native pastorate one of its central goals. Although they possessed a near monopoly on Protestant evangelization in the English Atlantic during the seventeenth century, Puritans received some competition at the turn of the eighteenth century when several new Anglican missionary societies were organized to spread the gospel throughout the British empire and beyond. The Society for Promoting Christian Knowledge (SPCK) was established in 1698 while The Society for the Propagation of the Gospel in Foreign Parts (SPG) was created in 1701. The SPG would eventually become the best funded, most widely scattered, and most tightly organized British missionary organization of the eighteenth century, sending out around 300 missionaries to stations throughout the Caribbean, British mainland colonies, and Africa. Most of these "missions" were churches in well established areas, but some of them were farther afield. Both the SPG and the SPCK were the brainchildren of Dr. Thomas Bray; the SPCK was designed to distribute books and establish schools while the SPG was primarily a missionary organization. Additionally, The Society in Scotland for Propagating Christian Knowledge (SSPCK) was founded in 1709 as a Presbyterian missionary organization that both distributed books and supported missionaries throughout the Atlantic. Some of Thomas Bray's associates also founded their own missionary branch in 1723, creatively naming it The Associates of Dr. Thomas Bray. This new collection of organizations attempted to spread Protestantism in places where Puritan missions failed to reach. In spite of the confusing array of titles, names, and responsibilities, all of these organizations would compete, correspond, and sometimes cooperate with Puritan missionary efforts. Like other evangelical enterprises before them, they too would tap into a long tradition of using native agents in their own missions.

The Anglican approach to missionary work was different from that of their Puritan counterparts in several ways. Praying towns, which were crucial to how Puritans envisioned and framed their civilizing and Christianizing mission, were less important among Anglican divines. Anglicans tended to be more hierarchical in their organization than Puritans, and Anglican ministers and missionaries had to travel to London to be ordained. By contrast, Puritans could ordain preachers anywhere they saw fit, making spiritual authority more decentralized. Some Anglicans begged for the establishment of an American bishopric so that they might ordain native preachers in the Americas. One Anglican even declared in 1718 that "it will be highly necessary to transfer the Center of this great Work to that side [the Americas], where it may rest, as in its proper place."[35] The creation of an American bishopric, however, was a thorny problem, and preachers would continue to be ordained only in England. The result was that, while Puritans had officially ordained Indian ministers by the 1670s, Anglicans did not ordain a native preacher until almost a century afterwards.

In spite of these differences, Puritans and Anglicans still had much in common, as both participated in a larger effort to spread Christianity, in their own unique ways, to the unconverted. They corresponded with one another frequently and both utilized the same rhetorical devices to justify evangelical work among Indians. While the Massachusetts Bay Colony seal showcased a naked Indian citing the sixteenth chapter of the Acts of the Apostles and begging Puritans to "come over and help us," the Indians in the SPG's official seal made the exact same request, but in Latin: "transiens adi uva nos." The SPG also viewed itself as an exceptionally benevolent organization that would be a model for others. "Corporations erected for Charitable uses," one Anglican divine reminded the SPG in 1717, "are as that City set on a Hill, which cannot be hid."[36] The implication was that the SPG was something akin to John Winthrop's Puritan community of the seventeenth century: a model for future evangelization and a beacon for the rest of the Christian world. Importantly, both groups also despised and feared Catholics. When they heard about French Jesuits' intrusions into Iroquoia and saw frontier wars explode in New York, they blamed themselves for failing to win the hearts and minds of Indians there. Even Cotton Mather, the most puritanical of all Puritans, urged the SPG to become more involved in evangelical efforts in Long Island and frontier New York.[37]

Like the Puritans before them, Anglicans would come to rely upon the very people whom they were trying to convert. When Thomas Bray began drumming up support for the SPCK and SPG in the 1690s, he suggested that every English colony should have at least one or two schools "for the Instruction of half a dozen *Indian* Youth, to be sent afterwards amongst their own People, to civilize and convert them."[38] Both Puritans and Anglicans hoped that the basis for this native evangelical leadership class would be rooted in already existing Indian leadership. In particular, the Puritans of the seventeenth century had, like the Anglicans after them, hoped that the conversion of native royalty would effect the conversion of all others. John Eliot revealed this missionary fantasy by publishing a fictional account of the conversion of powerful chief King Philip in the 1670s. At the same time, experience had shown Puritans that Christian leadership need not *always* come from the top down, and they often simply worked with the indigenous peoples who were willing to work with them.

Anglicans, on the other hand, assumed that indigenous political leaders would be the chief agents of conversion. This was partly due to the social and cultural milieu in which they lived, including their faith that they had created the best government in the world, a balanced government capped by the figure of a benevolent, magisterial monarch. For the English, royalty commanded respect, reverence, and especially deference, and some ministers believed that Indians possessed "the best of all Governments, *Monarchy*."[39] The English assumed that hierarchy, kingship, authority, and royalty were part of a common social grammar that Englishmen and Indians alike could respect and understand. Just as the conversion of New England sachems like King Philip might have resulted in the widespread Puritanization of countless Indian souls, Anglican missionaries began their efforts among America's native population with the working assumption that the conversion of a "king" would result in a general Christianization of the rest of his people. This trickle down evangelical policy did not account for demographic and generational change, nor did it acknowledge the long tradition of consensus (as opposed to hierarchical rule) that characterized Indian polities. Nevertheless, the figure of a converted Indian king was an attractive and

Seal of the Society for the Propagation of the Gospel in Foreign Parts. (Image courtesy of the John Carter Brown Library at Brown University.)

powerful icon that was just as appealing to Anglicans in the eighteenth century as it had been to Puritans in years prior. When Anglicans tried to employ native preachers in Indian missions, they began at the top.

One of the earliest efforts to cultivate a cohort of native preachers was the construction of Brafferton Hall at the College of William and Mary at the turn of the eighteenth century. Virginians and Anglicans believed that Brafferton would become an Indian Oxford, from which native preachers would set out to convert and "civilize" their Indian kin throughout Virginia and beyond. Enrollment, however, was always meager, and native parents often refused to part with their beloved sons. It probably did not help that the college's promoters tried to supplement the student body—composed mainly of the sons of existing Indian leaders—with Indians who had been captured in war. There were few examples of success even after willing Indians had been educated there. One Virginian noted that Brafferton's Indian students had indeed "been taught to read and write, and have been carefully instructed in the Principles of the Christian Religion, till they came to be men." And yet, soon after they returned to their people, the observer complained, "instead of civilizeing [sic] and converting the rest, they have immediately Relapst [sic] into Infidelity and Barbarism themselves." In the end, Brafferton failed to become the Indian college that Anglicans hoped it would become.[40]

In spite of Brafferton's dubious legacy, Anglicans still put their faith in native preachers. In the 1710s Anglicans began to invest a tremendous amount of time, money, and effort on cultivating native preachers who came from "royal" Indian families. The earliest and most prominent examples were the Four Indian Kings of Iroquoia and George, the Yamassee Prince of South Carolina. In the spring of 1710, four representatives from the Iroquois Confederacy (one was actually a Mahican) visited London to secure a diplomatic alliance with the English. The English relished the idea of using four native sachems whose power, charisma, and leadership would help them transition easily into models of Anglican spiritual leadership. In reality, these men were really not Indian kings, but rather diplomatic ambassadors. Nevertheless, the visit was seen by contemporaries as a crucial moment in linking the interests of England and Iroquoia. It was accompanied with pomp and majesty, and they even had an audience with Queen Anne. Newspapers reprinted the kings' dramatic speeches to the Queen while ballads and poems romanticized their visit. The Indian representatives asked Queen Anne not only for her military protection, but also for Christian missionaries to instruct the Indians, claiming that any person they sent to Iroquoia would be given a "most hearty Welcome."[41] The SPG obliged, and two years later

William Andrews arrived at Fort Hunter, a recently constructed outpost located in the heart of the Mohawks, one of the groups that made up the Iroquois Confederacy. The English were clearly trying to graft a Christian empire onto a Mohawk polity, and a key agent in that effort would be Hendrick. The most prominent of the four sachems, Hendrick would assist Andrews as a lay preacher in this new Anglican mission on the Iroquoian borderlands.

Hendrick's claim to Indian "royalty" may have been dubious, but he was no hack, for he and the three other "kings" understood how to prey upon English anxieties to achieve their diplomatic goals. The French Jesuits had been a significant force in Iroquoian diplomacy for decades, and any English mission would have to account for the complications of competing against Iroquoian Indians who allied themselves with the French and prayed for the Pope. One Anglican commentator dubbed the Iroquois "The Praying Indians of Canada" and, in his letter to the SPG, Hendrick signed his name with a Frenchified "Henrique."[42] In their speech to the Queen, the kings admitted that they had been "importuned by the *French,* both by the insinuations of their Priests, and by Presents, to come over to their interest." As allies to the English, however, the Indian kings assured the Queen that they had always looked upon French missionaries as *"Men of Falsehood."*[43] To make things even more complicated, the first Protestant missionaries among the Mohawks were not Anglicans, but rather a Dutch immigrant and a Calvinist minister, and the Indian kings who visited England were attached to the Dutch Reformed Church. Any Anglican missionary who began working among New York's Indians therefore had to factor in not only the persistence of Iroquoian traditional religion, but also the strength of French Catholic, Dutch Reformed, and Calvinistic influences among the Mohawks.[44]

Even as Anglican preachers railed against Jesuit efforts among Iroquoian Indians, they paradoxically looked to them as a model for how to best evangelize Indians. One commentator noted that the SPG might not be able to sustain a mission among the Indians unless they were "able and willing to live with the Indians in their own Country, and according to their Way and Manner, which is the Method the French take."[45] All of these exigencies, in addition to the sensitivity of Iroquoian politics, made native intermediaries like Hendrick absolutely necessary to any Anglican missionary attempts in New York. Williams Andrews could not hope to navigate the treacherous waters of Iroquoian cultural encounter without him.

Tee Yee Neen Ho Ga Row, also called Hendrick Tejonihokarawa, was born into a Mahican family in the last half of the seventeenth century. The Mahicans were an Algonquian-speaking people who traditionally inhabited lands south and east of the Mohawks. Hendrick became a Mohawk leader by the turn of the century, and his visit to England only bolstered his reputation—at least among the English—as a man of import. Like his Anglican sponsors, Hendrick argued that Christian missions were opportunities to solidify diplomatic and political allegiances. In their letter to the Archbishop of Canterbury, the four Indian kings noted that the construction of a chapel and the presence of English ministers would not only spread the light of the gospel, but also "occasion a credit to our Six Nations."[46] And yet, Hendrick was not just an anglophile, for he seemed to be a man of many overlapping and sometimes contradictory identities. A Mahican Mohawk who signed his name in French, allied himself with the Dutch Reformed Church, and begged for English missionaries, Hendrick was a product of the interlocking cultural matrices that transatlantic religious interaction fostered in the Iroquoian borderlands.

After his trip to England, Hendrick began to recast himself as a cultural broker, an intermediary who could slip between Indian and English worlds rather easily. His self-representation became an essential component of this identity. As one English commentator noted, by 1722 Hendrick had fashioned himself into a "polite Gentleman . . . apparall'd as we, Speaks pretty good English and Scarcely distinguishable from an Englishman but by his tawny complexion."[47] In fact, a series of portraits of the Indian kings—painted by Dutch artist John Verelst—demonstrate a visual representation of Hendrick as not only an Indian leader, but a Christian icon. While most scholars have emphasized the diplomatic characteristics of the Verelst portraits, Hendrick also stands out from the other three Indian kings because of the obvious Christian symbolism and iconography inscribed in the image. For example, Hendrick is the only Indian out of the four painted without a weapon, decorative tattoos, or a scene of battle or hunting in the background. Instead of a weapon, Hendrick carries a wampum belt, an icon of indigenous economic exchange and diplomacy. Interestingly, the belt is not decorated with traditional Amerindian imagery, but with crosses, symbolizing his newfound identity as a Christian diplomat. Perhaps more illustrative of Hendrick's new identity were his clothes. Instead of Indian clothing and moccasins, which the other Indians sport in their paintings, Verelst painted Hendrick with English-style stockings and shoes. The final touch was Hendrick's other vestments. Instead of a shirt or waistcoat, he was dressed in a black robe, similar to the clothing worn by the French missionaries he claimed to distrust. John Verelst painted Hendrick just as much as a preacher as a statesman. While Hendrick was certainly not deracinated, the portrait does suggest the ways in which Hendrick's image reconciles and makes compatible the worlds of the Iroquoian Indian and the English Christian.[48]

Hendrick assisted the Anglican mission at Fort Hunter by serving as a lay reader, an unordained member of the laity who read sacred texts but did not officially have the authority to administer any other sacred functions. It is difficult to ascertain exactly what impact Hendrick's assistance to missionary William Andrews meant, either to Hendrick, Andrews, or even the Mohawks who heard him. In spite of this, Andrews did record that he had some small successes during the initial period of Hendrick's tenure as a native evangelist. Within the first six months of Andrews' arrival, he and Hendrick oversaw 100 Mohawk baptisms. By 1716, about one-third of the Mohawks living near them had been baptized in the rites of the Anglican Church. Even if the Mohawks began attending religious services because of the "victuals" that Andrews offered them, this is certainly not a paltry number, and there is a great chance that Hendrick was personally responsible for many of these baptisms. Hendrick's position as an established leader probably helped the cause, as some Mohawks might have found it inspiring that their military leader, diplomat, and orator had already been baptized and converted. Language might have also played a critical role in these early successes, for the Mohawks had historically expressed an antipathy towards, and utterly refused to be taught, the English language. This was because the worst people they knew—the rapacious traders who sought to exploit them—spoke English. Because William Andrews spoke very little Mohawk, it was up to Hendrick—who could speak English, Mahican, Mohawk, and probably a little French—to communicate the religious doctrines necessary for Christian baptism. Hendrick thus wore many hats in Mohawk country: as a political leader, orator, interpreter, broker, leader of religious meetings, catechist, and preacher.[49]

Mohawks' suspicion of the English language not only made Hendrick all the more critical to the Anglican mission, it also spurred the publication of an Indian primer in the "Mahaque" tongue. It is likely that Hendrick utilized this primer as a tool for teaching the Lord's Prayer and preparing Mohawks for baptism. Indeed, prayer was no alien concept to the Mohawks, as they and other Iroquois frequently offered up prayers of thanksgiving and supplication to the spiritual forces that guided the universe. When Anglicans included a "Prayer in the time of War and Tumult" in the Mohawk primer, native Christians like Hendrick could seize upon this opportunity to see Christianity confronting the problems of international and intertribal warfare that plagued Iroquoia throughout

Hendrick, or Tee Yee Neen Ho Ga Row. (Image courtesy of the John Carter Brown Library at Brown University.)

the eighteenth century. Hendrick might also have used the primer to introduce Christian psalms into existing constructions of Iroquoian song-singing. The most prominent psalms in the primer were Psalms 23 ("the lord is my shepherd"), 67, 100, and 117. Psalm 103, also included in the Mohawk primer, spoke directly to the material advantages that Christian neophytes like Hendrick expected from their newfound covenant with the English God. "Praise the Lord . . . and forget not all his benefits," Psalm 103 declares. It then proclaims that God alone forgives sins, heals diseases, and satisfies true believers' desires so that their youth is "renewed like the eagle's." The eagle analogy certainly would have struck a cord with Mohawk audiences, for many Eastern Woodland Indians respected and revered animals that demonstrated the most physical freedom and were the least constrained by their environment. We do not know the extent to which Hendrick employed these psalms in his reading and preaching, yet their inclusion in the Mohawk primer at precisely the time that Hendrick was preaching to other Mohawks is worth noting. It suggests the ways in which native neophytes might have understood Christianity as accruing not only spiritual benefits, but temporal ones as well, protecting them from disease, hunger, and old age. The Mohawks even developed their own word for the personage responsible for protecting them: "Neoni," or Jesus Christ. In this and many other ways, native preachers like Hendrick translated Christianity—literally and figuratively—into a framework of Iroquoian spiritual concerns and temporal needs.[50]

In spite of these opportunities for religious translation, and in spite of the initial successes they seemed to have, Hendrick and Andrews still faced innumerable dilemmas in attempting to convert the Mohawks to Christianity. Hendrick was partially to blame for some of these failures. As early as 1710 one Anglican noted that the great Indian "King" was not really royalty at all, and that he "cannot command ten men."[51] Hendrick was noticeably and inexplicably absent from a conference of Christian Iroquois held at Schenectady in the summer of 1711. His power and faith may not have been as prominent as Anglicans hoped. Some of the fault lay with Andrews' high expectations for the mission. He complained incessantly about the Mohawks' roving lifestyle, affinity for liquor, constant swearing, and inattentiveness to the Sabbath. Less than a decade after he began his mission, Andrews angrily observed that the Mohawks were little more than a "sordid, mercenary, beggarly people, having but little sense of religion, honour, or goodness among them; living generally filthy, brutish lives: they are of an inhuman, savage nature; kill and eat one another." "Heathens they are, and heathens they will still be," Andrews summarily concluded.[52] Andrews abandoned his Hobbesian nightmare in 1719, taking a post in a more congenial New Jersey parish and leaving Hendrick in the lurch. There were a few sporadic attempts to rekindle the missionary fire after Andrews' departure, but it was not until the 1740s that the Anglicans would reestablish a more permanent presence among the Mohawks. Until then, native Christians like Hendrick were left to preach to the Mohawks on their own.[53]

Hendrick was critical to the development of the Anglican mission to the Mohawks, but Anglicans had missionary aspirations elsewhere. Indeed, Anglicans latched onto one Yamassee "Prince" in particular, and they hoped that the conversion and evangelical training of the Prince would catalyze a general conversion of Indians in the Carolinas. For his own part, the Yamassee Prince's participation in this experiment offered him access to English alliances while simultaneously putting him in the middle of Indian and English conflicts. The son of a Yamassee sachem, Prince George was seventeen years old in 1713 when he accompanied Gideon Johnston to England. He resided there for a year and a half while the SPG, the same organization that funded Hendrick's mission in New York, paid for his instruction, housing, and even clothing. As was the case with Hendrick, the SPG's intentions were both diplomatic and evangelical. George Stanhope explained in 1714 that the SPG spent so much money supporting the Yamassee Prince because they believed he would not only further British interests in South Carolina, but also "promote the Christian Religion" among other southeastern Indian tribes.[54] The Prince, however, did not fare very well in England. He struggled with his studies, flunked his scholarly examinations in 1714, and was often homesick. In spite of these challenges, he continued his instruction and was baptized as "George" after giving the SPG proof of his learning in 1715.[55]

Just as Hendrick's metamorphosis into a Christian preacher required his dressing the part, the redressing of the Yamassee Prince was also a crucial component of converting native royalty into Anglican evangelist. The SPG paid for the Prince's coat (a necessity in the cold English winters), breeches, socks, shoes, pants, a new cravat—essentially a whole new wardrobe. The redressing of the Prince was impelled by a desire to civilize Indians, as well as a more specific effort to make the Yamassee Prince presentable to the upper crust of English society in an attempt to procure funding. As noted earlier, the Prince was even presented to King George I just before he returned to South Carolina in 1715.

At the same time, the redressing of the Yamassee Prince was intended to prepare him for his re-entry into South Carolinian Anglo-Indian relations. Recast as an educated gentleman, it was important that the Yamassee Prince be both represented and re-presented to the Indians as a figure of honor, class, and respectability. In a society as highly structured as eighteenth century South Carolina, where race trumped all, the Yamassee Prince could possibly transcend racial boundaries (admittedly by supplanting them with Christian ones) if only given the proper education and attire. Furthermore, Anglican missionaries truly believed that clothing was an important tool for converting Indians, one that spoke volumes about a person before that person even spoke. Indigenous peoples, it was believed, understood hierarchy, honorific titles, and status, so dressing the Yamassee Prince was vital to recasting his identity as an Anglican missionary. Gideon Johnston, the Prince's mentor, observed that "Indians in Generall are most affected with that kind of garb, which is gawdy and makes the finest shew."[56] When the Yamassee Prince arrived in Charles Town after his year and a half away, his education, language, and attire made him, at least in appearance, partly an Englishman, a gentleman, and a Christian.

The Prince's conversion promised to fulfill the fantastical expectations of Protestant missionaries. Prince George was fitted with a new education, new wardrobe, and importantly, a newfound sense of gratitude towards the SPG. Even as they trained indigenous peoples in the complexities of Anglican theology and offered them a significant degree of spiritual and cultural power, SPG ministers still expected deference from their students. The Prince did not disappoint. Writing to the SPG upon his return to Carolina in the winter of 1715, he thanked his Anglican sponsors and appeared grateful for all "their Favours which I never forget."[57] From their vantage point in 1715, the future looked promising. They baptized a member of native royalty, indoctrinated him in English culture and Anglican Christianity, and forged a key alliance with a critical member of indigenous society. They had the missionary; now they just needed a mission for him.

Unfortunately for both George and the SPG, the Yamassee War of 1715 alienated the Prince from his Anglican sponsors and catalyzed a colossal diaspora of the same people that English missionaries were trying to convert. Gideon Johnston, who sailed back to the Carolinas with the Prince in 1715, reported to the SPG that when war broke out the Prince suddenly became "Extremely Sunk and dejected."[58] The drowning of Johnston in April of 1716 might have made him feel even more despondent, for Johnston had vowed to treat the Prince as one of his own children during this period of tribulation. Yet the most grueling challenge the Prince faced was the fate of his father, the Yamassee sachem. Although the sachem had offered up his own son for Anglican training, English officials in South Carolina did little to protect their valuable ally during the war. Rumors circulated that the sachem had been taken prisoner by enemy Indians, killed at the hands of his own tribe, or that he had fled to St. Augustine, seeking refuge with Spanish Catholics. By 1716 the Prince's father was captured by the English, and he and his men were shipped off as slaves. In all of this confusion the SPG lost track of the Prince, who most likely abandoned his English mission, followed his people to Spanish Florida, and disappeared out of the purview of Anglican missionaries. For all of their efforts to train Indian royalty, the Anglicans could not stop the wave of war that swept them away.

The Yamassee prince's experience did leave an important legacy. The support that Gideon Johnston received from the SPG, clergy in South Carolina, and well known Anglican missionaries like Francis Le Jau for his work with the Yamassee Prince, inspired him to turn to other native royalty even before his untimely death in 1716. No sooner had he stepped off the ship in Charles Town than he asked the "Emperour of the Cheriquois, to let me have his Eldest Son." The Cherokee sachem allegedly "most willingly and cheerfully consented" to this proposition because "he saw how well the Yammousea youth had far'd, by his being among us; and he has promised to bring him to me."[59] The Yamassee War and Johnston's death conspired to make this attempt into Cherokee royalty little more than a pipe dream, but several years later another schoolmaster in Charles Town brought an Indian youth to school to try to "make a good Use of him." Predictably, this youth was none other than the "Son to one of the Chiefs of the *Creek* Nations."[60] Like all the experiments with native royalty before it, this enterprise never materialized. In fact, none of these efforts even came close to creating long-lasting success, let alone an embryonic mission. Although the Anglicans had gained the trust of a few members of Indian royalty by the 1740s, they learned the same lesson that Puritans had learned generations before: war would always hamper missionary efforts, leaving native evangelists with little but torn identities, difficult choices, and displaced families.

Anglican efforts to develop a native pastorate in the Atlantic were uneven. Hendrick and Prince George appeared promising, but they never generated the kind of long term, sustainable, widespread conversions that the SPG had envisioned. In spite of these failures, most Anglicans never wavered from the conviction that indigenous peoples themselves would be key instruments of conversion. In fact, that conviction may have been strengthened when Anglicans began to participate, somewhat vicariously, in a mission to India beginning in the first decade of the eighteenth century. A group of German Lutherans, led by a missionary named Bartholomew Ziegenbalg, received permission from the Danish crown to establish a Protestant mission at one of its imperial posts in southern India. Interestingly, these missionaries also received books and financial support from the Anglican SPCK. Ziegenbalg and his cohorts sent the SPCK letters and missionary reports, many of which were published and broadcast throughout the Atlantic world. Not surprisingly, stories of native Indian preachers held a prominent spot in these publications. One of these was Tondaman Mudaly, a Hindu leader who adopted Protestantism, much to the alarm of his family members and associates. The rise of visible neophytes like Mudaly highlighted the early successes of this mission and provided evidence that, although the Anglican experiment with indigenous missionaries in the Americas was floundering, native missionaries were thriving in other places.[61]

The lackluster record of early Anglican missions in the Atlantic, especially when compared to the apparent successes of the Protestant missions in India, forced Anglican divines to propose new, creative, and more ambitious plans for the evangelization of Indians and Africans in the Atlantic world. The Indian royalty model certainly had staying power, and Anglicans continued to hope for the kind of trickle down evangelism that the conversion of Indian political leaders could potentially produce. And yet, new alternatives emerged that did not necessarily reflect such dependence on native royalty.

By the middle of the 1720s Anglican cleric George Berkeley had concluded that the expansion of British dominion abroad represented only a missed opportunity for spreading Christianity. Naturally, he blamed the SPCK and SPG for the "very inconsiderable progress" the gospel had made among blacks and Indians throughout the Atlantic world. Berkeley then drafted his own ambitious plan to convert the world's indigenous peoples and rescue Christianity from its failures: he would create a college where Indians and Africans alike would be educated, trained as missionaries, and sent back among their people to affect a general conversion.[62] In the middle of the 1720s, Berkeley secured funding, Parliamentary backing, and had even decided on Bermuda (a place he had never visited) as the location for his college. Situated at the crossroads of the British Atlantic, Bermuda appeared to be a perfect locale for the convenient intermingling of English preachers with Amerindian and African students. Although the Berkeley Plan was a fantastical and utopian scheme that became ensnared in the politics of competing Protestant personalities, it was also much more than that. Berkeley's scheme, in fact, represented a key moment in larger transatlantic debates about the propriety and efficacy of using native missionaries.[63]

In letters to his colleagues and in *A Proposal For the Better Supplying of Churches in our Foreign Plantations* (1725), Berkeley explained why native missionaries would be more effective than the English ones already in the colonies. Even the most zealous and skilled Anglican missionary, Berkeley claimed, "must find himself but ill qualified for converting the American Heathen, if we consider the difference of language, their wild way of living, and above all, the great jealousy and prejudice which savage nations have towards foreigners." "Children of savage Americans," he continued, would "make the ablest and properest missionaries for spreading the gospel among their countrymen: who would be less apt to suspect, and readier to embrace a doctrine recommended by neighbours or relations, men of their own blood and language, than if it were proposed by foreigners." His plan was to secure Indians while they were young and keep them at the Bermudian college until they were ready to be transported to England for ordination. They would then be sent back to their own nations and serve as "powerful instruments" to convert their brethren. Although Berkeley suggested that his ambitious scheme had "never been tried," this was not entirely accurate. By calling upon and explaining the need for native missionaries, Berkeley was participating in a much older transatlantic conversation about the best means for propagating the gospel. Still, two characteristics made his plan unique. The first was that this was one of the first times in which Anglicans did not fawn over native royalty. Second was Berkeley's plan to isolate Native Americans and Africans on a distant island 600 miles from the American coast. Secluded from the traders, merchants, and vulgarity of the world, Berkeley's students would serve as spokes in the hub of a transatlantic, Anglican evangelical effort centered in Bermuda.[64]

Berkeley and his supporters also believed that the Bermuda Plan would finally give Anglicans the opportunity to strike back at Catholics and provide an institutional framework for competing against Spanish, Portuguese, and French rivals in the Americas. Berkeley implied that the SPG was weak when contrasted against the veritable army of Jesuit and Franciscan "regulars" who did the bidding of the Catholic Pope. Their numerical advantage, Berkeley anticipated, would "be over-balanced by our employing American missionaries." Given their understanding of local languages and cultures, native preachers "would in all probability have much greater influence on the Americans, than the utmost endeavours of popish emissaries can possibly have."[65] Paradoxically, Berkeley's plan for native missionaries tried to emulate, and replicate the successes of, the Catholic missionaries he claimed to despise. Even one of Berkeley's friends applauded his scheme and predicted that Berkeley's reputation would "in some time exalt your name beyond that of St. Xavier."[66]

Berkeley eagerly tapped into anxieties about anti-popery even as he drew obvious parallels between Catholic missionaries and the army of native preachers he expected to graduate from his Bermuda school. Native missionaries, in other words, would operate like an evangelical army of Jesuit and Franciscan missionaries, an army that Protestants never really had.

Although Bermuda had many advantages, it lacked the two main ingredients that Berkeley needed: Indians and Africans. Berkeley thought he developed an easy solution to that obstacle: if peaceful methods could not be used to procure potential students, he might obtain some by "taking captive the children of our enemies."[67] This controversial suggestion aroused the indignation of Anglican missionaries and American settlers alike. Thomas Bray, the key Anglican divine who helped mastermind the creation of the SPCK and SPG years before, called it not only "un-Christian" but "anti-Christian," and declared that it would provoke "an Eternal War" between Indians and English.[68] William Byrd, a wealthy Virginia planter, lampooned the idea of using enemy Indians as future missionaries. He declared that the only way Berkeley could succeed would be if he had "the command of half a dozen regiments, with which he or one of his professors in the quality of Lieutenant General must make a descent upon the coast of Florida and take as many prisoners as he can." Byrd sarcastically concluded that such a maneuver would "be as wise, and as meritorious, as the Holy War used to be of old."[69] Byrd was right. George Berkeley's enemies-as-missionaries proposal exposed his naiveté in engineering this scheme. The idea of native missionaries was neither novel nor controversial, but the proposal to kidnap potential evangelists and take them to a barren island for training certainly was.

In some ways, Berkeley's ignorance about his own plan doomed it. He had never been to the island where he proposed to construct this seminary and he was inexperienced in missionary work. The fantastical scheme of taking Indians 600 miles from their homes to an island was improbable, if not impossible. Contemporaries agreed. Even though Berkeley had plenty of clout in the Anglican community, many believed that the plan was ludicrous and absurd. The Bishop of Salisbury said it was a "ridiculous project," and William Byrd thought it was simply a "romantic" musing engineered by a veritable "Don Quixote," and that it would only result in a "religious frenzy."[70] Even Berkeley himself acknowledged that some of his colleagues would think he was "mad and chimerical."[71] A further setback occurred when King George I died (he apparently supported the plan) and Prime Minister Sir Robert Walpole blocked the scheme.

Berkeley's plan also represented an implicit affront to the SPG itself. Thomas Bray, the influential founder of the SPCK and SPG, wrote

Missionalia a few years after Berkeley's plan went public to persuade readers that Berkeley's scheme was bizarre and impossible. Bray was the same person who in 1699 supported the creation of colonial colleges for the training of native preachers.[72] By 1727, when Bray published *Missionalia,* he had changed his tune. Casting doubt on the practice of using native preachers itself, Bray used several examples from missionary efforts in Africa to demonstrate how nominally converted indigenous peoples would only return to the rude and barbaric cultures they reveled in before they were exposed to Christianity. Two "Black Princes" from Mozambique, Bray explained, were "sorry Fellows" who were baptized and trained in Bray's parish in the early eighteenth century. One of them committed suicide in England and the other converted to Christianity, only to cast it off as soon as he returned home. For Bray, these examples demonstrated the futility of using native Christians to preach the gospel. Berkeley's plan was, in Bray's eyes, silly and impractical because natives would not travel far from home to be educated by Christian strangers, they may never return home if they did travel, and their return to savagery was practically inevitable if they did return home. Any indigenous student attending Berkeley's school or any other native missionary program would, in Bray's imaginative phrasing, eventually "return like the Dog to his Vomit, to the former Wild and Savage Ways." Bray believed this was equally evident for Africans as it was for Indians, and that "artificers" (people who could teach indigenous peoples civilization before Christianity would be introduced) should be the focus of any missionary project.[73]

Bray's voice, no matter how loud and influential it had been in the past, was actually in the minority. Berkeley's Bermuda scheme might have seemed preposterous, but few agreed with Bray that native preachers were the problem. Some Anglican ministers even urged the SPG to employ black evangelists in the south, especially since the plantations were so distant from one another. Edmund Gibson, the Lord Bishop of London, suggested in 1728 that plantation masters and SPG officials should begin selecting specific slaves and targeting them as future missionaries. "Some of them, who are more capable and more serious than the rest," Gibson argued, "might be easily instructed both in our Language and Religion, and then be made use of to convey Instruction to the rest in their own Language." The minister even coolly anticipated that this "may be done with great ease."[74] In spite of the alleged "ease" that would accompany such a plan, Gibson's scheme remained a pipe dream well until the 1740s, when a school for young black evangelists would be overseen by slaves owned by the SPG. In the meantime, it was one thing to educate a few

Indian kings, but to give slaves access to such spiritual authority and opportunity for social outreach seemed foolhardy, if not suicidal.

At the center of this debate over black missionaries was the problematic relationship between missions and slavery.[75] By the eighteenth century there was a veritable black majority in South Carolina, making the evangelization of that colony's slaves a matter of utmost importance to most ministers and an issue of extreme sensitivity to others. Although a few missionaries, most notably Samuel Thomas and Francis Le Jau, established schools and preached to some slaves, Christian instruction was usually left to the masters. The SPG faced an uphill battle in convincing slave masters that Christianization would not make their slaves more likely to rebel. The majority of plantation owners and overseers assumed that the slaves who harnessed the most spiritual and intellectual acuity would be the ones most prone to lead a bloody rebellion.[76] This assumption appeared to be correct when, in 1712, New York City experienced a brief but famous rebellion. Not surprisingly, rumors circulated that the rebellion originated among the slaves who attended Elias Neau's Anglican school. This ended up being a false accusation, and SPG commentators gloried in the fact that the slaves who started the rebellion were the property of men who were "declared Opposers of *Christianizing* Negroes."[77] Nevertheless, New York passed a law that limited slave mobility and curtailed blacks' access to education. Some masters even threatened to send their slaves south if they attended Neau's school. Such an angst-ridden social climate made it difficult, if not impossible, to suggest the creation of a black evangelical corps. Even if they remained slaves, black preachers still threatened to undermine the racial hierarchies that formed the backbone of colonial American society.

The root of the problem was the doctrine of Christian liberty, and masters feared slave instruction because of the rebellions that could result from it. The SPG responded to this suspicion (and neglect) of black instruction by drafting thousands of sermons and personal addresses to remind masters of their biblically-mandated injunction to spread the gospel. In each of these texts, SPG missionaries explained that conversion did not imply worldly freedom, and that Christian instruction in no way defied the racial boundaries of American society.[78] Edmund Gibson, the same Anglican who supported a black slave missionary program, assured masters that "Christianity, and the embracing of the Gospel, does not make the least Alteration in Civil Property, or in any of the Duties which belong to Civil Relations; but in all these Respects, it continues Persons just in the same State as it found them."[79] Christianized slaves disagreed. In a letter written in 1723 to Gibson, who had recently become the Bishop of London, an anonymous Christian mulatto slave from Virginia contended that all Christians were legally free. The petitioner proclaimed that enslavement of Christians was not only illegal but cruelly irreligious, and that their "task mastrs are has hard with us as the Egypttions was with the Chilldann of Issarall."[80] By invoking the celebrated story from the book of Exodus, this slave framed American slaves as modern-day Israelites, God's chosen people who were in desperate need of deliverance.

Nevertheless, many Anglicans lambasted the "horrid" and "erroneous" notion that Christian spiritual liberty implied temporal freedom.[81] In his famous sermon advocating the Christian instruction of black slaves, William Fleetwood asserted that "the Liberty of Christianity is entirely Spiritual." Fleetwood and his colleagues had little concern for the temporal status of slaves, for the spiritual consequences of remaining in heathenish darkness were significantly more ominous than the earthly conditions of southern slavery. "Let the Christians," Fleetwood proclaimed, "be Sold, and Bound, and Scourg'd, condemn'd to Bonds and Imprisonment, to endure all Hardships and Disgrace, and *to enter into Heaven, Blind, and Halt, and Maimed,* rather than having Two Eyes, and Hands and Feet entire, to perish miserably."[82] SPG ministers even suggested that slaves would be "much better servants to their earthly masters" if they had a sense of a divine master residing above. In this way Anglicans contributed to a planter ethos that demanded obedience while fashioning a kind of "Christian absolutism" in American slave society.[83]

Anglicans had several reasons to speak so unequivocally regarding the relationship between slavery and Christianity, not the least of which was that the SPG itself was a corporate slaveholder. When Christopher Codrington bequeathed his Barbados plantation to the SPG in 1710, the missionary organization accepted the donation with glee. The plantation held about 300 African slaves, and the SPG envisioned this windfall as a Protestant utopia, where they could demonstrate to other slaveholders that Christian instruction did not inevitably result in outright rebellion. In fact, the Christianization of the SPG's slaves (who later had the word "SOCIETY" branded upon them) was of the utmost concern to the Anglican organization precisely because they could not chastise American colonists for failing to instruct their slaves if they exhibited the same neglect. As William Fleetwood put it, "if all the Slaves throughout *America,* and every *Island* in those Seas, were to continue Infidels for ever, yet *ours alone must needs be Christians.*"[84] Anglicans thus looked to Barbados as an ideal place to begin a fresh, more ambitious missionary endeavor, with a new college structure as the backbone of this enterprise. This scheme was part of Codrington's last wishes, as he requested that students emerging out of the College would be either missionaries or doctors. The training of blacks for missions in the West Indies and Africa was one of the College's founding principles. Codrington College would serve as a "sort of perpetual *Seminary* for *Catechists* and Missionaries" and establish Barbados as a new beacon of Protestant missionary energy.[85]

The SPG started construction on the college in 1714, but the unprofitability of the plantation and other distractions barred it from opening before the fall of 1745. Unfortunately for the Anglicans, and against the designs of Christopher Codrington, it never served as a factory of native missionaries. Nevertheless, the Codrington bequest was an important moment in Anglican missionary history, for it created an opportunity for the SPG to use Barbados as a springboard to get involved in evangelical work in the rest of the West Indies.[86] By the middle of the eighteenth century they had missionaries stationed on Barbados and the Mosquito Shore, as well as in the Bahamas and several enclaves dotting the Caribbean. Codrington's bequest also left Anglicans with a legacy of deep involvement in slavery and the slave trade, a legacy with which the Anglican Church is still coming to grips. In spite of their attempts to nurture a native pastorate through royalty, and in spite of the ambitiously utopian schemes conceived of by Berkeley, Gibson, Codrington and others, Anglicans would enter the 1740s without a single indigenous missionary on the payroll.

Puritans and Anglicans learned important lessons about native preachers from 1700 to 1740. The first was that war would always transform or challenge native missionary work. In New England, native evangelists helped to refashion Christian missions after King Philip's War, but imperial wars around Anglican mission sites took their toll on native missionaries. Meanwhile, Anglicans found that obsessing over Indian "kings" and "princes" was neither productive nor effective. Indigenous leadership was never as stable as English missionaries hoped, and native preachers proved just as unpredictable as the wars that disrupted them. While this obsession with royalty produced meager results, the overly ambitious utopian schemes were also failures. Plans like Codrington College and Berkeley's Bermuda scheme never generated the elite corps of native preachers that they had promised. In fact, neither plan created so much as one native minister in the eighteenth century. These early failures forced Anglicans to recast, revise, and revisit their formula for missionary work, but indigenous preachers usually remained a central component of that formula. By the time of the First Great Awakening (in the 1730s and 1740s), Puritans and Anglicans alike had moved away from the royalty-centered approach and towards one that focused on the education of Indian and African children throughout the Atlantic world. Not surprisingly, Anglicans envisioned Africans and Indians teaching these children.

For their own part, indigenous missionaries throughout the Atlantic world and beyond tried to create sustainable Christian communities, preserve their sense of cultural autonomy, and carve out a space where being Indian *and* Christian was not a contradiction in terms. The Amerindian royalty supported by the Anglicans was never as productive as hoped, but preachers like Hendrick began a tradition of native Christian leadership that would be cultivated by other Indians later in the eighteenth century. By translating texts, singing psalms, leading prayer groups, and pushing for their own ordination, Christian Indians situated themselves within a sacred genealogy that had always reserved a space for native conversion of the gentiles.

Anglican experiments from 1700 to 1740 were crucial to establishing a precedent for future employment of native missionaries by Anglicans. As such, this period set the stage for an explosion of native missionaries after 1740. George Berkeley's failed Bermuda plan serves as a perfect example of these connections. Although Berkeley's proposed project never materialized, it did have some long-term repercussions. Berkeley never went to Bermuda, but he did land in Rhode Island, mailed his books there, and purchased a plantation just north of Newport. When he left Rhode Island and returned to England, he donated many of these books to Harvard and Yale Colleges. He even let Yale receive a portion of the profits from his plantation because he revered it as an institution that bred "the most clergymen and most learned of any in America."[87] Yale honored the generous donation by offering a post-graduate scholarship (the first in Yale's history) in Berkeley's name. One of the first Yale graduates to win this prestigious award, supported by the funds from Berkeley's donation, was a determined and imperious young man named Eleazar Wheelock. Wheelock's first Indian pupil would be a famous Mohegan preacher named Samson Occom, and Wheelock would engineer the most ambitious, and eventually the most controversial, native missionary project in the history of the early modern Protestant Atlantic world. In a bizarre, unpredictable, and indirect way, Berkeley did help fashion a corps of native preachers after all.

CHAPTER THREE

Slave Preachers and Indian Separatism

ARRY MAY HAVE HAD a case of "first-day-of-school" jitters. That universal sensation of nervous excitement that accompanies every new school year would have been exacerbated by the circumstances of the school he was in, for his school was part of an exceptional experiment in colonial South Carolina's race relations. Built several weeks earlier in the summer of 1742, Harry's "Charleston Negro School" was envisioned as the backbone of a new Anglican effort to evangelize South Carolina's black majority. The sprawling geography of the Carolina plantation system, fierce resistance from slave owners, and repressive laws against the education of bondspeople conspired to make the evangelization of the rice country's slaves nearly impossible. This new educational institution was anticipated as a seminal moment in the history of black Christianity, for the students themselves would be the ones to spread the word of Christ, hopefully succeeding where white missionaries had failed. Trained in the fundamentals of Christian doctrine by Anglican missionaries, Harry was not there to learn, but rather to teach. Like the students walking into his classroom on that first day, Harry was also a slave.[1]

From 1735 to 1770, Protestants witnessed and participated in a transatlantic explosion of evangelical revivalism that had an immense impact on indigenous missionary work. Before 1735 only New England Congregationalists had a substantial number of native preachers in their missions. Anglicans supported native preachers in India and even tried to train Native American royalty as missionaries in the first decades of the eighteenth century, but incessant imperial wars interrupted this program.

By 1770, however, native preachers had become vital to missions in the Caribbean, North America, Africa, and elsewhere, especially in missions run by Moravians, a group of Pietist evangelists from central Europe. Anglicans had purchased slaves to teach other slaves, employed Mohawk catechists in New York mission schools, and began training a few young Africans for the propagation of the gospel in West Africa. Eleazar Wheelock started training Samson Occom, Joseph Johnson, and other Algonquian Indians to serve as missionaries to the powerful Iroquois to the west. New England Indians were even beginning to form their own separate congregations under native pastors. The years from 1735 to 1770, therefore, witnessed an astonishing burst of indigenous missionary work. But such evangelical fervor was a mixed blessing. Moravians, Anglicans, and Congregationalists all came to realize that the appropriation and translation of Christianity by blacks and Indians during a period of revivalism could be encouraging and inspiring, but also socially destabilizing and theologically problematic. Even as black and Indian preachers became the backbone of the Protestant missionary enterprise, their access to ecclesiastical and spiritual authority became increasingly controversial. The genesis of Afro-Moravian preachers in the Caribbean, the rise and fall of the Charleston Negro School, and concerns over Indian separatism all immersed missionaries throughout the Protestant Atlantic in the problems of race, slavery, dispossession, and religious separatism during a period of Christian revivalism.

The Unitas Fratrum had a peculiar relationship with other Protestants. While their history, theology, and approach to evangelization made the Moravians, as they were commonly called, a unique component of the evangelical revivalism of the mid-eighteenth century, their rapid spread and alleged successes among Indians and blacks throughout the Atlantic world made them both a competitor of and model for other Protestant missionaries. When Ezra Stiles, a Congregationalist minister in Newport, Rhode Island, rejected his long-held belief that civilization should precede conversion among indigenous peoples, he attributed the change of heart to reading the history of the Moravian mission to Greenland.[2] David McClure, a contemporary of Stiles and a missionary among New York Indians, reported that Moravians practiced the "best mode" for converting the unconverted: "They go among them without noise or parade, and by their friendly behaviour conciliate their good will. They join them in the chace [sic], and freely distribute to the helpless and gradually instil [sic] into the minds of individuals, the principles of religion." McClure, like Stiles, suggested that the culturally flexible approach to Protestant evangelism might ultimately be more successful than previous attempts had been.[3] Stiles and McClure were not the only ones paying attention to Moravian missions. Moravian evangelical strategies heavily influenced those of the Methodists working among the slave populations of British North America. These relationships went both ways, of course. Moravian missionaries possessed Anglican sacred texts, including the daily prayers, litany, catechism, and chapters of the Bible that the Church of England printed into the "Mohoque" language. Although Moravians were distinct from other Protestant groups, Anglicans and dissenting Protestants were well aware of each others' movements, successes, and failures. As such, Moravians were a part of British Atlantic missionary history even as they weaved in and out of it.[4]

Moravians owed their origins to a wave of German pietism—a movement within Protestantism that emphasized personal emotion and devotion—that developed well before their eighteenth century missions were even conceived. Originally inspired by Jan Hus, a pietist martyred in 1415, Moravians found sanctuary with a wealthy patron named Count Nicholas Ludwig Von Zinzendorf. The community they formed in Herrnhut, Germany became a base for missionary work. Well organized, adequately funded by Zinzendorf and other donors, and driven by an insatiable evangelical enthusiasm, Moravian missionaries spread throughout the globe with astonishing rapidity. By 1740, they had missions in Bern, Stein, Malhausen, Schaffhausen, Estonia, Swenia, Lapland, Muscovy, Wallachia, and Constantinople, and the Danish islands of St. Thomas, St. Croix, and St. John. They began preaching to slaves in the British colonies of Jamaica in 1754, Antigua in 1756, and Barbados in 1765. While they failed in their attempt to settle a mission in South Carolina in 1737, they established themselves in Georgia by 1735, New York and Pennsylvania by 1740, Connecticut in 1743, New Jersey in 1751, North Carolina in 1753, and Ohio in 1772. In addition to these European, Caribbean, and North American missions, Moravians could also boast, by 1740, that they had sent missionaries to Greenland, the Cape of Good Hope, North Africa, Surinam, and even Sri Lanka. One commentator reported that the Moravians had ambitious plans to convert "the other Parts of the *East Indies,* the Savages of *New-York,* and the *Magi* of *Persia.*"[5] The reference to Asians, Iroquois Indians, and Persian clerics in the same sentence illuminates the global aspirations of this rapidly expanding Moravian missionary endeavor. Virtually stateless, Moravians weaved in and out of the British Atlantic world as easily as they did in the German, Danish, and Dutch.

Moravian theology was dramatically different from that of their British counterparts. While they shared many common doctrines with other denominations, Moravians' "blood and wounds" pietism situated them at an extreme fringe within Protestantism. Moravians emphasized, and indeed celebrated, the temporal suffering of Christ for the forgiveness of sinners. They highlighted the physical anguish and excruciating pain that Christ underwent during his last hours in order to draw attention to the ultimate sacrifice he made for humanity. They thus focused on everything from Christ's crown of thorns and his spilled blood to the massive gash made by a spear during his last hours on the cross. Moravians also stressed the nearness of Jesus Christ to their neophytes, noting that he was not simply a historical figure or theological abstraction, but rather a potent spiritual force that was constantly serving as their protector. Suffering under the traumatic realities of colonial wars, dispossession, slavery, disease, and racial violence, Indians and slaves alike could find in Moravian doctrine a spiritual alternative that spoke to the lived experiences of oppressed peoples throughout the Atlantic world. Unlike other Protestant denominations, Moravians sent men and women into the missionary field together and German Moravian missionaries married Indian and slave women.[6] Women had their own separate religious meetings with female spiritual advisers and played a major role in their congregations. Moravians even described Christ as an "eternal husband" to female converts and even went so far as to compare the wound on the side of Jesus' body to a woman's vagina.[7] These unique Moravian beliefs helped to craft an inclusive community that emphasized spiritual egalitarianism, the ubiquity and nearness of Christ, emotive qualities of Christian pietism, painful suffering of Christ's last hours on the cross, and the female dimensions of Christianity.

Moravians placed a significant degree of authority in local, native preachers. Invoking the fourteenth chapter of the Book of Revelation, Moravians believed that the "first fruits," or the small segment of the gentile population that first received the Gospel, would be the ones to carry the message of Christ's salvation to all the peoples of the earth. When Moravians set out from Germany in the 1730s, they aimed to create a base of "national helpers" to serve as the foundation of a new church among blacks and Indians. The ascension of these first fruits into positions of Moravian spiritual leadership was seen as a preparatory moment in the gradual conversion of the world. John Valentine Haidt's *First Fruits,* painted in 1747, reflected both the global ambitions and reliance on converted Moravians that characterized Moravian evangelical practices by depicting Moravian converts from places as far-reaching as Greenland, Persia, New England, Armenia, St. Thomas, South Africa, South Carolina, Suriname, and Pennsylvania.

For Afro-Moravian preachers in the Caribbean, these positions of evangelical authority were not necessarily new. Most of the slaves on St. Thomas were Kongolese, and Catholic missionaries had been preaching among the Kongolese in West Africa generations before St. Thomas' slave suppliers began to import them into the Caribbean island. As a product of Catholic missionary work and traditional Kongolese spirituality, Kongolese Catholics expressed a unique and syncretic set of Afro-Catholic beliefs and practices, including the veneration of the Virgin Mary. In fact, the Africans sold into slavery and sent to St. Thomas were pulled from the same cultural groups who used the birth of the Virgin Mary to time the notorious Stono Rebellion in South Carolina in 1739.[8]

Kongolese Catholics possessed a rich tradition of Christian leadership, even well before any of them set foot in the New World. Jose Monzolo, a Kongolese slave shipped across the Atlantic to Cartagena, was chosen as a catechist there because he had learned the catechism well from other

Johann Valentin Haidt, *First Fruits,* 1747. (Image courtesy of The Moravian Archives, Bethlehem, Pennsylvania.)

black preachers when he was a child in West Africa. Catholic priests maintained only an itinerant presence among the West African Kongolese in the sixteenth and seventeenth centuries; their duties were more sacramental than evangelical, as they conducted mass baptisms, oversaw marriages, and fulfilled other sacramental offices. The real evangelical work in the Kongo was done by local African catechists who often participated in missionary activities even when European missionaries were not around. For many Afro-Moravians, their work as national helpers was not a dramatic departure from their religious experiences in Africa. Prepared by a strong tradition of indigenous African spiritual leadership, Afro-Moravians probably expected—and may have even *demanded*—that their missionaries be Africans.[9]

Even the national helper system—where Moravians divided Africans into different "nations" and assigned black evangelists to instruct them—would not have been a novel concept to Kongolese Catholics. When ships full of Africans sailed into the harbor of Cartagena in the seventeenth centuries, Jesuit priests performed mass baptisms and administered last rites to any Africans who were on death's door. The rest were divided into national (ethnic and linguistic) groupings and were led by "a catechist of their own nation." These African catechists translated the Jesuit missionaries' message while the Jesuits stood on a makeshift altar. One Jesuit missionary showed a picture of Christ's last moments, "with blood flowing from his wounds." Another Jesuit used fake blood to baptize Africans. The catechists would teach their Christian pupils the Lord's and other prayers while employing a picture book to show images of sinners burning in hell as demons tortured them. The blood and wounds rhetoric that so defined Catholic missionary work in Africa and the Americas was, in reality, not terribly different from the Moravian theology that Kongolese Africans would embrace in the Danish Virgin Islands.[10]

Just as Catholics did in their missions throughout the Atlantic world, Moravians used national helpers as key evangelists in their attempt to convert Africans in the Caribbean. The role of a national helper was to lead groups of five to ten potential converts in theological reflection and teach them Moravian doctrine and rituals. In his 1777 history of the Moravian mission to the Danish Caribbean Islands, C. G. A. Oldendorp noted that national helpers were charged with "looking after the Negroes who lived near them, of coming to know them in regard to their internal condition, of remembering them diligently in their prayers before God, and of reporting on them to the white workers." These helpers met with white missionaries, as well as each other, at least once a week to report on the activities of the groups they led, the spiritual development of baptismal candidates, and the possibilities of bringing new national helpers into positions of leadership. They also filled in for white Moravian missionaries when they visited other mission stations, returned to Germany, or passed away. When there were too many communicants at a religious service on St. Croix in October of 1744, a white Moravian missionary asked four black national helpers to distribute communion. St. Croix was notoriously difficult to traverse, so German Moravians relied upon helpers like Maria Magdalena and Catharina Barbara to travel southward and westward in the sultry summers to try to convert slaves who lived far away from Moravian religious activity. The national helper system thereby gave Afro-Caribbeans access to the performance of the "important services" of religious mentorship, distributing communion, and serving as evangelical missionaries. It was through black national helpers that most Caribbean slaves experienced and expressed their developing sense of Afro-Christian identity.[11]

Although there were dozens of national helpers in Moravian Caribbean stations by the 1760s, the most important ones were the "first fruits": initial converts who helped bring other Afro-Caribbeans into the fold. The first national helpers in St. Thomas were Andreas and his brother Johannes, Petrus and his brother Christoph, and Anna Maria. They were officially installed by the Moravians in 1738, but these helpers were established spiritual leaders in their own slave societies. Perhaps the best known Moravian account, published in 1770, noted that they "had already been busy among their people, inspired by the divine grace bestowed upon them by the Savior." Their role as national helpers was therefore not a break with the past, but rather a continuation of previous religious mentorship that certainly had its roots in Afro-Caribbean spirituality. Although Moravianism was a form of Western Christianity, there were aspects of Moravian doctrine that these first fruits might have found emotionally or spiritually satisfying. On the one hand, slaves were drawn to the Moravian message because it emphasized equality and friendship while simultaneously privileging the spoken word over biblical exegesis. One national helper, for example, explained to a group of young catechumens that religious experience was more a matter of the heart than of the head. "You must not think," he assured his listeners, "that I know what I know and say what I say merely from my head and that I have learned it from a book. No, I say it out of my own experience and out of the feeling in my heart." Personal experience, rather than biblical scholarship, was at the center of Moravian theology, and Afro-Caribbeans could easily participate in religious experiences that privileged orality over literacy.[12]

Moravian spirituality and African cosmology were not entirely oppo-sitional. Africans taken to the Americas could often draw upon a rich and diverse religious heritage that was comprised of Muslim, Christian, and traditional African cosmologies. This diversity makes it difficult to generalize about the precise religious vocabulary that Afro-Moravians would be employing when translating Christianity into existing spiritu-alities. West Africans who had embraced at least some elements of Christianity or Islam before enslavement might have found pegging Christian Moravianism into their existing cosmologies relatively easy. At the same time, West Africans who were neither Christian nor Muslim also had religious cosmologies upon which Moravianism might be grafted. Although traditional West African religions were technically not monotheistic, they ultimately articulated a belief in a higher, supreme power that governed the universe. Many West Africans also believed in a series of lesser divinities that were much more active in their individual lives. Afro-Moravians could recognize the sovereignty of an all-powerful God above but would approach that God through the lesser deity of Jesus Christ. Christ was therefore translated by black preachers into a minor divinity who was constantly active in the temporal and spiritual experiences of Caribbean slaves. "He sees us all the same," one black preacher observed, "both when we are awake and when we sleep, at home and in the field."[13] The physical experience of racial slavery made Christ all the more impressive. Slaves could identify with someone who suffered as they did under the scourges of oppression and violence. For black slaves, Christ's suffering was not a passage from a text, but rather a lived episode of intense physical suffering that paralleled their own experiences within the Caribbean plantation system.[14]

This helps explain what Moravianism meant to national helpers in the Caribbean missions, but it also hints at the spiritual meanings that black preachers inscribed into their rapidly developing Afro-Moravianism. Black Moravians took the opportunity to preach during class lectures, funerals, morning prayers, and Sunday meetings. Yet the most important times came when they were asked to instruct baptismal candidates or catechumens on the saving grace of Christ. Although the speeches for these events varied in substance and style, they still followed a somewhat formulaic pattern. The image of Christ's personal suffering, for example, was the central theme. Jesus' "blood, wounds, and death," one national helper named Mingo explained, struck his "evil heart." "My heart lives in that experience, and that is the sole ground on which I base my exis-tence," he recalled. After acknowledging the sinfulness of his heart and the physical anguish his wrongs had caused, Mingo turned to the redemptive power of Christ's personal suffering. He proclaimed that "His blood and His death constitute more than adequate means to compensate for all my sins. My heart sings: Wounds and blood have bound us to God!" The blood, wounds, death, and heart rhetoric were classic Moravian tropes. Yet the reliance upon Christ as a spiritual intermediary between sinners and God was also rooted in West African cosmologies of lesser divinities. The emphasis on personal suffering and Christ's corporeal experiences, of course, struck a chord with Afro-Caribbeans living in a slave society. Like other national helpers, Mingo translated Moravianism into an Afro-Caribbean context, grafting Moravian theology onto African cosmology while forging it in the fire of Caribbean racial slavery.[15]

There were around forty national helpers on the island of St. Thomas by 1740, and two of the most prominent were Abraham and Petrus. Both men led their own spiritual meetings, addressed catechumens and candidates for baptism, spoke at weekly gatherings, and sermonized at funerals. "Their presentations," one Moravian historian explained, "were evangelical: they stressed the redemption of sinners through Jesus' death and their acquisition of Grace in Christ." Yet their styles could not have been more different. While Petrus had some prestige within Moravian circles because he was one of the first fruits, Abraham's "extraordinary gift" of oratorical prowess, combined with his ability to speak several African dialects, put him head and shoulders above other black Moravian preachers. Abraham's lectures were remarkable events that had "fire" and "were charged with a special force that swept his listeners along with him." When Abraham preached his listeners were not only struck with "pleasure and blessings" but frequently "broke into loud crying." His reputation as a preacher skyrocketed in the 1740s, but there were also temporal advantages that Abraham's fiery preaching accrued to him. After complaining that his slave labor was getting in the way of his work as a preacher, white Moravians negotiated a deal whereby they exchanged Abraham for another black slave that was more capable of doing hard manual labor. Although Abraham was still a slave, his avoidance of hard work ensured that he could "dedicate himself fully to his tasks as a helper in the work of God among his people." Membership in Christ's kingdom had its privileges.[16]

Unlike Abraham's powerful speeches, Petrus' lectures were "filled with love and gentle feelings." If Abraham exhorted his neophytes with a commanding voice, Petrus' lectures were softer, more emotive, and introspective. Like Mingo before him, Petrus fused Moravian blood and wounds theology with a sentimental reflection on his own status as a sinner. Christ's blood, Petrus confessed, "has redeemed me from the darkness. Now I have peace in my soul. All I am concerned about is to remain a poor sinner before Him forever." For Petrus, his personal experience with God's grace also mandated that he preach to others. "I feel in my heart," he admitted, "a great urge to search for souls which I can bring to the Saviour, souls which are as much in the dark as I once was." Whereas Abraham's lectures were manly and fiery, commentators described Petrus' sermons as "more motherly." In most denominations this observation might have been an insult, but for Moravians the description of Petrus as "motherly" reflected yet another way in which Moravian theology was highly feminized. Petrus could maintain his revered status as a preacher even while his lectures expressed the softer, more maternal tone common in women's preaching. This was just one of several models of Christian discourse that national helpers could draw upon to help fashion Afro-Caribbean Moravianism.[17]

Generational change made a difference in Moravian messages as well. Cornelius, for example, was born to an enslaved woman named Benigna, one of the national helpers who—along with Abraham, Petrus, and others—operated as the spiritual foundation of Afro-Moravianism in the Danish Virgin Islands. Cornelius became a master mason, purchased his own and his mother's freedom, and helped Abraham and other national helpers broadcast Moravian beliefs throughout the slave and free black population of St. Thomas and St. Croix. Cornelius drank from the same emotive cup as Petrus and Abraham, and his spiritual reflections demonstrate this. "For my part," Cornelius assured some young black Moravians in the 1760s, "I feel very miserable and needy. However, at today's prayer day I have experienced His grace in my heart and felt His love." The emphases on misery, spiritual longing, and the physical experience of God's penetration into the heart were classic Moravian rhetorical devices as well. And yet, as a second generation Afro-Moravian, Cornelius had more practice with and access to scripture, and he pulled generously from different biblical texts in order to craft a Moravian message based upon both penitent emotionalism and scriptural history. Invoking the Pauline rhetoric of universal spiritual equality, Cornelius assured his young black audience that access to God's salvation was not limited to the free, the wealthy, and the educated, but available to all. "My dear people!," Cornelius exclaimed, "Each of you should come to Him just as you are," for "The heathens shall see His light and become His people." Cornelius updated this Christian message in order to translate it into the transatlantic Afro-Moravianism that had been germinating in the Caribbean for over a generation. Instead of describing heathens as Jews and Gentiles, he characterized them as "Moors." The "Moors shall come to Him," Cornelius told his audience of young Moravians, "and He will accept them." For a community of slaves and free blacks who witnessed thousands of Muslim Africans being imported into their midst, the discussion of Moors converting to Christianity spoke to the powerful heritage of Islam

Cornelius, an Afro-Caribbean Moravian preacher. (Image courtesy of Moravian Archives, Herrnhut, GS 419.)

in Africa as well as the unsettling potential for religious competition on Moravian turf. As such, second generation Afro-Moravians like Cornelius built upon the tradition of black spiritual leadership while simultaneously refining, revising, and emphasizing Moravian messages in different ways and for different audiences.[18]

No other Christian denomination offered black women as much authority to preach and lead as did the Moravians. The basis for this authority was the gender-segregated meetings that served as the backbone of Moravian evangelicalism and that encouraged black women to be national helpers. Although Afro-Moravians would congregate weekly for larger gatherings, they had daily meetings with the national helpers, nearly half of whom were women. These included Benigna, Johanna, Magdalena, Maria, Anna Sophia, Susanna, Rosina, and others. Many of these women were older and some were free blacks, but they all operated as missionaries to other black women. In spite of Magdalena's age, for example, she visited unconverted black slaves and "took it upon herself to further the growth in Christ of those Negroes living nearby with whom she associated."[19] Like Magdalena, Rebecca Protten embraced the tremendous influence she had on other women. She led spiritual meetings, discoursed with friends about their own religious travails, and served as a conduit through which the Moravian clergy and black female slaves could be connected. Once again, the national helper system tapped into African religious spiritualities and practices, for West African women often possessed a tremendous amount of spiritual power as "sacred specialists."[20] These specialists used divination, healing, and spirit mediumship to lead the spiritual lives of Africans on both sides of the Atlantic. Often mistaken by white observers for witches, African women practiced the same kind of magic, fortune-telling, and astrology that was so evident in popular folk Christianity throughout the early modern Atlantic world. Afro-Caribbean women like Rebecca and Magdalena found in Moravian doctrine a system of theology that could not only be grafted onto existing African cosmologies, but also offered them opportunities for social and religious leadership that were unavailable to them through either the Caribbean plantation system or other Protestant missions.[21]

The status of Caribbean Moravian preachers, however, was always tenuous. Although most of the "national helpers" came from the rank and file of the slave societies on St. Thomas, St. Croix, and St. John, several active preachers were either assistant overseers or free blacks. In these highly stratified slave societies, the status of freedom and the position of authority within the social hierarchy could crystallize spiritual relationships just as it did social ones. The resulting fear was that black

Moravian preachers would represent themselves as superior specimens of the slave class. The national helper system probably exacerbated these tensions by nurturing a class of elite black preachers in a rigidly hierarchical system. German Moravians therefore had to constantly remind national helpers like Abraham and Mingo that "nothing would be more contrary to the purpose of their orders than if they were to imagine that they enjoyed an advantage over their fellows." But they almost certainly did. Abraham, who had Moravian leaders exchange another slave for himself so he could avoid hard manual labor, was not the only convert to use his role as a preacher to improve his temporal standing. Mingo was an assistant inspector who looked after blacks, possessed his own household, and was allegedly "as good as free" because of the temporal and spiritual benefits of his preaching. In spite of its professed egalitarianism, Moravian missionary activity could also intensify the already uneasy social tensions in these slave societies.[22]

The strains and pressures within the Afro-Moravian community paled in comparison to the tensions between black Moravians and the agents of racial slavery, including plantation owners, free whites, and even black overseers. Moravians made a "devil's bargain" with slavery: they accepted the institution of slavery, participated in it, and even negotiated with and depended upon slave owners to gain access to thousands of souls of black folk.[23] Like Anglicans, Moravians owned plantations and even their own personal slaves. They anxiously tried to assuage any fears that missionary work would upset the racial status quo. They assured masters as well as neophytes that baptism, conversion, and religious instruction would make blacks better slaves, not worse. A group of national helpers reported to the King of Denmark that, before their embrace of Moravianism, "we stoll [sic] before from our Masters, we run away to Porto Rico, have been lazy, and have cheated our Masters." "But," they concluded, "now it is quite otherwise with us."[24] Another neophyte noted that, as long as his name was Harry (before his Moravian baptism), "I was a bad negro." But after he heard Moravian preaching, changed his name to Heinrich, began going to church and talking about the evil things he had done, he became certain of his spiritual salvation. After his peaceful and faithful conversion to Moravianism, Heinrich admitted that he could now "promise my master that I shall be a faithful slave in God's grace."[25] When a national helper named Nathanael gave a speech to young students at one of the Moravian mission stations, he observed that they would be "doubly slaves, if we remain in sin, for, if we are not redeemed, we are also the slaves of Satan and will also remain as such if we depart from this world in that state." Nathanael focused on the horrors of spiritual enslavement to Satan, making a subtle comparison between plantation owners and the devil while simultaneously implying that spiritual salvation, rather than the trauma of temporal slavery, should be the main focus of Afro-Caribbeans' thoughts and efforts.[26] These Afro-Moravians peddled the classic convention that Christian slaves were obedient slaves.

Everyone in the Caribbean plantation system knew better. The conversion of thousands of slaves to Moravianism, and especially the rise of an elite black preacher class, certainly threatened to undermine the social, racial, and psychological anchors that kept the plantation system tied down. In fact, the Danish island of St. John had experienced a short-lived but violent rebellion in the early 1730s, just as Moravian missionaries were becoming established in the Danish Caribbean. When a black Englishman came to the Moravian mission station from Groot Hanslolk Cay (now Hans Lollik Island), he reported that "white residents of the cay were eager to hear the preaching of the Negroes' teachers."[27] This could mean that white residents of the cay were either requesting instruction *from* blacks or to be taught *like* blacks. Both scenarios threatened to invert the precarious power relations upon which racial slavery was built. Even when Afro-Moravianism did not subvert the plantation system explicitly, the presence of elite black preachers threatened to do so implicitly.[28]

National helpers were attuned to the racial implications of their preaching, and they often used their oratorical skills and sacred authority to situate themselves as God's chosen people. Not only could Moravian doctrine remind African slaves of their humanity, it could also pose a challenge to the social order of plantation slavery. The rhetoric of property serves as an ideal example. When Mingo wrote to other Moravians in the Pennsylvania missions, he said that he sincerely hoped that Christ would "not abandon us, for although we are poor, we belong to Him. He has earned us." "We beg you," Mingo continued, "to think of us continuously and pray to the Savior that He might wish to keep us as His property."[29] This was not a casual reference to property, but rather a racialized theological critique that challenged the rigid hierarchy of racial slavery. By invoking the concept of faithful slaves as Christ's property, Mingo offered a spiritual challenge to the temporal power of white masters and overseers. God was, of course, the ultimate "master," for he reigned above even the seemingly all-powerful white planter class. Black preachers' relationship with God, generated as it was through the conduit of Christ, promised to circumvent the racial hierarchy of plantation slavery and create a new spiritual hierarchy where God and Christ were the ultimate overseers of a benevolent kingdom of believers.

White planters understood these problems. Only a few years after the arrival of German Moravians they launched a sustained attack on Afro-Moravianism. One group of national helpers from St. Thomas wrote a letter to the King of Denmark in 1739, outlining the religious persecution they faced and appealing to the King's Christian sensibilities to encourage him to help. Writing on behalf of over 650 black Moravians, Abraham, Mingo, and the other authors of this letter lamented that white planters and overseers "come to beat and cut us." They also "burn our Books and reject our Baptism, they miscal [sic] the Brethren for Beasts; saying, a *Negroe* ought not to be baptized, and a baptized *Negroe* be like a Piece of burnt Wood in Hell."[30] When another master chained up his slave "until he promised that he would learn nothing more from the brethren about Christianity," he tacitly recognized not only the egalitarian impulses of Afro-Moravianism, but also the subtle ways in which slaves could invert the power relations within plantation slavery and reorient them along the axis of Moravian theology.[31] Opposition from slave masters was a constant reminder of the dangers of using black preachers in a slave society.

The problem, of course, was the doctrine of Christian liberty, a concept that made slave evangelization astonishingly problematic. Christian liberty complicated and obscured the relationships between slaves and masters, oppressors and oppressed. It could empower slaves and threaten to undermine the racial conventions, colonial laws, and imperial authority upon which slave societies rested. When Mingo invoked the trope of property to identify slaves as Christ's belongings, he expressed a version of Christian liberty that simultaneously circumvented and overrode the racial hierarchies upon which his society was built. When a Scottish woman named Janet Schaw spent Christmas on Antigua in 1774, she recalled how African slaves celebrated the holiday season. Slaves apparently believed that "good Buccara God," or the white man's God, would punish masters who physically battered their slaves during this time of celebration. The sanctity of the holiday season and the image of God punishing slave masters naturally resulted in heightened racial tensions and anxieties about slave rebellions. Schaw slept uneasily during "this season of unbounded freedom," even as white patrols constantly surveyed the island to ensure that no slaves employed the doctrine of Christian liberty to secure their worldly liberty or harm their masters.[32] When slaves rebelled in Demerara in 1823, the rebellion was fueled partially by an internalization of Christian liberty rhetoric that members of the London Missionary Society unwittingly helped germinate.[33] Even though Protestant missionaries throughout the early modern Atlantic tried to shift the focus away from Christian liberty and towards obedience to one's master, slaves nevertheless picked up on, translated, and employed Christian liberty in ways that white missionaries often predicted but rarely approved.

Although tensions over slavery could both sustain and challenge Afro-Moravianism, there were other basic, more logistical problems with Moravian missions. The vast distance between missions and potential converts was often insurmountable. As the first fruits got on in age in the 1760s, their evangelical trips to the outskirts of the missions became much less frequent. The grueling sugar harvest cycle also kept Afro-Moravians in the fields and away from the churches, as did periodic bouts of epidemic disease that wracked the slave population and perennial storms that destroyed roads, paths, and churches. All these natural—for Moravians, providential—events conspired to hinder the gathering of Afro-Moravian communities on the Danish Caribbean Islands. But the biggest problem was within the core of national helpers itself. Death and old age of the first fruits, the models of Afro-Moravian piety, certainly took its toll, as did a significant degree of religious backsliding. Petrus, that "motherly" preacher and one of the first fruits, was eventually expelled from the Moravian church in the spring of 1762 "on account of his bad behavior."[34] One Moravian historian recalled that *bombas,* or former Moravian converts who held positions of authority within the plantation system, were partially responsible for spiritual backsliding in the Caribbean. These apostates "could abuse their power that went along with their position to harass the others for as long as it took to make them as faithless as they."[35] In spite of these problems, German Moravians and national helpers collaborated from the 1730s onward to create the most successful missionary effort that the Caribbean had yet seen. Most importantly, this was the first time in the history of Protestant missions that black slaves were used as agents of evangelism. Even if Anglicans, Congregationalists, and other groups disapproved of this radical move, within years they would be doing the same thing.

The Moravian national helper system was not limited to the Danish Caribbean. In 1753 Mingo addressed a letter to his "white and brown brethren" in the Moravian settlements of Bethlehem and Nazareth, Pennsylvania. Speaking to whites and Indians alike, Mingo hoped that the Pennsylvania Moravians would "never forget us." "We are poor," Mingo lamented, "and it is necessary that you think often of us."[36] Mingo's letter was not the only thing that passed between the Moravian communities of the Caribbean and North American mainland, for German Moravian missionaries as well as recent converts frequently migrated to and from Caribbean mission stations throughout the Atlantic world, ensuring that pens, paper, and people would always keep these communities connected. Indeed, the Native American encounter with Moravianism paralleled, in many ways, what was happening in the Caribbean from the 1730s to the 1760s.[37]

Moravians had established a praying community in Bethlehem, Pennsylvania by 1741, and within five years they had built half a dozen settlements within a day's journey of that town. The Indians who lived there, of course, were suffering through the same problems that other Indians had experienced: territorial dispossession, forced migration, disease, and being pulled into the endless imperial wars between France and Britain. But some Indians discovered in Moravianism a way to address both the spiritual and temporal concerns of indigenous peoples trying to work through the troubles of colonialism. Moravian Indian preachers and their listeners crafted and articulated a syncretic Christianity, a blend of traditional Indian culture and new innovations from their Moravian counterparts.[38]

Like Afro-Caribbeans, Native American preachers indigenized Moravian doctrine by fusing it with their own spiritual rituals, traditions, and beliefs. Like African cosmologies, Native American cosmologies had much in common with Moravian theology. Moravian Indians in the Housatonic and Delaware Valleys, like their counterparts in the Afro-Caribbean missions, understood Christ as an ever-present "guardian spirit" that offered Indians protection and watched over their lives.[39] The ritual indigenous practices of torture and bloodletting fit easily with Moravian concepts of Christ's corporeal suffering, and even Indian rites of passage into manhood and womanhood melded with rituals of Moravian baptism. Indian women, like female Caribbean slaves, embraced Moravianism because it offered them opportunities for social status and spiritual leadership. Indian Moravians tried to cultivate an ethos of spiritual communitarianism by having husbands and wives construct written salutations (which praised the piety and faith of their spouses) to one another.[40] One commentator noted that, for Indian men, the taking on of new names signaled a transition into full manhood. When Indian Moravians changed their names and were brought into a larger community of Moravians, the act might have symbolized for many another rite of passage akin to making the shift from childhood to adulthood.[41] Even if they did not believe in any aspect of Moravian theology, many Indians accepted Moravian education to improve their physical and spiritual health, maintain a sense of kinship and community, and acquire literacy skills. While many Native Americans rejected the Moravians, others embraced some elements of Moravianism by fusing them with their own traditional beliefs, practices, and rituals.[42]

Indigenous spiritual leaders were central to the development of Indian Moravianism in the middle of the eighteenth century, for they served as church elders, teachers, and exhorters. One example was Nicodemus, the elder of the Moravian Indian Congregation at Gnadenhütten (just north of Bethlehem). In his writings, orations, and prayers, Nicodemus merged Moravianism with Indian spirituality by employing naturalistic metaphors to explain the value of Moravian cosmology to his fellow Indians. He confessed that "My heart is just so as a little run, which flows down from a mountain, if there is a little fish in the water, it will be carried along down with the water, and so is it with my heart, it swims always in the wounds and is carried away by the blood." He went on to employ metaphors from the animal world to elucidate his point. "At first my heart was like a young Pidgeon, which can not yet fly, but does try so long, till it can fly. And such is my heart now, I always fly into the wounds." But Nicodemus finished his confession with a reference to the centrality of military security on the Anglo-Indian frontier, for he noted that, "I feel my heart is nowhere better preserved than in the wounds of the Saviour, therein I find myself just as if I was in a Fort."[43] By variably describing his heart as a fish floating down a mountain river and a young pigeon flying into the wounds of Christ, Nicodemus grafted Moravian theology onto Native American understandings of the (super)natural world. In invoking the metaphor of Christ's wounds as a fort, Nicodemus implied that Moravian Christianity might, at the very least, offer some veneer of physical protection from settlers, soldiers, traders, and speculators who wished to harm and dispossess his Indian brethren.

Also like their Afro-Moravian counterparts, membership in Christ's kingdom gave Moravian Indians access to some skills and opportunities that other Indians did not possess. The most basic was their attempt to use Christian identity as a wedge against the voracious colonization of Indian lands. When a Moravian Indian named Tishcohan and another Christian Indian named Moses Tatami petitioned the government of Pennsylvania to protect Indian lands, they did so by using the idioms of Christian supplication. They suggested that, because they "embraced the Christian Religion and attained some small Degree of Knowledge therein," they should have the chance to live "under the same Laws with the English." They hoped that "some place might be allotted them where they may live in the Enjoyment of the same Religion and Laws with them." Instead of being moved by the language of Christian humanitarianism, the colonial government simply called these Indians "rascals" who possessed the "impudence to subscribe themselves, 'Your Honour's brethren in the Lord Jesus.'"[44] This attitude, as well as periodic massacres of Moravian Indians, tensions between Indian converts and one another, and conflicts between white Moravian missionaries and Indian ones, revealed the fragile nature of Christian missionary work. In spite of some Native Americans embrace of Christianity, by the 1760s many Moravian converts on the Anglo-Indian frontier began to realize that even if their appropriation of Christianity might help save their souls, it could save neither their lands nor their lives.[45]

Success can beget praise, but the ascension of the Moravians from the 1730s onward also drew severe criticism. Although later ministers like Ezra Stiles and David McClure would suggest that Moravian evangelical techniques among blacks and Indians were more effective than those tried by previous Protestant missionaries, others saw in Moravian expansion a grave danger. Referring to the Moravians' distinctive theology, George Whitefield complained that Moravians introduced "a whole Farrago of superstitions, not to say idolatrous Fopperies" into the Protestant Atlantic.[46] In spite of such criticism, the Methodists who followed Whitefield ended up incorporating much of the Moravian pedagogical repertoire into their own missionary work in the 1760s and 1770s. There was no denying that the Moravians had made some headway into the Caribbean and the North American frontier. They counted over 11,000 converts in British mission stations by the end of the eighteenth century and had cultivated a national helper system that had hundreds of blacks acting as spiritual leaders. This system and other Moravian practices provided a model for later Protestant missionary groups engaged in the debate over whether to use black slaves and Indians as preachers, teachers, and catechists. Every Protestant denomination eventually did.[47]

Like the Moravians before them, Anglicans began using black slaves as evangelical agents in the 1740s, and they did so when they founded the "Charleston Negro School" in South Carolina. One of the most unique educational experiments in early American history, the school was opened in September 1742 under the auspices of the Society for the Propagation of the Gospel in Foreign Parts (SPG), and was designed to instruct black children in the tenets of Anglican Protestantism. The ultimate goal, of course, was to have those black children then "diffuse their Light and Knowledge to their Parents, Relations, Countrymen, and Fellow Servants."[48] Yet the most remarkable characters in the school were the teachers. Indeed, both Harry and Andrew, the teachers charged with instructing these Carolina slaves, were slaves themselves, purchased by the SPG for the important task of educating others. Although it closed in 1764 and had a negligible impact on the Christianization of Carolina's slaves, the school's history nevertheless demonstrates major changes in the tenor of missionary work during a period of transatlantic revivalism. By purchasing slaves to teach other slaves, Anglicans walked a slender line between reinforcing and destabilizing the fragile racial hierarchies that ordered southern society. The ascension of slave teachers in South Carolina was therefore simultaneously innovative and socially dangerous.

The origins of the school lay in two historical developments within South Carolina. The first was the explosion of racial tensions in the 1730s. In 1731 there were two rumored slave rebellions in South Carolina, and in both of them it was feared that Christianized blacks had used their training to interpret their own doctrine of Christian liberty in their fight against slavery. In 1736 South Carolina papers reported on a slave uprising in Antigua, where some slaves apparently "administered the Sacrament . . . according to the rites of the Bishop's Church," before beginning their rebellion.[49] But the threat of rebellion became most palpable in 1739, when the Stono Rebellion erupted. In September of 1739, about twenty slaves started a slave rebellion with the aims of achieving their freedom by heading south into Spanish Florida, which had guaranteed freedom to runaways from British colonies. The rebellion failed, but dozens of white victims and rebelling slaves were killed during the rebellion and afterwards. Importantly, there was a common ideology, indeed a religious spirituality, that motivated and defined Stono. This ideology was a widespread Afro-Catholic religiosity—rooted in Africans' previous experience with Catholicism back in West Africa—that gave Carolina slaves the organizational ability, means of communication, and even sense of sacred timing (the rebellion began around the time of the Virgin Mary's birthday) to begin the revolt. It also explains why the Stono rebels chose Spanish Florida—a Catholic colony—as their getaway destination. The violence of the event struck fear into the hearts of southern masters. When the South Carolina legislature wrote new slave codes in the wake of the 1739 rebellion, they outlawed teaching a slave to write or even using an already literate slave as a scribe.[50] Paradoxically, Anglicans turned to literacy and Christian instruction as a method to demand slave obedience, spread the Gospel, and maintain peace in the Carolinas.[51]

The second development that provided the foundation for the Charleston Negro School was the itinerancy of John Wesley and George Whitefield in the late 1730s and early 1740s. Wesley, who was friends with the most influential Anglican clergymen in South Carolina, began working in Georgia in the late 1730s to put together a parish of slave congregants. While he was only marginally successful, he cleared the way for George Whitefield, who would also extend his evangelical itinerancy to include southern blacks. Whitefield was irate at the lackluster record of Anglican evangelization in the Carolinas, arguing that withholding Christian instruction from slaves was sinful, unchristian, and "Evil." Questioning the popular convention of innate African inferiority, Whitefield argued that blacks were "just as much, and no more, conceived and born in Sin, as White Men are." If both white and black men were "born and bred up here," then they were also "naturally capable of the same Improvement."[52] Equal under sin, blacks also had the same access to spiritual rebirth, regeneration, and divine judgment as their white counterparts. Like his predecessors and contemporaries, however, Whitefield also argued that slaves would be more faithful, obedient, and docile if they were Christian slaves.

In fact, Whitefield suggested that the Stono Rebellion and even the recent spread of smallpox were products of God's displeasure towards Carolinians for their lack of missionary zeal. Whitefield's remedy was "to buy" some of that "despised Generation" and set aside a large plot of land for the construction of a black school.[53] The evangelical preacher anticipated that, at this school and in other orphan houses that he constructed, several blacks with "suitable abilities" would eventually be "bred to the Ministry." Whitefield claimed that, by 1740, he already had one or two "in view for *that* Purpose."[54] In 1740 the Bryan family took their cue from Whitefield and raised their own funds to open a school for black children in St. Helena Parish, hoping that the school's graduates would teach other slaves about the blessings of Christ. In short, Whitefield and his followers believed that the rise of black preachers would serve as a panacea for South Carolina's lackluster reputation in preaching to slaves while easing the social tensions that threatened to tear that society apart.

Whitefield put the Anglicans on the defensive, blaming both licentious slave owners and lazy missionaries for failing to make any headway into South Carolina's slave population. The Anglicans responded in kind by attacking Whitefield's theology, especially the kind of ecstatic revivalism and excessive enthusiasm that more traditional Protestants found abhorrent. The biggest problem was the debate about conversion. While revivalists generally understood conversion as an immediate, life-changing experience, traditional Protestants (including Anglicans and Puritans) believed that conversion was instead a protracted and gradual process characterized by intense self-scrutiny, biblical study, and intellectual reflection. Although these debates were theological and scriptural in nature, when placed within the fire of South Carolina race relations, they became even more controversial. How should slaves be converted? Who was primarily responsible for their conversion, and what did this mean to their status as slaves? Although Anglicans had been debating these questions for decades, the rise of evangelical revivalism just as the Stono Rebellion shook the south made the question of black Christianity all the more pressing. As such, Anglicans scrambled to mount a defense of their own missionary tradition.[55]

The man who would spearhead the Anglicans' defense and renew missionary work in the Carolinas was Alexander Garden, an Anglican missionary and commissary to the Bishop of London. Garden thought Whitefield was a "very wicked man" who, even as he helped orphans in his schools, still had a nasty reputation for underfeeding his students, or "*Pinching* their Bellies."[56] Personal animosity aside, Garden found himself in the awkward position of rebutting Whitefield's claims that masters were oppressive towards their slaves while simultaneously explaining why so many slaves were still unconverted. Garden addressed the first point by invoking the classic trope of the paternal slave owner, noting that masters and overseers were not violent tyrants to their slaves, but rather benevolent fathers who constantly treated their charges with gentle love. Garden then suggested that the reason why Carolina's slaves were ignorant of the Gospel was because the Anglicans lacked a "certain uniform Method of teaching them."[57]

Garden found his uniform method in the pedagogy and practices of Whitefield himself, for in the early 1740s he began to develop an idea of a school for young black children. Like other Protestants throughout the Atlantic world, many Anglicans were beginning to believe that the education of adult blacks and Indians was futile. They believed that children were the future of Christian missions and that the only way to make any advances was to focus on a younger generation; a generation less sullied by the pagan rituals of their forefathers. Garden expected that, with two black teachers at the head of the class, his school might produce upwards of forty graduates per year. Those graduates would subsequently preach to the thousands of slaves that had formerly been so hard to reach. Slaves, Garden explained, were a kind of "Nation within a Nation," and the only way to introduce Christianity to the thousands of slaves in the rice country was to infiltrate their ranks with other, Christianized slaves. "Parents and Grand Parents, Husbands, Wives, Brothers, Sisters, and other Relations," Garden hoped, "would be daily teaching and learning of one another." Anglican Christianity would thereby spread throughout the Carolinas like a kind of virus, being transmitted via the hundreds of students that Garden expected to graduate from the school. Garden even anticipated that, within twenty years, "knowledge of the Gospel among those other Slaves . . . would not be much inferiour to that of the lowest Sort of White People." On Monday the 12th of September in 1742, the Charleston Negro School officially opened, and within a few weeks the total enrollment of black slaves was up to thirty. Garden's dream of using slaves to convert slaves seemed to be coming to fruition.[58]

If the creation of a school for blacks was not particularly controversial—Elias Neau had a school for black children in New York in the 1710s—the choice of teachers was. Rather than relying upon white Anglican instructors for the maintenance of the school, Garden instead envisioned a group of three to five slaves serving as the teaching corps for this school. In Garden's view, these slaves had to be between twelve and sixteen years old and must have had "sober and Docile Dispositions." The age requirement and the emphasis on sobriety and docility certainly went hand in hand. These teachers in training needed to be young enough to be molded but old enough to understand some of the complexities of Christian theology. In the end, Garden settled on two boys—Harry and Andrew—who were fourteen and fifteen years old, respectively. Formerly slaves of Alexander Skene, the two boys were born in Carolina, had been baptized, and could say the Church Catechism from memory. Although neither could read, Garden hoped that, with sufficient schooling, they could become teachers within the span of about a year. "This," Garden bragged, "is the only method, at least the most Efectual [sic] . . . that the whole ever will, or by Ordinary Human means, can be done." Most importantly, the identity of the two teachers as slaves would protect Garden's school against any claim of intellectual elitism while simultaneously guarding against social divisions within slave society itself. Garden believed that the two teachers "must be . . . Negroe Schoolmasters Home born, and equally property as other Slaves." In the wake of the Stono Rebellion, ensuring the status of these slave teachers as property was crucial to insulating the school from potential attacks from anxious masters. Indeed, it was precisely because Anglicans understood the liberating effects of Protestant evangelism that the Charleston School had to exhibit the classic pattern of slave domination that characterized the wider plantation society.[59]

The benefits of Garden's plan were both spiritual and temporal. While the school would help spread Christianity among slaves, that Christianity itself would serve as a protection against future slave revolts. As Anthony

Ellys noted in his 1759 sermon to the SPG, the Christianization of slaves could result in a paradigm shift in southern race relations. "Instead of needing to be always watched in order to prevent their doing any mischief," Ellys argued, "they may become guards, and defenders of their masters; and there will be no longer any such revolts and insurrections among them as have sometimes been detrimental, if not even dangerous, to several of the colonies."[60] Garden peddled this argument and conceived of his school as a cure-all for Anglican anxieties. The school would help offset the Catholic menace from Spanish Florida, redeem the Anglican reputation from the attacks of revivalists, ensure slaves' fidelity to their masters, and provide a new mechanism for slave instruction in the Carolina plantations. Garden also believed that the school would be a weapon for offsetting the gains made by the kind of evangelical Protestantism that could undermine Carolina's fragile racial, religious, and social order.[61]

Most importantly, the school was going to be very cost effective. Indeed, Garden purchased the two boys for the SPG on the cheap, buying them both for fifty-two pounds sterling, a sum the Anglicans found completely reasonable. One of the most tangible benefits of using slaves to teach, of course, was that, unlike teachers, catechists, and missionaries who frequently complained about their insufficient salaries, once slaves were purchased there would be "no further charge about them."[62] The SPG was learning the lessons that American slavery had been teaching planters for decades: African slaves could be much more profitable than comparable white labor. Despite decades of combined service for the SPG from the 1740s to the 1760s, Harry and Andrew never appeared on the payroll. In fact, Garden had explicitly calculated that the service of a "young healthy slave" could be counted on for three to four decades and he hoped that none of his successors would request from the SPG "any Charge for [Harry's] Maintenance."[63] This was not the first time that the SPG dabbled in slavery. They owned approximately 300 slaves at their Codrington plantation on Barbados and purchased individual slaves as assistants and domestics to Anglican missionaries.[64] The Anglicans' growing status as slave owners required that they continue attacking the "vulgar error" that Christianity implied temporal freedom.[65] When Philip Bearcroft boasted that the Charleston school would *"make them free indeed,"* he was implying that Christian education would free them from the chains of Satan rather than the yoke of American chattel slavery.[66] The kind of freedom that the school would bring about was spiritual, not worldly.

Like a contemporary slaveholder, Alexander Garden exhibited the classic paternalistic ethos that served to justify the enslavement of millions of Africans in the Americas. Although the SPG technically owned the two slaves, Garden guaranteed his bosses that he would take special care for their education and maintenance. In short, there was no question that Garden and the SPG embraced the role of benevolent slave masters. Assuring his superiors that these slaves would not enjoy any special privileges due to their role as teachers, Garden compared them to rank and file slaves, noting that Harry and Andrew would be "employed in it during life, as the others are in any other Services whatsoever."[67] Garden's slaves worked in a classroom instead of the fields, wielded books instead of hoes, and cultivated unconverted minds instead of rice. By 1740, Anglicans were fully participating in and contributing to the realities of racial oppression by purchasing Harry and Andrew to teach in their budding school. Garden played the role of the slave master while Harry and Andrew, in spite of their status as Christian teachers, nevertheless remained chattel slaves.

There is no better evidence for the Anglicans' embrace of their role of slave master than their treatment of Andrew, the older teacher who eventually became the forgotten son of the project. While Harry, the younger slave, was an "Excellent Genius," Andrew was "of a somewhat slower Genius."[68] Even though he was more mild-mannered than Harry, served as an assistant to Harry when enrollment became too overwhelming to manage alone, and even though another Anglican missionary asked Garden to place Andrew in his own parish, Garden concluded that Andrew could never teach on his own.[69] Therefore, and because Andrew apparently had shown "so weak an understanding" of Christian doctrine, in the fall of 1744 Garden asked his superiors for "discretionary Power to Sell him, and to purchase another of a better Genius in his Room." The committee in London instead directed Garden to ship him to the SPG plantation in Barbados, where he would work as a servant at Codrington College.[70] For reasons still unclear, Garden was unable to send Andrew away. Andrew spent the next six years in Carolina in limbo, suffering from a "Bruise in his Breast" and eventually being sold by Garden in 1750 for twenty-eight pounds sterling. Like the scores of other slaves who proved to have lackluster performance in the fields, Andrew was sold when he could not adequately serve his Anglican masters. Harry was on his own.[71]

It is difficult to determine exactly what Harry taught his students, and the inner workings of the school remain unclear. The list of books needed for the school—one hundred spelling books, fifty Testaments, fifty Bibles, and fifty Psalters with the Book of Common Prayer inside them—

reveals that the students probably focused on the basics of Christian instruction: literacy, psalm-singing, the lord's creed, and other essential lessons from scripture. By 1744, Alexander Garden claimed that enrollment had jumped from thirty to sixty, fifteen could read the testament very well, twenty were in the Psalters, and the rest were in the alphabet and spelling books.[72] Harry and Andrew (before the latter was sold) apparently examined the students twice a week to determine their progress and graduated about ten to fifteen students every year. The Charleston Negro School even expanded its enrollment to include "grown Slaves," who were given the same Christian instruction at the conclusion of the slaves' workday.[73]

In spite of Garden's contention that the Charleston Negro School was instrumental in "spreading the Light of the blessed Gospel among these poor heathens" of South Carolina, the school never achieved the kind of success that Anglicans hoped for.[74] Andrew's intellectual shortcomings and eventual departure was only a portent of the many challenges the school would face in the future. A hurricane tore the school down in 1752, enveloping the students' books and forcing them to start anew.[75] Garden, the main catalyst behind the program, suffered from increasingly ill health and died in 1755, forcing an apathetic Richard Clarke to replace him. Clarke resigned four years later. Smallpox struck Charleston in 1760, once again temporarily closing the school. When Harry died in 1764, the school officially stopped operating and was never reopened by the SPG. The Charleston Negro School disappeared from the records of the SPG by 1765.

Even though it eventually closed, Harry and Andrew's school was both a product of and catalyst for indigenous missionary work in the British Atlantic. Alexander Garden founded the school in response to evangelical revivalism, racial tensions after Stono, and concerns about Catholic Spanish influence in the Carolinas. Garden also called upon a longer history of using black and even Indian missionaries in the field, for he was certainly aware of the Moravian use of "national helpers" in their Caribbean plantations. As commissary to the Bishop of London, Garden might have also been tapping into a history of Anglican employment of non-whites in their Carolina missions. Indeed, it should be remembered that Garden's predecessor—Commissary Gideon Johnston—was the man who sponsored and directed the education of the Yamassee Prince in the 1710s. The Charleston school was therefore a product of transatlantic revivalism, Caribbean mission history, and Anglican experimentation with native missionaries.

The school was illustrative of a major shift in Anglican missionary policy, for this was the first time that Anglicans had employed black slaves in their missions. By 1765, however, another Anglican group known as the Associates of Dr. Bray had opened up schools for black children in Philadelphia, Newport, New York, Williamsburg, Norfolk, Yorktown, and Fredericksburg, as well as Chester, Maryland, Edenton, and Wilmington. Their missionaries also employed black intermediaries to teach other slaves. Jonathan Boucher, a Virginia missionary, reportedly trained Aaron to teach other slaves in "Reading & some of the first Principles of Religion."[76] Using slaves as teachers, Boucher argued to his bosses, was "the only practicable Method" for propagating the Gospel among slaves in Virginia.[77] John Barnett, a contemporary and colleague of Boucher who was preaching in North Carolina, gave some slaves several copies of Anglican tracts because they "promised me to take pains to instruct such of their fellow Slaves as are desirous to learn."[78] During these same years a young African named Philip Quaque was trained in London to become a missionary in his own home near Cape Coast Castle in West Africa. He would become the first African ordained in the English church. Indians, too, became central to Anglican missions. Beginning in the 1740s and lasting through the Revolutionary war, Mohawks like Daniel, Cornelius, and Paulus officially worked for the SPG as schoolmasters, catechists, and readers in the New York missions.[79] The Anglicans had no Indian or black teachers on their payroll in 1739. By 1765, they had recently closed a school that had used slaves as teachers for over two decades. They also had several black teachers working for the Associates of Dr. Bray, half a dozen Mohawks operating in New York as catechists and lecturers, and were finishing their training of Philip Quaque to return to West Africa. If native preachers were a pipe dream for Anglicans before 1740, they were vital to Anglican missions by 1770.

The introduction of native preachers in such numbers and with such rapidity was a major change for Anglicans, who still believed that literacy and formal education were the most important keys to conversion. Anglicans were afraid (and rightfully so) of losing their grip on the ecclesiastical and spiritual conduct of religion in the Americas and beyond, and they watched their control slipping away as uneducated speakers took to the pulpits, preached to Indians and slaves, and even performed as evangelical imposters.[80] The Charleston Negro School was just one of several attempts to address these problems by changing the direction of Anglican missions, maintaining control over the development of Afro-American spirituality, and ensuring that education—rather than an ill-defined "conversion experience"—be the centerpiece of black spirituality. In the

Charleston Negro School the Anglicans created a program that promised to provide the kind of viral evangelism that Great Awakening preachers were producing while simultaneously ensuring that its preachers—the slaves—were instructed within the circumscribed confines of an Anglican education.

While the rise of black slaves into positions of spiritual authority was a cause for both celebration and concern, the same might be said for the development of Indian Christianity during this period. Early modern Protestants throughout the Atlantic world viewed the appropriation of Christianity by black and Indian preachers ambivalently. On the one hand, the ascension of native evangelists could not only justify the pains taken to evangelize indigenous peoples, but also anticipate the eventual gospelization of the globe. Missionaries were particularly elated when indigenous peoples *themselves* sought out or promulgated Christianity. Moravians rejoiced to hear about a "converted Negroe" living in Genoa and "endeavouring to erect Schools in the neighbouring Parts, with a View to the Propagation of Christian Knowledge."[81] In New England, Benjamin Colman noted with glee that Indians suddenly exhibited a "surprising concern" for their souls in the early 1740s, as they earnestly began "voluntarily applying to the ministers" for Christian instruction.[82] One commentator recounted the 1741 reformation among the Montauk Indians in Connecticut and Long Island and observed that almost all of them had "renounced their heathenish idolatry and superstition, and many of them became true Christians."[83] Much of this is overstated, of course. The First Great Awakening did not engulf all of New England, and Indian religious affiliations were often sparked by a search for education and socio-political concerns. Indians joined churches well before and well after the First Great Awakening. Nevertheless, this period did witness the rise of powerful native preachers who offered new ways for Native American preachers to craft constantly evolving spiritual meanings out of Christianity.[84]

Protestant divines feared the permeability of the boundaries between sincere piety and excessive enthusiasm. The ecstatic revivalism that accompanied the 1730s and 40s—among both white and Indian populations—was often described by religious conservatives as a dangerous forecast of spiritual anarchy that threatened to subvert the fragile religious order. One of the most pressing problems was that many native preachers, exhorters, and prophets led their own meetings, followings, and congregations away from the eyes of white authority. One Anglican complained that, by 1750, "even the ignorant *Negroes* and *Indians* have set up preaching and praying by the Spirit, and they have their Meetings, in which such of them as can neither write nor read, hold forth in their Turn."[85] Like other Old Light divines who rejected the enthusiasm of the First Great Awakening, Charles Chauncy scoffed at this democratization of sacred authority. There was a risk, Chauncy lamented, of having "so many *Exhorters*"—who one of Chauncy's Anglican contemporaries called "false teachers"—preaching in the colonies.[86] In Chauncy's view, these new evangelists had:

> no *Learning*, and but *small Capacities*, yet imagine they are able, and without Study too, to speak to the *Spiritual Profit* of such as are willing to hear them: Nay, there are among these Exhorters, *Babes in Age*, as well as Understanding. They are *chiefly* indeed *young Persons*, sometimes *Lads*, or rather *Boys*: Nay, *Women* and *Girls*; yea, *Negroes*, have taken upon them to do the Business of *Preachers*. Nor has this been *accidental* only, or in a *single Place*, or at a *private House*; but there is scarce a Town in *all the Provinces*, where this Appearance has been, but there have been also *these Exhorters*, in smaller or greater Numbers.[87]

The problem was that, in an era of intensively divisive evangelical revivalism, Indians, slaves, and others began incorporating elements of revivalist theology and practice into their own, thereby complicating the boundaries between Christianity and indigenous religions while simultaneously offering an implicit rebuttal to entrenched church authority.

Few exemplified these tensions better than Samuel Niles. Born around 1701, Niles eventually became a spiritual, cultural, and social leader of the Narragansett people. His propulsion into a position of indigenous leadership was the result of two major developments in eighteenth century Narragansett history: the crisis in Indian dispossession of land and the outburst of Christian revivalism. Although English settlers were unapologetically buying up Indian lands in the first decades of the eighteenth century, the Narragansett sachemship was partly responsible for this dispossession. Niles, along with other Narragansett leaders, blamed Thomas Ninigret, the Narragansett sachem, for drinking too much, selling land without the consultation of the rest of the tribe, and using those land sales to resolve his personal debts. Niles even corresponded with Sir William Johnson, the British Superintendent of Indian Affairs, and complained that Narragansetts were quickly losing land, had no access to the sea, and that Indian children would eventually "come into bondage to the English."[88] He also petitioned the colonial government for assistance and even tried to depose Ninigret and replace the sachemship with a system of Indian counselors. It was within this context of dispossession, internecine power struggles with the sachem, and colonial apathy that Niles tried to use his spiritual authority as a preacher to preserve the land, power, and cultural identity of his Narragansett people.[89]

The other major development that inaugurated Samuel Niles' rise to power was the spread of evangelical revivalism in southeastern New England in the 1730s and 40s. Some of the first Christian missionaries to actively court the Narragansetts were Indians. Japhet Hannit of Martha's Vineyard and William Simmons of Dartmouth both undertook several evangelical trips to Narragansett in the first decades of the eighteenth century. While several Anglican missionaries and a handful of Congregationalist ministers also tried to proselytize the Narragansetts, the rise of New Light preaching in the wake of Great Awakening itinerant James Davenport's 1741 evangelical tour through southeastern New England marked the moment when some Narragansett Indians began to embrace revivalist evangelism. Previous Protestant missionaries had emphasized scriptural knowledge and ecclesiastical deference as fundamental components of Christian spirituality. Davenport and his successors—most notably Westerly, Rhode Island's Joseph Park—instead introduced "revelations, visions, trances, and emotional participation in services."[90] In doing so, New Light preaching amounted to a sustained attack on ministers who relied upon literacy and learning to maintain their positions. Personal feelings from the heart, rather than scholarly intellectualism, were to be the new basis of spiritual experience and church authority. Davenport, Park, and the growing number of Indian converts opened up new opportunities for Christian Indians to redefine what Christianity meant, where sacred authority originated, and how God's revelation was to be understood. Samuel Niles and other native preachers would combine the new evangelicalism's emphasis on personal spiritual revelation with a critique of traditional indigenous authority to become one of the strongest forces in Narragansett society.[91]

For both of these reasons—the failure of whites to respect Indian lands and the genesis of new models of Indian spiritual leadership—southeastern New England Indians consistently demonstrated a preference for indigenous preachers. The rise of native evangelists gave Indians who were suspicious of white ones an alternative form of leadership that, they believed, spoke directly to the unique problems of being a Christian Indian during a period of dispossession. One Anglican preacher, for example, complained that his Indian flock would not receive him because they feared "I would get their Land from them."[92] Narragansetts were irate when an Anglican minister hired a Mr. Cross to oversee the construction of, and future instruction in, a new school. Because Cross had recently bought up some of the best Narragansett fishing lands, Indian leaders rejected the offer and preferred to have nothing to do with him.[93] But Indians' growing suspicion of white preachers was not only about land, for they also distrusted English ministers because they accepted payment for their spiritual labors. Joseph Fish, a minister at Charlestown, Rhode Island and Stonington, Connecticut, complained that Indians would not attend his services because "I take Money of my Own people, for preaching; so Am a Hireling, And therefore cant be a true Minister of Jesus Christ."[94] Native preachers like Samuel Niles often took the opportunity to exploit these sentiments to recruit new congregants to their own churches. Niles reportedly told Indians to cease attending Fish's congregation because all learned ministers were "Thieves, Robbers, Pirates, etc." "They steal the word," Niles argued. "God told the Prophets the words they Spoke: and These Ministers Steal that Word."[95] By describing white ministers as burglars of revelation, Niles and other preachers tapped into psychological anxieties about dispossession and market interactions with white settlers. This strategy was so effective that, by the 1760s, native preachers were beginning to replace white ones. Joseph Fish complained in 1762 that Narragansett Indians had "a great Fondness for the Indian Teachers" and preferred to hear lectures and attend services by Indians rather than Englishman.[96] One instructor named Robert Clelland filed a truly pathetic complaint to his superiors in 1764. He asked to be dismissed from the "Low and Melancholy Situation" of trying to teach Indians who refused to hear him. Clelland admitted that in spite of his best attempts to generate an Indian congregation, he was still "forc't to make way for an Indian master."[97] The rise of native preachers in an era of revival gave Indians new figures for spiritual leadership and left some English missionaries out of a job.

These tensions manifested themselves and culminated in the creation of a separate Christian congregation under Samuel Niles in the 1750s. The origins of Niles' separate church lay in a post-Great Awakening schism within Joseph Park's congregation at Westerly. At the same time that Niles was being chastised for "exhorting" in Park's church, a white deacon named Stephen Babcock was establishing his own separatist congregation. Niles joined Babcock but, to the dismay of Niles and other Narragansett Indians, Babcock ordained a Pequot preacher named James Simon as their Indian minister. The Narragansetts expressed their dismay, either for placing a Pequot as minister of a Narragansett church or for having a white Englishman decide who their pastor should be. Either way, the Narragansetts threatened to separate again, but Simon's eventual migration out of Narragansett avoided the conflict and elevated Niles to the position of pastor within the newly formed church by the early 1750s. Samuel Niles was now at the head of his own congregation.[98]

One of the problems that Old Lights faced when dealing with someone as controversial as Niles was that he was not only supported by the majority of Narragansett Indians, but was also a celebrated preacher. Joseph Fish, who became Niles' nemesis in the 1760s, conceded that Niles was "a Sober Religious Man, of Good Sense and great Fluency of Speech; and know not but a very honest Man. Has a good deal of the Scriptures by heart, and professes a Regard for the Bible."[99] Even at the height of the Niles separation controversy, one New England divine told Fish that Niles should be "treated and Spoken of with great tenderness."[100] Ezra Stiles, an Old Light minister in Newport, Rhode Island, entertained Niles at his home in the spring of 1772. Although Stiles found it "extraordinary" (and not in a good way) that Niles could not read, the former was nevertheless impressed with his guest's theological and scriptural knowledge. "He is however acquainted with the Doctrines of the Gospel," Stiles observed, "and an earnest zealous Man, and perhaps does more good to the Indians than any White Man could do." Stiles also concluded that his Indian guest was "of an unblameable Life as to Morals and Sobriety" and generally had a "very great Influence over the Indians."[101] By the 1760s Niles had become a wildly popular and widely respected Narragansett pastor.

In spite of his popularity, there were several serious theological and ecclesiastical complications that Niles' ascension into ministerial authority exposed. The first was his unique ordination. Because no white ministers would officiate at his ordination, Niles' church instead "chose and appointed three Brethren Indians to ordain him." Niles told Ezra Stiles that, during his lengthy ordination (it lasted an entire afternoon), the "3 Brethren laid their Hands" on him and one of them "prayed over him and gave him the charge of that Flock." "Such a Spirit was outpoured and fell upon them," Niles recalled, "that many others of the Congregation prayed aloud and lift up their hearts with prayers and Tears to God." In the meantime, white witnesses, who probably mistook this entire process for utter confusion, "were disgusted and went away." At the end of the ordination the Indian congregation sang a few psalms and exited the meeting house.[102] Joseph Fish told a friend the same ordination story and emphasized that the Indians who ordained Niles were definitely "not in any Office."[103] When Niles was baptized for the second time in his life—the first by sprinkling and the second by total immersion— Stiles made note that it was conducted "by an Indian not an Elder."[104] Although his congregation had accepted him by incorporating some

elements of Christian ordination, the foundation for this ecclesiastical exercise was suspect. Indeed, the laying on of hands not only symbolized a transfer of spiritual authority, but also bound all ministers into
a sacred genealogy that could trace itself back to the first apostles and
even Christ himself. Employing lay Indians—who had no claim to this
spiritual lineage—to ordain Samuel Niles highlighted the pressing question of where ultimate authority originated. Niles' popularity within
Narragansett society, his unblemished personal record, and his church's
separate establishment away from the Congregational mainstream ensured
that irritated white ministers could only complain about Niles' dubious
claim to ministerial power. They had neither the will nor the authority
to depose him.

For conventional Congregationalists, the most infuriating aspect of
Niles' pastorate was his illiteracy. "He *cannot read a word*," Fish complained to a friend, "and So is wholly dependant [sic] Upon the (too
Seldom) Reading of others: Which exposes him, (doubtless) to a great
deal of Inacuracy [sic] in using Texts of Scriptures, if not gross Mistakes
in the Application of them."[105] For Protestants who understood scripture as God's revelation, the inability of a pastor to read and communicate those divine truths to his congregation could be unorthodox at best,
heretical at worst. Fish contended that separatists of all pales (including
Indians) generally lacked any knowledge of scripture and were patheti-
cally weak in biblical exegesis. This not only made them poor scholars
and teachers, but also resulted in "low and empty performances" in the
pulpit.[106] Fish heard from one source that Niles' lectures were filled with
"gross Error . . . Ignorance, Railing," and "outpourings of Ignorance."[107]
"These Indian Teachers," Fish complained to Andrew Oliver, "were very
ignorant: some of them, especially the Chief Speaker . . . could not read
a word in the Bible."[108] Literacy was one of the reasons why Indians
turned to Niles in the first place. At least one Narragansett reported that
Fish told Indians they could not hope for a saving conversion if they
could not read. They therefore concluded that, because they were illiterate, they "Were All going to hell."[109] Although Fish tried to reassure
Indians that literacy was ultimately not necessary for salvation,
Narragansetts still preferred to turn to a person like themselves: an illiterate Indian who claimed that his own spiritual authority derived not
from a sacred text but from personal revelation, visions, and dreams.

If Niles' inability to read was problematic, the source of his spiritual
knowledge was even more so. Although he did have scripture read to
him, Niles also relied upon personal revelation, including visions and
dreams, to access what he believed was God's message. In doing so, Niles

called upon an established indigenous tradition of using dreams and vision quests to communicate with the spirit world. Indian men often undertook vision quests in order to gain access to spiritual knowledge.[110] For Niles and other Christian Indian preachers, the guardian spirit they were trying to communicate with was probably Christ himself. Indeed, Manitous, or sacred spirits who possessed a wealth of spiritual power, served as advisors and guardians to those who needed assistance. Furthermore, Manitous were known for their "ultimate power of metamorphosis." As a spirit who multiplied loaves of bread, converted water into wine, and himself became transubstantiated during communion, Christ could have been interpreted and perceived as the ultimate Manitou for Narragansett Indians. Like Afro and Indian Moravians, Narragansetts approached the ultimate deity—God—through the lesser spiritual force of Christ. Christ was therefore a gateway and intermediary between humans and the creator of all things.

Dreams could also reveal visions of heaven that reflected the sociohistorical realities of colonialism. One Indian named Tobe had a dream where he went to heaven and saw "the Great God" as well as Jesus Christ (whom he described as a "handsome Man"). Tobe also dreamt that he saw "a Multitude of Folks in Heaven, Resembling Butterflies of Many Colours."[111] While Tobe's dream certainly could have been subconscious nonsense, it may have had its origins in Rhode Island's vibrant multicultural population, as Indians, whites, and blacks intermingled in the Narragansett region. It is noteworthy that Tobe's vision of heaven was an inclusive one that welcomed all souls, regardless of race, ethnicity, or class. In their dreams, vision quests, and recounting of scripture through memory, Niles and other Christian Indians creatively translated Christianity—including the personage of Christ and their visions of heaven—to incorporate it into a framework of indigenous cosmology and spirituality.

Congregational contemporaries, of course, did not see Niles' reliance upon dreams and visions as a creative translation of Christianity. Joseph Fish thought Tobe's dream was "Strange," "Horrible," and even "Gross."[112] Fish and his colleagues also scoffed at the "inward impressions," "*False Religion*," "wild Imaginations," "visionary things," and "idle dreams" of Indian separatist preaching.[113] Andrew Eliot told Fish that he was sorry that Niles threatened to lead his Indian congregants "from the Sacred oracles to his own whims and imaginations."[114] As if this was not clear enough, Niles' reliance upon personal revelation, rather than biblical study, threatened to undermine the very fabric of New England's spiritual order. Fish feared that Niles was "in imminent danger of leaving the *Word*, for the Guidence [sic] of *Feelings, Impressions, Visions, Appearances* and *Directions* of Angels and of Christ himself in a Visionary Way."[115] If Fish did not put it directly enough in his letters to friends and colleagues, he stated it plainly in his diary: Indians threatened the status quo because they were "taught by the Spirit, immediately from Heaven: So have teachings above the Bible."[116] It was one thing to create congregations separate from English ecclesiastical authority, but quite another to cast off thousands of years of scriptural tradition to find new revelations in dreams. Samuel Niles and other Indian separatists thereby represented not only a challenge to Congregational orthodoxy, but also an implicit threat to biblical authority itself. As such, Fish could only interpret his battle with Samuel Niles theologically. When Niles urged his Indian congregation not to attend any of Joseph Fish's services, the latter recorded that "Satan has a hand in Stirring up *Sam Niles*."[117] While Fish attributed the rise of separate native churches under Indian pastors to Satan's malicious designs, the roots of Niles' spiritual leadership lay instead in Narragansett concerns over dispossession as well as a wider effort to fuse indigenous spirituality with Christian revivalism.

Joseph Fish's invective towards Samuel Niles and his followers should not be mistaken for a general distrust of all Christian Indians. In fact, one of the more remarkable aspects of this entire conflict between Fish and Niles was that Fish continued to train, employ, and cultivate native preachers on his own, partially to combat the influence that Niles had among the Narragansett people. Fish employed Sampson Woyboy, Charles Daniel, and John Shattock, Jr. as teachers in his Indian school in Stonington, Connecticut. The rise of Indian separatist churches led by Indians like Niles urged Fish to find other, more manageable, native preachers who could combat Niles' unusual theology with their own form of intellectual Indian Congregationalism. This probably explains why, in the fall of 1770, Fish urged Indians to establish yet another Christian congregation, this time under the tutelage of James Daniel and the rest of Ninigret's sachem party. Although this attempt to break Niles' influence among the Narragansetts failed, it does reflect the power placed in the hands of indigenous preachers, as Fish used them to combat the gains of other native preachers.[118]

While the line between sincere piety and ecstatic excess was certainly thin, the boundaries between Christian preacher and native revitalist, or someone who sought a revitalization of indigenous culture to respond to colonization, were quite porous. Samuel Niles might be viewed as a kind of native revitalist, a spiritual leader who used his sacred authority as a tool to try to maintain Indian land and preserve Narragansett culture. As was the case with Niles, native preachers who were members of established Protestant congregations or trained in English schools had the potential to use Christianity in diverse ways that white ministers might not approve. Puritan divine Charles Chauncy rejected the idea of bringing Indian children to English schools because, after the great expense paid for their education, there was no guarantee that they would not be "viciously turned" into renegade preachers or apostates.[119] Although Presbyterian missionary David Brainerd rejoiced that his interpreter, Moses Tatami, had taken up preaching to other Indians in the Delaware Valley, he noted that the specter of Indian separatism always abounded when offering spiritual authority to indigenous peoples. "*Spiritual Pride,*" Brainerd recounted, "also discover'd itself in various Instances; and in one or two an unbecoming Ambition of being Teachers of others." This "unbecoming Ambition," however, was an attempt on the part of Indian neophytes to apply elements of Christian doctrine or ritual to the menacing realities of Native American experience in a colonial world.[120]

Native revitalization movements among Indians borrowed from indigenous traditions as well as Christian cosmologies. Papunhunk, for example, was a Munsee spiritual leader who, along with several colleagues, preached to a community of Indians on the Susquehanna River in 1752. Although his message was nativist—he deplored the use of liquor, demanded that the English continue fair gift exchanges, and was infuriated by the loss of Indian land—he also borrowed from his Quaker contemporaries by proclaiming himself an avid pacifist.[121] Moravian missionary John Heckewelder recalled an Indian preacher working around Cayuga in New York in the early 1760s. This preacher proclaimed that the "Great Spirit" had chosen him to not only point out the sins of Native Americans, but also to communicate how Indians could redeem themselves and regain the favor of the Great One. The Cayuga revivalist employed a map within a book of deerskin to make his message clear. The map was a sacred geographical outline of Indian lands, where Indians were blocked into their lands by an evil spirit restricting them from accessing "the heavenly regions." Calling it "the great Book or Writing," the Cayuga preacher held up the book and its contents during his orations, urging his listeners to abstain from drinking liquor, repent for their sins, and return to the old ways. The preacher even suggested that each Indian family create and preserve a book just like the one he was using in his sermons. This emphasis on the repentance for sin and the reference to a sacred text as a source of spiritual revelation about Indian lands illustrate how native revitalization movements fused indigenous traditions with Christian idioms, cosmologies, and practices.[122]

Many literate blacks within the African diaspora had experienced a parallel encounter with literacy. Often invoking the trope of the "talking book" in their autobiographies, black Atlantic writers believed that literacy was a sacred power which granted them access to divine revelations that illiterate persons did not possess.[123] Many Africans believed that books, like the Cayuga preacher's deerskin book, could help them navigate the complicated pitfalls of racial oppression within a framework of indigenized Christianity. It is supremely ironic that this preacher employed, and indeed embraced, an idea of sacred texts while Samuel Niles was doing just the opposite. Niles, who had been exposed to and trained within institutionalized Congregationalism, rejected the book as the only source of spiritual authority and instead incorporated his own memories, dreams, and visions into a capacious understanding of revelation. The Cayuga preacher, who lacked any formal Christian training, embraced his book as a sacred text from which Indians could direct their spiritual and temporal lives. The problematics surrounding literacy and text as spiritual authority thus reveal how separatist preachers and native revivalists selectively translated Christianity into their own indigenous frameworks. For Protestant ministers throughout the Atlantic, this rise of native preachers was both an opportunity and a problem. Although white ministers depended upon and cultivated indigenous spiritual leaders, they had little control over how these preachers would use Christianity to craft their own messages of salvation and redemption. The cases of Samuel Niles and the Cayuga preacher demonstrate how native religious figures appropriated Christianity for their own political, cultural, and spiritual agendas.

The Moravian missions of the 1730s, Anglican efforts in the 1740s, and the controversies within southeastern New England Indian churches in the middle of the eighteenth century appear, on the surface, to have little in common. But the rise of Afro-Moravianism in the Danish Caribbean, the creation and collapse of the Charleston Negro School, and the increase of separatism among Indian congregations all resulted from and promulgated a larger, transatlantic period of revival that offered new ways for blacks and Indians to appropriate and translate Christianity. These three episodes reveal the major shifts occurring in transatlantic Protestant missionary activity during the middle of the eighteenth century.

This period witnessed a veritable explosion in the use of black and Indian evangelists in Protestant missions throughout the Atlantic from 1735 onwards. While there were already dozens of Puritan Indian preachers in New England villages by this time, the only other denomination to follow their lead was the Anglicans, and they failed in their efforts to cultivate a royal Indian pastorate in the first half of the eighteenth century. By the third quarter of that century, however, New England preachers were not only continuing to lead their congregations, but also creating new ones, as Samuel Niles did. Anglicans began using Mohawk teachers in their missions to the Iroquois, as when David Brainerd allowed his interpreter to continue to preach in the Delaware Valley when his own services were over. Another Indian named Good Peter began taking up the task of preaching to his fellow Oneidas, and Indian revitalists like the Cayuga preacher incorporated elements of Christianity into their own nativist critique of Indian historical experiences. Perhaps most importantly, Eleazar Wheelock began Moor's Charity School in the 1750s, an institution which would train dozens of Indians to serve as missionaries to other Indians on the New York frontier. By the middle of the eighteenth century there were Afro-Moravian national helpers in the Danish and English Caribbean missions, slave teachers in Charleston as well as throughout Virginia, and an Anglican African beginning his mission on the Gold Coast.

This led to another major shift in missionary policy. While no denomination had considered training blacks for evangelical positions in the early eighteenth century, by the 1760s that policy had changed dramatically. There were black preachers in the Caribbean, American south, and West Africa. And yet, Moravians and Anglicans understood that the rise of an elite black preacher class in a slave society threatened to subvert the precarious social hierarchies upon which racial slavery was built. Good Christians could make bad slaves, and missionaries and slaves alike understood the tenuousness of their relations and the potential explosiveness of evangelical rhetoric.

Similarly, Indian separatism, while always a concern, became ever more immediate during this period. Not only did Indians begin to break away from mainstream Protestant churches in the middle of the century, they also embraced new forms of spiritual leadership that offered both explicit and implicit critiques of traditional secular and spiritual power. Indeed, Amerindian preachers who exhorted against dispossession, alcoholism, and the waning spiritual condition of their fellow Indians effectively blurred the boundaries between nativist revitalization and Christian revivalism. Like their black counterparts, Indian preachers found unique ways to participate in the revivalism of the eighteenth century, even as they translated evangelical Christianity to fight their own secular and spiritual battles.

CHAPTER FOUR

A Black among Blacks

THE TWO ANGLICAN MISSIONARIES who became pen pals during the third quarter of the eighteenth century seemed to have little in common. While one was stationed in the idyllic town of Newburyport, Massachusetts, the other was assigned to Cape Coast Castle, West Africa's brutal and notorious slave trading fort. Nevertheless, the men became fast friends when the New Englander wrote to his colleague across the Atlantic to inquire about the progress that the gospel had been making in Africa since his arrival there in the 1760s. As two employees of the Society for the Propagation of the Gospel in Foreign Parts (SPG), they could certainly relate to one another's problems. They lamented the slow spread of Christianity in Africa, expressed disappointment at the state of religion in America, and complained about the constant need for more books, stationery, and other supplies. They signed their letters affectionately and their wives exchanged polite greetings through their husbands. Unfortunately, the revolutionary fervor of the age undid this relationship as it did to so many other transatlantic ties that seemed to bind.

While the missionary in Africa was a clear supporter of the British empire, the minister in Newburyport seemed less fervent about his own loyalty. In the spring of 1775 he wrote to his friend in Africa to complain about the bitter injustices that American colonists faced under the yoke of British tyranny. He appropriated the revolutionary rhetoric of the era and argued that American colonists were careening towards oppression and, of course, slavery. Expecting an empathetic response, the Massachusetts man instead received a harsh scolding by the missionary in Africa for his protests. His friend wrote back, "In your Epistle You seem to lament bitterly of your Mother Country for Universal Liberty. You, upon whom the light of the Gospel flourishes and abound[s] . . . advancing daily towards the seat of Bliss, find the Hardships of Bondage and Oppression! Good God can this be possible!?" The African missionary was particularly irate at his colleague's tired use of the metaphor of slavery to explain the colonists' relationship with the empire. As a missionary on the Cape Coast, the Anglican had witnessed firsthand the horror and cruelty of the transatlantic slave system. Naturally, he compared the "slavery" of the American colonists with the actual enslavement of Africans all around him. He asserted that "When I behold with Sorrowful sighing, my poor abject Countrymen over whom You without the Bowels of Christian Love and Pity, hold in cruel Bondage . . . I could wish that the Conviction of this Practice would spring first from the Breast of us all, particularly *you*, since We know perfectly well the heinousness of it." The African missionary, Phillip Quaque, was clearly drawing attention to the paradox of liberty and slavery. He was also reminding his friend, Edward Bass, that the "oppression" of the British empire paled in comparison to the oppression of actual, physical, racial enslavement. But the choice of "countrymen" for his description of Africans was not a rhetorical trick, but rather a statement of fact, for this missionary was an African born on the same slave-trading coast he now hoped to convert.[1]

Philip Quaque is not as celebrated today as writers like Olaudah Equiano or Phillis Wheatley, but he was a transatlantic celebrity in the eighteenth century, a converted African who was trying to convert Africans in Africa. He hailed from the Gold Coast region, in modern-day Ghana. Originally named Kweku, he was one of three Africans selected for missionary training by a white Anglican missionary named Thomas Thompson. He and his colleagues sailed for England, where he received evangelical training and ordination. He even married a white English woman before they returned to the Cape Coast in 1766. Philip Quaque remained in Africa for another half century, dying in 1816. By all accounts, his attempts to convert Africans were ultimately unsuccessful. However, the rich documentary trail that Quaque left, featuring dozens of letters that run to almost 200 pages, provides an unprecedented opportunity to explore how native missionaries attempted to balance the tensions between European imperial ambitions, Christian evangelical aspirations, and African motivations. Quaque, a black among blacks, struggled to envision a world where Christian and African were not incompatible, contradictory, and mutually exclusive.

Philip Quaque's mission was based in West Africa, but the origins of his mission rested in both African and American missionary history. From the 1740s onward, both black and Indian preachers became increasingly visible in the British Atlantic world. One of the products of and catalysts for this transformation was Thomas Thompson, a Cambridge-educated Anglican missionary stationed in Monmouth County, New Jersey from 1745 to 1751. Thompson was certainly aware of the changes in missionary work over the decades prior to his work, as the SPG printed annual sermons with timely updates on missionary activity throughout the Atlantic world. They then sent the sermons and yearly overviews to their widely dispersed missionaries, creating an Atlantic-wide network of information that notified each missionary of other evangelical activities. Indeed, just as Thompson heard of and likely read missionary accounts from other places, he too would become a subject of transatlantic evangelical conversations.

In his *Account of Two Missionary Voyages*, published in 1758, Thompson recalled his attempts to expose local slaves to Christian doctrine as soon as he arrived in New Jersey. He instructed some of them after services on Sundays and even held occasional meetings in his own home, using Lewis's *Exposition* and the psalms to introduce Christian precepts into slave culture. The students that Thompson and other Anglican teachers proselytized were not from the rank and file of slave society. Instead, Thompson drew from American-born, English-speaking, domestic sectors of the slave population. His reasons were clear. Teaching Christianity in a highly stratified slave society would be potentially dangerous, so courting the most Anglicized slaves could help temper some of the more radical elements of Christian theology. However, Protestant Christianity required a concrete understanding of scripture, a fair amount of literary competency, and the ability to recite key Christian texts. Protestant missionaries had always prided themselves on how seriously they took conversion, especially in contrast to the ritual and casuistry that Jesuits and Franciscans employed to "convert" hundreds of thousands of native peoples in the Americas. Baptism and conversion were affairs of the utmost importance, demanding the intellect and *gravitas* of an acculturated Christian. Circumscribed by both theology and the educational limitations of a slave society, and dedicated to the instruction of an elite few, Thompson made little impact on the spiritual transformation of New Jersey's slaves. His greater legacy would be found in Africa.[2]

Thompson came to believe that Africa was in more need of his spiritual labors than New Jersey, and he requested a transfer to the West

African coast in 1750, effectively becoming the first Anglican missionary to spend a considerable amount of time on West Africa's shores. Interestingly, he was also an early advocate of the belief that American missionary experience would be an appropriate model upon which to base African missions. He looked to the American historical past for guidance, implicitly comparing Indian evangelical activities with his future African one. He countered those who suggested that his African mission would probably fail by arguing that the mission to Native Americans also had slow beginnings. Drawing upon missionary history, Thompson recalled, "The *Indian* Mission in *North America,* which was begun about the Year 1704, did not succeed at first." After the introduction of new missionaries and native catechists in the 1740s, however, Thompson could confidently claim that the New York mission "has since flourished, and many of those Heathens have been added to the *Lord*." The fact that his missionary voyages to both New Jersey and Africa appear next to each other in his *Account* also suggests the extent to which Thompson's evangelical activities in Africa might have seemed like a continuous, fluid expansion of his previous missionary duties across the Atlantic. In his mind, as in the minds of many other missionaries, Native Americans, African slaves, and Africans would all be central components in the spread of Christian religion throughout the world, regardless of where they lived.[3]

In spite of the explicit comparisons and connections, most contemporaries acknowledged that Africa and Africans were somehow quite different. In eighteenth century European thought, there was no place darker or more in need of Christian enlightening than Africa. David Hume, the famous philosopher who had little positive to say about Africa or Africans, observed that the continent was covered with "barren sands" and "sterile uncultivated lands." He believed the landscape and people there were "struck with one common curse" and that the entire coast was filled with "unhappy negroes" and "wretched men."[4] In his anniversary sermon for the SPG, Isaac Maddox paraphrased from previous descriptions of Africa to describe the people there as "all without Exception crafty, villainous, and fraudulent; being sure to slip no Opportunity of cheating an *European,* nor indeed one another; They seem to be born and bred Villains." Maddox continued by claiming these people were characterized by innumerable "degenerate Vices," the least not being "Sloth and Idleness."[5] In many contemporaries' minds, there was simply no worse place in the world than Africa.

The British Atlantic world had multiple "zones of law" and "zones of violence." This mapped out a "legal geography" of the Atlantic, but there was also a form of "sacred geography" at work in Protestant missionary enterprises.[6] Christian missionaries considered England and the expanding American settlements as zones of Protestant piety, where the light of the gospel shined more brightly than anywhere else. The Native American borderlands and the entire continent of Africa, on the other hand, were zones of intense irreligion, in spite of (or perhaps because of) the presence of both Catholicism and Islam in many communities on Africa's coast. Africa was usually portrayed as a land of brutish idolatry, rampant crime, and primordial evil. As Isaac Maddox noted in his anniversary sermon, "Murder, Adultery, and Theft, here are accounted no Sins."[7] When Thomas Thompson preached to English traders on the African coast in 1752, he reported that his audience was glad to hear the gospel, since the traders were "in that melancholy State of Exile from true Religion."[8]

Philip Quaque, the Anglican missionary born in Africa, would eventually come to embrace this rhetoric of Africa as an irreligious space, describing it as a "wicked and degenerate land," a "barren land," a "strange place," or even "these distant Clymes [sic]."[9] He complained to his friends and colleagues throughout the Atlantic world about the "wretched state of Africa."[10] By most accounts, Africa was clearly a religious periphery. If London was the "*Jerusalem* of *England*," as itinerant preacher George Whitefield once claimed, then Africa was certainly a modern-day Sodom or Gomorrah.[11] In fact, it was the very climate of Africa that marked it as distinctly different from missions anywhere else in the world. Africa was understood as a sultry, hot, exotic place containing climatic and epidemiological conditions that would wreak havoc on European bodies. Thomas Thompson stayed in Africa for only four years before he departed in 1756 on account of the climate and its impact on his health. The SPG readily acknowledged that "a longer Stay in that Climate would deprive him of his Health, if not his Life," and agreed to reassign him to England. He hoped that some other missionary "with better Health" might be able to succeed him after he left.[12] Philip Quaque and other young Africans certainly seemed like they would have "better Health" there. After a decade of training in England, Quaque returned to Africa with an English wife and another female friend. Perhaps the women should have followed in Thomas Thompson's footsteps and left early. Succumbing to tropical diseases, both women experienced premature deaths in Africa. Quaque lived for another fifty years.

Ideas about the body played a crucial role in cultural encounters between Europeans and Africans. In fact, the African climate's effect on the body would serve as both a metaphor and physical marker of racial difference between Europeans and Africans. William Bosman, an English traveler to West Africa at the beginning of the eighteenth century, observed that the region's sudden change from soaring heat during the day to bone-chilling cold at night "occasions several contrary Effects in our [English] bodies." He also believed that West Africa's mountain mists were to blame for spreading infections across the peoples of the coast. This mist, Bosman complained, fell "too thick on the Earth" and made it so that it was "almost impossible to escape the infection." Bosman even admitted that "our Bodies [are] more susceptible to it than the Natives." Bosman and other English commentators after him perpetuated the not wholly incorrect idea that West Africa was simply a white man's grave.[13] Anthony Benezet, a leading abolitionist during the last quarter of the eighteenth century, explained that "Altho' the extream [sic] Heat in many Parts of *Guinea,* is such, as is neither agreeable nor healthy to the *Europeans,* yet it is well suited to the Constitution of the *Negroes.*"[14] As such, the bodies of English missionaries would be particularly susceptible to the climatological and epidemiological hazards that the land contained. Native Africans would presumably not face such challenges.

Although Africans had successfully adapted to this exotic climate, European commentators nevertheless agreed that the climate had left its imprint on Africans' faculties, attributes, and behavioral patterns. Thomas Thompson suggested that even though Africans on the coast were not completely savage, most were still "hot and choleric." This choleric nature produced in them a natural "Impetuosity in their Temper which makes them speak their Words very quick." Thompson then applied his body metaphor to African culture, describing traditional African religions as a kind of "Deformity" that they had carried all their lives and were visibly ashamed of.[15] Indeed, it was the African body that made the prospect of establishing a native pastorate so appealing to Protestant missionary interests. The theory was that native Africans could not only retain the language of their upbringing but also survive the harsh disease environment, maintain strong constitutions in the exotic climate, and endure the physical toll that African missionary activity would entail. Ironically, the same kind of logic that made African bodies appear destined for perpetual slavery in tropical climes also gave promising young Africans access to Christian spiritual authority.

Thomas Thompson therefore had several good reasons to try to establish a native pastorate in Africa. His deep knowledge of American missionary experiments clearly demonstrated that native preachers could be more effective, especially in the borderlands, than English ones. African bodies seemed particularly well-adapted to a climate and environment that would easily crush less sturdy European bodies. Thompson was aware that he was not the first to try to train an African pastorate. Catholics had cultivated local African religious leaders for centuries, especially in places like the Congo.[16] But several Africans had also been sent to Europe and trained up as Protestant missionaries to return to their own countries. The most famous of these were Jacob Protten and James Capitein, both of whom were brought from Africa, educated in continental Europe, and returned to their respective posts on the Gold Coast and Elmina Castle just before the middle of the eighteenth century.

Jacob Protten, the son of a Danish soldier and an African woman, was sent from his home near Accra to Copenhagen for an education. Protten met Moravian leader Nicholas Ludwig Von Zinzendorf in 1735 and Protten agreed to return to Africa as a Moravian missionary. After several unsuccessful attempts to preach the gospel there he returned to Germany and then traveled to the Caribbean island of St. Thomas, where he met and eventually married a slave girl named Rebecca. Protten and Rebecca crossed the Atlantic to Germany, traveled to modern-day Liberia, relocated to the Danish fort at Christiansborg, went back to Germany, and then returned again to Christiansborg by 1763. Jacob Protten died in 1769, but his crossings—geographic and cultural—are a testament to the intercultural exchanges that knit the Atlantic world together. Jacobus Eliza Capitein, on the other hand, was educated in the Netherlands, ordained in the Dutch Reformed Church, and traveled to Africa's Elmina Castle in 1742, where he served as chaplain for five years before he died. In his attempt to employ native missionaries, the Anglican Thomas Thompson was building upon a securely laid foundation of American missionary history, ideas about African bodies, and West African evangelical experience.[17]

As soon as Thompson arrived at Cape Coast Castle he attempted to instruct local Africans in Christian precepts. He believed that the Africans living immediately on the coast—as opposed to those from the African interior—were more civilized and better prepared to accept Christian instruction. He employed the time-honored policy of looking to the children who came from elite indigenous families to form the backbone of his missionary experiment. He initially hoped that four or even six Africans could be sent back to England for training. He tried to extend his ambitious scheme to the Africans living near the slave castle, or a European-controlled fort where slaves were held before being shipped to the Americas, at Annamaboe. Although it is unclear whether

Thompson was directly involved in their selection, two West Africans (John Aqua and George Sackee) were sent to England around 1753 for religious education and baptism. Neither, however, panned out as missionaries.[18]

For his project, Thompson eventually settled on three young Africans: William Cudjo, Thomas Caboro (also called Cabinah), and Philip Quaque. They were all sons of prominent African families, all under 12 years old, and they all set out together for England in 1754. Trained under SPG tutors, the boys fared well for the first few years, but Cabinah died soon after his smallpox inoculation and Cudjo had apparently suffered a breakdown by 1764. By 1766, when Quaque returned to Africa, the SPG had concluded that Cudjo had no family members left, did not possess the mental capacity for travel, and would not be going home anytime soon. Taken from his African home as a young boy, Cudjo spent the rest of his life at St. Luke's Hospital in England. When Quaque returned to Africa, he did so not with his African compatriots, but with an English wife, her English friend, a bible, and a decade of Anglican training under his belt. He was a new man, a physical embodiment of the cultural transformation that a decade of Anglicization had wrought on an African body.

The experience of being transported to and living in England had destroyed the bodies and minds of Cudjo and Cabinah, Quaque's African colleagues, but Quaque survived. However, he found upon his return home that he too was not immune the epidemiological afflictions that ran rampant on Africa's soil. Even though his African birth would have presumably made Quaque impervious to native diseases, his first letters back to the SPG after his return to the coast reveal how his frequent maladies impeded missionary work. After only half a year, he lamented that, because of repeated sicknesses, "the state of my Constitution is very much altered for the worse." Disease was ruining his ability to even stand, let alone to give rousing sermons, and he was perplexed as to why he suffered so much like an Englishman. He concluded that "This Country is very destructive to the Health of many of the British Constitutions, and tho' myself being a Native by Birth, yet am not exempted from undergoing the common fate equally with those who are not."[19]

A wave of smallpox epidemics struck the slaving fort and surrounding area from 1769 to the early 1770s, leaving hundreds of dead Africans and English traders in its wake. Quaque survived the pox only to be infected with some "tormenting and wasting Guinea Worms." Otherwise known as *Dracunculiasis*, Guinea worms were a parasitic worm that would enter a human's body if they drank still and infected water. The worms would then remain in the body for up to a year, becoming as long as three feet and eventually exiting the body, often through the legs or the feet. One commentator even noted that the worst victims could suffer from up to ten guinea worms infesting their bodies, leaving them "inexpressibly tormented." Quaque understood that the worms could literally paralyze himself and his mission, and he admitted he was "very timorous about this Disorder, as many have been known to lose the use of their Limbs by it, and many others become a Cripple."[20] The worms probably caused Quaque a "grievous pain," as they had done to so many other victims.[21] Luckily for Quaque, the worms exited before doing any serious damage to either his body or his mission.

In 1778 Quaque connected a temporary rise in religious sentiment with climate change. When he wrote to the SPG in the summer of that year, he noted that the frequency and sincerity of devotion was greater in the past three months than he could ever remember. He then bragged about "how widely different the Climate appears to be to what it was a few Years ago," arguing that this "amazing Alteration" had been felt by every English settler and every African native.[22] The implication was that, just as the climate could shape African and European bodies, the introduction of civilized Christianity might also ameliorate the African climate. In Quaque's view, the transformation of Africa from a land of death to a Christian land was therefore marked not only by changes in the religious sentiment of the people, but also in the climate itself. Embracing the idea that the advance of human civilization could alter climate, Quaque pointed to climate as proof that Christianity was on the advance among his people.

Early modern ideas about the climate, the body, and disease accentuated the differences between Europeans, Africans, and Native Americans and demonstrated the necessity of native evangelists. Just as American missionaries relied upon Native American preachers because of their perceived ability to endure the harsh lifestyle in the wilderness, so too did African bodies became a central advantage to using native African evangelists and opened a window for black missionaries to be employed as evangelists to other Africans.

Even if Philip Quaque was immune to African diseases (he was not) and even if he retained his native tongue to speak fluently in indigenous African languages (he did not), he still would have faced immense challenges in converting Africans. Although he spent nearly half a century on the Cape Coast, the success of his mission was slim at best. By the time he was writing to his friend in New England in 1775, he could only boast of 52 baptisms over almost a decade of work, and that included European and mixed-race children.[23] Quaque had always doubted whether his unique position as an African preacher on the Cape Coast would make any difference in the religious temperament of Africa's population. He constantly complained about the irreligion of the English traders and officials in the slave fort and was even more shocked by the seemingly idolatrous customs of native Africans. He even admitted to the SPG that his failure to generate any spiritual transformation often made him wish that he had been sent somewhere else. He was beginning to understand that, instead of using his identity to his advantage, to his "great Sorrow and Astonishment [he had] found it quite the reverse." He eventually became convinced that "Something more than a Human effort must work that effectual Cure of their Bigotry and Superstition."[24] The SPG agreed that Quaque produced less than stellar results, lamenting that "It was natural for the Society to hope for better fruits from the ministry of a Black among Blacks . . . this has not been the case."[25] But Quaque did write letters. There were hundreds of native teachers, catechists, and missionaries throughout the early modern Atlantic, but only a handful left written records that illuminate exactly how they perceived non-Christian native peoples and positioned themselves between European and indigenous cultures. Quaque's letters to the SPG offer a remarkable opportunity to assess how converted Africans attempted to convert others and perceived the peoples they were trying to save.

Quaque was ashamed of his African neighbors. Like other Christianized blacks who populated the Atlantic world, he described Africa as a kind of pagan wasteland, bereft of the light of Christianity and devoid of any semblance of civilization. England, on the other hand, was a "blessed Christian country," and Quaque imbibed many of the rhetorical conventions that Christian contemporaries used to describe Africa.[26] Africans, Quaque believed, were "poor unthinking and lamentable Creatures" who inhabited a "barren country" that was characterized by superstition, idolatry, and ignorance.[27] For Quaque, African funerals revealed the "Apish" nature of its participants, the use of sacred rocks confirmed the ridiculousness of pagan practices, and sacrifices to African deities proved the stubbornly childish nature of African religion.[28] It did not matter that eighteenth century coastal Africa was a veritable religious bazaar, strangely blending elements of Fetu, Akan, Fante, Ashanti, and even Islamic beliefs and rituals with those of competing European powers. For Quaque, the spiritual battle lines were clearly drawn: Africans were vicious pagans who were desperate for the light of Christian salvation. The recipients of Quaque's letters were his white

Cape Coast Castle. (Image courtesy of the John Carter Brown Library at Brown University.)

Anglican sponsors, so perhaps Quaque was telling his audience what they wanted to hear. And yet, these tropes are so redundantly consistent in Quaque's letters and actions, as well as in the descriptions of Africa and Africans by other blacks of his ilk, that it seems clear that Quaque viewed himself as uniquely situated to serve as an instrument of God's will to save his pitiable neighbors.

In spite of his negative view of the African spiritual landscape and the people that inhabited it, Quaque still believed that Africans were ultimately redeemable. Just as Anglican missionaries from previous generations believed that the conversion of Indian kings would produce a mass conversion of all indigenous peoples, Quaque began his evangelical campaign with a kind of top-down, hierarchical approach. He focused on Cudjo Cabosheer. This was the man who, like other coastal African leaders during this period, maintained his position of political authority through commercial networks with English traders, efficient politicking, and (sometimes) ruthless violence. This was the man who reportedly had a million people attend his funeral in 1777. He was Philip Quaque's kin, and he also happened to be the man who agreed to send Quaque to England in the first place. Cudjo likely sent Quaque to reinforce economic and diplomatic ties with the English. When Quaque returned as an ardent missionary, Cudjo was less than enthusiastic about taking an evangelical turn.

Quaque was not the first to try to get Cudjo's ear, for Thomas Thompson also believed that if the leader of coastal Africans at Cape Coast would convert to Christianity, scores of Africans would do the same. But both Quaque and Thompson underestimated the extent to which African leaders like Cudjo manipulated European ambitions and Christian evangelical techniques for their own gain. Cudjo never expressed a sincere interest in Christian *conversion*—he apparently told Quaque that he was too advanced in age to "enter into Covenant with God"—but he was a major proponent of Christian *education,* the kind of education that would provide his family and business associates with the linguistic, cultural, and economic skills necessary to secure their position of prominence in Euro-African relations.[29] Cudjo supported schools and other educational initiatives, but he neither converted to Christianity nor influenced others to do so. With an apathetic Cudjo dead by 1777, Quaque turned to other evangelical alternatives to spread the Word.

Like other missionaries throughout the Atlantic, Quaque railed against the superstitious customs he saw emanating out of Africa. As he recorded it, his sermons occasionally "exposed and ridiculed" the "absurd notions" of religion held by coastal Africans, including their "Superstitious

Customs." Quaque clearly tried to highlight the advantages of Christianity by exposing what he believed to be the foolishness of African religious traditions. Few took the bait. One local leader summarily rejected Quaque's efforts by stating that Africans were "but Black Men," and that traditional spiritual practices were just as legitimate a religious practice as relying on books.[30] Quaque believed that responses like these from local political leaders, known as penyins, represented not only a resolute stubbornness, but also a manifestation of Satan's evil presence in Africa. Indeed, Quaque quickly learned that neither intellectual nor emotional appeals would win him converts.

Quaque turned to two techniques that he believed would recruit more Africans to hear his services: the allure of liquor and the employment of sacred music. Quaque might not have been delighted about the prevalence of drinking in the Cape Coast region, especially when his audiences would come to hear him preach the gospel one moment and turn to drinking the next. However, he found himself essentially bribing Africans to come to his services by offering them liquor. To some of his neophytes he gave "a flask of Liquor," and told them that "now they must not neglect my coming, whenever I officiate in Town." He reported that the distribution of liquor to boost his audience was one way of "enticing" coastal Africans to hear the word of God. In addition to doling out liquor rations to his congregants, Quaque also began incorporating more of the psalms into missionary work. A very common evangelical technique, the teaching of the psalms introduced basic Christian precepts into indigenous communities without raising serious theological complications by using the vehicle of music to communicate Christian ideas. In fact, Quaque even suggested that it was Africans' inherent love of music that made sacred songs so effective.[31]

Quaque's opinions on African identity, including his critical remarks about their religion and even his propensity to use liquor and music to attract potential neophytes, seem rooted in a racialized perspective. But, even so, Quaque still believed that Africans could be exposed to the saving grace of Christianity. If race, a category being fashioned during the age Quaque lived in, outlined the immutable and inherent differences between biologically discrete groups, religion could be a uniting factor, no matter how much rhetorical ammunition it provided to buttress racial claims. Quaque believed that, although Africans were backwards, pagan, superstitious, and sunk in gross theological errors, these mistakes were ultimately surmountable through his own efforts and the grace of God. Quaque often reminded his Anglican sponsors that the English had formerly been just like Africans at one point: mired in superstition and lost without the saving light of Christian revelation. Like Africans, Quaque claimed, England had been "troubled with Idols and false Notions." This pagan savagery persisted until Christ came into being, and God "made some Pastors and Teachers . . . to instruct and bring over the Ignorant." In spite of his critical remarks about Africa, he still described the continent as an early England, a barbaric but ultimately salvageable continent filled with Christians in waiting.[32]

Like so many Atlantic creoles during his time, Philip Quaque was a product of the convergence and exchange of European, African, and American cultures. He was situated uncomfortably between the people he left behind as a child and the ones who supported his evangelical career. Perhaps he believed that, like so many other coastal African leaders who served as economic middlemen, he would be a kind of spiritual middleman, a cultural broker who negotiated the religious transplantation of Protestant Christianity into Africa. He was sorely mistaken, for he made little headway among Africans (even among his own family), and he was consistently attacked, scolded, and ridiculed by the traders and political officials who were operating on the Cape Coast. His loneliness might have been alleviated somewhat by the company of his first wife, but she died shortly after their arrival in Africa. Although Quaque's second and third wives were African, rather than English, he still had a problem viewing himself as truly African. He even complained that his own family made the foolish mistake of seeing him "in no other Light than as one of themselves."[33] White officials and traders on the Coast considered him an African while Africans considered him an Englishman. Sent to serve as a cultural broker between the two, Quaque ultimately held onto a friendless space located awkwardly between Europeans and Africans.

Many "Atlantic Creoles" successfully navigated the boundaries of slavery and freedom, African tradition and Western culture, and black religion and Christianity. Quaque appeared to have found such a middle ground between European and African cultures, but this ground left him lonely and isolated as a preacher. The relationships he had with white slave traders, the connections he forged with his African neighbors, and the correspondence he maintained with his Anglican sponsors all revealed him as a man on the outside. He frequently complained that his Anglican sponsors did not correspond with him enough and grumbled that he did not even get "so much as a Line from my Worthy Benefactors." He compared himself to American missionaries supported by the SPG and suggested that he needed even more support and encouragement, as he was "situated in a Bypath of Misprision," and therefore he needed "that Assistance more than most Missionaries."[34] The nature of African missionary work, Quaque concluded, was significantly more demanding than that of other sites, and his increasingly negative criticism of his own mission reflected the "lamentable Situation" that African missionary work had created for him.[35]

Even so, Quaque developed a tempered imperial ideology, one characterized by *both* a glorification of the Christian gospel and a harsh critique of the white Christians who plundered Africa. Indeed, Quaque would use his own identity as a Christian preacher to express his vision of the proper relationship between religion and empire. The correspondence between Quaque and Edward Bass suggests that the former clearly supported the British crown. Quaque spent the most formative years of his life in England, and his English training, wife (his first one), dress, and language all helped to situate him as a black Englishman, not as an African. And yet, although Quaque took great pride in his English identity, he was still critical of the missionary, commercial, and political agents and institutions that shaped the political and religious landscape of coastal Africa.

The most paradoxical aspect of Quaque's tenure on the Cape Coast was that he lived in, worked from, and was funded by the same slave trading castle that annually shipped thousands of Africans to the Americas. It is likely that Quaque married a slave and benefited from the range of slave labor that kept Cape Coast going. He even purchased an elderly female slave in 1785, although one historian notes that it is entirely unclear whether this was to "benefit from her labor" or was some kind of "act of charity."[36] Cape Coast Castle, which served as the hub of Quaque's evangelical activities, was a vital military and economic hub for the transatlantic slave trade. This commanding coastal fort, situated on a rocky shoreline along Africa's Gold Coast, was operated by the Company of Merchants Trading to Africa and consisted of governors, imperial officials, traders, and, of course, slaves. The SPG paid half of Quaque's salary, but the Company of Merchants paid the other half for Quaque to serve there as chaplain. Theoretically, Quaque would have been an invaluable asset because of his ability to oversee Anglican services among the white Christians while simultaneously using his identity as a Fetu to evangelize the Africans living near the fort. There is no better evidence of the duality of Quaque's patronage than the commemorative tablets that memorialized his life after his death. One is situated at Christ Church Cathedral and the other is located inside the Castle itself. The man who would come to lambaste Cape Coast Castle and everything it represented was eventually memorialized within its courtyard.[37]

Quaque's most acrimonious disputes were with the governors of the castle. These administrators supervised economic and political arrangements between African slave traders and English ones, but they also sought to secure the fort from rival attacks by the French, Dutch, and other European powers. If Quaque initially assumed the governors would be enthusiastic about the Christian conversion of Africans, he would be sorely disappointed. In fact, most of the governors he dealt with during his fifty year tenure—there were about seventeen of them—generally seemed as apathetic about the gospelization of Africa as Cudjo Cabosheer. For Quaque, the proof of this was not only in the way the governors treated Quaque, but also in the behavior of the white soldiers and traders who milled around the Castle. Some of them took African wives and mistresses, unbeknownst to their English wives at home. Others turned to heavy drinking to ease the tedium of waiting for weeks on end for their ships to sail. Still others neglected public worship and infuriated Quaque by refusing to hear him preach. Several gave him "very disrespectful treatment" during their encounters.[38] The most egregious sin, of course, was their complicity in the transatlantic trade of human beings.

To Quaque's surprise, the governors often appeared as immoral, vicious, and licentious as their own soldiers. Not all governors were completely terrible. When David Mill took over as governor in 1770, Quaque optimistically explained that the new governor was a "well-wisher of mine," a man of a "humane and peaceable Temper" who would support Quaque's Christian mission.[39] Like the other governors who came before and after, Mill would only disappoint Quaque. The governors appeared to be in such a position of power and authority that they could have had a significant effect on the religious development of West Africa. But, "love of gain and Ambition," Quaque argued, were all that they cared about.[40] The relationship between Quaque and the governors thus grew increasingly rancorous. Some kicked Quaque out of his quarters in the Castle to make room for more soldiers, evidently revealing that military expediency trumped Christian evangelism. Quaque even complained bitterly when he found out that one of the governors was not a member of the Anglican Church, but rather a "very rank Presbyterian born and bred."[41] In spite of his elite education and spiritual authority, Quaque was still rejected by Castle officials and governors.

Perhaps his most hostile conflict was with John Grossle, who only served as Governor from 1769 to 1770. In spite of his short tenure, he still drew the ire of Quaque. Grossle was a German governor who Quaque dubbed the "present reigning Monarch" because of his imperious nature.[42] He treated Quaque with disdain, but he also castigated not only Anglicanism, but the very idea of revealed religion itself. The missionary argued that the Governor gloried in making "a ridicule of religion, and a future state, as a trick and cheat." Grossle apparently claimed that he "never knew any one to chuse to go to heaven when he could live upon earth."[43] Quaque complained that the Governor never allowed him opportunities to preach, ridiculed his religion, and even sailed away from Cape Coast during a temporary epidemic, leaving his community in the lurch. This probably explains why, when Grossle suddenly died in 1770, Quaque rejoiced that "my Enemy is taken out of my way." He admitted to his sponsors that, with Grossle out of the picture, he was "in great hopes of seeing better Days."[44] But Grossle was never alone in his scorn towards Quaque. A previous governor apparently proclaimed that Christian missionaries like Quaque should not have been in Africa in the first place. "Clergymen have no Business in these Parts," the governor reported to Quaque, "unless come to be starved."[45] As bad as Grossle was, governors before and after him continued to neglect, reject, and humiliate Quaque and his evangelical efforts.

This could explain why Quaque hoped that Cape Coast would eventually transform into an official military outpost, operated by the British Navy, rather than a commercial port run by a private company and defended by hired guns. In 1769, just three years after his initial arrival in Africa, Quaque reported that his mission would be better supported if the British military were more actively involved. It would be "far more Advantageous" Quaque argued, "could this Settlement be more immediately under His Majesty's Protection." If there was any confusion about his argument, Quaque illuminated his position more precisely by explaining, "I mean a Military Establishment."[46] The Navy seemed more orderly, disciplined, and, given its official status as a military arm of the British Crown, was expected to be more devout and religiously sensible than the scoundrels and miscreants who governed the Cape Coast. This does not mean that the Navy would somehow compel Africans to convert at the point of a sword, but rather that it would introduce a semblance of order, decorum, and Christian respectability that the Company of Merchants sorely lacked. Indeed, a year after writing this letter, Quaque laid his eyes on two British ships—the *Phoenix* and *Hound*—off the Coast. He rejoiced that the arrival of "His Majesty's" vessels suddenly introduced to Cape Coast some English Christians who would at least hear what he had to say. Quaque later wrote that the fortuitous arrival of the British Navy "afforded Me an Opportunity on Sunday before Easter of Expatiating the little Talent I have by reading of Prayers."[47] If Quaque grew to despise the governors and traders operating the fort, he also looked to the ocean optimistically, anxiously awaiting a British ship of war to impose order and signify the coming of a new age of Christian decency at Cape Coast.

There were limits to his martial enthusiasm. When an African rebellion erupted in the 1780s near Annamaboe, another crucial slave castle in the nexus of British military outposts, Quaque was called on by the Company of Merchants to defend the fort and fight against the African rebels. He rejected their plea, later reflecting that such a decision would have been "highly inconsistent and injurious to my Profession."[48] In response, the governor kicked Quaque out of Cape Coast Castle, forcing him to find alternative housing. The problem, of course, was that Quaque was caught between two worlds. On the one hand was the world of the slave traders, officials, soldiers, and governors, who expected him to defer to them and generally ignored his pleas for them to pay more attention to the next world and less attention to this one. On the other hand, Quaque seemed to identify with the plight of Africans in this affair. He framed himself as an elite African, but he certainly could not abide putting down a rebellion by Africans who were fighting against the very slave traders and licentious imperialists that Quaque had grown to disdain.

Part of the inherent tension within Quaque's work was race. According to Quaque, race trumped Christian identity, especially in the highly racialized societies of coastal Africa. He knew that, although his status as an African explained why he had been sent to England for ministerial training, this status also undermined his evangelical efforts and circumscribed his activities at the Cape Coast. He even heard that some merchants, who were nominally Christian, would never attend religious services while Quaque was leading them. Merchants in the heart of the slave trade could not bear the thought of sitting "under the Nose of a Black Boy to hear Him pointing or laying out their faults before them."[49] For merchants plying their trade in Africa, listening to a sermon from a person who was the same color as those they sold as commodities created a cognitive dissonance that they ultimately could not confront or reconcile. Africans were slaves and (sometimes) slave traders, but they were not spiritual guides or models of Christian piety. Any example to the contrary was either comical or tragic.

Quaque was irate at the merchants' attitude towards revealed religion, not only because he found it personally insulting, but also because he believed that the merchants' failure to attend divine services, honor the Sabbath, and engage in rituals of Christian worship would ultimately hamper his efforts. He hoped to convert coastal Africans, but how could he convert them into good Christians if white Christians did not pay any attention to religion at all? In fact, Quaque argued that the licentious lifestyle of the slave traders, combined with the barbarity of the slave trade and irreligion of Africa itself, turned would-be Christian exemplars into worse Christians. "By their Behaviour," Quaque lamented, slave traders "have both changed the good Seeds sown, by the stain which they now shamefully cast upon the Profession wherewith they were called." The white Christians were far from the agents of evangelization that they might have been, and were now marked by "Corruption of Morals," "the Inhuman Practice" and "Love of Mammon."[50] "The stir of religion and its everlasting recompense," Quaque explained, was "not so much in vogue as the vicious practice of purchasing flesh and blood like oxens in market places."[51] If Quaque had expected white Christians living at Cape Coast to perform as willing evangelical partners, he instead found traders who had their minds set on the worldly profits that could be made from turning Africans into commodities, rather than the spiritual rewards that might be gained by turning Africans into Christians.

Philip Quaque witnessed firsthand the barbaric ferocity of the transatlantic slave trade, and his letters to correspondents in England and the British American colonies reveal a growing contempt for the institutions and people that bankrolled it. In fact, Quaque's mission coincided with a critical period in the development of conversations about transatlantic slavery, race, and Christianity. The Age of Revolutions helped to energize an embryonic but increasingly vocal and effective abolitionist movement that harnessed both natural rights and Christian humanitarian rhetoric. Unlike other black Christian contemporaries, Quaque never published an abolitionist tract or engaged in transatlantic anti-slavery campaigning. He did, however, articulate his views on slavery through his correspondence, and he and his contemporaries were at the center of the debate over the relationship between Christianity and slavery. Additionally, his first-hand accounts made their way, indirectly, into some of the most biting damnations of the slave trade. A host of social commentators, from religious figures and doctors to naval officers and imperial officials, relied on Quaque for information about the development, conduct, and character of the slave trade in West Africa. In the early 1790s, when several officials testified in England about the depredations that the slave trade had wrought on Africans at the Cape Coast,

Quaque's name was frequently invoked as an informant. He never published his thoughts or observations but, through the medium of his correspondence, his commentaries became quite public, helping to fuel the abolitionist cause. Quaque played a key role in the rancorous arguments over Christianity, race, and slavery towards the end of the eighteenth century.[52]

The moral conundrum of slavery often drove a wedge between Christian evangelists. Just as Quaque and other contemporaries rose to attack it, other Christian leaders sought to defend it. Thomas Thompson, the white missionary who preceded Quaque and initiated his London training, published a pro-slavery tract in 1772, entitled *The African Trade for Negro Slaves, Shewn to be Consistent With Principles of Humanity, and With the Laws of Revealed Religion*. Published the same year that Britain's famous *Somerset* case challenged the institution of slavery in England, Thompson's work contended that slavery and Christianity were entirely consistent, compatible, and reconcilable. Interestingly, it was not just whites publishing these works. Jacob Capitein, the Afro-Dutch evangelist who served as Chaplain at a Dutch fort in the 1740s, wrote a dissertation that provided much the same argument several decades before.[53]

Capitein's arguments notwithstanding, one of the most diabolical consequences of the slave trade was that it promulgated an entrenched sense of racial difference. As an African Anglican, Quaque certainly felt this notion of difference all around him, even as he served as a walking example for how bankrupt that idea was. Quaque's very identity was intrinsically contradictory to the race-based status system of the early modern Atlantic world. He complained, correctly, that many people rejected and ignored him not because of his theology or teachings, but rather because of "Distinction of Colours and Place of Nativity." These "upstarts" could not see what Quaque eventually came to envision: a *Christian* nation, bound by universal brotherhood and affection.[54] Quaque was critical of Africa and Africans, but his arguments were not based on some fictional self-identification as an African transformed into an Englishman. In fact, if Quaque believed in the deracination of Africans, it was not so that they might become white, but so white and black would eventually become categories that failed to have any intellectual meaning in the wake of Christian gospelization. He anticipated a world where the "Christian race" would unite Africans and Europeans together into a harmonious Kingdom of God. Christian faith, rather than skin color, would be the new marker of difference, the new symbol of status, in the kingdom that Quaque envisioned.[55]

In his articulation of a universal Christian kingdom that rejected the rigid racial hierarchies of the transatlantic world, Quaque represented one of a growing number of voices who hoped for a world characterized by universal Christian brotherhood rather than maliciously ruthless commoditization of human beings. These voices came from a range of sources—including Methodists, Quakers, Anglicans, and other religious groups—and their arguments attacked the slave trade as well as the very racial ideologies that underwrote it. In February of 1766, the same month that Quaque began his mission in Africa, William Warburton gave the anniversary sermon for the SPG, the organization that sent Quaque. Perhaps having Quaque in mind, Warburton argued that racial distinctions meant absolutely nothing in light of the grace and reason that God had implanted in all rational beings. Africans, he argued, were equal to Englishmen, as they were "endowed with all our Faculties" and possessed "all our qualities but that of colour."[56] Writing seven years later, Granville Sharp, perhaps England's most ardent white abolitionist, contended that Christianity shatters not only national divisions, but also racial distinctions between blacks and whites. "The glorious system of the gospel," he proclaimed, "destroys all *narrow, national partiality;* and makes *us citizens of the world,* by obliging us to profess *universal benevolence.*"[57] These two visions set out by Warburton and Sharp reveal the centrality of Anglican missions at the Cape Coast to transatlantic discourses on race. On the one hand, Warburton was articulating an ethos of African potential at the very moment that a London-educated African was returning to his land of birth to proclaim the gospel. On the other, Granville Sharp's polemical work was not just a standard abolitionist tract, but an invective-filled attack on the pro-slavery work produced by Thomas Thompson, Quaque's predecessor and supporter.

Quaque despised the slave trade and the slave traders that perpetuated it. Conversely, merchants disdained and ignored the black preacher who, by his identity, brazenly defied the racial hierarchies that supported the very business which sustained them. But Quaque also developed an acrimonious relationship with his own bosses: the SPG. While part of Quaque's salary derived from the Company of Merchants trading in Africa, the other portion was provided by the Anglican missionary organization. Also, Quaque's training—which took about a decade and was achieved with significant expense—was patronized and funded by the SPG. As such, the SPG expected Quaque to be an obedient servant of Christ, a humble and compliant cultivator of God's vineyard. The problem was that Quaque not only defied the SPG's expectations, but sometimes even blatantly ignored their directives. As tensions began to grow, Quaque doubted the SPG's support while the SPG likely regretted spending so much care and attention on his religious instruction in the first place.

Quaque rarely heard from the SPG, especially during those first few years when he believed that he needed institutional support the most. He persistently asked for raises. He received a few paltry ones, but never believed that he was compensated as much as he should have been. In fact, he would have been unhappy to learn that, while he earned only fifty to sixty pounds a year, his white predecessor earned seventy pounds nearly two decades prior. Quaque even asked that his own children be sent to England to be supported and educated by the SPG, likely for the purpose of becoming black missionaries or cultural brokers in Africa, like their father. Tellingly, the SPG flatly and repeatedly refused.

Because the SPG and the Company of Merchants split Quaque's salary—meaning he was both an SPG missionary and a chaplain to the slave fort—it was assumed that Quaque would simply stick to his post at the Cape Coast. But, after several years of combatting both African spiritual apathy and white Christian neglect, Quaque began to consider taking a more itinerant approach to evangelization. His decision reveals a central tension in Protestant evangelical efforts: while missionary work necessitated a certain degree of itinerancy, Anglican missionaries were usually rooted in certain parishes or chaplaincies. When Quaque's labors at Cape Coast began to appear fruitless by the early 1770s, he began aspiring for a more itinerant approach, or at least a change in venue. He wrote to the SPG in 1772 and asked to be relocated to a new position in Senegal, where he might be "more Serviceable" than he was "here amongst my own Kindred."[58] The SPG rejected his request, but that did not stop Quaque from travelling to other commercial and administrative centers on Africa's West Coast. He went to Accra in the winter of 1772. He was at Dixcove Fort for nearly a year from 1774 to 1775. Quaque would always return to his base at the Cape Coast, but his itinerancy became increasingly viewed by the SPG as highly unorthodox, if not downright insubordinate.

Part of the SPG's concern might have been because Quaque's audience was tinged by religions other than Anglicanism, suggesting that Quaque might have been developing a tear in his imperial or even spiritual allegiances. Quaque positively reported how Dutch evangelists at Dixcove Fort effectively taught African children and introduced a well-established routine for Christian spiritual worship. The relationship between Quaque and the Dutch seemed to be growing increasingly cozy. Quaque said that

Dutch evangelical efforts were "worthy of Imitation," and he was elated to report that whites and blacks alike came to hear him when he offered to lead religious services.[59] A Dutch governor even offered Quaque a gratuity for providing religious instruction. Quaque likely embraced this as an opportunity to finally achieve the recognition, respect, and appreciation that he had vainly hoped for at the Cape Coast. When the SPG received word of his evangelical wanderings, however, they tersely ordered that he should not "absent himself for so long from the Cape Coast without the Leave of the Society." Quaque was never recalled, reassigned, or repositioned, and he would officially remain at Cape Coast until his death in 1816, even if he dreamed of settling elsewhere.[60]

Another point of contention was that, although the major advantage of native missionaries seemed to be that they could offer a smooth entrance into the worlds of Africans and indigenous Americans, Quaque's identity cast him as an outsider among his family, former friends, and neighbors. This was particularly apparent when it came to the issue of language. Because Quaque spent such a critical part of his life training in London, he allegedly failed to maintain a firm command of the Akan-based language of his roots. Missionary organizations like the SPG valued native missionaries not only because they could translate Christian concepts into indigenous frameworks and cosmologies, but also because they could translate languages themselves. Quaque seemed to fail at both endeavors. In fact, he even had to hire another local African, a man named Frederick Adoy, to serve as his translator. This prospect must have seemed troubling for the SPG but comical to others. Here was an African being paid to translate for an African trying to spread the gospel to other Africans. Adoy refused to serve as Quaque's interpreter unless he was rewarded monetarily for his work, and there is even evidence that Adoy simply cut one of Quaque's sermons short because he was tired of translating.[61] It is unlikely that Quaque lost total command of his native tongue, and it is even more likely that, once grounded in Africa, he was able to recover some of it along the way. However, his failure to speak his African tongue *fluently* resulted in him being just as useless as the white missionaries who preceded and succeeded him. We might even wonder if he believed, as his white predecessor did, that Africans spoke a nearly unintelligible, "strange kind of jargon."[62] Realizing that Quaque's linguistic failures hampered his missionary efforts, the SPG reported that they strongly encouraged Quaque to "recover his own language."[63] It is unclear if he ever did, and it is likely that his inability to communicate with his fellow Africans in the local dialect represented and exacerbated the cultural chasm between the London-trained missionary and the Africans he hoped to convert.

Written in a moment when he was irate at the treatment he received from neglectful Anglican sponsors, tyrannical white traders, and apathetic African neighbors, Philip Quaque exclaimed that "a Prophet hath not Honor or Merit in his own Country."[64] Interestingly, Quaque was citing a phrase that appears in *all* of the Gospels—Matthew, Mark, Luke, and John—at a point in the passion narrative where Christ was discarded by his own people. As such, Quaque analogized himself to the ultimate preacher who also experienced depressing evangelical rejection. Quaque believed that he was, like Christ, a walking martyr. He perceived himself as a living testament to Christian truth but he also believed that his work was frustrated by native stubbornness and English neglect. Perhaps Quaque was overly ambitious, or perhaps he was tragically naïve. Either way, his mission was ultimately unsuccessful. He did make important contributions to the development of education in West Africa by attempting to create several small schools and establishing rudimentary pedagogical practices for the teaching of African children, but the Christian conversion of his people would happen in later centuries, not on his watch. Entering the 21st century, Ghana's millions of Christians made up the majority of the population. At the dawn of the 19th century, however, Quaque could only count a few dozen baptisms among his paltry successes.[65]

The legacy of Philip Quaque is an ambiguous one. In the generations after Quaque died, several commentators contended that he had died as an apostate who had forsaken Christianity to return to traditional African religion. Many Anglicans took these stories as proof of the ineptitude of native preachers.[66] And yet, for the majority of the period that Quaque was in Africa, he played a significant role in the development of transatlantic missionary activity. He personally corresponded with several evangelical figures throughout the Atlantic and summaries of his work and letters were disseminated throughout the wider world and were invoked as examples of Christian evangelical sacrifice. Stories about him were featured in Anglican reports, missionary accounts, and even more popular publications like the *Gentleman's Magazine*. Not surprisingly, later missionaries contacted him to inquire about the possibilities of launching native missionary programs in Africa, and others cited him while attempting to drum up financial support for some of these ambitious plans.[67] Quaque's legacy was therefore quite mixed. He was an unsuccessful missionary who nevertheless gained transatlantic recognition, a clear opponent of the slave trade who worked for a slave trading company, and a native missionary whose example simultaneously provided encouragement and dissuasion for missionary organizations considering the use of native missionaries in Africa. Yet his misfortunes, missteps, and misgivings should not detract from the value of the rich documentary record he left behind. There are few better records for detailing indigenous missionary work in the Atlantic world, and Quaque's story provides an unceasingly compelling account of what it was like to be an African missionary among Africans.

CHAPTER FIVE

Native Evangelists in the Iroquoian Borderlands

THERE MAY HAVE BEEN no better symbol of English civility in the eighteenth century than tea. Critically important for the British imperial economy, crucial to the networking of socialites and politicos, and the commodity of choice for Bostonian protestors to dump overboard, tea was universally understood as vital to the constitutions of English bodies and essential to the conduct of social life. This explains why, in February of 1765, a missionary named Joseph who was stationed among the Oneida Indians in southern New York complained bitterly about the absence of it. Writing to a colleague to beg him for more tea, coffee, and a new shirt, the evangelist grumbled that the Indian family he lived with had depleted most of these supplies during the frigid winter. While this evangelist was stationed at Onaquaga, an Oneida town that had actively invited Christian missionaries to settle there, his colleague, named Samuel, had settled himself among a group of Seneca Indians who were much less amenable to the idea of Christian missionaries than their Oneida cousins. Stuck among what he dubbed "the most savage and barbarous" Indians on the North American continent, Samuel was infuriated by Joseph's complaints. Although Joseph was distinguished by his "polished manners," Samuel nevertheless advised him to make use of the innumerable natural materials that the wilderness afforded to make his greatly desired tea.[1]

These materials included "*pine buds, sassafras bows* & the bark of the root *spice wood*," and "chips from the heart of the sugar maple." "These are more friendly to our constitution," Samuel observed, "than foreign teas & all more so to the natives." As for the deteriorating clothes, he added that his friend should procure a leather shirt and have "Indian breeches" made for him. "Disgrace or no disgrace," Samuel assured his colleague, "I expect to do it shortly for myself." Many Christian missionaries experienced a temptation to "go native" and adopt the foods, material comforts, clothing, and lifeways of their charges, but Samuel was actively endorsing it. What made this written exchange unique was that the man who directed Joseph to go native was an Anglo-American preacher named Samuel Kirkland. What made it even more peculiar was that his colleague was Joseph Woolley, an Indian evangelist. Here is an exceptional case where a white missionary insisted that a native one go native.[2]

While we do not have a record of Joseph Woolley's response, he must have considered Samuel Kirkland's suggestion with some trepidation. Woolley was a graduate of Moor's Charity School, an educational institution in Lebanon, Connecticut operated by the famous Eleazar Wheelock. Wheelock's "Grand Design" was to "purge all the Indian out" of his students and employ them as native preachers among the Iroquois in the 1760s.[3] Trained in husbandry and agriculture, indoctrinated in scripture, and fluent in Latin, Greek, and Hebrew, Woolley's education at Wheelock's school—as well as his identity as a Delaware Indian—set him apart from the Indians he was trying to convert. Woolley was not the only Native American to experience this tension, for there were a handful of other Montauk, Mohegan, and Delaware Indians who took up residence at Wheelock's school, received a classical education, and were sent out to open the door for the Christianization of the Iroquois, the most powerful Indian nation in North America. Caught between cultures, Woolley and other native preachers from Wheelock's school constantly struggled with this perpetual identity crisis while simultaneously hoping to change the identities of the people to whom they preached.

Eleazar Wheelock's effort to use Indian preachers was less a result of his own personal ingenuity than a product of the end of the Seven Years' War and the material and spiritual concerns of Oneida Indians. As a result of schools such as Wheelock's, native preachers wrote of their movements, attitudes, and evangelical efforts. Preachers involved in the Iroquois mission left nearly ninety letters that document their work among the Oneidas. These letters highlight the unique ways in which they translated Christianity, perceived other Indians, and situated themselves as *both* Indian and Christian. They also illuminate the many conflicts between native preachers and their superiors, between native preachers and Oneida Indians, and among native preachers themselves.

Such problems undermined the mission as a whole and cast doubt on the effectiveness of native preachers, but they did not necessarily cease native missionary efforts. In fact, Wheelock's mismanagement only reinforced other missionaries' belief that native peoples would be central to indigenous Christianization within the Atlantic world and beyond.

Protestant missionaries viewed 1763 as a seminal moment in the history of Christianity. The French had been defeated in the Seven Years' War, and a seemingly simple "scratch of a pen" on the Treaty of Paris left Canada, the Great Lakes Region, and the Mississippi Valley in the hands of the British and their colonial allies.[4] English divines understood this transition as a sign from God himself, a providential omen that offered Protestantism a unique opportunity to spread the light of Christianity where pagan darkness and Catholic popery once ruled. The metaphor of the open door was employed *ad infinitum* to characterize their future evangelical prospects. An Anglican divine named Edmund Keene had argued as early as 1757 that the war gave the English a "Prospect of seeing an effectual Door opened to introduce Missionaries into [Indian] Castles."[5] Samuel Buell reported that "a glorious door" was opening for the propagation of the gospel to the Iroquois by the end of 1763.[6] Eleazar Wheelock observed that there was a "door opening for a hundred Missionaries . . . and perhaps for ten Times that Number" to go among the Indians now that the French were gone.[7] An Anglican minister in the American colonies observed in 1762 that he and his Protestant colleagues should not miss the incredible potential for Christian evangelization that now lay before them. "The War being now happily concluded in that Country," he declared, "there will, in a short Time, be the best Opportunity of propagating the Gospel among the heathen Natives of that Part of the World, that was ever offered."[8] This appeared to be a crucial moment in Christian history. Protestant ministers had long been fantasizing about the conversion of the Iroquois nation, and in 1763 the opportunity to do so seemed imminent.

But the persistence of French Catholicism, as well as French Catholics, loomed large. The Jesuits had made inroads into Iroquoian villages during the seventeenth century, and Protestant ministers feared and envied their successes. They believed that the Indians of Iroquoia were "infected with the roman catholic religion" and "deeply tinctured with romish superstition."[9] Although the Treaty of Paris had ousted the French from Indian borderlands, many Catholic missionaries stayed. "We Expect one of the French Ministers here this season," one Mohegan missionary reported to Eleazar Wheelock in the spring of 1768, "for which Reason I don't love to leave the Indians."[10] Native preachers, as well as their white counterparts, were viewed as weapons in the fight against engrained French sympathies and even more stubborn French preachers. For their own part, Iroquoian Indians were highly selective of the Christian missionaries they brought into their lands before and after the war, and they understood that missionary influence could generate inter- and intra-tribal divisions along kinship lines. And yet, their unique circumstances at the end of 1763 encouraged them to invite Christian missionaries into their homes, lands, and lives, thus holding that metaphorical door open for native preachers.[11]

English divines and Native Americans understood Christianity as a fundamental component of diplomacy, and Eleazar Wheelock pushed his sponsors to think of the diplomatic and military benefits of his native missionary program. Wheelock informed Sir William Johnson, superintendent of Indian affairs and arguably the most powerful British official in North America, that indigenous missionaries might "guard [the Iroquois] against the influence of Jesuits; be an antidote to their idolatrous and savage practices; attach them to the English interest, and induce them to a cordial subjection to the crown of Britain, and it is to be hoped, to a subjection to the king of Zion."[12] One of Wheelock's colleagues declared that "20 Missionaries among the Indians would be better to keep them in peace than 5000 Men under Arms."[13] While Wheelock's plan was fundamentally evangelical in nature, he also believed that he could drum up support for his native missionary program by appealing to the anxieties of English policymakers and frontier settlers. He even suggested that procuring Iroquois students would be another safeguard against the ravages of the frontier, as Indian parents would be reluctant to attack English settlements if they knew their children lived among them. As Wheelock promoted his native missionary plan, he fused military and evangelical rhetoric to attract a wide swath of donors and supporters.

A Yale graduate who trained a Mohegan preacher named Samson Occom in the 1740s, Wheelock tried his hand with other Indian pupils after witnessing Occom's remarkable transformation from pagan Indian to celebrated preacher. Wheelock established a school in Lebanon, Connecticut and named it after its most generous donor. Moor's Charity School brought in dozens of Delaware, Mohegan, Montauk, Narragansett, and other Algonquian Indians in the 1750s and Wheelock actively recruited Iroquois Indians in the 1760s. The goal was to train these students in classical languages, civility, agriculture, husbandry, and scripture, and then to use them as instruments for the conversion of other Indians. As he told the nations of Iroquois beyond his borders, his primary objective was for the Iroquois students to return home, "and in their own language teach their brothers, sisters, and friends the way of Salvation Jesus Christ."[14] Wheelock sold his native missionary scheme as a fundamentally innovative and path-breaking method for spreading the gospel. He extolled "the Newness of the Thing" and later hagiographers would perpetuate the mistaken claim that the idea for a native school was "his and his alone."[15] Consequently, he gained the reputation as an innovator who introduced the use of native preachers in early America.

However, native evangelists had always been central to the Protestant missionary enterprise, and Wheelock was building on an older, transatlantic tradition of using indigenous preachers. He was, after all, a Berkeley Scholar at Yale, and his school in Lebanon looked strikingly similar to the one that Berkeley envisioned for Bermuda: a seminary of learning located far away from the vices of English and Indians alike. The Scottish Society for Propagating Christian Knowledge (SSPCK), the Edinburgh-based Presbyterian organization that initially lent tremendous support to Wheelock's plan, claimed that Wheelock's program was "begun and carried on with the same spirit with which the late Reverend and eminent Professor *Frank* founded the present famous orphan-house at *Hall* in *Germany,* so it hath been blessed with many suchlike remarkable smiles from Heaven."[16] Francke's program influenced Puritan missionary efforts in New England, George Whitefield's orphan schools in the Lowcountry, native evangelical programs in India, and countless other Protestant missionary efforts. And yet, Wheelock never conceded that he was not the first to introduce native preachers into missionary practice.

Wheelock was not even the first to introduce native missionaries into Iroquoia, for they already had a long tradition of using local Christian preachers among them. The early 1740s saw a period of extraordinary change in Anglican missionary policies. Anglicans' earlier experiments with native royalty had little effect, and growing religious competition from Methodists, Presbyterians, and Moravians compelled them to begin using black slaves as teachers in the Carolinas. By the 1750s they were even training West Africans—like Philip Quaque—for Anglican missionary work. The Iroquois Indians were part of this larger development, as Anglicans began employing native schoolmasters, catechists, and readers in their Mohawk missions in the 1740s. The earlier mission by William Andrews (from 1712 to 1719) was a failure, but in the 1740s Anglican missionaries from Albany began to return to the Mohawk "castles" of Tiononderoge (The Lower Castle near Fort Hunter) and Canajoharie (The Upper Castle), hoping to cultivate native Christians among the 500 or so Mohawks who lived there in the 1740s and 50s. Henry Barclay, the Anglican missionary stationed in Albany, petitioned the SPG to fund native schoolmasters at these two castles. By 1742 a Mohawk named Daniel was teaching at Canajoharie and Cornelius (apparently a Sachem) was teaching at Tiononderoge. Barclay's choices appeared to be good ones. He reported that Cornelius was "very faithful and diligent" in his teaching, and that Daniel was also very successful.[17] Because Barclay exercised only an itinerant presence among the Mohawks, Daniel and Cornelius were often left to their own devices, and both of them had leave to join the Mohawks when they went on their seasonal hunts. But their jobs were not simply educational in nature, for even schoolmasters were charged with teaching students the fundamental principles of Christianity. Barclay reported that Cornelius, the schoolmaster at Tiononderoge, "reads prayers in my Absence, and is much Beloved by his Countrymen."[18] Native preachers like Daniel and Cornelius exercised some of the spiritual authority that absent English missionaries possessed.

In spite of its early successes, the use of native schoolmasters among the Mohawks also produced its quarrels. An anti-English, anti-Christian Mohawk manipulated some of the tensions inherent in using native missionaries. Cornelius and Daniel were both paid seven pounds, ten shillings annually for their services, but the Mohawk told Cornelius that he had heard that the SPG was paying him twenty pounds per year. The rest of the money, the Mohawk declared, was being pocketed by Barclay, the English preacher.[19] Other Iroquois Indians opined that Barclay was "in League with the Devil, who was the Author of all the Books" that the SPG had given them. The Mohawks at Tiononderoge did not believe this story, but the ones at Canajoharie did, and by March of 1745, the Upper Castle was "all in a Flame" over Barclay's alleged fidelity to Satan.[20] When John Ogilvie, an Anglican minister working among the Mohawks in the 1750s, tried to train another Mohawk as a Christian missionary, his parents took him home, "as they said, [because] he might learn to despise his own Nation."[21] Such episodes demonstrate how precarious the use of native missionaries in Iroquoia was. In fact, Barclay's reputation never recovered from his rumored allegiance to Satan. Cornelius and Daniel quit their teaching jobs in 1746 and Barclay followed soon after, taking a less demanding post as a church rector.

By 1750 another Anglican missionary (John Ogilvie) was cultivating another corps of native preachers at Tiononderoge and Canajoharie. This time the Anglican relied upon Abraham, an older Mohawk sachem and brother to Hendrick, a celebrated Mohawk soldier and diplomat. Ogilvie reported in 1750 that Abraham prevented drunkenness, read morning prayers, visited other Indian nations, rejected religious solicitations from French Jesuits, and kept up "divine service among the aged people & children whilst the others are in the woods."[22] Jonathan Edwards reported that Abraham was a "remarkable man; a man of great solidity, prudence, devotion, and strict conversation." Edwards concluded that Abraham acted "very much as a person endowed with the simplicity, humanity, self-denial and zeal of a true Christian."[23] Abraham must have been quite the catch, for Edwards actively recruited Abraham and his Christian Mohawk allies to train them at his own community at Stockbridge, Massachusetts. The Anglicans, of course, anticipated this move and instead offered Abraham five pounds sterling to be a reader in the Mohawk congregation. Although Abraham toyed with the idea of going to Stockbridge, it never came to fruition. Instead, Abraham spent the last of his days reading and teaching his fellow Mohawks, following his brothers and cousins on the warpath during the French and Indian War, performing "Divine Service every morning and evening" during that war, and training his son, Paulus, to do the same.[24]

When the SPG was debating whether to give Paulus a teaching position, they admitted in 1750 that offering him the salaried post would "much engage his uncle Hendrick, who we are all sensible has been of the most material Service during the late War."[25] The SPG had mistakenly claimed that Hendrick was Paulus's uncle, but they were right to note that Paulus would have, like his father Hendrick, significant military and political clout. He fought alongside his fellow Mohawks during the French and Indian War and eventually took the sachemship at Canajoharie when Hendrick and Abraham died in 1755 and 1756, respectively. In the meantime, Paulus taught about forty children each day to read and write, instructed them in the Christian psalms, and even "read Prayers" in Ogilvie's absence.[26] He probably had the help of an Anglican catechism after 1763, but he had little support from spelling books, for a colleague of his noted that he taught Mohawk children the alphabet "by means only of little manuscript scraps of paper."[27] In short, Paulus took up the mantle of indigenous Christian leadership that Abraham left when he died. He would remain a reader throughout and after the American Revolution, when he migrated with some of his fellow Mohawks to Ontario. When Daniel Claus published a primer for the Christian education of Canadian Indians in 1786, he included an engraving of Paulus teaching young Indians on the inside cover.[28]

The conversion of the Mohawks was never viewed as an end in itself. The Mohawks occupied the eastern side of the Iroquoian "longhouse" of New York, and missionaries imagined Mohawk evangelists spreading westward to their Iroquoian brothers: the Oneidas, Tuscaroras,

Peter Paulus teaching Canadian Mohawks. (Image courtesy of the John Carter Brown Library at Brown University.)

Onandagas, Cayugas, and Senecas. We have become accustomed to using these monikers to distinguish between Iroquoian groups, but there was a tremendous amount of overlap, interconnection, and entanglement among them. Onaquaga, an "Oneida" town situated on the Susquehanna River in southern New York, was comprised of Oneidas, Shawnees, Delawares, Tuscaroras, Mohawks, and other mixed groups. Joseph Brant, the prominent Iroquois leader, was a Mohawk from Canajoharie who also owned land at Onaquaga.[29] Brant was not the only one to cross the permeable boundaries between Mohawk and Oneida, for the similarity of dialect and their geographic proximity ensured that other Iroquois travelers would work to knit these communities together. Missionaries hoped they could exploit these itinerant tendencies as a tool to expose Indians west of Mohawk territory to the fundamentals of Christianity. In 1751 Abraham, the Mohawk missionary, reported to Jonathan Edwards that the Mohawks were not the only ones interested in hearing the word of the Gospel. There were other, "considerable men," Abraham reported, "of the nation of the Oneiyutas, in other places, and also some of the Tuscarores, that are religiously disposed."[30] These "considerable men" were probably Good Peter, Isaac Dakayenensere, and Deacon Thomas, leaders of Oneida communities and later Protestant evangelists.

Good Peter was a leader among the Oneida Indians. A man of considerable import in his own right, he embraced a call to Christian evangelism after a series of New Light preachers visited his town of Onaquaga in the late 1740s. "Occasion'd partly by the death of his father, and by a blessing on the means of grace," Peter had a conversion experience in 1754 at the age of 21.[31] English missionaries undoubtedly viewed Peter's sudden "conversion" as divine providence, but Peter might have understood it as a change in his ever-evolving identity as an Oneida. A young adult coping with the death of his father, Peter might have seen his turn to Christian Indian, and even Christian evangelist, as a rite of passage, assuming a new adult identity along with a new name. When Gideon Hawley, one of the most active English preachers at Onaquaga, left the village in 1756, Peter took up the mantle of Christian evangelism that Hawley left behind. He learned to read the Mohawk bible, conducted itinerant missionary trips to other Iroquois Indians, and (with Isaac), "constantly led the people in the publick worship of God, ever since they have been destitute of a missionary."[32] Elisha Gunn, who witnessed some of Peter's sermons, reported that he "preaches excellently well."[33] Like other native preachers before and after him, Peter was no pawn. When English officials built a fort in his town in 1756, he urged them to take it down because it disturbed their peace and upset the Oneidas' practice of Christianity. "Some of our Warriors are foolish & some of our Brothers soldiers don't fear God," Peter explained, so the destruction of the fort would hopefully remind his brothers and cousins to pay more attention to their spiritual lives than their martial ones.[34] Peter

Good Peter. (Image courtesy of Yale University Art Gallery, Trumbull Collection.)

also made a name for himself as a warrior and scout for the English during the Seven Years War, hoping to purge the French and their Catholic influences out of Iroquoia. He understood the financial benefits of his cultural skills. While a group of Indians were collectively paid fifteen shillings for assisting Gideon Hawley in returning from Onaquaga, Peter alone was paid twelve shillings and two dollars for doing the same thing. Once again, membership in Christ's kingdom had its privileges.[35]

Indian missionaries were not motivated solely by money, and it would be difficult to overestimate the importance of Oneida preachers like Good Peter, Isaac Dakayenensere, and Deacon Thomas to sustaining Christian evangelical efforts in the absence of English missionaries. Isaac, for example, reported that as soon as he had his conversion experience, he "made it my Business . . . to learn letters, and as much of the Christian religion as I possibly could, and have endeavored all in my power to spread it amongst our people."[36] Isaac and Peter oversaw religious services at Onaquaga while Deacon Thomas led Christian meetings around Kanonwalohale in the 1750s and 60s, frequently preaching "with the Appearance of great Affection and Zeal . . . for an Hour and a half."[37] These Oneida preachers even scouted out evangelical opportunities among their Iroquois cousins. In 1765, Good Peter told Presbyterian missionary Samuel Kirkland that a mission to the Senecas at that time was a "bold if not hazardous enterprise," since they were still riled up from the Indian uprisings of previous years. Kirkland ignored Peter's advice and, predictably, his mission failed.[38] Oneida preachers were fully aware of their centrality to Christian missions and even pushed for more ecclesiastical authority. The Indians at Onaquaga assured Gideon Hawley that they "need no further instruction, and were Isaac or Peter ordained, they would be contented without an English missionary."[39] Neither Oneida preachers were officially ordained, but their power as cultural brokers and Christian missionaries only grew as the Oneidas and English became more dependent upon them to navigate the tempestuous waters of Christian missionary work among the Iroquois.

Oneida preachers like Good Peter, Isaac, and Deacon Thomas helped to interpret Christian concepts for their people, did damage control when English ministers floundered, and embraced opportunities to do some preaching of their own. When Samuel Kirkland used the word "Karoughyage" (Oneida for "heaven") for "Kanonwalohale" (the major Oneida town) in one of his sermons, Deacon Thomas stepped in to clarify Kirkland's meaning. "Brethren," Thomas reportedly told his fellow Oneidas, "don't take Offence at what our Father has said; you see his Mind is so much in Heaven, that he speaks it when he thinks nothing of it." Thomas then immediately gave what Kirkland dubbed a "lively, judicious and affecting Exhortation upon the Nature and Properties of a spiritual Mind." Kirkland remembered Thomas' intercession as a seminal moment in his mission to the Oneida, for he was in the midst of trying to get the town of Old Oneida (a traditional, anti-Christian town) to congregate with those at Kanonwalohale (a larger, more missionary-friendly settlement). The chiefs of Old Oneida met with Kirkland sometime later and entered into a long discourse, with Thomas witnessing the event. The Oneida chiefs then finished their discourse and awaited Kirkland's reply. But "before I had time to utter a Word by way of reply," Kirkland recalled, "Thomas . . . desired to speak a few Words, and gave a most judicious and striking Exhortation." Far from feeling upstaged, Kirkland seemed impressed, and reported that tears flowed quickly from the eyes of many Oneida chiefs. He even proclaimed that he had "never heard Words flow more easy, or with greater Propriety, from any Man in my life."[40] Although Kirkland might have envied Deacon Thomas' effortless ability to speak to the Oneidas, he never complained about the Oneida preacher overshadowing him. Instead, Kirkland probably realized that Thomas was a priceless cultural asset, even if he had the tendency to speak on Kirkland's behalf and engage in long, extemporaneous exhortations.

The Oneidas at Kanonwalohale, Onaquaga, and other towns possessed their own need for assistance, their own agendas for inviting Christian missionaries into their lives, and even their own "open door" metaphor. They viewed the Mohawks as elder brothers, but also as keepers of the "eastern door" of their Iroquoian longhouse, whereas the Senecas guarded the "western door." They actively recruited Christian missionaries to help them deal with the cataclysmic problems they faced in the wake of the Seven Years War. The warrior class had increased its power among the Oneidas throughout the eighteenth century, and the traditional leadership of older sachems and even Oneida women was constantly being challenged. The warriors looked to English missionaries as a way to secure diplomatic allegiances with the east and strengthen their own position in Iroquois society. The Oneidas were in the midst of a fundamental change in their lifeways as they were moving out of larger longhouses and into smaller homes, characterized less by extended kinship networks and more by nuclear families. The accoutrements of English "civilization" had also altered their material culture. By the 1760s the Oneidas were cooking in metal kettles and frying pans, eating their foods from pewter plates, sporting English silver broaches, and looking in glass mirrors as they combed their hair. The Oneidas embraced their reputation as outposts of

English culture. While one English commentator called Onaquaga "the finest Indian town I ever saw," Samuel Kirkland dubbed the Oneidas there "the most civilized Indians" in Iroquoia.[41]

But "civilization" had its discontents. Encroaching settlers carried not only an insatiable thirst for land, but also destructive vermin and diseases that wreaked havoc upon native crops and bodies. In the first years of the 1760s the Iroquois suffered from smallpox, vermin infestations, premature frosts, and failed crops. One of the Oneida chiefs warned David Fowler, a Montauk Indian on a Christian mission in the spring of 1765, that "some of the Indians would starve to Death this Summer. Some of them have almost consumed all their Corn already."[42] As English colonial settlers hunted in Iroquoian lands and fished on Iroquoian rivers, meat and fish were depleted precipitously, and Oneidas complained that they could not find fowl, beast, or fish within seventy miles of their settlements. This partially explains why Oneidas understood the introduction of agriculture and Christianity as "spiritual food" and asked Protestant ministers to help them "uphold our *Bodies,* our *lives,* lest our souls should unexpectedly leave both you and us, before we have time to set them in the right way."[43] The Oneidas had no intention of ceding their lands and understood the precarious position they would be put in once they accepted English missionaries. "We would have you Understand Brethren," the Oneidas proclaimed to Wheelock and his colleagues, "that we have no thoughts of selling our Land to any that come to live among us; for if we should sell a little Land to any, by & by they would want to buy a little more & so our Land would go by Inches till we should have none to live upon."[44] The Oneidas at the small village of Jeningo wanted a Christian missionary, but they utterly refused to have an English one settle among them. They therefore requested that Samuel Ashpo, a Mohegan preacher trained at Wheelock's charity school, initiate a mission there. The Mohawks at Canajoharie followed suit, expressing a strong preference for their own English-trained Philip Jonathan over a Euro-American teacher named Jacob Oel.[45] Native preachers would, in their eyes, provide the best of both worlds, as they could introduce Indians to the saving graces of Christianity while providing material relief. Because native preachers lacked the avaricious impulses that discredited white missionaries, they were expected to protect the very lands that English settlers eyed so jealously.

While missionary Christianity's association with English colonization marred it in the eyes of some Iroquois Indians, others viewed Christianity as a weapon to combat the epidemiological, territorial, and spiritual dilemmas they faced. If husbandry and agriculture accompanied

Christianity, as Wheelock and other Protestants claimed it would, then the starving Oneidas supported it. Furthermore, literacy and education were beginning to be viewed as cultural weapons, as tools for gaining access to English power and authority as well as the word of God himself. Baptism, for example, was not simply an arcane formality, but an important moment for securing the protection of an all-powerful God and gaining access to a kind of preventative medicine. Even if Iroquoian traditional religion and Christianity were not completely compatible—the Trinity, afterlife, and original sin were usually alien concepts for indigenous peoples—there were many other areas of religious overlap. Iroquois Indians and Christians both believed that God had created the earth, that good and evil were active forces in peoples' everyday lives, that lesser deities (like Christ) were also active in peoples' lives, that thanksgiving and charity would improve one's standing with spiritual forces, and that martial imagery was appropriate for understanding the battle between good and evil. The Oneidas were therefore not "passive recipients," but "demanding catalysts" for Protestant missionary work in the 1760s.[46] When they asked for help from Eleazar Wheelock's Indians, the Iroquois knew what they were getting into. Indeed, Wheelock's Indians traveled to the same places where Mohawk and Oneida native preachers had already been working: the Mohawk "castles" of Tiononderoge and Canajoharie, the Oneida towns of Kanonwalohale, Old Oneida, and Onaquaga, as well as smaller settlements like Cherry Valley, Lake Utsage, and Jeningo. In short, the Moor Indians' missions were designed to cultivate already well trodden ground. Native preachers among the Iroquois were not unique, unheard of, or exceptional, but important and long standing threads in the fabric of eighteenth century Iroquoian society and culture.[47]

One aspect of Wheelock's program was unique: this was the first time that Amerindians from one linguistic and cultural group were used to proselytize other indigenous groups. In that sense, Wheelock's Indians were not really "native" at all. Instead, they were Indians but outsiders, lying in a mercurial space between Indian and English, Iroquois and Algonquian, Western and indigenous. Fortunately, their frequent letters back to Wheelock describe their missions, their attempts to maintain their unique identity as Christian Indians and, most importantly, their efforts to use Christian evangelism to remold Iroquoian society in the 1760s. While these letters were predictable and formulaic, "exercises in penmanship and epistolary styles" that "rehearsed religious discourses" and "practiced a rhetoric of politeness and humility," they were also pragmatic and informational, revealing the subtle ways in which indigenous peoples tried to convert neighboring indigenous peoples.[48] Like Philip Quaque's letters detailing his mission in West Africa, the letters of Eleazar Wheelock's Indian missionaries illuminate how Native Americans functioned as evangelical agents during the eighteenth century.

These Moor Indians were certainly not alone, for Wheelock and his benefactors envisioned using native preachers alongside Anglo-American ones like Samuel Kirkland, Ralph Wheelock, and Theophilus Chamberlain. In their role as assistants, they often worked in conjunction with local Oneida Christians to protect English missionaries, who were much more suspect than their Indian colleagues. Samuel Kirkland, for example, had a volatile relationship with the Oneidas in the 1760s; some days he was embraced as a father, other days he was kicked out of his hosts' homes because of his battle against Indian drinking. When Kirkland confiscated some rum from an Indian named Jau-na-whau-na-gea, the Oneida demanded payment for his loss. Kirkland refused, and Jau-na-whau-na-gea approached the missionary and threatened to "gripe" him "upon the throat." Kirkland wrestled his adversary to the ground and called for Mohegan missionary Joseph Johnson to "assist in binding him." Jau-na-whau-na-gea's wife ran to the scene and tried to pry Johnson and Kirkland off her husband by hitting and biting them "like a Dog." Kirkland and Johnson released Jau-na-whau-na-gea, but the English missionary was so fearful of retribution that he wisely fled into the woods.[49] In the ensuing days, Deacon Thomas discovered more rum among the Oneidas, apprehended it, and destroyed it while Kirkland was in exile. Kirkland returned within a few days and resumed his normal pattern of preaching, having temporarily won this crusade against Indian vices. Although the threat of violence was ever-present for white missionaries, Joseph Johnson's physicality and Thomas' crusade against rum helped legitimize and, in some senses indigenize, Kirkland's work among the Oneidas. Kirkland may not have survived this encounter without the help of either native evangelist.[50]

Native preachers were among the Oneidas to stop their excessive drinking and protect English missionaries, but they were certainly not just the muscle of the operation. The most basic duty expected of the Moor Indians was to keep school regularly among their Mohawk and Oneida charges, teaching them the fundamentals of Christianity as well as the basics of language, the alphabet, and spelling. Schooling was a vital element of Christian spirituality, for it gave Christians access to sacred texts and religious truths that were unavailable to non-literate peoples. As such, native missionaries took schooling very seriously. Joseph Woolley, the tea-drinking Delaware preacher at Onaquaga, reported to Wheelock that "I hope Sir, I shall be enabled to walk before my School as it becometh, & teach them those Things that I ought which I wish, Long & Pray for."[51] A list of David Fowler's books suggests that the entrance into all things spiritual was literacy, for he had forty copies of spelling books at his mission at Kanonwalohale. He also had catechisms, discourses on the Lord's supper, and other sacred texts, but the small and cheap spelling books were the foundation of his educational program.[52] Other native preachers did not have the resources that Fowler had. Moses, a Mohawk teacher at an Iroquois community near Lake Utsage, had few books, taught his classes in "nothing but an open Barrack," and had his students sit around a "Bark Table" while he led classes.[53] In spite of their material wants on the borderlands, native preachers nevertheless pushed indigenous education as a way to better deal with English colonialism and gain access to divine revelation.

Iroquois students and parents, on the other hand, were ambivalent about literacy and schooling. While many saw the spiritual and temporal power that literacy could accrue, others believed that schooling was not the main benefit of having Christian missionaries. They constantly asked for help with agriculture and frequently requested Christian ministers, but schoolteachers were less in demand. They kept school very irregularly, and native schoolmasters complained bitterly about their inability to draw students on a daily basis. Montauk missionary David Fowler reported in May of 1765 that Iroquois Indians never sent their children to school because they "had too much work to do" and because Fowler came too early in the season. "I can't get but one Boy here," Fowler complained, because all the boys had gone to their seasonal hunt. Fowler was not alone in his frustration.[54] Hezekiah Calvin, a Delaware Indian sent to open a school among the Mohawks at Fort Hunter (near Tiononderoge, or the Lower Mohawk Castle), said that the Indians were "very loth to send their children" to Calvin's school. They would "make excuses," Calvin complained, "that they had work for [the children] to do." Calvin knew how to respond to what he perceived as blatant Iroquois laggardness. He threatened to leave the Indian settlement because, as he put it, he had no one to teach. The very next day the Mohawks sent five students to Calvin's school, hoping to keep him there and maintain the cultural and diplomatic link between themselves and the ministers to the east.[55]

What kept most students out of the schools were the seasonal hunts that formed a central part of the Iroquoian subsistence economy, especially when vermin and premature frosts destroyed their harvests. Iroquoian hunting patterns proved to be one of the most paradoxical aspects of native missionary work in New York: while the Iroquois demanded Christian missionaries, in part, to help solve their famine crises, missionary work was severely hampered by the Iroquois' frequent absences during their long, seasonal hunts. As the plentitude of game decreased dramatically in the eighteenth century, hunts had become more time consuming and less successful than ever before, thus keeping Iroquoian children (especially young boys) and men out of native missionary schools. Algonquian preachers complained constantly about these noticeable absences. David Fowler's class at Kanonwalohale, for example, was doing exceedingly well in the spring of 1765, so much so that he bragged to Eleazar Wheelock that he "never saw Children exceed these in learing [sic]." The problem, however, was that most of his children accompanied their parents on the lengthy spring hunts. "They are often/always roving about from Place to Place," Fowler complained, "to get something to live upon. Provision is very scarce with them."[56] One year later Hezekiah Calvin noticed that his Mohawk students at Fort Hunter were absent because the adults "are going out to hunt & that they must needs take their Children with them that they cant leave their Children alone &c &c."[57] One year after that, Joseph Johnson lamented that all his students were absent because they were off to "fetch some flesh from the Hunters." Iroquois hunting patterns undoubtedly hampered Indian educational efforts in New York.[58]

Unlike English missionaries, however, native preachers were less daunted by the prospect of accompanying Indians on these seasonal hunts. This was obviously true for Oneida preachers like Good Peter and Deacon Thomas, the latter of which aspired to participate in a spring hunt in 1768 to help pay off a personal debt. In fact, for most Native American societies, hunting was understood not only as a subsistence strategy, but also an opportunity to demonstrate masculinity, cultivate group cohesion, and contribute to the welfare of the community. As such, native preachers often took the opportunity to accompany the Iroquois on their seasonal hunts, hoping to strengthen cultural bonds while simultaneously carrying on some semblance of Christian education among them. During his missionary trip to the Oneidas in the spring of 1762, for example, Samson Occom opted to "wander about after" his students because they were scattered around, trying to find food.[59] Joseph Johnson, another Mohegan and Occom's son-in-law, went hunting with the Iroquois in May of 1768. This was because the ones who remained in his Oneida town during the hunt were, in his estimation, "hardly worth staying for." Native preachers were more opportunistic than

English ones in their attempt to use the hunt as a chance to prove their mettle, procure some food, and connect with the very people they were trying to convert.[60]

In spite of their willingness to join the Iroquois on their seasonal hunts, the eastern Algonquian Indians who comprised a large share of the missionary corps nevertheless emphasized agriculture, rather than hunting, as the true path to living like Christians. No one exemplified these attitudes better than David Fowler, the Montauk Indian who oversaw a school and worked alongside Samuel Kirkland at the Oneida town of Kanonwalohale in the mid-1760s. When Wheelock introduced Fowler to the Iroquois, he declared that the Montauk would not only be a missionary, but also a weapon against the periodic famines and starvation that plagued Iroquoian society in the eighteenth century. "I hope you will help him to get a house," Wheelock wrote to the Iroquois, "and let him have some of your land to plant and sow." Besides instructing schoolchildren, Fowler was expected to "help and instruct you in managing husbandry; with which you must learn if you expect God will increase your number, and build you up, and make you his people."[61] The Oneidas complied and promised Fowler free but temporary use of their lands as well as some help in clearing and fencing them. They understood this as an experimental move that could provide some relief from the temporal problems they were facing. Fowler understood his agreement with the Oneidas as a precious opportunity to transform the economic, religious, and social culture of the native peoples of New York. Well before Fowler had cultivated any crops on his lands, he proclaimed—perhaps prematurely—that his Indian neophytes "see now that they would live better if they cultivate their Lands than they do now by Hunting & fishing." Native preachers also viewed the males' neglect of the fields as a marker of laziness. Fowler dubbed Oneida Indian men the "laziest Crew I ever saw in all my Days" because the women farmed while the men slept late and took care of the children. When he brought his wife Hannah to Oneida, Fowler hoped his "other Rib" would serve as a model for Iroquois women and persuade Indian men to take to the plow while their women stayed in the homes. In urging Iroquois Indians to embrace sedentary agriculture and transform gender roles, native preachers invoked the same narratives of civilization that characterized English missionary discourses.[62]

If agriculture was one marker of difference between the Moor Indians and the Iroquois of New York, language was another obvious point of dissimilarity. Wheelock's program was original in that the Indian preachers traveling to Iroquoia in the 1760s were usually not Iroquois.

There were therefore dramatic linguistic differences between Wheelock's Indian missionaries and the people they were trying to convert. This is not to say that the Moor Indians lacked linguistic skills: they were familiar with Algonquian languages and English, as well as Latin and Greek. But their inability to speak the Iroquoian dialect made them ineffective and more socially isolated than they ever might have imagined. When Joseph Woolley relayed his troubles in speaking to his students at Onaquaga, Samuel Kirkland sharply rebuked him, noting that Wheelock depended much on Woolley's "proficiency in the Indian language." Urging him to labor harder to learn the Oneida tongue, Kirkland curtly reminded Woolley that "A faithful Missionary's life is no *lazy* one."[63] David Fowler, a much better scholar than Woolley, also admitted that he could "say very little" to his students and greatly needed an interpreter.[64] Hezekiah Calvin expressed dismay at his inability to communicate sacred truths to the Iroquois, going so far as to call himself a "dumb stump that has no tongue to use."[65] Calvin might have been too hard on himself, for the problem was not only in translating words into indigenous languages, but translating Christian concepts into native ones. David Brainerd, a missionary in Pennsylvania in the 1740s, felt the pain of this problem acutely and observed that there were no Indian words for concepts like "*Lord, Saviour, Salvation, Sinner, Justice, Condemnation, Faith, Repentance, Justification, Adoption, Sanctification, Grace, Glory, Heaven,* with scores of the like importance." While Brainerd complained about the "defectiveness" of indigenous languages, native peoples also suspected the English language itself as a source of social and cultural problems.[66] Iroquois Indians were understandably reluctant to send their children to learn under native preachers who spoke the same tongue as the English traders and settlers who constantly sought to deceive them.

In spite of these linguistic differences, or perhaps because of them, native preachers pursued other ways to ingratiate themselves into the hearts and minds of the Iroquois. Oratory was one way to do that. An English contemporary noted that, among Indians, "Orators are in the highest Esteem." "To be able to speak well in public," he continued, "is the shortest and most infallible Road to Honour and Influence among" the Indians.[67] Warriors might have taken issue with this argument, but the fact remained that public speaking skills were prized by Iroquois Indians. The Moor Indians also embraced the sacred power of oratory, even as their struggles with learning Iroquoian languages hampered their efforts. When Jacob Woolley wrote to Eleazar Wheelock in the winter of 1761, he complained that writing was but a "silent language" that could not convey exactly what he had to say as if they were conversing with one another face to face.[68] Samson Occom, reputed for his eloquence, was another native preacher who embraced the power of sacred oratory. Nearly blinded by years of intense reading and study, Occom often preached extemporaneously to Indian congregations from Iroquoia to Long Island. He complained that the sacred texts produced by Anglo-Americans were too often "written in a high and refined language . . . in a very high and lofty style." Occom's preaching, by contrast, was universally celebrated as powerful but plain, clear but eloquent, moving and articulate. Occom said that his oratorical style was "common, plain, every day talk," so simple that children, blacks, and especially Indians could understand him. He employed common phrases, metaphors, and incidents from everyday life in his preaching to Iroquois in New York, Mohegans in Connecticut, and Montauks on Long Island.[69] The Moor Indians' training gave them a chance to situate themselves as eloquent orators who wielded the power of speech and speaking, even if their audiences did not always understand what they were saying. Although Wheelock's training did not prepare its native missionaries to speak Iroquoian, it certainly trained them *how* to speak among this so-called "nation of orators."[70]

This aural self-presentation by the Moor Indians accompanied a visual representation, and clothing constituted an important medium whereby native preachers represented themselves as powerful cultural intermediaries. Part of this had to do with security, as native preachers changed their dress depending upon their location in English or Indian country. But, like oratory, it was believed that Iroquois Indians respected and understood clothing as a marker of social distinction and value. Hendrick, the Mohawk lay preacher of the early eighteenth century, was—at least in dress—reported to be barely distinguishable from an English gentleman. When Joseph Brant arrived at Wheelock's school in Connecticut, everyone knew he was from a "Family of Distinction" because he was "considerably cloathed."[71] This emphasis on status in clothing also explains why David Fowler was quick to lend fellow missionary Joseph Woolley his shirt when he discovered that his colleague was "almost nacked."[72] Nudity was a symptom of poverty, and native preachers could never appear wanting if they hoped to convert the thousands of Iroquois who expected Christianity to ameliorate their own poverty.

Some evangelists even expressed a preference for certain colored clothes. David Fowler, for example, asked in January of 1766 for some "blue Broadcloth and that which is good." Fowler repeated this request before he returned to Wheelock's school later that spring. He planned to stay at Wheelock's home for a week or so "to shed my Skin" and admitted that his clothes were so worn that he, like Woolley before him, was almost naked. Again, he wrote to Wheelock and demanded, "I want all my Cloaths to be blue and that which is good."[73] While Fowler's obsession with high quality, blue clothes might seem peculiar, it is possible

Samson Occom. (Image courtesy of Hood Museum of Art, Dartmouth College, Hanover, New Hampshire: gift of Mrs. Robert White Birch, Class of 1927W.)

that he was hoping to use his clothing as a reminder of his status as a Christian preacher. Eastern woodland Indians revered objects with a blue or blue-green hue because they believed that the translucent quality of these colors reflected their status as visual intermediaries between the natural and supernatural worlds. By aggressively demanding that he be outfitted in blue vestments, Fowler might have been seeking to remind his Iroquois audiences that he was an Indian of impressive power, a spiritual medium who exhibited a masterful awareness of and access to the natural and supernatural worlds around them. By asking for "good" cloth, Fowler was also hoping to remind his audiences that he was indeed an Indian of worldly value as well. Even Paulus, the Mohawk catechist, was reported in 1755 to be "splendidly arrayed in a suit of light blue, made in an antique mode, and trimmed with silver lace."[74] Like Paulus before him, Fowler sought to tap into Iroquoian understandings of the translucence of certain colors as well as the importance of clothing as a marker of social standing in indigenous societies.

The records of these missions also give us a sense of how native evangelists spoke, what messages they emphasized, and which rhetorical devices they used when preaching to Iroquois Indians in the 1760s. Oneida preachers like Good Peter and Deacon Thomas were particularly adept at describing Christian spiritualities with Oneida concepts and cosmologies. Good Peter, for example, called the Christian God "the great God, who created all things." In explaining Christ's divinity, Peter assured his Oneida audiences that God "walked on earth with men, and had the form of a man, but He was all the while the same Great Spirit; He had only thrown his blanket around Him."[75] By describing God as a kind of shape-shifter, Peter explained to his Oneida brethren that God was both human and divine, an active and ever-present force in their world. Peter, Isaac, and Thomas had the benefit of being Oneida insiders, but the Moor Indians had no such advantage and often acknowledged their precarious position as Indian Christians among other Indians. When Occom preached to the Iroquois, he complained little about "Indian fopperies, and manner of dress," and reproached them only for their use of painting as bodily decoration. Instead, Occom sought to "strike at the root of evil, and insist on heart religion." Although "heart religion" is a wonderfully vague description of Occom's preaching, he probably urged his listeners to embrace charity, humility, and a solemn reflection on their own humanity and spiritual frailty. Like other eastern Algonquian preachers, Occom preached delicately and trod carefully when trying to transform Iroquois Indians into devout Christians.[76]

Other native preachers emphasized the fire and brimstone approach of the First Great Awakening, advising Indian audiences to acknowledge their sins and consider the punishments they would face if they continued to live in pagan darkness. While we do not have records of Joseph Johnson's preaching to the Oneidas, his later sermons among other Indian groups are instructive. All people, Johnson proclaimed, were "children of wrath" and were destined to descend into a hell that "burns with unquenchable fire and brimstone." Christ's power could save Indians from this terrible fate, and Johnson cunningly described Christ as a kind of spiritual physician who could defend Indians against the diseases of evil.[77] In 1767 one of the Oneida preachers encouraged his audience to recognize the evils of drinking and the perils of ignoring their Christian missionaries. "Brethren I think we are poor miserable Creatures," the Oneida speaker declared. He then proclaimed that the only way to rise above their spiritual poverty was to confess their sins and find ways to enhance "the Glory of God."[78] At the same time, Oneida audiences sometimes found the constant talk of sin, wrath, fire, and brimstone to be excessive. One Indian complained to an English missionary that he was completely content until Christians introduced the concept of sin into his life. When he fell on hard times, he accused an English missionary of being "the cause of it, by your continual talk of sin, sin, sin, as tho' there was nothing else in the World." The Oneida concluded that the missionary was "a Plague to me, you give me all this trouble."[79] Sin was an alien concept for most eastern woodland Indians, so it was difficult for native missionaries to shoehorn it into existing Iroquoian cosmologies. When native preachers taught their students about sin or discoursed with their neighbors on the subject, it had the potential to backfire and make already unstable cultural relations increasingly more volatile.

Native preachers emphasized the eternal punishments of hell, but they also outlined the everlasting rewards of living a pious Christian life. Samuel Ashpo frequently spoke to the Oneidas of the glories of the "upper World." In other sermons among other Indians, Ashpo asked his audiences to "set their mind heavenward," and think of the eternal blessings they would receive once they were accepted into heaven. Avoiding the thorny issue of original sin in his sermons, Ashpo spoke to Indians "chiefly about the latter Day" and encouraged his listeners to prepare for the coming of Christ, the day when every man had to give an account of their lives, actions, and deeds.[80] Influenced by English ministers, Oneida preachers, and Algonquian evangelists like Samuel Ashpo, Oneida Indians began transforming their varying ideas about heaven, and not all of them were in tune with what English missionaries had envisioned.

Many listened carefully to their missionaries' words but did not understand the complicated subtleties of Christian theology. Samuel Kirkland observed in 1773, for example, that Oneida Indians had "conceived a notion, that an external good behaviour with learning the Decalogue as to repeat it without Book, was all the divine law intended or required" for them to obtain *"eternal life."* If this was truly the case, the Oneidas themselves were not the only ones to blame, for English and Indian preachers alike emphasized rote memorization in their schools and preached the doctrine of exemplary living in their sermons.[81]

Some Oneidas came to believe that, in order to be absolved of their sins, all they had to do was confess or undergo another baptism, which would wash away their misdeeds. Samuel Kirkland complained that loud and boisterous Indian feasts became an "essential part" of these baptisms. What Kirkland may not have realized was that name-changing was a frequent and important ceremony in eastern woodland Indian society, a rite of passage that was embraced and celebrated by the entire community. Samson Occom reported that Long Island's Montauk Indians, for example, understood name-changing as a central component of life's cyclical development, a celebration performed not only by the newly named Indian but also by the entire community. "They used to make great dances or frolicks," Occom reported, and the Montauks "made great preparations for these dances, of wampum, beads, jewels, dishes, and cloathing [sic], and liquor." Renaming was so common among them that it was not unusual for Indians to "name their children two or three times over by different names, and at different times, and old people very often gave new names to themselves." The celebratory nature of Indian name changing explains why Iroquois Indians "dance and frolic" after a baptism, where the newly baptized candidate took "part in the songs, and walk[ed] in the dance." Baptism was a definitively Christian sacrament, but it was situated relatively easily into eastern woodland Indians' traditions of name-changing as a central moment of personal development. Oneida Indians thus embraced some aspects of Christian evangelism, especially ones, like baptism, that were easily incorporated into their own religious worldviews. At the same time, native preachers like Samson Occom and Good Peter—who both experienced their own name changes in years prior—were active participants in helping Oneidas and other eastern woodland Indians translate Christianity on their own terms and into their own cultural vernacular. Baptisms and name changing were vital to this process of religious translation.[82]

Songs were central to expressions of Iroquoian spirituality, and native preachers used song as a medium through which to communicate Christian messages. In spite of the differences in their preaching styles, native preachers all used Christian psalms and hymns to engage Iroquoian audiences and tap into indigenous traditions of orality, song-singing, and community-building. "Psalmody," a Presbyterian missionary in Pennsylvania once observed, "is exceeding pleasing to the *Indians*," and the short structure of the psalms was particularly suited for integration into Iroquoian song culture.[83] One commentator noted that Indians' songs were sung "in short parts" and "in short lines or sentences."[84] Psalms and hymns, more than any other sacred text, were therefore easily adaptable to the Iroquoian cultural and ritual landscape. Good Peter and Isaac, who preached at several Oneida towns before the Moor Indians arrived, carried with them "no other book but the Psalms" when they undertook itinerant missionary trips to their neighbors.[85] Eleazar Wheelock's school had a renowned reputation for producing not only able missionaries, but excellent singers. It is no surprise that the native preachers who preached to the Iroquois also turned to psalms and hymns as a way to attract indigenous audiences to Christianity. David and Jacob Fowler both boasted that their singing schools were successful, and that their Iroquoian students could sing "many Tunes with all three Parts."[86] When Wheelock sent David Fowler a packet of new books, three of them were exclusively about sacred music. While Joseph Johnson could not keep his younger students in the day school, the singing school he ran every evening was characterized by "very full meetings."[87]

No native preacher was as ardent in his devotion to psalmody and hymnody as Samson Occom. Occom believed that singing was not just pleasant, but a critical ingredient of Christian spirituality. He thought it was the "Duty of Christians to learn the Songs of Zion, according to good Method or Rule; but the People ought not to be contented with the outward Form of Singing, but should seek after the *inward* Part." Not only did these songs of Zion comfort those with spiritual anxiety, Occom declared, they would also prove to be very "destructive to the Kingdom of Satan." This explains why Occom wrote handmade songbooks and even published original hymns in 1774. Iroquois Indians thus accepted Christian songs much more readily than they did Christian education, and native preachers understood the power of music to draw a crowd.[88]

And yet, Occom's distinction between *inward* and *outward* singing underscores the danger of singing, especially its potential for profane superficiality. English and Indian preachers like Occom understood singing as a serious task, one that demanded contemplation, reflection, and *gravitas* more than it did a good voice. John Witherspoon, a supporter of Wheelock's missionary program, president of the College of New Jersey, and later tutor of two African evangelists, agreed that music was not to be taken lightly. Music was one of the "fine arts," Witherspoon opined, but when it was applied for the purposes of "amusement only," music immediately becomes "wholly contemptible." Singing without religious purpose was "a disgraceful calling" that was "not consistent with the character of a gentleman."[89] Other observers agreed and noted that Iroquoian singing was not indicative of a serious turn towards Christianity, but rather showed that they only embraced the more zealous and extreme of evangelical Christianity's elements. Sir William Johnson, who initially supported Wheelock's native missionary program, declared that the Iroquois Indians had not made much progress in Christian knowledge since Wheelock's Indians began their cultural offensive. "Their whole time," Johnson complained, was spent "in Singing psalms amongst the Country people." Johnson believed that this not only caused the Iroquois to neglect their hunting and public affairs, but also forced them to imbibe "an air of the most Enthusiastical Cant" along with "Belchings of the Spirit." Instead of transforming them into truly pious Christians, Johnson believed that native preachers and their psalm singing only left Iroquois Indians with zealous religious enthusiasm and "a Sett of Gloomy Ideas." Singing could be evidence of sincere Christian piety, but it could also belie an excessive, ecstatic zeal.[90] Through their oratory and self-representation, preaching and teaching, and through their participation in seasonal hunts and employment of sacred music, the Moor Indians tried to plant the seeds of Iroquoian Christianity during a period of intense cultural encounter.

The eastern Algonquian Indians who embarked for New York in the 1760s never really succeeded in their mission. In Iroquoian society but not from it, markedly distinct from their own people by virtue of their education, and unique in their access to Christian spiritual authority, native preachers constantly struggled to understand their missionary labors and their potential converts. Their letters back to Eleazar Wheelock expose the challenges and conflicts that this native missionary project generated. The intermingling of ambitious Indian preachers, imperious English supervisors, and cunning Oneida audiences catalyzed a host of conflicts. Although these conflicts resulted in the downfall of Wheelock's program, they did little to dissuade other Protestant ministers from recruiting, training, and employing indigenous missionaries.

While Christian missions have been characterized by physical violence and cultural conflict, there were important opportunities for conversation, negotiation, and even mutual accommodation between the Moor Indians and their Iroquois audiences. The Moor Indians were certainly not coerced into traveling to Iroquoia and, in spite of their misgivings about Iroquoian culture, they truly looked upon their New York neighbors as Christians in the making, future brothers who might share in the glories of the gospel. David Fowler admitted that the main goal of his teaching was in "Spreading the Gospel among the Pagans," whom he considered to be "my brethren."[91] When Hezekiah Calvin contemplated leaving the missionary life behind, the only thing that made him hesitate was his loss of his Mohawk friends. "The state and condition of my Friends & fellow Brethren would be hovering in my mind daily," Calvin admitted, "so that I was almost ready to conclude to spend my life amongst them . . . if I could but have it in my Mind that I should be likely of doing them any good." He concluded that "I should be very glad . . . to see my Brethren become Christians and live like Christians."[92] Joseph Woolley also expressed a sentimental concern for the plight of Iroquoian souls. Three months after he arrived at his mission at Onaquaga, Woolley declared that "My Soul seems to be more and more upon the perishing Pagans in these Woods: I long for the Conversion of their Souls, and that they may come to the Knowledge of our Lord Jesus, and be saved."[93] Joseph Johnson entreated God to "make me a blessing to the Children which he has committed to my charge," while Samson Occom felt "a General Concern . . . riveted in my Heart, for my Poor Brethren . . . Both for their Bodies and Souls." When Occom undertook a famous but taxing fundraising trip to the British Isles, he claimed he did so not to boost his reputation or gain fame. Instead, as he said, he went "purely for the poor Indians."[94] These native preachers were not avaricious and self aggrandizing imperialists, and they appear to have truly cared about the lives and souls of their Indian brethren on the borderlands.

But the line between altruistic beneficence and condescending pity was extremely thin in the eighteenth century, especially in missionary discourses. As much as native preachers saw the Iroquois and other Indians as their "brethren," they also recognized that their unique position as indigenous evangelists had elevated them in English eyes. Some native preachers attributed this elevated status to their own intellectual acuity while others gave the glory to God. David Fowler praised and thanked God because he "distinguished me from many of my poor Brethren, in setting me up to be their Instructor."[95] David's brother, Jacob, thanked Wheelock (instead of God) for "his goodness to chuse [sic] me out from my stupid Brethren and to bring me into his School."[96] Jacob Woolley, a young Delaware Indian who left the College of New

Jersey because of his perpetual tantrums, was completely humiliated by and ashamed of his behavior. If he was a normal Indian, Woolley implied, his actions might have been understandable. But Woolley was ashamed because "of the peculiar Obligations I am under to God & Man, by whose Goodness & their Charity I have been so distinguished from all my Nation."[97] Native missionaries' sense of status and superiority derived partly from Wheelock himself, who described non-Christian Indians in the lowest of terms. He called them "poor stupid creatures" at the "level of brutal Creation." Their children were "little savage wretches" who lived in "little despicable bark huts." Wheelock viewed Indians as a whole as "poor, greasy, lousy, half starved creatures," and "the most ignorant, sordid, and miserable of the human Race."[98] While Wheelock's son dubbed Indians "a Swarm of tawny Immortals," another missionary described them as "little tawny Wretches."[99] Native preachers certainly imbibed some of Wheelock's invective against non-Christian Indians and harnessed it to forge their own identity as Christian Indians whose souls had presumably been saved.

These missionary discourses frequently sounded like racialized commentaries, and native preachers developed a host of examples to demonstrate that their Iroquoian neophytes were quite different from themselves. Some of this was subtle and nuanced. Samson Occom, for example, rejected the Anglo-American assumption that Indian bodies were particularly well-suited for evangelical work on the frontier. After several weeks in Iroquoia in 1762, he admitted that the "Climet and the way that I am obliged to Live here, will never suit my Constitution."[100] In these few words Occom differentiated himself from his Indian hosts while simultaneously staking claim to English bodily civility. As Occom's letter reveals, the material comforts they lacked played into this rhetoric, for native preachers frequently complained that they lived like dogs, ate the poorest of foods, verged on the edge of starvation, and were ensconced in unbelievable material poverty when in Iroquoia. Joseph Woolley was appalled by the way in which Indians neglected a famous Delaware chief named Squash Cutter, who had died from the smallpox. "This poor man was left destitute by all his Friend, & Relations, had nobody to tend him," Woolly recalled, and he was "sorry & greaved [sic] to see in the Indians so much Brutality, that they caired [sic] no more for each other than the Beasts do."[101]

When native preachers became frustrated at the ineffectiveness of their evangelical labors, they often blamed the stubborn nature of the Iroquois Indians for their failures. Hezekiah Calvin had hoped to do some good "among these Savages," but their refusal to embrace Christianity (at least along Calvin's lines), forced him to conclude that nothing could be done for them, for "Indians will be Indians."[102] Joseph Johnson—the same man who called an Iroquois student at Wheelock's school an *"Indian Devil"*—took it one step further by equating Iroquoian recalcitrance with demographic extinction. Replicating an argument he heard many times from Wheelock, Johnson declared that, "if the Indians now Refuse the Offered Gospel it will be wonder if God don't in his anger cut them off from his Earth."[103] Johnson's extinction trope also dovetailed with missionary discourses concerning the land: civilized Christians were destined to spread light into places of darkness while uncivilized indigenous peoples were destined to retreat before it. When Indian preachers described the Iroquoian landscape, they often called upon biblical allusions of non-Christian lands as a wilderness, a desert, and as "the Gall of Bitterness and the bond of Iniquity."[104] Moor Indians thus described Iroquoia as a barren country destitute of any religious light at exactly the same time that Anglican Philip Quaque was saying the same thing about West Africa. When David Fowler beat his Iroquois students so badly that it made "their Hands to Swell very much," his actions were a violent manifestation of the religious, geographic, and racial tensions that plagued the relationship between Moor Indians and their Iroquois hosts.[105]

Although these discourses appear overtly racist, pity, rather than racism, was at their core. Pity was a powerful rhetorical tool, for it helped colonizers craft imperial identities while defining them as distinct from the colonial "other." While the objects of colonization were objects to be pitied, colonial subjects fabricated their own imperial identities based upon their pity of another group. To be pitied was, in short, to lack power. Conversely, to pity another person was to possess power.[106] Pity therefore gave eastern Algonquian evangelists another way to distinguish themselves from their Iroquoian neophytes. Like their imperious English colleagues, native preachers dolled out pity, not received it. David Fowler described his Oneida hosts, for example, as "lazy and sordid Wretches." "But," he clarified, "they are to be pitied, not frown'd." Fowler had hoped that he could help these "poor creatures" cleanse their souls and "weaken the strong Holds of Satan in this Place."[107] Joseph Woolley explained in 1765 that "My heart feels sorry for the poor Indians, that they know no more about our crucified Saviour."[108] Fowler, Woolley, and other Moor Indians' efforts to bestow pity not only gave native preachers a chance to define the indigenous "other," it also afforded them the opportunity to simultaneously work out and articulate their own unique identities as Christian Indian preachers among non-Christian

Indians. For native preachers, pity was a sacred marker of difference, not necessarily a racial one.

In his sermon to an Indian who had been sentenced to death for murder, Samson Occom clarified what he and his colleagues meant when they described other Indians as pitiable beasts in the wilderness. For Occom, the distinction was not ultimately a racial one, but one delineated by the sacred workings of God's grace. "Sin," not race or culture, Occom implied, "has made him [man] beastly and devilish." In fact, the sinful man was not even on the level of beasts, for he was "sunk beneath the beasts, and is worse than the ravenous beasts of the wilderness." Occom's wilderness was less a physical place and more of a metaphorical space characterized by an absence of Christian revelation and a dominion of Satanic power. Even though the Indian murderer to whom Occom preached was a "poor miserable object" who had lived in "folly and madness, and enormous wickedness," he was ultimately redeemable. He was not to be pitied because he was an Indian, but rather because he was not a Christian and thus had no access to divine forgiveness for his wickedness.[109]

Occom had come to this conclusion about race and pity well before he gave this sermon in 1774. About thirteen years prior, during his first missionary trip to the Iroquois, Occom traveled across Indian and English lands. One thing that Occom took note of was the appalling lack of religious devotion from so-called English Christians. "I have thought there was no Heathen but the wild Indians," Occom recorded in his travel journal, "but I think now there is some English Heathen." He believed that these English non-Christians were "worse than ye Savage Heathens of the wilderness" because they had the light of the gospel all around them (in ministers, churches, and sacred texts), but neglected to embrace its saving power.[110] For Occom and other native preachers, the distinctions they noticed between indigenous peoples and themselves seemed overtly racial. In the end, however, they ultimately believed that these distinctions were superficial, able to be immediately lifted through the repentance of the sinner and the grace of God. While Europeans and Americans were beginning to think of racial differences as immutable, natural, and biological, native preachers believed that these differences were conditional upon the sentiment of the sinner and the benevolence of the Almighty. Native preachers pitied non-Christian Indians partly because it helped them work out their own thorny identity crises, but also partly because they truly believed that their neighbors and brethren could never share in the eternal glories of the afterlife if they continued to live and sin as they did.

Because native preachers depended upon the approval of Oneida Indians, the rapport between evangelists and traditional leaders was absolutely crucial to the development of this missionary project. Samson Occom's first trip to the Oneidas in 1761 may not have been a rousing evangelical success, but he did win the respect and affection of Oneida leaders. They told him that they were "glad from the inside of our Hearts that you are come here to teach the right way of God" and presented him with a ceremonial wampum belt before he departed.[111] When Samuel Kirkland introduced Delaware Indian Joseph Woolley as schoolteacher to the Oneidas at Onaquaga, the Indians widely approved and promised to adopt him into their tribe. After Woolley died later that year, Good Peter, Thomas, Isaac, and other Christian Oneida leaders wrote to Wheelock to declare that his former pupil was a "very Sober Man, a very good Teacher," and that Woolley "understood ye Book well." "We fear," the Oneidas concluded, "there are none will equal his place."[112] There were also opportunities for collaboration between existing Oneida preachers and the Moor Indians. David Fowler, for example, relied upon the logistical and spiritual assistance of Deacon Thomas during his mission to Kanonwalohale, so much so that Fowler proclaimed that Thomas had "done me more Service than all the Town."[113] If established Oneida preachers like Good Peter, Isaac, and Deacon Thomas felt threatened or overshadowed by their eastern Algonquian counterparts, they rarely showed it, for they often showered the Moor Indians with compliments and supported them in ways that were indispensable to their missions.

At the same time, the Oneidas were very discerning and particular in their expectations for native missionaries and were especially quick to show disapproval if their guests brought shame upon themselves or their calling. Samuel Ashpo, whom the Jeningo Oneidas requested for a preacher in the first years of the 1760s, was accused several times of "Drinking Strong Drink to Excess, & of Quarrellg [sic], Indecent, unChristian behaviour," during and after his mission. The Oneida Indians in that small town were infuriated with Ashpo's behavior, which discredited both Ashpo in particular and Wheelock's program in general.[114] Hezekiah Calvin had a difficult time trying to cultivate amicable relationships with his Mohawk hosts at Fort Hunter. Part of this might have been due to his imperious nature and his inability to heed certain Mohawk social mores. The Mohawks were appalled that Calvin refused to eat their food, greet them when entering their homes, or move out of the way of others. For his own part, Calvin believed that the Mohawks "think that I am their Servant." The *coup de gras* for Calvin's reputation was when he got drunk and threw a rampage among his Mohawk charges. Calvin later chalked his misbehavior up to the fact that he was in love. Although love may have driven Calvin crazy, his social isolation and insecurity about his spiritual authority among the Mohawks contributed to his fall.[115]

The Oneidas tolerated some missteps by their missionaries, but Ashpo's and Calvin's problems paled in comparison to the outbursts that Joseph Johnson instigated in the spring of 1768. Around that time, as he was teaching among the Oneidas, Johnson began exhibiting a remarkable lack of social and sexual restraint; he and another Indian drank three gallons of wine, destroyed household furniture, hired prostitutes (and bought them valuable trinkets), and wasted provisions. Summarizing the incident later, Kirkland reported that Johnson "turn'd pagan for about a week—painted, sung,—danc'd—drank & whor'd it, wh some of the savage Indians he cou'd find."[116] Johnson later admitted that his actions were completely inexcusable, writing to Wheelock and apologizing for indulging in "Brutish Ease whilst in the wilderness." His fall, he explained, was not an attempt to bond with the Indians, but was instead "Occasioned by the temptation of the Devil."[117]

What made the entire scenario even more problematic was that Johnson's debaucheries were "taken Notice of by the Indians." As word leaked that one of the arbiters of Christian morality lost all sense of it, Johnson's reputation became shattered. Deacon Thomas implored Johnson to salvage his character by making a public Confession, "as is their Custom." In an illuminating role reversal, the Oneidas demanded that Johnson—the Christian missionary—make a public confession of his sins. Johnson later explained that, after his confession, the Oneidas agreed to "Bury in Oblivion" everything that had happened and to act as it "never happened so."[118] In spite of their promise to forget his misdeeds, the Oneidas and Mohawks continued to look upon Joseph Johnson unfavorably and suspiciously, and he left his missionary post later that year in complete dishonor. "His name stinks," Samuel Kirkland reported, "from Kanajohare to Fort-Stanwix." Kirkland declared that even the road that connected Iroquoian communities in northern New York "smells very strong of his pride, falsehood, & diabolical Conduct."[119] Christian missions—and especially these native missions—were delicate affairs, and Johnson's erratic and undisciplined behavior did irreparable damage to the Moor Indians' objectives.

It was no coincidence that Oneida Indians began expressing a guarded suspicion of the Moor Indians at about this same time. In February of 1769, the Oneidas removed their children from Wheelock's school in Connecticut, partly because of Johnson's missteps and partly because they had heard how draconian a disciplinarian Wheelock could be. Iroquois Indians traditionally treated outsiders, even enemy captives, with relative kindness and even respect, and they expected Wheelock and other educators to reciprocate that relationship. A council of Indians at Onandaga, where the Iroquois traditionally held important meetings that involved all members of the Confederacy, told Wheelock's son that his father could learn much from the French Jesuits: "They don't speak roughly, nor do they for every little mistake take up a club & flog them."[120] This may have appeared like a sudden turn in attitude, but the Oneidas had always had their suspicions about Wheelock's program. Sir William Johnson reported that Iroquois Indians "despise" the Moor Indians because they appeared impoverished and constantly complained about their loss of land in the east.[121] After Johnson's fall, Kirkland earnestly warned Wheelock not to send any more of his revered Indian preachers. "It wont be acceptable to ye ppl here," Kirkland explained. Kirkland even begged Wheelock to keep native preachers out of Iroquoia "until there is good evidence to believe ye Indian Devil & evil spirit is gone out of him."[122] The Moor Indians were gradually developing a reputation as rabble rousers and intruders who had clearly worn out their welcome. Perhaps they wore out their necessity, too. After the arrival of the Moor Indians, the Oneidas began their own school, where boys and young men learned outside of the institutional framework of the missionary schools. The Oneidas had invited Algonquian preachers into their homes, lives, and lands as a way to secure their futures, but the Moor Indians had disappointed them.

To make things even more problematic, the intercultural conflicts were not just between the Moor Indians and their Iroquois audiences, but also between Indian missionaries and white ones, native missionaries and each other, and Moor Indians and Wheelock. David Fowler, for example, labored to establish his own authority as a teacher even as white ministers sought to boss him around. He complained that white missionary Samuel Kirkland, Fowler's colleague and housemate, thought he was better than indigenous evangelists and could "order us about where and how he pleased." It got so bad that Fowler demanded Kirkland never speak his name again, and he warned Wheelock not to give any preacher enough authority to order Indians about. "He can't order me," Fowler quipped, "nor no Missionary that shall come into these Parts. As I am an Instructor I am able to act for myself, without having a master over me."[123] Joseph Johnson had a similar encounter with Kirkland when the white missionary ordered Johnson to gather some firewood. Johnson refused, sparking a heated quarrel about their relative authority in the borderlands.[124] Even native preachers had petty rivalries with one another, like when Samson Occom demanded that Samuel Ashpo, another Indian preacher who had different political allegiances than Occom, not be allowed to enter Wheelock's school. Occom complained about Ashpo's "irregular steps" and sought to bar him from exercising the same spiritual authority that he himself wielded.[125] Even the indigenous Oneida preachers who were already well-established on the borderlands experienced some of these tensions and conflicts. When the Revolutionary crisis began to heat up, the Iroquois sometimes declared their allegiances based upon religious preferences: many of the Anglicized warriors (like Joseph Brant) sided with the Anglicans and the English, while some Christian Oneidas (who were friends with Kirkland) sided with the colonists. Isaac hoped to join the former while Good Peter opted to ally himself with the latter.[126]

The most problematic conflict that developed in the late 1760s was not between the Moor Indians and the Oneidas, but between the Moor Indians and their benefactor, Eleazar Wheelock. Wheelock's domineering comportment and inconsistent support led many of his former students to believe that they were only pawns in his effort to amass power and influence. Ever-willing to speak his mind, David Fowler strongly believed that Wheelock had not supported him as faithfully as he could have during his mission to the Oneida. He even contrasted his own intellect, successful training, and evangelical abilities with those of other Indian missionaries. Fowler protested that Wheelock spent too much time codling them while ignoring him. "I think it very strange," he complained to Wheelock, "that one who has done most should be forgotten." "All those which have been sent into those parts have not done any thing worth mentioning. All what they have done is only roving abroad and making the Indians angry," Fowler quipped.[127] Wheelock did not take Fowler's comments seriously, but instead attributed them to intrinsic Indian vices. For Wheelock, Indians were particularly susceptible to three distinct but overlapping sins: wandering, pride, and drunkenness. In Wheelock's mind, Fowler was clearly guilty of pride. But he was not the only one. From the late 1760s to the early 1770s, Wheelock recounted innumerable instances when the best of these native preachers (Jacob Woolley, Samson Occom, Hezekiah Calvin, and Joseph Johnson) got drunk, ran away, "turned pagan," became apostates, exhibited excessive pride, and brought shame upon Wheelock, his school, and his native missionary program. The origins of these falls lay not only in the anxieties and challenges that native missionaries faced, but also in the racial stereotyping that Wheelock had absorbed and expressed throughout his career. Wheelock had astronomically high expectations for his Indian pupils, and the stresses of undergoing grueling missions to the Iroquoian borderlands often caused ruptures in the relationships between all parties involved.

Wheelock's program was in trouble by the late 1760s. The Treaty of Fort Stanwix, which extended English jurisdiction westward and into Mohawk and Oneida lands, infuriated Indians and rightfully caused them to suspect Wheelock and any other English or allied Indians who professed a desire to help them. At the same time, Wheelock's Indians were dying, leaving missionary service, or engaging in such astonishing bouts of "apostasy" that it made him question whether Indians were even capable of missionary work. Wheelock confided to George Whitefield in the spring of 1769 that his missionary experiment had gone horribly wrong, and the only practical course was to turn away from training unreliable and vice-ridden Indians and towards more dependable and trustworthy English preachers. "I am convinced," Wheelock conceded, "that God does not design that Indians shall have the lead in the Affair at present."[128] Although Samson Occom and another English minister had recently raised over 12,000 pounds for Wheelock's native missionary program, Wheelock used the funds to build an elite seminary for white missionaries. The result was Dartmouth College, an institution that graduated only three Indians from 1770 to 1800 and only nine in the nineteenth century. Wheelock turned his attention to training English missionaries for the conversion of Canadian Indians, rather than Iroquois ones. As for the Iroquois Indians that he earlier professed to care so much about, Wheelock believed that their rejection of God's offer of salvation practically sealed their fate. They shared the same destiny as that of the native missionary program initially designed to help them. Wheelock believed they were simply destined to waste away "like a morning dew."[129]

Protestant ministers around the Atlantic world understood the fall of the French in 1763 as a providential moment in the history of Christianity. The door seemed open for the Iroquois to finally embrace the saving light of divine grace, and Eleazar Wheelock sold his native missionary program as a fundamentally innovative and original proposal for sending Christianity into those parts. Native preachers, however, had longstanding histories in Iroquoia, from Mohawk schoolmasters like Abraham and Paulus to the existing Christian leadership of Good Peter, Isaac, and Deacon Thomas among the Oneidas. When eastern Algonquian Indians entered Iroquoia in the 1760s, they were not entering a Christian *terra nullius,* but rather a religious landscape that had already been well trodden by indigenous Catholic, Anglican, and Presbyterian evangelists. Their methods of instruction and self-representation, their embrace of oratory and employment of the psalms, their willingness to join Indians on the hunt, and their preaching styles all reveal how this unique group of Indians tried to spread Christianity among their neighbors. Indeed, if anything was original about Wheelock's program, it was the fact that this was the first and most aggressive attempt to use one Native American group to convert another. The conflicts that erupted from these missions, including frequent lapses by native missionaries themselves, brought an end to this ambitious evangelical design. Even the man who professed to love the Iroquois and care for their souls could not understand or empathize with their historic trials and tragedies. He turned his back on them when he opened a school for white missionaries in New Hampshire, thereby acknowledging that his native missionary program had been an abysmal failure.

Although Wheelock was eminent and influential, few ministers shared his rejection of native preachers in the late 1760s. Scottish missionaries, Samuel Kirkland, Samson Occom and other Algonquian preachers, Christian Iroquois leaders, and other divines throughout the Atlantic world universally proclaimed that Wheelock's denial of native missionaries was unfounded, irregular, and wholly wrongheaded. They generally agreed that Wheelock's motives were suspect, and that he was hoping to boost his own reputation at the expense of the native preachers he claimed to patronize. The failure of the Moor Indians did little to stop other Protestant missionary groups from cultivating native preachers in other places and at other times. Anglicans still employed native evangelists like Paulus in their Iroquoian missions, Samuel Kirkland still worked with Good Peter and Deacon Thomas to spread the gospel among the Oneidas, missionary organizations working in Iroquoia still used native preachers in their missions well after the failure of Wheelock's program. Even Wheelock's native preachers returned to Oneida in the 1780s to establish an Indian community that would serve as a base for future native missionary work. Although Wheelock's program had not succeeded, the idea of using native missionaries was never in doubt for most ministers. In fact, later ministers would understand Wheelock's program as a model for planning other missionary efforts in other places. When two ministers from Newport, Rhode Island began advertising a native mission to Africa in the early 1770s, the inescapable legacy of the Moor Indian mission to the Iroquois loomed large in their minds.

CHAPTER SIX

Afro-Christian Evangelism and Indian Missions

J OHN QUAMINE WAS ONCE AGAIN on a merchant vessel, hoping and praying that he survived the "severe storm," "high Wind," and "very dangerous gale" that threw the ship violently in and out of the tempestuous New England waters. As he tried to avoid getting sick during his turbulent ride in November of 1774, Quamine must have contemplated what he was leaving behind in Newport, Rhode Island. Indeed, the past few years witnessed several dramatic life changes for Quamine and his growing family: he married a woman named Duchess, had a son named Charles, and bought his way out of slavery through a winning lottery ticket. An equally important change was his embrace of Protestant Christianity and his successful application to become a member of Newport's First Congregational Church. This decision explained why he was on the ship. Quamine and his companion, Bristol Yamma, were being sent to the College of New Jersey (soon to be Princeton) for training as African missionaries under the tutelage of John Witherspoon. Witherspoon was not only the president of the college but also widely recognized as one of the leading divines in the Protestant Atlantic world. The headiness of the entire scenario must have caused Quamine some trepidation, for he and Yamma had little academic training and seemed ill-prepared to be tutored by one of the brightest minds in the colonies. It is probable that the last time he was on a merchant vessel he was about to become one of the millions of slaves who were transported from Africa to the Americas. Although Quamine's wealthy African father had secured safe passage for his son to be educated in the American colonies in the 1750s, a conniving merchant sold him into slavery as soon as he got the chance. Now, after Quamine's rocky ride from slavery to freedom, he was traveling to New Jersey as an African missionary-in-training, his way paid to be educated by one of the most celebrated theologians of his time.[1]

Quamine's mission remains an overlooked episode in the tangled history of cultural encounter between Europe, Africa, and the Americas. This is because his mission was thwarted before it even began. The outbreak of the American Revolution had cut off communication networks and left Newport devastated. This forced the two Africans to find alternative ways to support the families they left behind. It all ended tragically when Quamine lost his life aboard a ship in 1779 while trying to earn money for his struggling family as a privateer. Yet, this African mission was a *cause célèbre* in its own day. Not only were Quamine and Yamma the first two Africans to be trained at any colonial college, but their supporters were intellectuals of the first order. These included divines such as Ezra Stiles, Samuel Hopkins, and John Erskine, famous notables like Anthony Benezet, John Witherspoon, and Elias Boudinot (the latter two were signers of the Declaration of Independence), Africans Phillis Wheatley and Philip Quaque, and missionaries among Indians, such as Eleazar Wheelock, Samson Occom, and David McClure. Their African mission was unlike any before it, if only because of the wide swath of ecumenical support it garnered from all corners of the Protestant Atlantic missionary community. It was not just the brainchild of one minister, but rather involved Indians and Englishmen, enslaved Africans as well as slaveholders, Radical New Lights, moderate Presbyterians, Anglicans, and Old Light Congregationalists. Anglicans and Dissenters certainly had their doctrinal differences, but when it came to the evangelization of non-Christians, they could seize upon opportunities to create cross-denominational networks of funding and correspondence.[2]

The transatlantic popularity of the enterprise is not the only reason why Quamine and Yamma's story is compelling. Although the two evangelists never set sail for Africa, their experience illuminates the development of indigenous evangelical enterprises in the eighteenth century British Atlantic. Most importantly, Africans *themselves* were co-creators of this mission. While Samuel Hopkins and Ezra Stiles are usually credited with forging this mission, evidence suggests that Quamine and Yamma had already conceived the idea well before Hopkins approached Stiles about it in the spring of 1773. The two Africans were not just participants in this project; they aided significantly in its birth. Equally important is the degree to which the African mission was influenced by Native American missionary history. Quamine and Yamma were selected for this experiment just as the failure of Eleazar Wheelock's Indian preachers became evident. The mission was thus not only an effort to Christianize Africa, it was also an attempt to redeem the failed Protestant missionary enterprise by learning from the lessons of previous Indian missions and avoiding the same mistakes. As such, this African mission was generally understood as a logical extension of Christian missions to Native Americans. John Quamine's failed mission illustrates how both Afro-Christian evangelism and Indian missionary history became equally vital to the development of African missions in the British Atlantic.

John Quamine's biography reads similarly to those produced by black Atlantic writers of the same era, including Olaudah Equiano, James Albert Ukawsaw Gronniosaw, and Phillis Wheatley. Quamine was born into a Fante family around 1743. He later reported that his father was a "rich man" who lived at Annamaboe, one of West Africa's most notorious slave-trading ports on the Gold Coast. Bristol Yamma, by contrast, was an Ashanti who lived further inland. According to Quamine's account, he was sent by his wealthy father (who might have been a slave trader or broker) to the American colonies to receive an education in the mid to late 1750s. Like so many Africans who were coerced into the transatlantic slave trade, Quamine was instead shipped to Newport, Rhode Island, and sold into slavery to Captain Benjamin Church, a prosperous merchant.[3]

The Newport that Quamine encountered in the 1750s was arguably the most religiously diverse town in the British Atlantic world. Rhode Island's religious toleration meant that Old Lights, New Lights, Baptists, Sabbatarians, Anglicans, Moravians, Quakers, and Jews all mingled in its streets. At the same time, the city's deep harbor and proximity to both the town's rum distilleries and the labor-hungry farms along the fertile Narragansett Bay ensured that Newport would become a major destination for West Indian and African slaves. Newporters were very active in the slave trade in the eighteenth century. By 1755 Newport's 1200 blacks comprised nearly one-fifth of the town's population, making Charles Towne, South Carolina the only colonial city that had more Africans per capita. Like Quamine and Yamma, African slaves who came directly to Newport were usually from the Ashanti, Fante, Mandingo, Mende, or Ibo peoples of the Gold Coast, though some could have originated from much further inland. The persistence of African traditions and culture, even in an urban setting where there was not as much comparative social autonomy as in the Deep South, revealed itself in the ubiquity of African naming patterns (Quamine meant "born on

Saturday" among Akan-speaking peoples) and the perpetuation of African cultural rites, coronation days, and funerary ceremonies. When Quamine set his foot on Newport's wharves for the first time, he was stepping into a complex world filled with a wide range of Protestants, Jews, Africans, and Native Americans, and an equally diverse range of beliefs and rituals.[4]

Quamine and Yamma may not have even been the first Africans trained for missionary work to come out of Newport. Philip Quaque— the African Anglican missionary stationed on the Cape Coast—reported in 1774 that he encountered an African who was "stoled away from his Country when very young" and shipped to Newport in the 1720s. He lived in that seaport for nearly fifty years as a slave to a Quaker named Samuel Collins. In time this African became a "member or professor of Quakerism." Even as he was sitting in the segregated balconies of Newport's Quaker meeting house, confessing his sins publicly, searching for his own inner light, and engaging in the outward performances of Quakerism, he was nevertheless drawn to the remarkable religious pluralism of Newport. He became a faithful "Spectator" of the Anglican Church, though the natural antipathy between Anglicans and Quakers probably restricted him from officially joining the Anglican congregation there. His master died in 1772, presumably freeing this slave upon his death. The newly freed slave found his way back to Africa, sought baptism under Philip Quaque, and hoped to "become a Proselyte of Christianity." Although the documentary record of this African Quaker turned Anglican disappears after Quaque's mention of him, the story nevertheless anticipates the ways in which transatlantic slavery, black participation in religious activity, and religious pluralism in Newport formed the basis for transatlantic Afro-evangelism.[5]

Given the paucity of records—there is only one recorded letter written by Quamine, and that has subsequently gone missing—it is impossible to say for certain exactly what Christianity meant to either John Quamine or Bristol Yamma. Like the millions of Africans pulled into the vortex of the early modern slave system, they probably dealt with their plight by carving out a life for themselves within the circumscribed social boundaries of New England family slavery. Given their later preparation as missionaries, Christianity probably became a central component of that life. And yet, their introduction to Christianity would not have begun in Newport, but rather in Africa. Slaves' exposure to Christianity only rarely began on the American side of the Atlantic, as they often had encounters with Christianity, or at least with Christians, well before their slave ships hoisted anchor. As a coastal African who was the son of

a wealthy man at Annamaboe, there is no doubt that he had some interaction with the nominally Christian slave merchants who plied their
trade there.[6]

Quamine may have approached Christianity in the same ways that
other Christian slaves did throughout the Atlantic world: not by erasing
an African cultural past, but by fitting Christianity into existing spiritualities and cosmologies. West Africans were technically not monotheistic. They did, however, believe in a supreme power, one that created
and governed the universe. More importantly, they also believed in an
assortment of lesser divinities. Unlike the supreme and powerful God,
these divinities were very active in Africans' spiritual and temporal experiences. Many Afro-Christians understood Christ as one of these lesser
divinities; an intermediary between man, the lowest of spiritual beings,
and God himself. Christianity thus could have fit easily into a West
African cosmological system. While Afro-Christians recognized the
authority of an all-powerful Christian God, many also approached that
God through lesser divinities, especially Jesus Christ or, in the case of
Kongolese Catholics, the Virgin Mary.[7]

The physical experience of being enslaved might have only made
Christ more relevant. In Christ, slaves could identify with someone who
suffered as they did under the weight of oppression, violence, and death.
For black slaves, Christ's suffering was not just a passage from a text,
but rather a lived episode of intense physical suffering that paralleled
their own personal experiences within the transatlantic slave system.
Quamine might have applied stories from scripture to explain his own
terrible fall into this system. When Ezra Stiles asked him in 1773 which
biblical texts he read the most, he replied that he read John, Matthew,
Romans, and Corinthians. Paul's letter to the Romans and Corinthians,
as well as other Mediterranean communities, emphasized that Christian
salvation was open to everyone, and not just the Jews. Paul's letters thus
framed Christianity as an inclusive, expansive religion, rather than an
exclusive, restrictive one. Stiles then asked Quamine to read out of the
tenth book of John. "All who came before Christ," the text reads, "were
thieves and robbers." The passage explains that, while a thief plunders,
steals, slaughters, and destroys, Christ remains the faithful shepherd,
laying down his own life for his flock. As someone who not only witnessed the theft of so many African bodies from his home at Annamaboe,
but became one of those bodies himself, the story of Christ's faithfulness in a world full of duplicitous robbers would have had spiritual reso-
nance for Quamine. This might explain why, when Quamine changed
his name from Quaum to John Quamine in the early 1770s, the new

name combined both his African identity and the name of the author of one of his favorite gospels.[8]

This was certainly not a spontaneous change, for it is likely that Quamine's encounter with Christianity was a long, uneven, and protracted process within a larger trajectory of spiritual transformation. Quamine apparently "fell under serious Impressions of Religion" in 1761 and by October of 1764 he had given a local schoolteacher named Sarah Osborn an account of his Christian conversion. By 1765, Quamine had been baptized and admitted into the First Congregational Church. Bristol Yamma, his missionary colleague, followed suit three years later.[9] In 1769, Quamine sank his roots deeper into Newport's black community by marrying Duchess, an African slave four years his senior. Although they were members of the First Congregational, they had their children baptized by Ezra Stiles, who headed the Second Congregational. Their infant Charles was baptized in 1772, Violet in 1776, and Katharine in 1779. Although they were slaves, Quamine and his wife participated in the Christian rituals of conversion, baptism, and marriage.[10]

Few of these episodes would have been more important than the Newport Revival. Sarah Osborn, the teacher who recorded Quamine's first conversion narrative, was at the center of this revival. She had been influenced by the evangelical preaching of George Whitefield, James Davenport, and Gilbert Tennent years before and began leading her own religious meetings in her home in the mid-1760s. These were not religious services within the institutional framework of the church, but rather informal bible study sessions, where participants met weekly to discuss passages from scripture and relate them to their own spiritual longings, sufferings, and travails. While Osborn was painfully aware of the gendered repercussions of holding meetings at her home, her status as a well-established and older woman helped guard her against potential accusations as a religious upstart.[11]

Race was a problem, however, and the fact that Africans embraced Osborn's teaching made her both praiseworthy and dangerous. In fact, Africans initially approached Osborn to request Christian instruction. As Osborn noted to a friend in 1765, there were "several Ethiopians thotful [sic] who Having their Liberty to go where they like on Lords day Evenings have ask'd Liberty to repair to our House for the benefit of family prayer reading etc."[12] In spite of the resistance she might have received from the community, Osborn thought it her Christian duty to lead these meetings. By the summer of 1766 she had 300 people—white and black—attending her meetings. By the beginning of 1767 that number rose to 525, literally filling her house with freedmen and slaves in search of spiritual elucidation. While some members of the community accused her of keeping a "Negroe House," she responded that "I only read to them talk to them and sing a Psalm or Hymn with them, and then at Eight o clock dismiss them by Name as upon List."[13] Her list of names, the highly structured timing of the meetings, and the Africans' promise that they remain orderly and would not "come without the consent of their masters" all helped Osborn situate herself as a benevolent teacher rather than a religious exhorter.[14] Not surprisingly, two of the people who soaked in such teachings every week were John Quamine and Bristol Yamma. If Osborn dismissed her charges alphabetically, Quaum (as he was then called) and Yamma would have been among the last to leave.

And yet the significance of the Newport Revival was not only in Quamine and Yamma's participation in it, but also their developing role as spiritual advisors outside the boundaries of Osborn's weekly meetings. Although there is no evidence to indicate that either African participated in public speaking, Osborn revealed that some slaves had begun organizing their own private meetings. She observed that those who had families living in separate households (like John and Duchess Quamine) sometimes held "secret prayer." She further knew of "two or three of these [Africans] Meeting privately together to read pray and converse." Osborn even admitted that, "now I Heard Last week they are drawing up into a Little society for prayer at one of their Houses on Thursday Nights. They dont know I know any thing about it." Afro-Christians were holding clandestine religious meetings and organizing themselves around a core of black spiritual leaders. It is quite likely that Quamine or Yamma—or both—participated in these exercises well before they were hand-picked for missionary work. These two African missionaries were participating in at least some form of Christian evangelization years before they were recruited to continue it in Africa.[15]

While the growing religious autonomy of Quamine, Yamma, and other black Christians was pregnant with spiritual potential, others found it fundamentally problematic. Joseph Fish, who was not only Osborn's confidant but also the preacher at Stonington, Connecticut, knew something about the porous boundaries between revivalism and separatism. When Osborn and Fish were writing, Fish was in the midst of a dispute between himself and Indian separatist preachers in southern New England. Samuel Niles, the Narragansett Indian charged with exhorting in another congregation, had split off and formed his own independent church. Niles was "ordained" by a committee of Native Americans, a move which was viewed by most Protestants as somewhere between highly unorthodox and completely heretical. Niles was dependent upon personal and direct revelation, rather than biblical exegesis, for spiritual knowledge. Any minister worth his salt would have easily seen the problem with an illiterate Indian preaching the gospel to other Indians. When Fish admonished Osborn to be careful when preaching to blacks, he understood the separatist tendencies that Christian Indians and Africans could embrace, appropriate, and employ to secure their own spiritual independence. While it could be liberating for blacks and Indians, separatism had the potential to be dangerously democratic.[16]

This fear of separatism might also explain Ezra Stiles' sudden interest in black spirituality after 1770. That year, the same that Osborn's Newport Revival died down, Stiles began holding weekly religious meetings for blacks at his house. These meetings were smaller than Osborn's, but he sometimes had seventy to eighty blacks in attendance, many coming from outside his Second Congregational Church. Perhaps Stiles was sincerely interested in the fate of Africans' souls, or perhaps he was simply trying to use his preaching as a form of social control. Stiles' recollection of his preaching among Newport's blacks revealed their own volition in these spiritual exercises. One time in 1773, for example, they held their meeting at "Brother Primus's House" instead of Stiles'. It is highly probable that Quamine and Yamma were present at these meetings; they had already begun the first stages of their missionary training and Stiles probably assumed that any extra instruction, even practice in leading bible study, would prepare them for their mission. By 1773, Quamine and Yamma had been exposed to nearly a decade of extra-ecclesiastical Christian instruction from Sarah Osborn and Ezra Stiles, not to mention the lessons they learned weekly at Hopkins' First Congregational Church. Chances are that, in their own clandestine and subaltern meetings, they expressed some form of spiritual leadership for themselves. At the very least, their religious experiences in Newport demonstrated that spiritual leadership need not originate within the hierarchical structure of the church but rather could be generated from below.[17]

Given Quamine's transformation, then, it might have been difficult for him not to view the sudden stroke of fortune he experienced in 1773 as anything but providential. In that year he and Yamma collaborated to buy a lottery ticket. When they won, Quamine purchased his freedom and Yamma used the winnings to commence saving for his own. Such a seemingly miraculous turn of events, as well as the Christian transformation of these two Africans, demonstrated to Samuel Hopkins, Ezra Stiles, Quamine, and Yamma that the two Africans were destined for greater things than urban slavery in Newport. Only a few months later it became public knowledge that these two exceptional men were to be groomed for a mission "back" to Africa. Former African slaves, God now seemed to be smiling down on the two budding evangelists.[18]

While Quamine and Yamma's religious development remains speculative, other Afro-Christians of their ilk frequently explained their journey from African slavery to Christianity through the idea of the "fortunate fall," a literary device frequently employed by black Atlantic writers of the eighteenth century. The fortunate fall explained the horrors of their personal enslavement by suggesting that such trials were only part of God's plan to bring them to the saving grace of Christianity. This approach to black suffering neither excused nor justified slavery, but instead offered a powerful explanatory device for why bad things happened to them.[19] When James Albert Ukawsaw Gronniosaw wrote about his religious experiences within transatlantic slavery, he summarized his life as a spiritual pilgrimage that hopefully ended in salvation. "As Pilgrims," Gronniosaw commented, "and very poor Pilgrims, we are traveling through many difficulties towards our Heavenly Home, and waiting patiently for his gracious call, when the Lord shall deliver us out of the evils of this present world and bring us to the Everlasting Glories of the world to come."[20] Phillis Wheatley expressed similar sentiments in a letter to a black friend in Newport. Wheatley wrote, "let us rejoice in and adore the wonders of God's infinite Love in bringing us from a land semblant [sic] of darkness itself, and where the divine light of revelation (being obscur'd) is as darkness."[21] Perhaps the most eloquent articulation of the fortunate fall approach to black enslavement was put into verse by Wheatley:

> 'Twas mercy brought me from my *Pagan* land,
> Taught my benighted soul to understand
> That there's a God, that there's a *Saviour* too:
> Once I redemption neither sought nor knew.
> Some view our sable race with scornful eye,
> "Their colour is a diabolic die."
> Remember, Christians, Negros, black as Cain,
> May be refin'd, and join th' angelic train.[22]

Wheatley later told Samuel Hopkins that she supported Quamine's mission—which she learned of via an integrated network of evangelical printing and correspondence—precisely because of her own spiritual transformation. She admitted that her heart expanded with joy to see "the thick cloud of ignorance dispersing from the face of my benighted country. Europe and America have long been fed with the heavenly provision, and I fear they loath it, while Africa is perishing with a spiritual famine." According to Wheatley, Quamine and Yamma were the instruments whom God had selected to save the African race: "O that [Africans] could partake of the crumbs, the precious crumbs, which fall from the table of these distinguished children of the kingdom." While there is no evidence to suggest that Quamine and Yamma believed in their own fortunate fall, the evidence from other black Atlantic figures is illuminating. Gronniosaw, Wheatley, Quamine, and Yamma all hailed from the West Coast of Africa, had comparable experiences within Atlantic slavery, converted to Christianity, and understood their lives as a spiritual journey with many travails. The fact that Quamine and Yamma lived in such a religiously vibrant city suggests that they might have imbibed this fortunate fall theory, even if they did not articulate it themselves.[23]

The fortunate fall device certainly could not justify slavery itself. As Samuel Hopkins argued in 1776, enslaving Africans in order to Christianize them was a "direct and gross violation of the laws of Christ."[24] And yet, Hopkins, Stiles, and other ministers, including the two African missionaries, might have looked to African oppression as an example of how God operated in mysterious ways. Perhaps, Hopkins mused, "all this past and present evil, which the Africans have suffered by the slave trade and the slavery to which so many of them have been reduced, may be the occasion of an overbalancing good."[25] Furthermore, the use of two African missionaries seemed a wholly appropriate way to begin atoning for the sins of the slave traders. Hopkins and Stiles both spoke of missionary work as a kind of early modern reparations program. This was certainly nothing new. Anglicans had long been arguing for the conversion of black slaves as "the only righteous Recompence [sic] that can be made them for their being forc'd from their native Country into a strange Land."[26] While Stiles suggested that sending two natives was "the best compensation we are able to make the poor Africans," Hopkins later observed that the native missionary project was "the best and only compensation we can make."[27] At least for Hopkins and Stiles, there seemed no better way to absolve Christians of the sins of slavery than to send some of Africa's sons back home to help their people share in the glories of God.

Every individual involved in this mission had been touched by slavery. Quamine and Yamma were former slaves, Hopkins had a slave before he arrived in Newport in 1770, Stiles owned one for twenty years before he became the president of Yale College in 1778, and John Witherspoon possessed a slave at his death in 1794. Hopkins' battles against slavery and the slave trade have been well-documented, and Stiles also became involved in anti-slavery campaigns after the Revolution.[28] For Newporters, who depended on the transatlantic slave trade for their economic survival, slavery was the "first wheel of commerce" that transformed the idyllic port town into what Hopkins called a "Tower of Slavery."[29] It is therefore no surprise that, for Quamine and Yamma, the problem of slavery was at the core of their missionary impulse. The natural rights and republican rhetoric that pervaded college campuses, taverns, and print culture in the 1760s and 70s only stoked this abolitionist fire, as blacks throughout the Americas began appropriating the language of liberty for their own fight against slavery and racism. When Quamine and Yamma returned from Princeton in the spring of 1776, the war had already been going on for a year and the Declaration of Independence was only weeks away from being proposed. In this milieu Quamine used his newfound literary ability to express thanks to one of the colonies' most ardent abolitionists: Moses Brown. Quamine wrote that he had heard through several sources of Brown's "noble and distinguished character, and boundless benevolent engagements, with regard to the unforfeited rights, of the poor unhappy Africans." As "one of that nation," and though an "utter stranger" to Brown, Quamine wanted to present him "with gratitude and thanks . . . for all your ardent endeavours for the speedy salvation of his poor enslaved country men."[30] Although Quamine's letter to Brown is brief, it showcases the natural rights and Christian redemptive rhetoric that permeated evangelical circles in the 1770s. Perhaps Quamine anticipated that he might have a major role to play in a historic transformation. Not only would he bring Christianity back to the land of his birth, but he might also employ his newfound cultural skills to end African suffering within the transatlantic slave system.

Hopkins and Stiles are usually credited with being the sole originators of the African mission, but it seems clear that Quamine and Yamma were as much catalysts as participants. They had apparently been discussing it amongst themselves well before Hopkins asked Stiles to help advertise the mission in 1773. Conversion and missionary activity was not necessarily forced upon them; indeed, the evidence suggests that they requested education, evangelical training, and the opportunity to return to Africa as preachers. Ezra Stiles noted that the two Africans were "not only *willing*, but very *desirous* to quit all worldly prospects and risque their lives, in attempting to open a door for the propagation of christianity [sic] among their poor, ignorant, perishing, heathen brethren."[31] Quamine reported to Stiles that he began to learn to write, on his own, in the winter of 1772/73. Stiles recorded that, on April 12th of 1773, "*Quaum* came to see me to discourse upon the scheme of his becoming a Minister." "He tells me," Stiles recalled, "that ever since he tasted the Grace of the Lord Jesus he conceived a Thought and Earnest Desire or Wish that his Relations and Countrymen in Africa might also come to the knowledge of and taste the same blessed Things."[32] Quamine and Yamma were not just instruments in the mission, but rather originators and co-authors of this ambitious experiment.

The best evidence for the two Africans' authorship of this mission comes from a manuscript produced by Samuel Hopkins in 1784, when he was trying to drum up support for another African mission after this one failed to get off the ground. Although Hopkins never published the piece, it reveals that Quamine and Yamma had planned to pursue an African mission years before Hopkins and Stiles jumped on board. Hopkins admitted that, before he arrived in Newport, the two Africans "had talked of this matter between themselves." "And," Hopkins recalled, "as the gospel had never been offered to their brethren in Guinea, they said to each other, it would be agreeable to them to spend their lives in attempting to spread the knowledge of salvation among that perishing people." Hopkins took his Newport pulpit in April of 1770 and the plan was officially underway in 1773. Quamine and Yamma had been conversing about and planning this African mission at least three years before any white minister became involved. Although Hopkins and Stiles would be the ones raising money for, and acting as the public faces of, this missionary experiment, the genesis of this African mission lay in the two Africans' themselves.[33]

Quamine and Yamma might have had more personal, worldly motives for pursuing a mission to West Africa. In fact, we might read Quamine's initial adoption of Christianity in the 1760s as a response to the problem of racialized power struggles within New England family slavery. Quamine was a slave of the Church family, who attended Ezra Stiles' Second Congregational Church. When he decided to join a church, Quamine opted for the First Congregational, a decision which would not have produced the kind of conflicts that a conversion to Quakerism might, but nevertheless belied a degree of spiritual autonomy. Although the two churches were affiliated, the First Congregational had more of a New Light pedigree than the Second. Furthermore, Stiles recorded that the Church family attended religious services only three times a year, so Quamine's masters were neither particularly active in their congregation nor showy in their piety. Quamine's conversion therefore might have been a kind of power play. Slaves could certainly resist by running away, poisoning their masters, or inciting rebellion. But they also found more subtle, nuanced ways to upset and complicate the power dynamics of slavery. Quamine's admission into the First Congregational might have been *both* an act of surreptitious resistance as well as an assertion of his rights to spiritual liberty. Quamine carefully navigated the racial politics of conversion within a city founded upon the idea of religious freedom.[34]

Quamine may have conceived of the African mission because he was impelled by a sincere evangelical desire, but he also understood the mission as a way to renew contact with his African family and rejuvenate his connections to an ancestral past. Just as Indians used a network of native preachers to find information about and secure the safety of their families during King Philip's War, Quamine relied upon a transatlantic network of correspondence between native preachers, white ministers, Africans, and Americans to learn about his family back in Annamaboe. The backbone of this network was Philip Quaque, the Fetu African who had been ordained an Anglican minister and sent back to Cape Coast Castle as a missionary in 1766. While most victims of the African diaspora would never have had the chance to reunite with their families back home, their correspondence with Quaque—mediated as it was through Samuel Hopkins—gave Quamine and Yamma this unusual opportunity. When Quaque reported to Samuel Hopkins that Quamine's father (Coffee Yangoe) was dead, but that his mother (Mansa) and uncle (Eucone) were both alive and well, Quamine must have felt some joy to know that his surviving family waited impatiently for his return. Quaque even compared Quamine's mother's joy to Joseph's return to his father, Jacob, in the Book of Genesis. "The bowels of maternal affection," Quaque wrote, "seem ready to burst; and break forth in tears of joy." He continued, "The joy it kindled, on the occasion, in expectation of seeing once more the fruit of her loins, before she with her grey hairs goes to the grave, throws her into ecstasies . . . in rapture she breaks forth and says, 'It is enough! My son is yet alive! I hope, by God's blessing, to see him before I die!'"[35] Quamine's wealthy uncle, who inherited his brother's property upon his death (per West African custom), told Quaque that "nothing shall be wanting Conducive to make him and all about him Happy, and live Satisfactory amongst his own Kindred."[36] Quaque even secretly suspected that Quamine's missionary project was designed only so that the latter might begin "seeking Shelter amongst his own Kindred."[37] At the very least, these transatlantic missionary connections informed Quamine and his African family about the state of each others' welfare. At best, the African mission gave both Quamine and Yamma an opportunity to return to their native land, be embraced as prodigal sons, and live a life of comparative comfort and freedom. Not only did Quamine's spiritual transformation give him access to education and literacy, it also offered him the chance to connect with his African family in a way that few black Atlantic slaves ever could. For Quamine and Yamma, volunteering for the African mission could reap at least some temporal rewards.

Stiles and Hopkins might have wondered if Quamine and Yamma were spinning a kind of trickster tale by bankrolling their Christian conversion into secular opportunities, for both ministers revealed some doubts about the Africans' sincere conversion to Christianity. While Stiles noted that the two of them were "hopefully converted," Hopkins later recalled that Yamma and Quamine "hopefully became real Christians."[38] Given the magnitude of the mission, one could understand why Hopkins and Stiles were somewhat circumspect when discussing the conversion and piety of their African recruits. Many Protestants, especially after the First Great Awakening, understood that sincere conversions were not simply used for admittance into a church, but were instead at the core of religious experience. Conversion experiences formed the basis of all future spiritual activity, so it was important that these two evangelists had undergone legitimate ones. At the same time, Hopkins and Stiles understood the temporal advantages that missionary work could offer to former slaves, so they tempered their grammar of conversion with "hopefully" in order to guard themselves against the kind of backsliding that Eleazar Wheelock saw in his own Indians in years prior.

Hopkins and Stiles attempted to insulate the African mission by extolling their Africans as having "good character" and "good proficiency," and assuring others that they were "remarkably steady, discerning, and judicious."[39] The advantages of these native missionaries seemed obvious to the Newport ministers, especially since Quamine and Yamma were originally part of "the same nation, and speak the same language" as their future neophytes.[40] Nevertheless, doubts about the efficacy of these two Africans persisted. Even Stiles admitted in 1773 that Quamine was "not communicative, and I am doubtful whether he would be apt to teach." Stiles further noted that Quamine needed "much Improvement to qualify him for the Gospel Ministry."[41] Quamine might have become a Christian teacher, but even Stiles doubted that the African evangelist had the aptitude to become a fully ordained minister.

The most vociferous critics attacked the Quamine mission on both racial and theological grounds. One of the plan's biggest detractors was Boston's Charles Chauncy, a man whose reputation as an Old Light curmudgeon made it unclear whether the nickname "Old Brick" referred to his church building or himself.[42] When Stiles and Hopkins published a narrative of the mission and a request for donations in 1773, Chauncy and his Boston ministers balked at sending in contributions. Chauncy explained that one of the reasons why he failed to donate any funds to the training of the Afro-evangelists was because there was little hope of success *"unless they should go under the conduct of some well pointed and well qualified white person."*[43] Like Thomas Bray and Eleazar Wheelock before him, Chauncy became a voice against the use of native preachers partially on the basis of race. But the biggest problem for Chauncy was theological, not racial.

It was well-known in religious circles that Samuel Hopkins was a controversial figure, and not only because he was apparently "devoid of all the gifts of oratory."[44] His system of divinity, which became known as Hopkinsianism, was an extension of Jonathan Edwards' radical theology. One of Hopkins' most contentious arguments was that conversion must happen *before* one could pray for their own salvation. In other words, sinners who had yet to convert could do nothing to save themselves. This was a dangerous position for most Congregationalists, for many believed that such a view would alienate congregants and push them out of the church. When Hopkins was about to take his Newport pulpit in 1770, Chauncy told Stiles that Hopkins was "a troublesome, conceited, obstinate man," and that he knew of "no worse system of thot [sic] in any pagan nation, in any age" than that preached by Hopkins.[45] Another minister said Hopkins' ideas were "false, absurd, and dangerous, tending to overthrow all Religion natural and revealed."[46] When Stiles asked Chauncy for money to support the African mission, the Boston minister suggested that the Africans would be better off without Hopkins' help. He noted that Hopkins' theology was "far more *blasphemous* than were ever ones broached among the Pagans in every part of the World." Chauncy sincerely hoped that Quamine and Yamma would not get their education from Hopkins himself. If they did, and then set out to propagate that system of theology among Africans, he was *"fully of the opinion, the African Negroes had much better continue as they are."* In Chauncy's view, going from African "paganism" to Hopkins' system of divinity would "only exchange bad for worse."[47]

Stiles recognized that Chauncy's complaints would be shared by other clergy, so he assured his Boston friend that Hopkins had promised not to indoctrinate the Africans into his system. Stiles also sarcastically noted that Quamine and Yamma had "as much probability of their Learning the theory of Gravity or the intricate principia of the Newtonian system as of their making any kind of real proficiency in metaphysical erudition." Quamine and Yamma, Stiles conceded, were simply "not capable of being initiated into the metaphysical subtleties" of Hopkins' system. In this rare instance, assumptions about racial inferiority guarded the mission against Chauncy's attacks. Certainly the Africans were capable enough to merit supporting the mission, but Stiles believed they also lacked the intellectual acuity to understand the complexities and nuances of Hopkins' hazardous theology.[48]

That a conservative Old Light resisted the native missionary enterprise on racial and theological grounds is not terribly surprising. That an African missionary stationed at Cape Coast Castle would do the same thing is worth exploring. Although Philip Quaque was happy to serve as Quamine and Yamma's connection to information networks on the West Coast of Africa, Quaque had serious reservations about the ethnic makeup and religious sentiments of the future missionaries. When Hopkins initially sent Quaque a copy of *To the Public* (their fundraising pamphlet), the Anglican missionary's heart was moved "not a little" to learn that there were "still Numbers of Africans, the supposed Race of Ham, able to embrace Christianity were they in a country that yields that Light and Knowledge."[49] Quaque might have viewed Yamma and Quamine as kindred spirits, but he was nevertheless wary about the institutional origins of this mission. When Quaque discovered that Hopkins was not a Presbyterian but rather the minister of Newport's First Congregational, he reported to his Anglican benefactors that "it should be held in Everlasting scorn and Contempt by unminded Men, that those Men whom [Hopkins] spoke of as having more than common Knowledge in Theological Sciences prove at last to be Dissenters." In spite of their shared identity as African preachers, institutional and doctrinal boundaries between Anglicans and Dissenters still tore Quamine and Quaque apart. From the moment that Quaque learned of their theological leanings, he refused to help the project in any way besides gathering information about Quamine's family. In fact, he sternly warned Hopkins that "were they to put their feet again on Afric's [sic] Shore without the Support and Concurrent Testimony of both the African Committee, and my Great Benefactors the Venerable Society, they bitterly would rue the Day on which they with Reluctance parted with their happy Place of aboad [sic]."[50] Without the consent and support of English merchants and the Anglican missionary organization that supported him, Quaque believed, Quamine's mission would inevitably fail.

Interestingly, race was another reason why Quaque backed down from offering Yamma and Quamine any assistance in their mission. When

Quaque discovered that Quamine was from Annamaboe and Yamma was an Ashanti, he articulated his vitriolic hatred for those two African groups. "Those gentlemen," he said of Quamine and Yamma, "could not spring from a Race more Vicious, villainous, Revengeful, Malicious and none more brutal and obdurate in their Dispositions, than the Natives of Annamaboe [and] the adjacent Places on the interior parts of that Country." Their "delight and practice," Quaque opined, was in "shedding of Blood and distressing their fellow Brethren by frequent Disputes . . . merely to ruin their inferior Brethren." Quaque was not only referring to the practice of slave trading, but also to the intense, brutal, and violent intertribal conflicts that perennially devastated the Ashanti, Fante, and other Akan-speaking peoples of the Gold Coast. As a Fetu *and* an Anglican, Quaque expressed his scorn towards a mission of Ashanti and Fante Dissenters coming to the Gold Coast. Drawing from his perception of other Africans as impulsive, greedy, and blood-thirsty, Quaque anticipated that the two evangelists would hastily succumb to their ethnic proclivities and would "be enticed into many Vices and irregularities that they would find not so easily Eradicated."[51] These "debaucheries" included the giving of exorbitant gifts to friends, the allure of wealth and power, the spiritual backsliding that Quaque perceived all around him at the Cape Coast, and the inevitable participation in the slave wars that had engulfed the region for generations. While Quaque faintheartedly wished the Newporters the best of luck, he conceded that Quamine and Yamma had little hope of success, especially without the assistance of the Anglicans. As a proud Fetu and devout Anglican, Quaque could certainly not allow a Fante and his Ashanti companion to establish a Dissenting mission only a few miles from his own.[52]

Although the resistance of Chauncy and Quaque came from very different sources—an old Boston Congregationalist and an African Anglican stationed in the epicenter of the slave trade—their complaints reveal much about the nature of the mission. This was certainly a mission to Africans, by Africans, and the theological and racial reasons for resistance only highlight that point. Detractors described Quamine and Yamma as incapable, vulnerable to Hopkins' system of divinity, as religious upstarts, or from the most savage tribes in Africa. Furthermore, Quamine and Yamma took ownership of this mission, conceiving of it from the beginning and acting as its most important participants. Their motivations likely ranged from Afro-Christian evangelism and abolitionism to a desire to maintain connections with Africa and see their families again. Yet despite the fact that Quamine and Yamma were at the center of the mission, they certainly could not have organized it alone. Instead, Hopkins and Stiles provided the fundraising, networking, and publishing force behind the mission. When they did so, they relied upon a different missionary past—a Native American missionary past—to understand and explain why an African mission by Africans was so important.

In March of 1771 a Native American urged a woman in Boston, Massachusetts to part with her slave. This was certainly a bold request, but the Indian and the slave were not typical people. The slave was Phillis Wheatley, an African whose reputation as a celebrated poetess had sky-rocketed in the 1760s and early 70s, marking her as an example of black "genius" and making her a lightning rod for heated debates about the intellectual and spiritual capacities of black people.[53] Her would-be emancipator was Samson Occom. Occom, who urged Susanna Wheatley to emancipate her slave, Phillis, wanted Phillis to return to Africa as a Christian evangelist. "Pray Madam," Occom implored Susanna, "what harm would it be to Send Phillis to her Native Country as a Female Preacher to her kindred?" "You know," he continued, that "Quaker Women are alow'd to preach, and why not others in an Extraordinary Case?"[54] Of course, Wheatley never returned to Africa. When Samuel Hopkins asked Wheatley to participate in another African missionary project based out of Newport, Rhode Island just a few years after Occom's proposal, Wheatley graciously declined.[55] Occom's effort to recruit Wheatley as an African missionary therefore reveals a striking convergence: like other Anglo, African, and Indian missionaries in the early modern Atlantic world, the Mohegan preacher believed that Native American missionary history could serve as a working model for the future evangelization of Africa. Importantly, he also posited that African missionaries like Wheatley would be central to that effort.

The histories of Native and African Americans were certainly distinct, but early modern Protestant missionaries also emphasized their entanglements and similarities. Christian evangelists saw many connections between Native American and African missions, and their belief was rooted in early modern assumptions about the cultural histories of blacks and Indians. Many ministers believed that, despite a few obvious cultural differences between Africans and Indians, they could still be uniformly categorized as savage gentiles awaiting their conversion. John Witherspoon admitted that what struck him about the Indians of North America were the same things that characterized other indigenous peoples throughout the world: "gravity and sullenness of deportment, love of hunting and war—that is to say, depredation; ferocity to their captives, laziness and aversion to habitual labor, tyranny over the female sex, passive courage, and, if it may be called so, active cowardice, and strong passions both of lasting gratitude and unextinguishable [sic] resentment."[56] If Protestants could crack this cultural code and discover a way to convert Native Americans, it was widely presumed that the same strategy might work for Africans and other non-Christians throughout the globe.

Anglican Thomas Bray, the founder of several missionary organizations around the turn of the eighteenth century, observed that "Both the American and African Indians," were "upon the same Level, as to Matters of Religion." Any evangelical effort, therefore, may be "as proper to be pursu'd in the instruction of the one, as well as of the other." Bray even sent over a copy of evangelical instructions originally intended for South Africans to missionaries working among Indians in the American colonies. According to Bray, "African Indians"—a perplexing turn of phrase—had much in common with their indigenous counterparts in the Americas. "The Heathen in both Quarters of the World, Africa and America," he argued, "seem to us as like in Way of Living, and Sentiments of Religion, as two Eggs. And therefore we suppose, the very same Method must be taken with both."[57] Protestant ministers assumed that any perceived differences between indigenous peoples were, in the long run, superficial. They claimed that Native Americans, Africans, Asians, and even Scottish Highlanders possessed generally the same behavioral and cultural qualities. The history of missions among one would certainly have a lot to say about the success or failure of others.

It was not just white, Anglo-American missionaries who emphasized the historical comparisons and religious entanglements between Africans, black slaves, and Indians during this period. Native Americans and black evangelists (African as well as African American) frequently placed both groups within the same sacred continuum even as they were more circumspect about, and sensitive to, the salient religious differences between them. Samson Occom's attempt to free Phillis Wheatley from bondage so that she might return to Africa as a missionary was just one instance of this phenomenon. In fact, the Wheatleys, which included Phillis' mistress and master, were well informed about the native preachers working among the Indians of New England and New York, as they were family friends of Occom. The Wheatleys also served as agents for missionaries and philanthropists throughout the Atlantic world, linking Indians, Africans, and Anglo-American Protestants to a wider network of transatlantic conversations and epistolary exchange. John Thornton, a wealthy philanthropist who counted William Wilberforce, The Countess of Huntingdon, and George Whitefield among his colleagues, distributed funds to Occom via the Wheatleys. After Susanna Wheatley died in 1774, Phillis reported to Thornton that "We [meaning she and John, Susanna's husband] received and forwarded your Letter to the rev'd Mr. Occom, but first took the freedom to peruse it, and are exceeding glad, that you have order'd him to draw immediately for twenty-five pounds." Perhaps in the days following Susanna's death Phillis became a *de facto* agent of her own, an African who operated as a financial middlewoman between English philanthropy and Native American evangelism.[58]

While Phillis Wheatley's exact role in mediating between Anglo-American philanthropists and Indian missionaries remains speculative, she nevertheless placed both Indians and Africans within the same sacred history. In another letter to Thornton, Wheatley invoked the oft-cited concept of spiritual equality to stake a claim to universal Christian fellowship among both blacks *and* Indians. She noted that God was "no respecter of Persons, being equally the great Maker of all." Since God had fashioned all of his creatures equally, Wheatley argued, he would "disdain not to be called the Father of Humble Africans and Indians; though despisd [sic] on earth on account of our colour, we have this Consolation, if he enables us to deserve it. 'That God dwells in the humble & contrite heart.'" Wheatley's evangelical worldview was therefore not just oriented towards Africa and Britain, but also facing west, into Indian country. Wheatley—that celebrated poet and international epistolist—actually wrote one of her first known letters to Samson Occom, the Indian missionary.[59]

Wheatley was not alone, as other Christian evangelists encouraged religious connections between blacks and Indians. Many of the earliest Black Atlantic authors ascribed to Native Americans a vital role in their spiritual development as Christian preachers. John Marrant, a popular black minister who became pastor of a black church in Nova Scotia in the latter part of the eighteenth century, counted his alleged "conversion" of a Cherokee King in the late 1760s among his most prized accomplishments. As a teenager, Marrant had wandered into the Carolina backcountry, was taken to the Cherokees by a hunter, and was summarily sentenced to death by the king. However, in a formulaic narrative that could have drawn equally from both the story of the persecution of Christ as well as John Smith's "miraculous" rescue by Pocahontas, Marrant's prayers just moments before his execution suddenly turned the hearts of his executioner, the king's daughter, and eventually the king himself. Marrant noted the change that his prayers and God's grace had on the Cherokee people: "the king's house became God's house; the soldiers were ordered away, and the poor condemned prisoner had perfect liberty, and was treated like a prince." Marrant stayed with the Cherokees for several weeks, learning their language and even dressing the part. When he returned home, he claimed that his "dress was purely in the Indian stile [sic]; the skins of wild beasts composed my garments, my head was set out in the savage manner, with a long pendant down my back, a sash round my middle without breeches, and a tomahawk by my side." The wandering black teenager who left his home in Carolina returned a successful itinerant missionary, dressed in his Indian finest. Perhaps his experience among the Cherokees explains why, when he became a preacher at Nova Scotia, he traveled frequently to baptize, lead services among, and preach to several Indian villagers there.[60]

Like Marrant, Olaudah Equiano, the abolitionist, autobiographer, and perhaps the most famous person of African descent in the eighteenth century, also identified Indian missionary history as crucial to his own spiritual development. In fact, Equiano counted two Indian missionary books among the most formative texts in his spiritual journey to Christianity. The first was Thomas Wilson's *The Knowledge and Practice of Christianity Made Easy to the Meanest Capacities: or, an Essay Towards an Instruction for the Indians: . . . Together with Directions and Prayers* (1741), which took the form of a fictional dialogue between a missionary and an Indian. Interestingly, the "Indian" was not a real, historical character, but rather an archetypal indigenous mold that could be applied to any non-Christian within the Atlantic world. Designed for white audiences as well as black and Indian ones, Wilson's conversational format made Christian doctrine more accessible than other, more abstruse, theological treatises. Equiano also treasured another text, entitled *The Conversion of an Indian, in a Letter to a Friend.* Written by Lawrence Harlow and also recounting the spiritual journey of a faceless "Indian," this book narrated one Indian's effort to find the Christian God in England. Perhaps the text resonated with Equiano because the story of leaving one's home and finding redemptive religion overseas, as well as Harlow's characterization of many white Christians as hypocrites and scoundrels, spoke to Equiano's personal experience as a black Christian in the Atlantic world. Indeed, Equiano even noted that Harlow's account of the conversion of this fictional Christian Indian was "of great use to me, and at that time was a means of strengthening my faith."[61]

Equiano might have applied the lessons he learned from Wilson's and Harlow's conversion accounts when attempting to Christianize a Mosquito "prince" who shared a voyage with him from England to the

West Indies. Equiano was irate that the prince had not undergone a rigorous Christian education in England, for he had only been taught some rudimentary English and a few general Christian principles. Equiano lambasted the "mock Christianity" that characterized the Indian's understanding of revealed religion. In order to address this deficiency, Equiano "took all the pains that I could to instruct the Indian prince in the doctrines of Christianity, of which he was entirely ignorant." According to Equiano, the prince appeared to have a sincere conversion, but then abandoned Christianity because of the behavior of white sailors and, in Equiano's view, the guiles of Satan. Nevertheless, the experience left an indelible mark on Equiano. When the British governor of a West African post asked Equiano to be a missionary, Equiano responded by citing his experience as a Christian mentor to the Mosquito Indian. Like John Marrant, Equiano probably understood Native Americans as both future recipients of the gospel as well as a golden opportunity for him to enhance his missionary credentials.[62]

We do not know if John Quamine and Bristol Yamma thought deeply about Indian missions as they were preparing for their African one. The records are simply silent. And yet, the white supporters of this mission—particularly Samuel Hopkins and Ezra Stiles—certainly did. Hopkins and Stiles had their personal agendas for supporting the African mission, but both of them approached it via their personal involvement in and understanding of Native American missionary history. Indians from Stockbridge, a Christian Indian town in western Massachusetts, sent Samuel Hopkins a "particular message" in 1749 to ask him to be their minister after John Sergeant died.[63] He seemed like a logical choice for a range of reasons, including the fact that his uncle actually published a history of the mission in its earliest years.[64] Hopkins considered the position but then relented upon anticipating that his spiritual mentor (Jonathan Edwards) would take the post. Instead, Hopkins remained the minister at Housatonic (later known as Great Barrington), just a thirty minute ride from Stockbridge. He resided within riding distance of the Christian Indian town for over a quarter of a century before relocating to Newport in 1770. Throughout his career at Newport he maintained a friendly correspondence with Stephen West (the later pastor at Stockbridge) and Gideon Hawley, a missionary who had proselytized among the Iroquois of New York and Mashpee of Cape Cod. Hopkins even suggested to Hawley in 1761 that the best way to preach to Iroquois Indians would be to bring "some Mohawk boys" to New England "to be educated in order to make interpreters or missionaries as they appear qualified." Hopkins discussed native Iroquois missionaries so frequently it compelled Hawley to observe that he "seemed to have it at Heart in every letter he writes."[65]

Like Hopkins, Ezra Stiles was deeply interested in Native American missionary work, but his interests were far more wide-ranging than Hopkins'. Stiles was famous for having an insatiable curiosity for anything that was "historical and curious," including everything from astronomy and geography to smallpox and silkworms.[66] Stiles grew increasingly interested in Indian demography, ethnography, and missionary history throughout the 1760s and 70s. This understanding of Native American history would serve as a model for how he interpreted his role in the African mission. As soon as he graduated from Yale College, Stiles, like Hopkins, was recruited for the ministerial position at Stockbridge.[67] Although he never took the job, he kept his eyes on the development of Stockbridge for the rest of his life. He also revealed his interest in John Eliot's seventeenth century mission to the Indians when he copied Eliot's narrative of the rise of Indian churches in Massachusetts, a text which emphasized the role of indigenous Christian leaders in Indian praying towns.[68] During the spring of 1762 Stiles took a journey to several Indian settlements in southern New England, stopping by the native Christian community of Mashpee, noting its prevalence of Indian preachers, and establishing a long-standing correspondence with Gideon Hawley. It might have been during this tour that Stiles learned about Martha's Vineyard's Japhet Hannit, whom Stiles called "an excellent Indian Minister."[69] In 1772, just a year before he became involved in the African mission, Stiles edited and republished a history of King Philip's War, a conflict which devastated New England and dramatically transformed native missionary efforts.[70]

Stiles used his extensive contacts to keep in touch with Samson Occom, who provided information about the demographic and religious state of the Montauk Indians on Long Island. Eleazar Wheelock, David McClure, Samuel Kirkland, and Carolina minister Elam Potter all sent Stiles information about Native American natural symbols, demography, and spiritual beliefs. Stiles even made sketches of Indian wigwams and drew maps that noted the locations of Indian tribes throughout New England.[71] He was also personally acquainted with Samuel Niles, the Narragansett separatist preacher that Joseph Fish was likely thinking of when he warned Sarah Osborn to be cautious while teaching Newport's blacks. Stiles and Niles met a few times, but the most memorable meeting was in the spring of 1772, just a year before Stiles became involved in the African missionary project. Stiles not only recorded the history of Niles' strange path to ministerial power in Narragansett, but also took the Indian preacher into his study, read him the history of a Moravian mission to Greenland, and showed him a globe "To give him a better Idea of Things." He concluded the visit by giving his guest "An Account of the Sarepta Brethren and the prospect of introducing Christianity among the Kalmuks and Tartars." As Samuel Niles learned that day, Stiles was an early modern embodiment of the global citizen. His efforts to expose the Narragansett Indian pastor to the histories of missions from Greenland to Central Asia demonstrate that many early modern Protestants perceived Christian missions as connected, if not contiguous, evangelical enterprises.[72]

From his quiet study in Newport, Rhode Island Stiles researched the religious state of affairs throughout the world by corresponding with other ministers in Mexico City, Surinam, and even Russia. He knew about Catholic missionary efforts in China and Japan, as well as the Danish mission to India, which relied significantly upon native preachers and teachers. He took stock of Anglican missionaries stationed in Africa, Barbados, the Mosquito Shore, the Bahamas, and the Carolinas. He believed that the Moravians, who had missions throughout the Atlantic world and beyond, were the most successful missionary force among Indians and Africans.[73] By 1774 Stiles could confidently claim that he had studied "the history of almost all nations and empires on earth."[74] When he sat for his 1771 portrait, the image reflected the cosmopolitanism of its subject: the books in the background included Livy, Newton, and Plato, as well as J. B. DuHalde's *The General History of China*. By the time Stiles became involved in the African project in 1773, his correspondence with other missionaries throughout New England and the world, as well as his own research into Indian missionary history, all demonstrated that there were native missionaries on Martha's Vineyard, in John Eliot's praying towns, at Mashpee and along the southeastern New England coast, in Narragansett, Iroquoia, Japan, China, India, the Caribbean, and even Greenland. While the use of native ministers in Africa might have seemed novel to some, Stiles' studies into the demography, culture, and missionary history of indigenous peoples throughout the world taught him otherwise.

When Stiles outlined his motivations for participating in the Quamine mission to Charles Chauncy, he pointed to the failures of Protestant evangelical efforts among Indians as a guiding lesson for how to continue this work. He noted in 1773 that for twenty years he had "no hope" of converting Indians to Christianity. Nevertheless, he believed it was their "bounden duty as Christians" to "spare no expence [sic] towards effectually carrying the Gospel" to Indians and continuing to offer them saving grace, "till they shall have vanished & their Nations

shall all be swept off the Earth." The next line in his letter moves immediately to his reasons for participating in the African project, making
both a textual and rhetorical connection between Indian and African
evangelical work. He observed that Europe's merchants had been selling
Africans for nearly eighty years, and that it was the duty of Protestant
ministers to convert Africans in order to compensate them for the "injury

Ezra Stiles. (Image courtesy of Yale University Art Gallery. Bequest of Dr.
Charles Jenkins Foote, B.A. 1883 M.D. 1890.)

and injustice" they had suffered at the hands of nominal Christians. For Stiles, at least, African missionary work was directly connected to the failures of evangelical efforts among Indians. Sending Quamine and Yamma to Africa would not only redeem the failures of earlier Puritan efforts, but the Protestant missionary enterprise as a whole. As an extension of Native American missionary efforts, Quamine's mission might succeed where previous Indian missions had failed.[75]

In a period marked by intense theological bickering, the ecumenical support that the mission generated was remarkable. The friendly collaboration of Stiles and Hopkins undoubtedly fueled this interdenominational cooperation. The two men must have made strange partners; the former was the son of Isaac Stiles (an Old Light minister) and the latter was the most notable student of Great Awakening firebrand Jonathan Edwards. Yet when Hopkins first arrived in Newport in 1770, Stiles vowed to "endeavour to live with him as a brother."[76] "I have a mind," Stiles informed a colleague, "that there should be one Instance on this Continent, where two Churches in the same place and of the same denomination should live in harmony. In most Instances they hate one another most heartily." Stiles practiced what he preached, for he and Hopkins—in spite of their institutional and doctrinal differences—became fast friends. Stiles delivered Hopkins' ordination ceremony and frequently attended his lectures.[77]

The project helped unite other missionaries throughout the Atlantic world, for Protestant ministers of all stripes could agree that missionary work was central to the health and vivacity of Christianity. Although they might have disagreed about the goals, means, and nature of missions, they could easily rally behind a plan like this because of its potential as a conciliating force. When Stiles and Hopkins published *To the Public* in 1773 and again in 1776, they relied upon an interconnected, transatlantic network of Protestant ministers from England, Scotland, the Americas, and Africa to raise money for the cause. The nominal and monetary support they received throughout the Atlantic world demonstrated that indigenous missionary efforts could be a unifying force in an era of divisive religious strife. They received money and support from one religious society of women in Newport and from another in Boston. They opened letters of approbation from the Presbyterian synod in New York. Stockbridge's John Sergeant (the son of the first missionary to that Indian town) informed Stiles that he was "much pleased with your Negro Mission" and promised to donate to the experiment.[78] They also received money from a collection taken throughout Berkshire County, as well as from an organization called the North Association in Connecticut.

Other Connecticut clergy supported the idea and volunteered to train the aspiring African missionaries. Elias Boudinot, a powerful New Jersey lawyer and politician who would later sign his name on the Declaration of Independence, offered to board and tutor the two Africans. Hopkins and Stiles received five pounds from a gentleman in London and Anthony Benezet, a famous abolitionist and social activist, agreed to help raise money for the Africans' education.[79] While Philip Quaque's letters expressed suspicion towards the mission, they praised it just enough for Hopkins and Stiles to include parts of them in To the Public, giving the entire affair an even more ecumenical luster. As Stiles summarized in a letter to a colleague, this mission might, at the very least, temporarily bridge the doctrinal and ecclesiastical divides that had historically torn the American religious community apart. "We ought all to joyn [sic]," Stiles concluded, "in carrying the glorious Gospel to the Heathen in all parts of the Earth."[80] Most of the donations, of course, came from individuals and organizations very much accustomed to supporting missions to American Indians.

Nowhere was this clearer than within the halls of The Scottish Society for Propagating Christian Knowledge (SSPCK), based in Edinburgh. The SSPCK contributed their financial and moral support to the mission mainly because its members viewed it through the lens of previous missionary work among Scottish Highlanders and American Indians. The SSPCK had long supported American missions; white evangelists like David Brainerd and Samuel Kirkland were on their payroll and sent them periodic summaries of their efforts. The members of the SSPCK—especially John Erskine, who was in touch with Indian and African missionaries throughout the Atlantic world—certainly knew about Moses Tatami, David Brainerd's interpreter who became a part-time preacher when Brainerd went home after delivering his sermons. In fact, the SSPCK agreed to pay for the education of Tatami's son, Peter, at the College of New Jersey in the 1750s—precisely the same place where Quamine and Yamma were headed in 1774. The college's board members were not only trustees, for they also served as the Commissioners of Indian Affairs for the SSPCK. In other words, the college's trustees (along with the missionaries in the field) were the eyes and ears of the Scottish missionary enterprise among Indians. They acted as a circuit of information and even dispensed funds for the training of a native evangelical corps. They would have been aware of the ascension of Deacon Thomas, Isaac, and Good Peter in Oneida, where SSPCK associate Samuel Kirkland was stationed for much of the 1770s. The members of the SSPCK therefore knew of and supported indigenous missionary efforts.[81] In this way the SSPCK, like other Protestant groups, conceived of missionary work as a linear, almost genealogical exercise, where each mission was directly connected to all others. When an SSPCK member expressed "great satisfaction" that two native missionaries were going to "extend the Mediator's kingdom to those nations who dwell, at present, in the habitations of cruelty, and in the land of the shadow of death," he could have been speaking equally about Highlanders, Indians, or Africans. Indian missionary history was central to the SSPCK's participation in the project.[82]

The most important model for this African mission was the cadre of Indian preachers who attended Eleazar Wheelock's Charity School in the 1750s and 60s. The narratives that Wheelock published annually, Samson Occom's famous fundraising campaign in the British Isles, and the fallout that ensued when Wheelock used those funds to create a college for English children (rather than Indian ones), all made Protestant ministers painfully aware of the accomplishments and failures of Wheelock's program. But the direct connections between the organizers of the Quamine mission and Wheelock's Indian missionaries were many. Wheelock was personally acquainted with John Witherspoon, who administered funds to Wheelock on behalf of the SSPCK. One of Wheelock's friends once reported that Witherspoon had accepted to pay some unknown expense of Wheelock's missionary plan, noting that "In this affair, you are not a little indebted to the Connections & Influence of Dr. Witherspoon who took the most prudent & affectual [sic] steps to serve your Interests." Whenever Wheelock's missionaries were in need, his friend concluded, "they will draw on the Doctor."[83] Witherspoon thus distributed funds for Wheelock's Indian missions well before he became engaged in the African one. When Ezra Stiles wrote to Wheelock in 1767 to congratulate him for recently receiving the Doctor of Divinity from the University of Edinburgh—an accolade which Stiles had been awarded two years earlier—he took the opportunity to praise Wheelock's school as a "noble Institution." Stiles added that Wheelock's ambitious plan of training Native Americans as Christian missionaries was "the almost only prospect of Christianizing the American Aboriginals."[84] Wheelock returned the favor when the African mission became public, sending Stiles and Hopkins complimentary copies of his narrative of the Indian School and informing the Newport ministers of his "approbation, and readiness to promote the design; so far as lies in [his] power."[85] The most striking gesture of cooperation between Wheelock's Indian missionary program and the African one was when Wheelock volunteered to train Quamine and Yamma himself at Dartmouth College.[86]

The African mission even harnessed the evangelical rhetoric that animated Wheelock's earlier Indian program. The open door, which was such a powerful rhetorical tool for Wheelock's Indian mission program, also found its way into the evangelical discourses concerning Africa. While Wheelock believed that the 1760s witnessed "a Door opening for a hundred Missionaries" in Iroquoia, Hopkins and others repeatedly used the open door metaphor to describe the potential of their African mission.[87] Hopkins suggested that Quamine and Yamma employed that rhetoric themselves when they assured him that "if a door should be opened for them to go, they thought it was their duty, in such a case, to forsake wife and children, and go and preach the gospel to the perishing heathen."[88] Perhaps this explains Hopkins' analogous choice of title for his history of the African mission. While Wheelock published *A Plain and Faithful Narrative of the Original Design, Rise, Progress and Present State of the Indian Charity-School at Lebanon, in Connecticut,* Hopkins titled his "A Narrative of the rise & progress of a proposal and attempt to send the gospel to guinea." The actual, rhetorical, and literary connections between Indian and African missionary projects partially explain the rumor circulating in 1778 that Wheelock had hand-picked Ezra Stiles, rather than his own son, to be president of Dartmouth College when he died.[89]

While the organizers of this African mission were undoubtedly influenced by, and had many connections to, Wheelock's Indian missionary project, recent controversies surrounding Indian missions also provided a model for how *not* to organize a mission. In the late 1760s, Mohegan preacher Samson Occom and another minister set out across the Atlantic to raise money for Wheelock's native missionary program. This experiment aroused the pity and philanthropy, as well as the wallets, of hundreds of individuals, and Occom eventually collected an astronomical 12,000 pounds for the enterprise. However, when Wheelock used the funds to establish Dartmouth College—designed mainly for English students rather than Indian ones—donors became irate that they had freely given money to establish yet another white colonial college. This entire scenario caused a public, messy, and controversial rift between Wheelock and Occom as well as between Wheelock and Samuel Kirkland, his most dedicated white missionary. The Newport ministers were fully aware of this imbroglio as they planned their African mission only five years later. Agitated by Wheelock's turn against native preachers, Stiles remarked that Wheelock had "much of the religious Politician in his Make," a "very ambitious" and "haughty" man. The funds that Occom helped raise, Stiles noted, were intended mainly for the education of Indian preachers at the college. "Yet the only Indian that has graduated there," he protested, "was obliged to beg elsewhere towards supporting him the last year of his College Residence." Stiles concluded that it would have "been better to have left the Funds in the Hands of the London Board," rather than to give it to Wheelock *carte blanche*.[90] According to Stiles and other Protestants throughout the Atlantic, Wheelock's deception had wasted a very promising native missionary project. Stiles and Hopkins hoped to keep the African mission an interdenominational one, one that would avoid the pitfalls of Wheelock's failures while simultaneously learning from them.

When Stiles, Hopkins, Quamine, and Yamma collaborated to raise money for their African mission, they had the failures of the Wheelock controversy fresh in their minds. Stiles even quietly worried that the African mission might share the same fate as the Indian one. Even if they had thirty or forty black preachers, Stiles admitted to Hopkins, he feared the mission "would be taken up by the public and secularized—as Dr. Wheelocks Indian College, which has already almost lost sight of its original Design."[91] Donors would have expressed the same fears about the potential of party politics, egos, and duplicitous fundraising to ruin this native African mission, just as it had divided the Indian one. The organizers of the African mission assured potential donors that "Whatever shall be given to this end, and put into the hands of the subscribers," they would "engage faithfully to improve to this purpose only, and to promote the proposed mission, according to their best discretion; and to be at all times ready to give an account to those who desire it, of all they shall receive, and the manner in which it has been expended."[92] To further distance themselves from Wheelock, they rejected his offer to train the two African missionaries at Dartmouth. As Hopkins noted in February of 1774, Quamine and Yamma could enjoy free schooling and cheap living in Newport while staying close to their families. Such collaboration between Wheelock and the Newport ministers, Hopkins concluded, "cannot take place to any advantage."[93] Hopkins and Stiles were clearly distancing themselves from the sour reputation that Wheelock had amassed in recent years. By the time that Hopkins wrote those words, Quamine and Yamma had probably learned that they were heading to New Jersey, rather than New Hampshire, for their training.

Although there were more prestigious colonial colleges that were closer to Newport, the choice of the College of New Jersey as a site for Quamine and Yamma's training made sense. By the early 1770s, the institution had built for itself a reputation as a destination for the education and missionary training of Indians and Africans. Before his death in

1764, the popular evangelical preacher Gilbert Tennent had received 200 pounds from a man in Scotland for the education of an Indian youth to be trained for "instructing his countrymen in the English language and the Christian religion, or preaching the gospel to them."[94] It is unclear whether this ever materialized, although the anonymous Scot would have been pleased when two Delaware Indians named Jacob Woolley and Bartholemew Scott Calvin attended the college. While Stiles had personally heard about Woolley's education there, Witherspoon was president by the time that Calvin began matriculating. As noted earlier, Peter Tatami was the son of David Brainerd's Indian interpreter, and the SSPCK offered some funds for his education at the college. In addition, The College of New Jersey experienced a religious revival in the early 1770s, a fact which might have assured Stiles and Hopkins that the two Africans would not suffer from any spiritual backsliding when they left Newport. Indeed, Witherspoon publicly bragged that his college was not only "one of the healthiest places" in the Atlantic world, but also that its distance away from licentious English traders, merchants, and conmen virtually guaranteed that students would preserve their religious piety while avoiding the temptation to be pulled into uncouth, worldly affairs.[95] This was not the first plan for African missionaries to attend the college. Twenty years before Quamine and Yamma arrived at John Witherspoon's doorstep, college president Samuel Davies devised a plan for "some three or four young Africans, who still retained their native language, were pious, and of good abilities, to be educated at the College of New Jersey for missionaries."[96] Although the scheme failed to materialize, it nevertheless reflected how this college, rather than Harvard or Yale, had historically been understood as a training ground for both Indian and African evangelists.

John Witherspoon's prestige and reputation were the final reasons why he was asked to prepare Quamine and Yamma for the rigors of the African mission. Although Witherspoon did not have much missionary expertise, he was a ranking member of the Presbyterian SSPCK (he gave the organization's anniversary sermon in 1758) and had argued for the necessity of Indian missions in his sermons. Witherspoon noted that there was not a "more noble, a more important, or more necessary exercise of Christian charity, than enabling the Society to carry on their useful and salutary schemes, especially to extend their mission to the *Indian* tribes."[97] Ezra Stiles also assured his colleagues that Witherspoon was not only of a "catholic, charitable spirit," but was probably the finest theologian in all of the colonial colleges.[98] Unlike other Protestant theologians of his time, Witherspoon had few enemies, and he seemed to be the perfect person to head such an ecumenical and collaborative effort. On the one hand, he was generally against the teachings of Samuel Hopkins, so Old Lights like Charles Chauncy might have donated more readily knowing that Quamine and Yamma were not going to be indoctrinated into Hopkins' system. At the same time, the ascension of Witherspoon and the recent popularity of his college gave it the opportunity to situate itself as an anti-Anglican institution in a growing Anglican mid-Atlantic. While intense rivalries between Anglicans and other American Protestant ministers heated up over the issue of an American bishopric in the 1760s, the competition over Indian missions provided the ammunition in a clerical cold war between Anglicans and Dissenters. Witherspoon's ecumenicalism could bridge the divides that tore Dissenting communities apart and unite them against the growing aggressiveness of the Anglican Church. "Our Jersey College," reported a friend to Stiles in 1769, "is now talking as if she was soon to be the bulwark against Episcopacy: I should rejoice to see her Pistols, like honest Teagues, grown up into great Guns. The President is an active man, & a good Preacher; & has done much to procure funds."[99] With Witherspoon at the helm, there was little chance that the African mission would devolve into the rancorous type of conflict that Wheelock engineered years before.

The education of the two Africans was also influenced by changing perceptions of how to properly train indigenous peoples for evangelical work. While Wheelock had demanded that civilization, husbandry, familiarity with classical languages and texts, and biblical erudition were all equally important, the organizers of Quamine and Yamma's mission approached African education with an eye towards the main goal of the mission—Christianization—rather than civilization. Ezra Stiles, for example, had an organic view of the role of civilization in converting native peoples. He initially believed that Indians had to be civilized before they could be converted, but by the late 1760s he had changed his mind. This was for two reasons. The first is that he was influenced by the writings of his colleague, Charles Chauncy, who argued in the early 1760s that missionaries should not think themselves "obliged to convert measures to effect an alteration in that way of civil life they have been used to for ages immemorial."[100] English civility and Christianity were not necessarily dependent upon one another, for the history of civilization plans had only shown that they resulted in the disruption of native lifeways and rarely made good Christians. Quamine and Yamma would therefore miss the training regimen that Wheelock put his Indians through, as they would never be trained in husbandry, blacksmithing, agriculture, or any of these material arts. Theology, rather than civilization, would be at the heart of their training. At the same time, Stiles' research into Moravian missions demonstrated in a very practical way that civilization need not accompany conversion. After reading the history of the Moravian mission to Greenland, Stiles wrote to Eleazar Wheelock to inform him of the implicit comparisons between the native peoples there and those in New York. "Perhaps your missionaries," Stiles suggested to Wheelock, "might learn from these volumes more advantageously to address the Indians. Perhaps it is a Mistake that Civilizing is necessary to Christianizing the Heathen. If the divine truth can find admission into their hearts, the rest follows of course."[101] By the time of his involvement in the project, Stiles had rejected centuries of Protestant missionary assumptions by arguing that civilization need not precede conversion. If Christian conversion could come first, the rest would follow.

Quamine and Yamma's training might have reflected this change in direction. Wheelock's Indian missionaries studied classical texts, learned Latin, Greek, and maybe even Hebrew, and were constantly engaged in agriculture and husbandry. Students at the College of New Jersey spent their first years studying Latin, Greek, rhetoric, geography, philosophy, and mathematics. It is likely that Witherspoon's personal regimen for Quamine and Yamma looked to, but differed significantly from, both educational models. The first major difference was that, while Wheelock's students complained bitterly about the harsh, physical, and draconian punishment at the hands of their schoolmasters, Witherspoon was proud of the fact that "no correction by stripes is permitted" at his college. Those who could not be governed by reason and maintain control of their passions, Witherspoon argued, "are reckoned unfit for residence in College."[102] This pedagogical stance, in addition to the fact that his two students were former slaves, highlighted the problems involved with the corporeal punishment of black students. Unlike Wheelock, Witherspoon never resorted to such measures. Part of this could have been the missionaries' age. By the time that Quamine and Yamma arrived at the College of New Jersey, the missionaries were far from children, as both were well over thirty years old. As Witherspoon observed in a sermon on religious education, "You may bend a young twig and make it receive almost any form; but that which has attained to maturity, and taken its ply, you will never bring into another shape than that which it naturally bears."[103] As grown men, rather than young children, the Africans' education would have prepared them for the duties of their future evangelical calling rather than expose them to classical texts or arm them with academic erudition. Their training therefore would have been much more practical, even vocational. In the year and a half that they spent with Witherspoon from November of 1774 to the spring of 1776, Quamine and Yamma allegedly became "very good in reading and writing." In addition to acquiring the skills of literacy, they also gained "a pretty good notion of the Principles of the Christian faith."[104] By 1776, the organizers of the mission could boast that Quamine and Yamma had excelled so quickly in their studies that they were fully prepared to begin the African mission they had been preparing for—and spearheading—for years. The timing, however, could not have been worse. Just as Quamine and Yamma had successfully finished their training under John Witherspoon, the American Revolution began to undo the years of work leading up to this African mission. Yamma eventually moved to Providence and, when John Quamine died aboard a privateer's ship in 1779, the mission effectively died with him.

We could point to nearly a dozen reasons why Quamine's mission failed. The American Revolution cut off most communication and interaction with Africa, during which the slave trade reached a temporary nadir and some states even made it illegal. Interestingly, the organizers of this African mission viewed this development as a mixed blessing. While most of the donors to and participants in the project abhorred the slave trade, the transportation connections that the trade wrought would have made mobilizing African missionaries much easier. When given the choice between having the slave trade and Christian missions or losing both, some ministers preferred to accept the evil of slavery in order to accomplish what they thought was a greater spiritual good. Scottish divine John Erskine rejoiced to hear that Massachusetts was abolishing slavery in the 1780s, but admitted that he "shall be sorry if that otherwise desirable event shall hinder any probable scheme of sending the Gospel to the natives of Africa."[105] Even some of the project's organizers and central participants had their doubts about whether Quamine and Yamma could ever hope to succeed. Ezra Stiles had admitted as early as 1773 that the project was a "discouraging" enterprise and that "Success may be doubtful."[106] Quamine and Yamma's tutor came to agree with Stiles. By 1782, with the project fully behind him, John Witherspoon reflected on the indigenous people trained at the College of New Jersey. He noted that his educational experiences with Indians, in particular, demonstrated that they would never attain a civilized life. Witherspoon concluded that "There have been some of them educated at this college, as well as in New England; but seldom or never did they prove either good or useful."[107] Although John Erskine and Samuel Hopkins would try to revive the project in later years, hopes of a native mission to Africa faded as the American Revolution began and participants like Stiles and Witherspoon succumbed to their own doubts about indigenous missionary work.

Although this mission ultimately died aboard a privateer's ship, the failed plan says a great deal about indigenous missionary work in the eighteenth century British Atlantic. Afro-Christians were not simply participants in, but rather organizers and initiators of, African missions. Fueled by local revivals, an anti-slavery impulse, and wider spiritual transformations among people of African descent throughout the Atlantic world, Quamine and Yamma's mission was certainly a mission to Africans, by Africans. While Ezra Stiles and Samuel Hopkins were the public faces of the project, it ultimately sprang from Quamine and Yamma, who were themselves its catalysts. Additionally, Native American missionary experience played a crucial role in how this African project was understood, framed, and conducted. Indeed, many Protestant missionaries thought of Indians and Africans as "two eggs," and that missionary work among the Indians would have much to say about the prospects of spreading the gospel among Africans. Quamine and Yamma's mission was influenced by Eleazar Wheelock's missionary program, which showed later evangelists the opportunities and challenges associated with placing indigenous peoples at the center of the Protestant missionary program. Quamine's mission was rooted in Afro-Christian religious transformations within the Atlantic world as well as the history and challenges of Native American missionary experience. But, like countless indigenous missionaries before them, these two Africans never realized their chance to return to Africa and "preach the gospel to the people from which they sprang."[108]

Conclusion

OLAUDAH EQUIANO'S ATTEMPT to secure a position as an Anglican missionary in West Africa in 1779 coincided with an extraordinarily turbulent period in the Atlantic world. Equiano was writing his application at the dawn of an era of transatlantic revolutions, an era marked by a loosening of imperial bonds, declarations of independence, and appeals to universal rights of justice, equality, and self-determination. These ideals animated not only the American Revolution, but also the French, Haitian, and a bevy of Latin American revolutions in the early nineteenth century. These are political events, but black and Indian Christians also used the Revolutionary moment to forge independent communities away from the institutional oversight of white churches. In the Christian Indian communities of upstate New York, the pulpits of black churches in Philadelphia, the pews of southern Baptist congregations, and on the shores of black settlements at Nova Scotia and Sierra Leone, black and Indian evangelists tried to create spiritual communities that would provide them with political sovereignty and offer hope for future generations. Equiano's attempt to become an Anglican preacher in West Africa is therefore such a paradoxical and challenging story because he was trying to bind himself to a white church at the same time that blacks and Indians throughout the Atlantic world were creating their own. Their efforts represented nothing less than declarations of independence.

Joseph Johnson, the Mohegan preacher who conducted an ill-fated mission to the Oneida Indians in the 1760s, championed the idea of moving eastern Algonquian Indians—particularly his own Mohegans—

to land within the territory of Oneidas in New York. The plan got under-way in the 1770s, but the American Revolution and Johnson's premature death derailed it until the early 1780s. Samson Occom, Johnson's father-in-law, took the mantle of community building from Johnson and set about constructing a settlement on the post-Revolutionary New York frontier. Eeyawquittoowauconnuck, or Brothertown, was officially incorporated in November of 1785 and a neighboring town of New Stockbridge was also established.[1] Occom and other New England Algonquians who moved west believed that this migration paralleled the celebrated journey of the Israelites out of Egypt as told in the book of Exodus. When Occom undertook his momentous trip from his Mohegan home to the budding community at Brothertown, he found himself con-stantly preaching from Exodus along the way.[2] For these Christian Indians, Brothertown represented not only political sovereignty and independence, but also an opportunity to fashion lasting Christian com-munities that might serve as bases for future evangelical work among the Indians.

About 250 miles directly south of the Indian community at Brothertown lay Philadelphia. And, while Christian Indians were building communi-ties in New York, black preachers were also building churches—both in terms of the people and in terms of the physical structures—in the city of brotherly love. Black ministers like Richard Allen, Absalom Jones, and Daniel Coker forged independent congregations in Pennsylvania and Delaware while simultaneously riding itinerant evangelical circuits to spread the gospel. This was both a push and pull process, as white clerical leaders often discriminated black congregants out of their churches just as a black spiritual leadership class emerged to pull them into their own. Black Methodist preachers were especially active in building their ranks. As Richard Allen explained, Methodism was appealing to blacks because the founders of these churches were gener-ally in opposition to slavery and they explained Christian doctrine through emotional appeals. Their camp meetings were ecstatic and reve-latory, and (most importantly), they cultivated black leadership. Allen observed in his autobiography that Methodism was suited perfectly for blacks because:

> The plain and simple gospel suits best for any people, for the unlearned can understand, and the learned are sure to understand; and the reason that the Methodist is so successful in the awakening and conversion of the coloured people, [is] the plain doctrine and having a good discipline . . . The Methodists were the first people that brought glad tidings to the coloured people. I feel thankful that ever I heard a Methodist preach. We

are beholden to the Methodists, under God, for the light of the Gospel we enjoy; for all other denominations preached so high-flown that we were not able to comprehend their doctrine. Sure am I that reading sermons will never prove so beneficial to the coloured people as spiritual or extempore preaching. I am well convinced that the Methodist has proved beneficial to thousands and ten times thousands.[3]

The most famous church was Allen's African Methodist Episcopal Church, founded in 1794, but there were dozens of other churches, societies, and organizations led by black Christians. And, like their Native American counterparts to the North, black church leaders invoked the Book of Exodus frequently to articulate their newfound identity as God's chosen people, a sovereign community escaping the scourge of Egyptian slavery. When Absalom Jones, one of Philadelphia's key black leaders, preached a thanksgiving sermon in 1808 to celebrate the official ending of the transatlantic slave trade, the starting point for his sermon was, naturally, the book of Exodus.[4]

The same process of declaring religious independence was underway in the south. Black Baptist and Methodist preachers had been traveling itinerant circuits as early as the 1740s, but it was not until the 1760s and early 1770s that they began to appear in larger numbers. Harry Hosier (Black Harry), Jacob Bishop, Moses Wilkinson, George Liele, David George, and Andrew Bryan were celebrated black Christian leaders after the Revolution. But there were also lesser-known figures, most of whom were or had been enslaved. These included preachers by the names of Jupiter, Primus, Jem, Jacob, Simon, Lewis, and Martin. George Liele and David George founded a Baptist church in Silver Bluff, South Carolina by 1773, but other Baptist and Methodist churches with black leaders were quickly popping up throughout the south immediately afterwards. The collective labors of black preachers within the newly formed United States generated an astronomical surge in the number of black adherents to Methodist and Baptist Churches. In 1786 the Methodists counted 1,890 blacks among their ranks, but by 1797 that number had grown to 12,215. By 1793 the Baptists counted around 18,000 black congregants, a number which grew to 40,000 by 1813. Black preachers and religious leaders—both male and female—were absolutely crucial to the development of independent Protestant congregations in post-Revolutionary black communities.[5]

Many of the black preachers who started their evangelical careers in the American south ended up in places like Nova Scotia, Jamaica, and the Bahamas. Runaway slaves flocked to British lines during the American Revolution—largely as a result of Dunmore's Proclamation, which promised freedom to any slave of an American patriot—and when the British left after the war thousands of blacks went with them. One of the most common destinations was Nova Scotia, and black Christian leaders like David George, John Marrant, and Boston King immediately began forging independent Christian congregations there upon their arrival. However, and in spite of their newfound independence, poor land, white racism in Nova Scotia, material poverty, and unbearably cold winters

Richard Allen. (Image courtesy of the Library Company of Philadelphia.)

forced them to consider alternatives. When a British abolitionist named John Clarkson asked the community's black leaders for migrants to establish a colony in West Africa for free blacks, many readily signed up.[6]

Sierra Leone, established as a colony for freed blacks in the late 1780s, had three main sources of black migration: poor blacks from England, the black Nova Scotians, and runaway slaves from the Caribbean. Just as Native Americans and urban black leaders analogized their experiences to the tale of the Israelites escaping Egypt, so did the migrants to Sierra Leone understand their own migration in light of the Exodus story. Tellingly, one of the most dynamic of these evangelical leaders was a charismatic preacher named Moses. The powerful narrative of Israelites escaping persecution, following a prophetic leader to the Promised Land, and becoming God's chosen people resonated with blacks throughout the Atlantic world. They believed Sierra Leone represented a fresh start, a place where blacks could escape the scourge of white racism, establish a sustainable lifestyle through agriculture and trade, and evangelize the native Africans who, they believed, were suffering under the brutish chains of cruel superstition.[7]

Native American and Afro-American evangelists experienced unique conditions in the wake of revolution. And yet, their simultaneous attempts to create independent Christian communities away from the problems of dispossession and racial slavery, their understanding of those communities as missionary bases for future evangelization of others, and even their invocation of scriptural texts like the book of Exodus to explain their plight all mark out similarities rather than differences. Most importantly, a reliance upon native evangelical leadership, in the form of people like Samson Occom, Richard Allen, David George, and Moses Wilkinson, became central to the development of these communities and the people who sought their future in them. It was no coincidence that, when Paul Cuffee attended a black Baptist meeting in Sierra Leone in December of 1811, the meeting read a letter from Christian Oneida Indians "to good satisfaction." The very next day Cuffee delivered this letter to the Methodist congregation, so that both Baptists and Methodists in West Africa might learn from their Indian counterparts "for the improvement of the people."[8] In spite of the vast distances and historical circumstances that separated them, Indians and Africans could recognize the common bonds that knit them together. By the end of the eighteenth century, Native Americans, American blacks, and Sierra Leonean migrants had all struggled to wrestle ecclesiastical and spiritual authority from the clutches of white, Christian denominations. Their congregations and communities spoke to the problems of a people in motion, a people in exodus, just as their hopes for the conversion of Native Americans, Africans, and black Americans outlined their visions for a shared Christian destiny.

While blacks and Indians continued to fight to protect their political sovereignty as well as their spiritual independence, British based evangelical organizations like The Baptist Missionary Society (1792), London Missionary Society (1795), and Church Missionary Society (1799) all began active missionary efforts within Britain's second empire at the turn of the century, fanning out to Africa, India, and East Asia. Missionaries often viewed this new stage in British evangelical expansion not as a complete break with the past, but one that depended significantly on the history and practices of prior missionary work in the Atlantic. One Anglican asked rhetorically in 1786, if Anglicans had previously treated American Indians and the "savage African" as "objects worthy of our attention; ought not the same charitable disposition animate our hopes and excite our zeal towards the conversion of the Mahometan or the Gentoo?"[9] As the American Revolution ended and as the British Empire reconstituted itself, missionaries began to frame their focus more on the east. In all of these missions, native preachers would continue to be central figures in their development.

Indigenous missionaries were ubiquitous in the British Atlantic world. From the early seventeenth century to the late eighteenth, one could find hundreds of native missionaries from New England to the Caribbean, from South Carolina to West Africa, and from the Indians of New York to the Indians in India. While the conventional image of a missionary has been that of a white, middle-class Anglo-American who was often ignorant of the culture and peoples he was attempting to convert, the astonishing ubiquity of native preachers compels us to rethink the ways in which native peoples not only encouraged Christian missions, but actually led them. They drew from Christianity to frame new identities, amass spiritual power, preserve their cultures, and protect their peoples during a period of unprecedented change. In doing so, they became pivotal players in Protestant missionary activity and cultural exchange in the early modern Atlantic world.

Appendix: Table of Native Missionaries

This table, though not an exhaustive list, represents the aggregate research for *Native Apostles,* but not all of the missionaries that appear in the following table are discussed in the book. The total number of black and Indian missionaries is around 275, but many evangelists certainly went unrecorded. Seventeenth century Indian missionaries are mentioned throughout the famous Eliot tracts, and the collection of New England missionary accounts published in the seventeenth century. See Michael P. Clark, ed., *The Eliot Tracts: With Letters from John Eliot to Thomas Thorowgood and Richard Baxter* (Westport, CT: Praeger Publishers, 2003). For later New England Indian missionaries, see Frederick L. Weis, "The New England Company of 1649 and its Missionary Enterprises," *Publications of the Colonial Society of Massachusetts,* Volume 37 (Boston: Colonial Society of Massachusetts, 1959), 134–218. For Iroquoian and Algonquian Indians of the eighteenth century, see James Dow McCallum, ed., *The Letters of Eleazar Wheelock's Indians* (Hanover, NH: Dartmouth College Publications, 1932). See the endnotes, as well as the "Note on Sources," for other suggested scholarly works.

Name	Time frame	Denomination	Notes
Mass. praying towns			
John Speen	Mid 17th C.	Congregational	Brother to Anthony—both were teachers. John was at Natick from 1669 to 1675.
Anthony Speen	Mid 17th C.	Congregational	God "broke his head." At Natick, with his brother John, from 1669 to 1675.
Abraham Speen	Mid 17th C.	Congregational	Preacher at Natick from 1669 to 1675.
Nishokon	Mid 17th C.	Congregational	Gave a sermon on Noah's flood, supposedly a bashful person.
Caleb Cheeshah-teaumuck	Mid 17th C.	Congregational	Originally from Martha's Vineyard. Harvard trained but died (went by many last names).
Joel	Mid 17th C.	Congregational	Originally from Martha's Vineyard. Harvard trained but died (Hiacoomes's son).
Monequessin	Mid 17th C.	Congregational	Trained by Eliot as a schoolteacher.
Daniel Takou-wompbait	17th/18th C.	Congregational	Teacher at Natick from 1685 to 1700. Gravestone still in South Natick.
Benjamin Larnel	17th/18th C.	Congregational	Trained at Harvard but he died in the 1710s. Last Indian to attend Harvard in the eighteenth century.

Name	Time frame	Denomination	Notes
John Nessnumun	Early 18th C.	Congregational	Preacher at Natick from 1709 to 1719. Expert linguist who assisted Mayhew family in translating the Psalter.
John Thomas, Jr.	Early 18th C.	Congregational	Preacher at Natick from 1714 to 1727.
Joseph Tuckappawillin	Mid 17th C.	Congregational	At Hassunnimesut (Grafton). His brother was the ruler there. He served as a scout in King Philip's War (KPW).
James Printer	Mid/Late 17th C.	Congregational	Indian printer and teacher at Waeuntug. Fought English in KPW. Returned to Natick, then Grafton, after the war.
James Speen	Mid/Late 17th C.	Congregational	At Pakachoog (Auburn) from 1672 to 1676. Preacher who also set the tune for the Psalms.
William Awinian	Mid 17th C.	Congregational	Teacher at Punkapog (Canton) from 1656 to 1672.
William Ahaton	17th/18th C.	Congregational	Punkapog (Canton) from 1674 to 1717.
Amos Ahaton	18th C.	Congregational	Punkapog (Canton) from 1717 to 1743. Possibly took over his father's position.
Aaron Pomham	18th C.	Congregational	Punkapog (Canton) around 1742.
John Thomas, Sr.	Mid 17th C.	Congregational	At Nashope, or Nashoba (Littleton) from 1669 to 1714. Alias Naamishcow.

Name	Time frame	Denomination	Notes
Jethro	Mid 17th C.	Congregational	Panatucket. Mentioned in Mary Rowlandson's captivity narrative.
George	Mid 17th C.	Congregational	At Wamesit (Lowell) from 1669 to 1675.
Samuel	Late 17th C.	Congregational	At Wamesit (Lowell) from 1670 to 1675. Apparently spent some time at Harvard College.
Simon Beckom	Mid/Late 17th C.	Congregational	At Wamesit (Lowell) from 1675 to 1685. Led Sabbath meetings during King Philip's War.
Job Nesutan	Mid 17th C.	Congregational	At Okkokonimesit (Marlboro) from 1669 to 1675. Helped Eliot with Bible translations.
Nausquonit	Late 17th C.	Congregational	At Okkokonimesit (Marlboro) from 1669 to 1675, when he retired.
Sampson	Late 17th C.	Congregational	At Okkokonimesit (Marlboro) from 1669 to 1675.
Solomon	Late 17th C.	Congregational	Teacher at Okkokonimesit (Marlboro) from 1675 to 1676.
Samoset	Late 17th C.	Congregational	At Waeuntug (Uxbridge) around 1674.
Wohqohquoshadt	Mid/Late 17th C.	Congregational	At Magunkog (Ashland) in 1669.
Job Kattenanit	Mid/Late 17th C.	Congregational	At Magunkog (Ashland) in 1675. Noted for his "piety and ability."

Name	Time frame	Denomination	Notes
Simon	Mid 17th C.	Congregational	At Magunkog (Ashland) in 1716.
Waabesktamin	Late 17th C.	Congregational	At Manchaug (Sutton) around 1674, and this was a very small village with only about twelve families.
Joseph	Late 17th C.	Congregational	At Chaubun-agungamaug (Webster) from 1672 to 1676. He lived in Grafton with everyone else.

Southeastern Mass.

Name	Time frame	Denomination	Notes
John Sassamon	Mid 17th C.	Congregational	At Nemasket (Lakeville) from 1673 to 1675. At Assawompsett (Lakeville 2) from 1673 to 1675.
Stephen	Late 17th C.	Congregational	At Nemasket (Lakeville) from 1685 on, but this could also be the Stephen from Martha's Vineyard.
Jocelin	17th/18th C.	Congregational	At Assawompsett (Lakeville 2) from 1698 to 1711.
Charles Aham	17th/18th C.	Congregational	At Titicut (Middleboro) around 1698. Also at Cokesit (Rochester) at some point.
Joseph Joshnin	Early 18th C.	Congregational	At Titicut (Middleboro) from 1710 to 1718.
Thomas Sekins	Early 18th C.	Congregational	At Titicut (Middleboro) around 1712.

Name	Time frame	Denomination	Notes
Thomas Felix	Early 18th C.	Congregational	At Titicut (Middleboro) around 1712. Alias Wanamahkohkowit.
Nehemiah Abel	Early 18th C.	Congregational	At Titicut (Middleboro) Ponds around 1712. 1718.
Joseph Wanno	Early 18th C.	Congregational	
John Symons	Early 18th C.	Congregational	At Titicut (Middleboro) from 1747 to 1757.
Charles of Mannamit	Late 17th C.	Congregational	Probably the son of John Simon.
John Hiacoomes	17th/18th C.	Congregational	Son of Hiacoomes, at Assawampsit (Lakeville 2) from 1698 to 1718. Also at Quittabut.
Ralph Jones	17th/18th C.	Congregational	
Indian John	Late 17th C.	Congregational	At Cooxisset (Rochester) around 1685.
Isaac	Late 17th C.	Congregational	At Acoaxet (Westport) around 1685. Associated with the Little Compton Indians congregation.
Jacob Hedge	17th/18th C.	Congregational	
Daniel Wicket	Late 17th C.	Congregational	At Acoaxet (Westport) around 1698.
John Briant	17th/18th C.	Congregational	Teacher at Acushnet (New Bedford) from 1693 to 1713.
William Briant	Early 18th C.	Congregational	At Achushnet (New Bedford) around 1713.
William Simmons	17th/18th C.	Congregational	At Nukkehkummees (Dartmouth) from 1695 to 1718. Ordained by Japhet of Martha's Vineyard.
Samuel Holms	18th C.	Congregational	At Nukkehkummees (Dartmouth) from 1711 to 1718.

Name	Time frame	Denomination	Notes
Thomas Simmons	18th C.	Congregational	At Nukkehkummees (Dartmouth) around 1770 or so. Related to William Simmons (or Simons).
Samuel Church	17th/18th C.	Congregational	At Watuppa Ponds (Fall River) from 1706 to 1716. Also at Sakonnet (Little Compton) from 1685.
John Simons	Early 18th C.	Congregational	At Sakonnet (Little Compton) from 1714 to 1718. Also at Titicut (Middleboro) from 1698–1714.
Benjamin Nompash	Early 18th C.	Congregational	At Sakonnet (Little Compton) from 1714 to 1718.
George	Late 17th. C.	Congregational	At Sakonnet (Little Compton) around 1685.
Will Skipeag	Late 17th C.	Congregational	At Saltwater Pond (Plymouth 2) around 1685, acting as a teacher and preacher.
Wuttananamattuk	Late 17th C.	Congregational	At Bourne 2 (Mannamit Praying Town) around 1674.
Meeshawin	Late 17th C.	Congregational	At Bourne 2 (Mannamit Praying Town) around 1674.
Peter (Sakantucket)	Late 17th C.	Congregational	At Bourne 2 (Mannamit Praying Town) around 1674.
Isaac Jeffrey	Mid 18th C.	Congregational	At Bourne 2 (Mannamit) from 1757 to 1767, then Bourne 1 (Herring Ponds) from 1767 to 1770.

Name	Time frame	Denomination	Notes
William Nummuck	17th/18th C.	Congregational	Preached at Manomet Ponds around 1698. Alias Wanatnuhkuhkowit.
Joseph Wanno	Early 18th C.	Congregational	At Manomet Ponds from 1713 to 1718.
Esther	17th/18th C.	Congregational	Teacher. Wife of John at Manomit Ponds.
Charles of Mannamit	Late 17th C.	Congregational	At Bourne 1 (Herring Ponds) from 1674 to 1685.
Ralph Jones	17th/18th C.	Congregational	Indian Preacher with Thomas Tupper in Sandwich. At Herring Pond in Eastham (or Bourne) around 1698.
Jacob Hedge	17th/18th C.	Congregational	Indian Preacher with Thomas Tupper in Sandwich. At Herring Ponds from 1698 to 1709.
Simon Wicket	Late 17th C.	Congregational	At Skauton (Sandwich) around 1685.
Old John	17th/18th C.	Congregational	At Succonesit (Falmouth) from 1685 to 1709.
John of Falmouth	18th C.	Congregational	At Succonesit (Falmouth) from 1708 to 1719.
Simon Papmonit	17th/18th C.	Congregational	Preacher in Mashpee from 1682 to 1725. At Canaumet (Mashpee 2) from 1685 to 1725 as well.

Name	Time frame	Denomination	Notes
Isaac Papmonit	18th C.	Congregational	At Mashpee, son of Simon, a deacon in the church, lived until 1758, when he was at least 83.
Josiah Papmonit	18th C.	Congregational	At Mashpee, son of Simon, school teacher, blind, born around 1685 and died in 1770.
Deacon Pamonit	18th C.	Congregational	Son of Caleb, deacon at Mashpee, died in October of 1770, which was a huge loss to the community.
Solomon Briant	Mid 18th C.	Congregational	Preacher at Manomet, Herring Pond, and Mashpee from 1720 to 1775. Mostly in Mashpee.
Josiah Shanks	Late 17th. C.	Congregational	At Mashpee around 1685. At Canaumet (Mashpee 2) around 1685.
Joseph Papener	Mid 18th C.	Congregational	Briant's Deacon at Mashpee. Preacher at Falmouth and Pocasset (Bourne 3) from 1758–1762.
Joseph Briant	Mid 18th C.	Congregational	Solomon's Brother. At Mashpee from 1725 to 1759. Also at Portnumicut.
Joshua Ralph	Mid 18th C.	Congregational	Succeeded Joseph Briant but was teacher, not pastor. At Potanumaquut from 1719 to 1760.
Manessah	17th/18th C.	Congregational	Preached at Nobscusset (Dennis) from 1685 to 1698, as well as Satucket from 1685 to 1714.

Name	Time frame	Denomination	Notes
Jeremy Robin	Late 17th C.	Congregational	At Matakees (Yarmouth) around 1685.
Hercules	Early 18th C.	Congregational	At Satucket (Harwich) from 1711 to 1714.
Menekish	Early 18th C.	Congregational	At Satucket (Harwich) around 1714.
John Ralph	18th C.	Congregational	At Satucket (Harwich) from 1762 to 1770. At Potanumaquut (Orleans 2) from 1762 to 1770.
Nicholas	Late 17th. C.	Congregational	At Monimoy (Chatham) around 1685.
John Cosens	17th/18th C.	Congregational	At Monimoy (Chatham), preaching and teaching around 1698.
Daniel Munshee	17th/18th C.	Congregational	At Eastharbor and Billingsgate. At Nauset (Orleans) around 1698.
Great Tom	Late 17th C.	Congregational	At Nauset (Orleans) around 1685.
Thomas Coshaumug	Late 17th C.	Congregational	At Potanumaquut (Orleans 2) around 1698.
Elisha Ralph	18th C.	Congregational	Probably at Potanumaquut (Orleans 2) from 1762 to 1770.
Potanummatack	Late 17th C.	Congregational	At Meshawn (Truro) from 1674 to 1685. At Punonakanit (Wellfleet) from 1670 to 1685.

Name	Time frame	Denomination	Notes
Unnamed Indian teacher	Mid 18th C.	Congregational	Worked at Stockbridge and was being groomed to be a preacher among other Indians.

Southern New England

Name	Time frame	Denomination	Notes
Wequash	Mid 17th C.	Congregational	Converted out of fear during Pequot War, but became preacher in Connecticut afterwards.
Wohwohquoshadt	Late 17th C.	Congregational	At Quantisset (Pomfret, CT) around 1671.
Daniel	Late 17th C.	Congregational	At Quantisset (Pomfret, CT) around 1674, when Eliot and Gookin visited.
Monatunkanet	Mid 17th C.	Congregational	At Quantisset (Pomfret, CT) around 1669.
John Moqua	Late 17th C.	Congregational	At Manexit (Thompson, CT) around 1674. Eliot presented him to this congregation.
Sampson	Late 17th C.	Congregational	At Wabquissit (Woodstock, CT) from 1674 to 1676. Brother of Joseph of Chaubuna-gungamaug.
Charles Daniel	17th/18th C.	Congregational	Employed by Joseph Fish (Stonington) as Teacher
John Mettawan	18th C.	Congregational	Taught at Samuel Whitman's Farmington, CT school in the early/ mid 18th century.

Name	Time frame	Denomination	Notes
Weebox	Late 17th. C.	Congregational	At Mohegan Mission in Norwich, CT around 1674.
Tukamon	Late 17th. C.	Congregational	At Mohegan Mission in Norwich, CT around 1674.
John Cooper	Late 18th C.	Unclear	At Mohegan Mission in Norwich, CT around 1790.
Samuel Niles	Mid 18th C.	Sep. Baptist	Fighting with Joseph Fish, Separatist leader who defended Narragansett lands. Illiterate.
Simon James (James Simon)	Mid 18th C.	Sep. Baptist	Pequot minister preaching at Narragansett for three to four years before Niles took over.
Martha's Vineyard			
Hiacoomes	Mid 17th C.	Congregational	First native preacher on Martha's Vineyard. Preached at Chappaquidick (Edgartown 1) from 1659 to 1690.
Joshua Tackanash	17th/18th C.	Congregational	At Nunnepoag (Edgartown 3) around 1698.
Josiah Thomas	17th/18th C.	Congregational	At Nunnepoag (Edgartown 3) around 1698.
Job Russell (Peosin)	17th/18th C.	Congregational	Preached at Edgartown. Also at Sanchacantacket (Oak Bluffs) from 1698 to 1723.

Name	Time frame	Denomination	Notes
Joshua Momatchegin	17th/18th C.	Congregational	Preached at Chappaquidick (Edgartown 1) from 1670 to 1703. Ruling elder who died in 1703.
Jonathan Amos	18th C.	Congregational	At Chappaquidick (Edgartown 1) from 1703 to 1706. Also sporadically at Gay Head until 1706.
Mittark	Mid 17th C.	Congregational	Sachem turned Pastor. Founded Gay Head Church in 1666.
David Wutto-manomin	Late 17th C.	Congregational	At Gay Head Indian Church from 1683 to 1698.
Elisha (Paaonut)	17th/18th C.	Congregational	Preached at Gay Head from 1683 to 1714, when he died. Also at Gay Head 2 (smaller congregation).
Abel Wauwom-puhque, Jr.	17th/18th C.	Congregational	A deacon in the Gay Head church from 1712 to 1722, when he died. Also occasionally at Chilmark.
Isaac Decamy	18th C.	Baptist	At Gay Head from 1708 to 1720.
Joash Panu	Mid 18th C.	Congregational	At Gay Head from 1713 to 1720. Succeeded Sowomog as Pastor.
Peter Ohquanhit	Mid 18th C.	Congregational	Preached at Gay Head around 1724 or 1725. His will is in Ives/Goddard, *Native Writings*.

Name	Time frame	Denomination	Notes
David Capy	18th C.	Congregational	At Gay Head around 1770.
Zachary Hossueit	Mid 18th C.	Congregational	Minister at Gay Head around 1770. Left a marriage register in Ives/Goddard, *Native Writings*.
Thomas Setum	17th C.	Congregational	Petty sachem of Sanchekantacket (Oak Bluffs) around 1667. Went to the mainland to preach.
Wompamog	17th C.	Congregational	Alias Mr. Sam. Sachem and minister at Oak Bluffs. Died around 1689.
John Nohnoso	Late 17th. C.	Congregational	At Sanchacantacket (Oak Bluffs) from 1670 to 1678.
Paul Mash-quattuhkooit	Late 17th. C.	Congregational	At Sanchacantacket (Oak Bluffs) around 1688, when he died.
Momonequem	17th C.	Congregational	At Nashakemmuck (Chilmark 1) from 1651 onward. Descendents also preached.
John Tackanash	17th/18th C.	Congregational	At Nashakemmuck (Chilmark 1) from 1670 to 1684 and Nashamoiess from 1670 to 1684.
William Lay	17th/18th C.	Congregational	Alias Panunnut, urged Experience Mayhew to learn the Indian languages and become a preacher.
Wuttinomanomin	17th C.	Congregational	Alias David. Deacon of the Chilmark Church who died around 1698.

Name	Time frame	Denomination	Notes
Thomas Sogko-hkonnoo	17th/18th C.	Congregational	Schoolmaster in Tackanash's church. Deacon from 1698 to 1703, when he died. At Sanchacantacket.
Amos	17th/18th C.	Congregational	Another schoolmaster.
Janawannit Hannit	17th/18th C.	Congregational	Uncle to Japhet Hannit (his Brother was Pamehannit—a Sachem in Chilmark).
Japhet Hannit	17th/18th C.	Congregational	At Nashakemmuck (Chilmark 1) from 1683 to 1712. At Gay Head from 1683 to 1712.
Sowomog	17th/18th C.	Congregational	Succeeded Japhet as Pastor.
John Momanequin	17th/18th C.	Congregational	Preacher at Chilmark and then later preacher at Dartmouth. Son of Momonnequem.
Panupuhquah	17th C.	Congregational	At Muckuckhonnike (Chilmark 2) and died around 1664. Very small village.
Stephen Shohkow	17th/18th C.	Congregational	At Seconchgut (Chilmark 3) from 1698 to 1713. Possibly brother to Daniel.
Daniel Shokau	17th/18th C.	Congregational	At Seconchgut (Chilmark 3) from 1698 to 1718 but was also at Gay Head.
Wunnanauhkomun	17th C.	Congregational	At Christiantown Indian Church (West Tisbury) from 1660 to 1676.

Name	Time frame	Denomination	Notes
John Amanhut	17th C.	Congregational	At Christiantown Indian Church (West Tisbury) from 1670 to 1672.
James Sepinnu	Late 17th C.	Congregational	At Christiantown Indian Church (West Tisbury) from 1680 to 1683. Brother of John Tackanash.
John Shohkow	Late 17th C.	Congregational	At Christiantown Indian Church (West Tisbury) from 1683 to 1690.
Micah Shohkow	Late 17th C.	Congregational	At Christiantown Indian Church (West Tisbury) around 1690 or so.
Isaac Ompany	17th/18th C.	Congregational	Elder, minister, and magistrate at Christiantown, 1713–1717.
Jabez Athem	Early 18th C.	Congregational	At Christiantown Indian Church (West Tisbury) from 1718 to 1719.
Hosea Manhut	Early 18th C.	Congregational	At Christiantown Indian Church (West Tisbury) around 1724. Was an ordained minister.
Daniel	17th/18th C.	Congregational	Tisbury. Taught with brother Stephen.
Stephen Nashokau	17th/18th C.	Congregational	Minister at Sechonchqut and Christiantown (1698–1713). Died 1713.
Samuel Cosanan	Early 18th C.	Congregational	Last name also Coshomon, Indian minister living in 1724.

Name	Time frame	Denomination	Notes
Stephen Tackamasun	17th/18th C.	Cong./Baptist	Son of a mainland Indian. Pastor of Nashakemmuck (Chilmark 1) from 1690 to 1708. Later Baptist.
Josias Hossuit	18th C.	Baptist	At Gay Head Baptist Church around 1702.
Josias Hossuit, Jr.	18th C.	Baptist	At Gay Head Baptist Church from 1720 to 1727.
Ephraim Abraham	Mid 18th C.	Baptist	Minister of Gay Head Baptist Church sometime after 1727.
Silas Paul	Mid 18th C.	Puritan	At Gay Head Baptist Church from 1763 to 1787. Has the gravestone, died when he was only 49.
Samuel Kakenehew	Mid 18th C.	Baptist	At Gay Head Baptist Church and died around 1763.
Thomas Jeffers	18th/19th C.	Baptist	At Gay Head Baptist Church from 1792 to 1818.

Nantucket and Islands

Name	Time frame	Denomination	Notes
John Gibs	17th/18th C.	Congregational	Preached at Occawan (Nantucket) from 1665 to 1698.
Job Muckemuck	17th/18th C.	Congregational	Took over at Occawan (Nantucket) when John Gibs died. Preached around 1698.

Name	Time frame	Denomination	Notes
Jonah Hossueit	Early 18th C.	Congregational	Also called Nonahauwasuit. Nantucket Preacher at Occawan Church at Nantucket from 1710–1718.
Benjamin Tarshema	18th C.	Congregational	At Occawan (Nantucket) around 1770.
James Momog	Unclear	Congregational	Minister and justice of the peace for the Indians at Nantucket.
Caleb	17th C.	Congregational	Could be the Caleb Cheeshahteaumuck, from Vineyard and Harvard. At Second Indian Church on Nantucket ca. 1674.
John Asherman	17th/18th C.	Congregational	Nantucket Preacher at Second Indian Church around 1698. This was a smaller congregation.
Quequenah	17th/18th C.	Congregational	Nantucket Preacher. Maybe same as Quequenomp, son of Nantucket Sachem named Wanachmamak.
Peter Hayt	17th/18th C.	Congregational	Nantucket Preacher at Wammasquid (Nantucket 3).
Wunnohson	17th/18th C.	Congregational	At Wammasquid (Nantucket 3).
Daniel Spotso	17th/18th C.	Congregational	At Wammasquid (Nantucket 3).
Netowah	Unclear	Congregational	At Wammasquid (Nantucket 3).
Codpoganut	17th/18th C.	Congregational	Nantucket preacher.
Noah	17th/18th C.	Congregational	Nantucket preacher.

Name	Time frame	Denomination	Notes
Asa	17th/18th C.	Congregational	Teacher on Gosnold, the Elizabeth Islands, around 1698.
Jannohquosso	17th/18th C.	Congregational	On Gosnold, the Elizabeth Islands, around 1700.
Sampson Natusoo	18th C.	Congregational	On Gosnold, the Elizabeth Islands, around 1711.
Unnamed Indian teacher	17th/18th C.	Congregational	On Sandford's Island.
Moor's/Brothertown			
Samson Occom	Mid 18th C.	Congregational	Best known native preacher, a Mohegan who undertook trips to London, Iroquoia, etc.
Joseph Johnson	Mid 18th C.	Congregational	Mohegan preacher who preached to the Oneidas, left Wheelock, and began Brothertown movement.
David Fowler	Mid 18th C.	Congregational	Trained by Wheelock. Montauk who taught (in 1765) among the Oneida.
Jacob Fowler	Mid 18th C.	Congregational	Trained at the Wheelock School. Was supposed to go with David McClure out into the frontier.
Joseph Woolley	Mid 18th C.	Congregational	Trained at the Wheelock School. Delaware Indian who taught at Onaquaga in 1765.

Name	Time frame	Denomination	Notes
Jacob Woolley	Mid 18th C.	Presbyterian?	Trained by Wheelock. Was the first Delaware (with Pumshire) to come to Moor's. Studied at the College of New Jersey.
Hezekiah Calvin	Mid 18th C.	Presbyterian?	Trained by Wheelock. Delaware. Came with Joseph Woolley in spring of 1757.
Abraham primus	Mid 18th C.	Congregational	Trained by Wheelock. Mohawk. Too young to teach but used anyway.
Abraham secundus	Mid 18th C.	Congregational	Trained by Wheelock. Mohawk. Too young to teach but used anyway.
John Pumshire	Mid 18th C.	Presbyterian?	Sent to Wheelock when he was fourteen in December of 1754. Sent with Jacob Woolley. Delaware.
Moses	Mid 18th C.	Presbyterian?	Trained by Wheelock. Mohawk. Too young to teach but used anyway.
Peter Johannes	Mid 18th C.	Presbyterian?	Trained by Wheelock. Mohawk. Too young to teach but used anyway.
Joseph Brant	Mid 18th C.	Anglican	Trained at the Wheelock School. Smith's interpreter, fought during Seven Years War, possibly preaching after it.

Name	Time frame	Denomination	Notes
Samuel Ashpo	Mid 18th C.	Puritan/Baptist	1718–1795. Trained with Wheelock. Taught at Indian schools in NY and later became a Baptist.
Jacob Reed	Mid 18th C.	Congregational	Trained by Wheelock. Oneida. Served as a schoolmaster.
Isaiah Uncas	Mid 18th C.	Presbyterian?	Trained by Wheelock. Mohegan Chief's son. Ill at the school—supported by London.
Joseph	Mid 18th C.	Presbyterian?	Mohawk brought to Wheelock in 1761.
Negyes	Mid 18th C.	Presbyterian?	Mohawk brought to Wheelock in 1761.
Center	Mid 18th C.	Presbyterian?	Mohawk brought to Wheelock in 1761.
John Matthews	Mid 18th C.	Presbyterian?	Trained by Wheelock at Dartmouth. Narragansett. Sent out to help Samuel Kirkland.
Abraham Symons	Mid 18th C.	Presbyterian?	Trained by Wheelock at Dartmouth. Intended to go to Oneida.
Tobias Shattock	Mid 18th C.	Presbyterian?	Narragansett, trained by Wheelock, went to England to protest King Tom's land policies.
John Shattock, Jr.	Mid 18th C.	Presbyterian?	Narragansett, trained by Wheelock, went to England to protest colonial land policies and agreements.

Name	Time frame	Denomination	Notes
SPG missionaries			
James Macquillan Mussoom	Early 18th C.	Anglican	Brought from Mozambique to England, learned at Bray's parish, then returned to Mozambique and vanished.
John Chaung Mussoom	Early 18th C.	Anglican	Brought from Mozambique to England, learned at Bray's parish, then committed suicide.
Prince George	1710s	Anglican	Yamassee Prince trained as evangelist before the Yamasee War. Met King George I.
Miranda	1740s	Anglican	Worked for Azariah Horton on Long Island, then preached to the Delawares and Susquehannocks.
Unnamed teacher	1760s	Anglican	Kept a school for a missionary named Carter on Harbor Island (Bahamas); had forty scholars.
Hendrick Tejon-ihokarawa	Early 18th C.	D.R./Anglican	Assisted William Andrews at Fort Hunter beginning in 1712. One of the "Four Indian Kings."
Paulus Sahonwadi	Mid 18th C.	Anglican	Mohawk. Schoolteacher and interpreter. Son of Hendrick. Different from Petrus Paulus.
Old Abraham	Mid 18th C.	Anglican	Mohawk. Uncle to Paulus Sahonwadi. Catechist. Died in 1757. Brother to Hendrick.

Name	Time frame	Denomination	Notes
Cornelius	Mid 18th C.	Anglican	Mohawk. Do not confuse with Cornelius Bennet. Quit in 1746.
Daniel	Mid 18th C.	Anglican	Mohawk. Quit in 1746.
Harry	Mid 18th C.	Anglican	Slave. Head of Charleston "Negro School." School disbanded when he died in 1764.
Andrew	Mid 18th C.	Anglican	Former Slave. Head of Charleston "Negro School." Eventually shipped to Codrington Plantation, Barbados.
Bray Associates			
Aaron	1760s	Anglican	Employed in Virginia for the Bray Associates. Teacher on a plantation there.
India (the SPCK)			
Aaron	Early/Mid 18th C.	German Lutheran	Part of an English/Danish/German enterprise to spread the Gospel in India.
Diego	Early/Mid 18th C.	German Lutheran	Part of an English/Danish/German enterprise to spread the Gospel in India.
Sattianadan	Early/Mid 18th C.	German Lutheran	Part of an English/Danish/German enterprise to spread the Gospel in India.
Rajanaikan	Early/Mid 18th C.	German Lutheran	Part of an English/Danish/German enterprise to spread the Gospel in India.

Name	Time frame	Denomination	Notes
Tondaman Mudaly	Mid 18th C.	German Lutheran	Former Hindu priest who converted and taught in Christian School.
Every Catechist	Early/Mid 18th C.	German Lutheran	According to the Christian Monthly History, every catechist is an Indian!

New York/Pennsylvania

Name	Time frame	Denomination	Notes
Good Peter	Mid 18th C.	Presbyterian	Worked with Gideon Hawley at Onaquaga and worked extensively with Samuel Kirkland.
Isaac Taukyyau-nauserau	Mid 18th C.	Congregational	Worked with Hawley at Onaquaga
Deacon Thomas	Mid 18th C.	Presbyterian	Oneida Deacon and spiritual leader upon whom Samuel Kirkland relied.
Tuscarora Catechist	Mid 18th C.	Presbyterian	Preached when Kirkland was not there.
Wirom	Mid 18th C.	Presbyterian	Indian catechist, younger than Peter, Thomas, and Isaac.
Ahsheggwanseri	Mid 18th C.	Presbyterian	Oneida, used by Kirkland in 1771 or so.
Thahnehtory	Mid 18th C.	Presbyterian	Ran a school for Kirkland. Taught the Psalms. Was also an Oneida Chief.
Doniat	Mid 18th C.	Presbyterian	Ran a school for Kirkland. Taught the Psalms.

Name	Time frame	Denomination	Notes
Stephen Calvin	Mid 18th C.	Unsure	Delaware interpreter, father of Hezekiah and Bart, schoolmaster at Brothertown, New Jersey.
Bartholemew Scott Calvin	Mid 18th C.	Unsure	Delaware preacher, College of New Jersey (1776), son of Stephen and brother to Hezekiah.
Papunhank	Mid 18th C.	Quaker/Moravian?	Munsee Indian preacher who established a Christian community in 1752.
Philip Jonathan	Mid 18th C.	Unsure	Canajoharie. Took over when Paulus Sahonwadi went away. In 1764 the community chose him over Jacob Oel.
Moses Tinda Tautamy	Mid 18th C.	Presbyterian	Worked for David Brainerd as interpreter in the mid 1740's. Born around 1695.
Unnamed	Mid 18th C.	Presbyterian	Was training in John Brainerd's school for the ministry at the expense of the SSPCK.
Peter Tatami	Mid 18th C.	Presbyterian	Probably the son or relation of Moses Tautamy. Aaron Burr drew money to educate him at College of New Jersey.
John Wauwaum-pequunnaunt	Mid 18th C.	Presbyterian	Former Student of Sergeant's at Stockbridge, David Brainerd's interpreter/teacher at Kaunaumeek.

Name	Time frame	Denomination	Notes
Miranda	Mid 18th C.	Presbyterian	A man who worked with Horton on Long Island but died shortly after being appointed in 1741.
West Africa			
James Capitein	Early/Mid 18th C.	Dutch Reformed	From West Africa, educated in Netherlands, and then sent to Elmina Castle in 1742.
Philip Quaque	1750s–1810	Anglican	Anglican African who was sent back to Cape Coast Castle, wrote over forty letters in fifty years.
Thomas Caboro	1750s	Anglican	Traveled with Quaque to England for ministerial training in the 1750s; died of consumption in 1758.
Cudjo	1750s	Anglican	Traveled with Quaque to England for ministerial training in the 1750s but went insane.
Frederick Adoy	1750s–1810	Uncommitted	Quaque tried to employ him as a preacher, but failed.
John Quamine (Quamino)	1772–1776	First Cong.	Sent to College of New Jersey but Revolution intervened with him being sent to West Africa.
Bristol Yamma	1772–1776	First Cong.	Sent to College of New Jersey but Revolution intervened. Died in January of 1794.

Name	Time frame	Denomination	Notes
Unnamed	1770s	Unclear	From Annamaboe and could have been employed, but was not.
Salmar Nubia	1790s	Second Cong.	Samuel Hopkins wanted to revamp the African missions and send him with Yamma. He eventually does end up going.
Newport Gardner	1790s	1790's	Hopkins wanted to revamp the African missions and send him with Yamma. He eventually does end up going.

Moravians

Name	Time frame	Denomination	Notes
Jacob Protten	Mid 18th C.	Moravian	Married to Rebecca Protten. From Accra, educated in Denmark/Saxony, returned to Gold Coast.
Rebecca Protten	Mid 18th C.	Moravian	Married to Jacob Protten. Began in the Danish West Indies (St. Thomas), went to Herrnhut, then Africa.
Frederick Pedersen Svane	Mid 18th C.	Moravian	Lived from 1710–1789, educated at University of Copenhagen, and preached on the Gold Coast.
Unnamed	Early/Mid 18th C.	Moravian	Planned to found a school in Genoa, Italy, and neighboring parts.
Jans Bafing	Mid 18th C.	Moravian	Deacon. Danish Atlantic—sent to petition Danish King on behalf of St. Thomas slaves.

Name	Time frame	Denomination	Notes
Andries	Mid 18th C.	Moravian	Deacon. Danish Atlantic—sent to petition Danish King on behalf of St. Thomas slaves.
Johannes	Mid 18th C.	Moravian	Brother to Andries. Moravian "helper."
Petrus	Mid 18th C.	Moravian	St. Thomas. Moravian helper, brother to Christoph. Actually expelled (behavior) in May of 1762.
Christoph	Mid 18th C.	Moravian	St. Thomas. Moravian helper, brother to Petrus.
Abraham	Mid 18th C.	Moravian	St. Thomas, teacher, had more "fire" than Petrus, but under him.
Mingo/David	Mid 18th C.	Moravian	St. Croix. Oldendorp says he was as "good as free." Kept meetings when white Moravians absent.
Cornelius	Mid 18th C.	Moravian	St. Thomas. Son of Benigna and a young but talented preacher.
Tabea	Mid 18th C.	Moravian	St. Croix. Wife of David and also a worker among women.
Stephanus	Mid 18th C.	Moravian	St. Thomas/St. Croix. Installed as helper in February of 1745.
Anna Maria	Mid 18th C.	Moravian	Moravian helper. With Rebecca she led women's religious groups.

Name	Time frame	Denomination	Notes
Magdalena	Mid 18th C.	Moravian	St. Thomas. Moravian helper, much older.
Maria	Mid 18th C.	Moravian	St. Thomas. Replaced Magdalena but then left for PA to get married.
Christina	Mid 18th C.	Moravian	St. Thomas. Replaced Maria when Maria left for PA to get married.
Every baptized convert	Mid 18th C.	Moravian	Many Moravian missionaries believed every baptized convert would have to be a preacher at some point or another.
Nicodemus	Mid 18th C.	Moravian	In Pennsylvania. An Elder of an Indian Church who wrote confessional texts.
Every national helper	Mid 18th C.	Moravian	Almost every national helper among the Moravians, black or Indian.
Abraham	Mid 18th C.	Moravian	A Mahican operating at Shekomeko, New York in the 1730s and 40s.
Johannes	Mid 18th C.	Moravian	A Mahican operating at Shekomeko, New York in the 1730s and 40s.

Post-Revolutionary

Name	Time frame	Denomination	Notes
Boston King	After Rev.	Methodist	Nova Scotia and Sierra Leone. Was a convert of Daddy Moses, but got his own congregation.

Name	Time frame	Denomination	Notes
"Daddy" Moses Wilkinson	After Rev.	Methodist	Blind by 1779. Operated in New York, Nova Scotia, and Sierra Leone.
Richard Allen	After Rev.	Methodist/Zionist	Itinerant preacher who later founded Philadelphia churches. Dates African Methodist Episcopal (AME) church to 1779 in his portrait.
Harry Hoosier	After Rev.	Methodist	Took part in 1784 Christmas Conference (with Richard Allen) in Baltimore. AKA "Black Harry."
John Jea	After Rev.	Methodist	Famous accounts of conversion.
John Marrant	After Rev.	Methodist	Preacher to Africans/Cherokee (account).
Olaudah Equiano	After Rev.	Uncommitted	Flirted with missionary activity before major success as author.
David George	After Rev.	Baptist	Converted by George Liele, established churches throughout Nova Scotia, missionary in Sierra Leone.
George Liele	After Rev.	Baptist	Converted many in South Carolina.
Luke Jordan	After Rev.	Methodist	Runaway slave who preached at Birchtown, then moved to Sierra Leone.

Name	Time frame	Denomination	Notes
John Chavis	Late 18th/19 C.	Unclear	Educated by John Witherspoon at College of New Jersey, went back to North Carolina to preach and teach.
Absalom Jones	Late 18th/19 C.	Methodist	Worked with Richard Allen to found Philadelphia churches.
Daniel Coker	Late 18th/19 C.	Methodist	Worked with Allen and Jones, but also spearheaded a missionary trip to West Africa.

Notes

Introduction

1. Olaudah Equiano to the Bishop of London, 11 March 1779, and Governor MacNamara to the Bishop of London, 11 March 1779, in Olaudah Equiano, *The Interesting Narrative of the Life of Olaudah Equiano, or Gustavus Vassa, The African, Written By Himself* (New York: W. Durell, 1791), 165–169.
2. Ibid.
3. Vincent Carretta, *Equiano the African: Biography of a Self-Made Man* (Athens: University of Georgia Press, 2005), 176–201. Carretta has suggested, here and elsewhere, that Equiano was born in the American colonies, not in Africa.
4. This statistic was estimated by Jeffrey Cox when he served as Chair of a panel entitled, "Religion, Empire, Indigenous Worlds," at the November 2006 meeting of the North American Conference on British Studies held in Boston, Massachusetts. See Jeffrey Cox, *The British Missionary Enterprise Since 1700* (New York: Routledge, 2008).
5. Norman Etherington, ed., *Missions and Empire* (The Oxford History of the British Empire) (Oxford: Oxford University Press, 2005), 7. Charles W. Forman, "The Missionary Force of the Pacific Island Churches," *International Review of Mission* 59 (1970): 215–226. Forman, *The Island Churches of the South Pacific: Emergence in the Twentieth Century* (Maryknoll, NY: Orbis Books, 1982). Peggy Brock, "New Christians as Evangelists," in Etherington, ed. *Missions and Empire,* 132–152. E. Palmer Patterson, "Native Missionaries of the North Pacific Coast: Philip McKay and Others," *Pacific Historian* 30 (1986): 22–37. Bonnie Sue Lewis, *Creating Christian Indians: Native Clergy in the Presbyterian Church* (Norman: University of Oklahoma Press, 2003). Louise M. Pirouet, *Black*

Evangelists: The Spread of Christianity in Uganda, 1891–1914 (London: Collings, 1978). Peggy Brock, ed., *Indigenous Peoples and Religious Change* (Boston: Brill, 2005).

6. See "Note on Sources" in the appendix.

7. See Joel W. Martin and Mark A. Nicholas, eds., *Native Americans, Christianity and the Reshaping of the American Religious Landscape* (Chapel Hill: University of North Carolina Press, 2010). David J. Silverman, *Faith and Boundaries: Colonists, Christianity, and Community among the Wampanoag Indians of Martha's Vineyard, 1600–1871* (New York: Cambridge University Press, 2005). Rachel M. Wheeler, *To Live Upon Hope: Mohicans and Missionaries in the Eighteenth-Century Northeast* (Ithaca: Cornell University Press, 2008). Linford D. Fisher, *The Indian Great Awakening: Religion and the Shaping of Native Cultures in Early America* (New York: Oxford University Press, 2012). Terrence Ranger, "Christianity and Indigenous Peoples: A Personal Overview." *The Journal of Religious History* 27 No. 3 (October 2003): 255–271.

8. Mary Louise Pratt, *Imperial Eyes: Travel Writing and Transculturation* (New York: Routledge, 1992), 7. Hilary E. Wyss, *Writing Indians: Literacy, Christianity, and Native Community in Early America* (Amherst: University of Massachusetts Press, 2000), 41–51.

9. Horacio De La Costa, S.J., "The Development of a Native Clergy in the Philippines," *Theological Studies* 8 No. 2 (June 1947), 219–221. Pierre Charles, *Missiologie: Études, Rapports, Conférences* (Paris: Desclée, 1939), I: 111–112.

10. Thomas Lechford, *Plain Dealing: or, Newes from New England. A short view of New-Englands present Government, both Ecclesiasticall and Civil, compared with the anciently-received and established Government of England, in some materiall points; fit for the gravest consideration in these times.* (London: W. E. and I. G., 1642), 53.

11. John Eliot, *A Brief Narrative of the Progress of the Gospel among the Indians of New England.* (Boston: John K. Wiggin & William Parsons Lunt., 1868), 5.

12. Henry Whitefield, *Strength out of Weakness. Or a Glorious Manifestation of the further Progresse of the Gospel amongst the Indians in New-England;·Held forth in sundry Letters from divers Ministers and others to the Corporation established by Parliament for promoting the Gospel among the Heathen in New-England: and to particular Members thereof since the late Treatise to that effect, formerly set forth by Mr. Henry Whitfield, late Pastor of Gilford in New-England. Published by the aforesaid Corporation* (London: M. Simmons, 1652), 6.

13. Matthew Mayhew, *The conquests and triumphs of grace: being a brief narrative of the success which the gospel hath had among the Indians of Martha's Vineyard (and the places adjacent) in New-England: with some remarkable curiosities, concerning the numbers, the customs, and the present circumstances of the Indians on that island: further explaining and confirming the account given of those matters, by Mr. Cotton Mather,*

in the Life of the renowned Mr. John Eliot (London: Nath. Hiller, 1695), 11–12.

14. SPG Journal in Society for the Propagation of the Gospel in Foreign Parts, *Records of the Society for the Propagation of the Gospel.* (East Ardsley, Yorkshire: Micro Methods, 1964), Volume 18, page 267.

15. Henry Whitfield, *The light appearing more and more towards the perfect day. Or, a farther discovery of the present state of the Indians in New-England, concerning the progresse of the Gospel amongst them. Manifested by letters from such as preacht to them there.* (London: T.R. & E.M., 1651), 22.

16. Thomas Shepard, *The Clear Sunshine of the Gospel Breaking Forth upon the Indians in New-England. Or, An historicall Narration of Gods Wonderfull Workings upon sundry of the Indians, both chief Governors and Common people, in bringing them to a willing and desired submission to the Ordinances of the Gospel; and framing their hearts to an earnest inquirie after the knowledge of God the Father, and of Jesus Christ the Saviour of the World.* (London: R. Cotes, 1648), 35–36.

17. John Eliot, *A further Account of the progress of the Gospel amongst the Indians in New England: Being a Relation of the Confessions made by several Indians (in the presence of the Elders and Members of several Churches) in order to their admission into Church-fellowship. Sent over to the Corporation for Propagating the Gospel of Jesus Christ amongst the Indians in New England at London, by Mr John Elliot one of the Laborers in the Word amongst them.* (London: John Macock, 1660), 10.

18. Society for the Propagation of the Gospel in Foreign Parts, *Classified Digest of the Records of the Society for the Propagation of the Gospel in Foreign Parts, 1701–1892* (London: Society for the Propagation of the Gospel in Foreign Parts, 1893), 837.

19. The Society in Scotland for Propagating Christian Knowledge, *Recommendation by the Society in Scotland for Propagating Christian Knowledge, in Favour of the Academy established by Mr. Eleazar Wheelock, of Lebanon, in Connecticut, in New England, for the education of Indian Missionaries* (Edinburgh: s.n., 1767), footnote on page 2.

20. Kenneth White, *The Lets and Impediments in Planting and Propagating the Gospel of Christ. A Sermon Preached before the Society for the Propagation of the Gospel in Foreign Parts, At Their Anniversary Meeting, In the Parish-Church of St. Mary-le-Bow; On Friday the 15th of February, 1711/12* (London: J. Downing, 1712), 41.

21. Eleazar Wheelock, *A Plain and Faithful Narrative of the Original Design, Rise, Progress and Present State of the Indian Charity-School at Lebanon, in Connecticut* (Boston: Richard and Samuel Draper, 1763), 27.

22. Letter from John Eliot to Unknown, 12 November 1648, in Edward Winslow, *The Glorious progress of the Gospel amongst the Indians in New England manifested by three letters under the hand of that famous instrument of the Lord, Mr. John Eliot, and another from Mr. Thomas Mayhew, Jun., both preachers of the word, as well to the English as*

Indians in New England . . . : together with an appendix to the foregoing letters, holding forth conjectures, observations, and applications, by I.D. . . . / published by Edward Winslow. (London: Hannah Allen, 1649), 10.

23. Eliot, *A Brief Narrative,* 5.

24. "An Account of Indian Churches in New-England, in a Letter Written A.D. 1673, by Rev. John Eliot, of Roxbury. Copied Under President Stiles's Inspection from the Original MS. Letter in Mr. Eliot's Own Hand Writing, in the Library of the Mathers at Boston," *Collections of the Massachusetts Historical Society,* First Series, Vol. X (Boston: Massachusetts Historical Society, 1809), 128.

25. Wheelock, *A Plain and Faithful Narrative,* 27.

26. I borrow this phrase from Edmund S. Morgan, *The Gentle Puritan, A Life of Ezra Stiles, 1727–1795* (New Haven and London: Yale University Press, 1962), 181.

27. Matthew 28:19 and Acts of the Apostles 16:9.

28. William Smith, *A Discourse Concerning the Conversion of the Heathen Americans, And the final Propagation of Christianity and the Sciences to the Ends of the Earth. In Two Parts. Part I. Preached before a voluntary Convention of the Episcopal Clergy of Pennsylvania, and Places adjacent, at Philadelphia, May 2d, 1760; and published at their joint Request. Part II. Preached before the Trustees, Masters and Scholars of the College and Academy of Philadelphia, at the first anniversary Commencement* (Philadelphia: W. Dunlap, 1760), 15.

29. John Wilson, *The Day-Breaking, if not the Sun-Rising of the Gospell with the Indians in New-England.* (London: Rich. Cotes, 1647), 16.

30. Letter from Sir John Percival to William Byrd, 3 December 1729, in George Berkeley, *Berkeley and Percival: The Correspondence of George Berkeley Afterwards Bishop of Cloyne and Sir John Percival Afterwards Earl of Egmont,* ed. Benjamin Rand (Cambridge: Cambridge University Press, 1914), 260.

31. St. George Ashe, *A Sermon Preach'd before the Incorporated Society for the Propagation of the Gospel in Foreign Parts; At Their Anniversary Meeting in the Parish-Church of St. Mary-le-Bow; on Friday the 18th of February, 1714.* (London: J. Downing, 1715), 15.

32. John Leng, *A Sermon Preached before the Incorporated Society for the Propagation of the Gospel in Foreign Parts; At the Parish-Church of St. Mary-Le-Bow, on Friday the 17th of February, 1726. Being the Day of their Anniversary Meeting.* (London: J. Downing, 1727), 20–23.

33. Experience Mayhew, *All mankind by nature equally under sin: a sermon preach'd at the public lecture in Boston, on Thursday, Dec. 3, 1724.* (Boston: B. Green, 1725), ii.

34. William Fleetwood, *A Sermon Preached before the Society for the Propagation of the Gospel in Foreign Parts, At the Parish-Church of St. Mary-le-Bow, on Friday the 16th of February, 1710/11, Being the Day of their Anniversary Meeting.* (London: J. Downing, 1711), 13.

35. John Egerton, *A Sermon Preached before the Incorporated Society for the Propagation of the Gospel in Foreign Parts; At Their Anniversary Meeting In the Parish-Church of St. Mary-le-Bow; On Friday February 18, 1763.* (London: E. Owen and T. Harrison, 1763), 11.

36. Smith, *A Discourse Concerning the Conversion of the Heathen Americans*, 18.

37. Ezra Stiles to Charles Chauncy, 8 December 1773, in Stiles, *The Papers of Ezra Stiles at Yale University* (New Haven: Yale University Press, 1976), Microfilm Reel 3.

38. Cotton Mather, *Magnalia Christi Americana, or The Ecclesiastical History of New England, From its First Planting In the Year 1620, Unto the Year of the Our Lord, 1698,* Vol. II (Hartford: Silus Andrus, 1820), 375–376.

39. Samuel Buell, *The Excellence and Importance of the Saving Knowledge of the Lord Jesus Christ in the Gospel-Preacher, Plainly and Seriously Represented and Enforced: and Christ preached to the Gentiles in Obedience to the Call of God. A Sermon Preached at East-Hampton, August 29, 1759; at the Ordination of Mr. Samson Occum, a Missionary Among the Indians. To Which is Prefixed, A Letter to the Rev. Mr. David Bostwick, Minister of the Presbyterian Church, in New-York, giving some Account of Mr. Occum's Education, Character, &c.* (New York: James Parker and Company, 1761), 32.

40. Joseph Sewall, *Christ Victorious over the Powers of Darkness, by the Light of His preached Gospel. A Sermon Preached in Boston, December 12. 1733. At the Ordination of the Reverend Mr. Stephen Parker, Mr. Ebenezer Hinsdell, and Mr. Joseph Seccombe, Chosen by the Commissioners to the Honourable Society for Propagating Christian Knowledge at Edinburgh, to carry the Gospel to the Aboriginal Natives on the Borders of New England.* (Boston: S. Kneeland and T. Green, 1733), 42.

41. Laura M. Stevens, *The Poor Indians: British Missionaries, Native Americans, and Colonial Sensibility* (Philadelphia: University of Pennsylvania Press, 2004).

42. Luca Codignola, "The Holy See and the Conversion of the Indians in French and British North America, 1486–1760," in *America in European Consciousness, 1493–1750,* ed. Karen Ordahl Kupperman (Chapel Hill: University of North Carolina Press, 1995), 216–217.

43. Ludwig von Pastor, *The History of the Popes From the Close of the Middle Ages Drawn From the Secret Archives of the Vatican and Other Original Sources* translated by Dom Ernest Graf Vol. XXIX (London: Kegan Paulo, Trench, Trubner & Co., Ltd., 1938), 214.

44. Quoted in C. R. Boxer, "The Problem of the Native Clergy in the Portuguese and Spanish Empires from the Sixteenth to the Eighteenth Centuries," in *Studies in Church History VI, The Mission of the Church and Propagation of the Faith,* ed. Geoffrey J. Cuming (London: Thomas Nelson and Sons, 1970), 85–99. John K. Thornton, "On the Trail of Voodoo: African

Christianity in Africa and the Americas." *The Americas* 44 No. 3 (January 1988): 263.

45. Boxer, "The Problem of a Native Clergy," 97.

46. Horacio De La Costa, S.J., "The Development of a Native Clergy in the Philippines," *Theological Studies* 8 No. 2 (June 1947): 222.

47. Boxer, "The Problem of a Native Clergy," 90.

48. Gerónimo de Mendieta, *Historia Eclesiastica Indiana* (Mexico: Antigua Librería, 1870). Thanks to Barry D. Sell and Cristián Roa de la Carrera for assistance on translating this text.

49. Robert Ricard, *The Spiritual Conquest of Mexico: An Essay on the Apostolate and the Evangelizing Methods of the Mendicant Orders in New Spain, 1523–1572,* Translated by Lesley Byrd Simpson (Berkeley: University of California Press, 1966), 222.

50. Ricard, *The Spiritual Conquest of Mexico,* 225–228 and 235. Steven W. Hackel, *Children of Coyote, Missionaries of Saint Francis: Indian-Spanish Relations in Colonial California, 1769–1850* (Chapel Hill: University of North Carolina Press, 2005).

51. Allan Greer, ed., *The Jesuit Relations: Natives and Missionaries in Seventeenth-Century North America* (Boston: Bedford/St. Martin's, 2000), 150.

52. Codignola, "The Holy See and the Conversion of the Indians," 217–219. Allan Greer, *Mohawk Saint: Catherine Tekakwitha and the Jesuits* (Oxford: Oxford University Press, 2005). Emma Anderson, *The Betrayal of Faith: The Tragic Journey of a Colonial Native Convert* (Cambridge, MA: Harvard University Press, 2007).

53. Caspar Sibelius, *Of the conversion of five thousand and nine hundred East-Indians, in the Isle Formosa, neere China, to the Profession of the True God, in Jesus Christ; by meanes of M. Ro: Junius, a Minister Lately in Delph in Holland. / Related by his good friend, M. C. Sibellius, Pastor in Daventrie There, in a Latine Letter. Translated to Further the Faith and Joy of Many Here, by H. Jessei, a Servant of Jesus Christ. With a Post-script of the Gospels Good Successe also amongst the West-Indians, in New-England. Imprimatur, Joseph Caryl* (London: John Hammond, 1650), 8.

54. Cotton Mather, *The triumphs of the reformed religion, in America. The life of the renowned John Eliot; a person justly famous in the church of God, not only as an eminent Christian, and an excellent Minister, among the English, but also, as a memorable evangelist among the Indians, of New-England; with some account concerning the late and strange success of the Gospel, in those parts of the world, which for many ages have lain buried in pagan ignorance* (Boston: Benjamin Harris and John Allen, 1691), 94.

1. Apostles to the Indians

1. John Eliot, *A further Accompt of the Progresse of the Gospel amongst the Indians in New-England, and of the means used effectually to advance the same. . . .* (London: M. Simmons, 1659), 14–15 and 53.

2. John Eliot and Thomas Mayhew, *Tears of repentance: or, A further narrative of the progress of the Gospel amongst the Indians in New-England. . . .* (London: Peter Cole in Leaden-Hall, 1653), 53.

3. Cotton Mather, *The Triumphs of the Reformed Religion in America. The life of the renowned John Eliot. . . .* (Boston: Benjamin Harris and John Allen, 1691), 119.

4. Constance Post suggests that Nishokon's sermon represents a form of cultural subjugation. See Post, "Old World Order in the New: John Eliot and the "Praying Indians" in Cotton Mather's Magnalia Christi Americana," *The New England Quarterly* 46 No. 3 (September 1993): 424–426.

5. Joshua David Bellin, "John Eliot's Playing Indian," *Early American Literature* 42 No. (January 2007): 4.

6. Henry Whitfield, *The light appearing more and more towards the perfect day. Or, a farther discovery of the present state of the Indians in New-England, concerning the progresse of the Gospel amongst them. Manifested by letters from such as preacht to them there.* (London: T.R. & E.M., 1651), 14–15.

7. Manasseh ben Israel and Moses Wall, *The Hope of Israel* (London: R.I., 1650) and Thomas Thorowgood, *Jews in America, or Probabilities, That Those Indians are Judaical, Made More Probable by Some Additionals to the Former Conjectures. An Accurate Discourse is Premised of Mr. John Eliot . . . Touching Their Origination, and his Vindication of the Planters* (London: Henry Brome, 1660).

8. Richard White, *The Middle Ground: Indians, Empires, and Republics in the Great Lakes Region, 1650–1815* (New York: Cambridge University Press, 1991).

9. Henry Steele Commager, ed., *Documents of American History*, 7th edition (New York: Appleton-Century-Crofts, 1963), 8.

10. Quoted from Robert Hunt Land, "Henrico and Its College," *The William and Mary Quarterly* 18 No. 4 (October 1938): 491. See Francis Jennings, *The Invasion of America: Indians, Colonialism, and the Cant of Conquest* (Chapel Hill: University of North Carolina Press, 1975). 53–56.

11. Henry Bowden and James P. Ronda, *John Eliot's Indian Dialogues: A Study in Cultural Interaction* (Westport, CT: Greenwood Press, 1980), 52. James Axtell, "Some Thoughts on the Ethnohistory of Missions," *Ethnohistory* 29 (Winter 1982): 36.

12. Mather, *The triumphs of the reformed religion, in America*, 80.

13. Cotton Mather, *Magnalia Christi Americana, or The Ecclesiastical History of New England, From its First Planting In the Year 1620, Unto the Year of the Our Lord, 1698.* Vol. I. (Hartford: Silus Andrus, 1820), from the epistle dedicatory.

14. Daniel Gookin, *Historical Collections of the Indians in New England* (Boston: Belknap and Hall, 1792), 14.

15. Letter from John Eliot to John Winslow (?), dated October 29, 1649, in Whitfield, *The light appearing*, 28.

16. Commager, ed. *Documents of American History*, 7th edition, 18. Acts of the Apostles 16:9.

17. Thomas Lechford, *Plain Dealing: Or, Newes from New-England. A short view of New-Englands present Government, both Ecclesiasticall and Civil, compared with the anciently-received and established Government of England. . . .* (London: W. E. and I. G., 1642), 21.

18. Anonymous, *New Englands first fruits: in respect, first of the conversion of some, conviction of divers, preparation of sundry of the Indians, 2. of the progresse of learning in the colledge at Cambridge in Massacusets Bay: with divers other speciall matters concerning the country.* (London: R.O. and G. D. for Henry Overton, 1643), 4.

19. John Wilson, *The Day-Breaking, if not the Sun-Rising of the Gospell with the Indians in New-England* (London: Rich. Cotes, 1647).

20. Thomas Shepard, *The Clear Sun-shine of the Gospel Breaking Forth upon the Indians in New-England. Or, An historicall Narration of Gods Wonderfull Workings upon sundry of the Indians. . . .* (London: R. Cotes, 1648), 33 and 15.

21. Shepard, *The Clear Sun-Shine*, 5.

22. Elise M. Brenner, "To Pray or to Be Prey: That is the Question. Strategies for Cultural Autonomy of Massachusetts Praying Town Indians" *Ethnohistory* 27 No. 2 (Spring 1980): 142–144.

23. Letter from John Eliot to a Gentleman of New-England, September 13, 1649, in Edward Winslow, *The Glorious progress of the Gospel amongst the Indians in New England manifested by three letters under the hand of that famous instrument of the Lord, Mr. John Eliot, and another from Mr. Thomas Mayhew, Jun., both preachers of the word, as well to the English as Indians in New England . . . : together with an appendix to the foregoing letters, holding forth conjectures, observations, and applications, by I.D. . . . / published by Edward Winslow* (London: Hannah Allen, 1649), 16.

24. "An Account of Indian Churches in New-England, in a Letter Written A.D. 1673, by Rev. John Eliot, of Roxbury. Copied Under President Stiles's Inspection from the Original MS. Letter in Mr. Eliot's Own Hand Writing, in the Library of the Mathers at Boston," in *Collections of the Massachusetts Historical Society*, First Series, Vol. X (Boston: Massachusetts Historical Society, 1809), 127.

25. John Eliot, *A Brief Narrative of the Progress of the Gospel Among the Indians of New England* (Boston: John K. Wiggin & William Parsons Lunt., 1868), 8.

26. Cotton Mather, *A letter, about the present state of Christianity, among the Christianized Indians of New-England. Written to the Honourable, Sir William Ashhurst, governour of the Corporation, for Propagating the Gospel among the Indians, in New-England, and Parts Adjacent, in America* (Boston: Timothy Green, 1705), 7. Gookin, *Historical Collections*, 40–45.

27. David J. Silverman, "Indians, Missionaries, and Religious Translation:

Creating Wampanoag Christianity in Seventeenth-Century Martha's Vineyard," *William and Mary Quarterly* 62 No. 2 (April 2005): 168–169. David J. Silverman, *Faith and Boundaries: Colonists, Christianity, and Community Among the Wampanoag Indians of Martha's Vineyard, 1600–1871* (New York: Cambridge University Press, 2005). James P. Ronda, "Generations of Faith: The Christian Indians of Martha's Vineyard," *The William and Mary Quarterly* 38 No. 3 (July 1981): 369–394.

28. Whitfield, *The light appearing*, 3–4.
29. Experience Mayhew, *Indian converts, or, Some account of the lives and dying speeches of a considerable number of the Christianized Indians of Martha's Vineyard, in New-England [microform] / by Experience Mayhew ; to which is added, some account of those English ministers who have successively presided over the Indian work in that and the adjacent islands* (London: S. Gerrish, 1727), 1–2.
30. Whitfield, *The light appearing*, 6.
31. Mayhew, *Indian Converts*, 9.
32. Ibid., 7.
33. Erik R. Seeman, "Reading Indians' Deathbed Scenes: Ethnohistorical and Representational Approaches." *The Journal of American History* 88 No. 1 (June 2001): 17–47. Erik R. Seeman, *Death in the New World: Cross-Cultural Encounters, 1492–1800* (Philadelphia: University of Pennsylvania Press, 2010), 143–184.
34. Whitfield, *The light appearing*, 1–2.
35. Mayhew, *Indian Converts*, 5.
36. Letter from John Wilson, October 27, 1651, in Whitfield, *Strength Out of Weakness*, 13–14.
37. Mather, *Magnalia Christa Americana*, 378–384.
38. Mayhew, *Indian Converts*, 14 and 21–23.
39. Mather, *Magnalia Christa Americana*, 384.
40. Mayhew, *Indian Converts*, 168. Ronda, "Generations of Faith": 384–385.
41. Ronda, "Generations of Faith": 369–394. Silverman, "Indians, Missionaries, and Religious Translation": 146–167.
42. Mayhew, *Indian Converts*, 26.
43. Axtell, "Some Thoughts on the Ethnohistory of Missions": 36.
44. John Eliot and Thomas Mayhew, *Tears of repentance*, 28.
45. Eliot, *A further accompt*, 10 (Anthony) and 4 (Nishokon).
46. Letter from Thomas Mayhew to the United Commissioners of New England, June 21, 1671, in Company for the Propagation of the Gospel in New England and the Parts Adjacent in America, *Some correspondence between the governors and treasurers of the New England Company in London and the commissioners of the United Colonies in America, the missionaries of the company, and others between the years 1657 and 1712, to which are added the journals of the Rev. Experience Mayhew in 1713 and 1714 [Edited by] John W. Ford [Governor of the New England Company]* (New York: B. Franklin, 1970), 42.

47. Eliot and Mayhew, *Tears of Repentance,* 12.
48. Anonymous, *New England's First Fruits,* 5–7.
49. Neal Salisbury, "Religious Encounters in a Colonial Context: New England and New France in the Seventeenth Century," *American Indian Quarterly* 16 No. 4 (Autumn 1992): 502. Silverman, "Indians, Missionaries, and Religious Translation": 147.
50. William Scranton Simmons, *Spirit of the New England Tribes: History and Folklore, 1620–1984* (Hanover: University Press of New England, 1986), 67.
51. Society for the Propagation of the Gospel in New England, *The New England Company of 1649* (Boston: The Prince Society, 1920), 34.
52. Eliot and Mayhew, *Tears of Repentance,* 6.
53. Wilson, *The Day-Breaking,* 17.
54. Shepard, *The Clear Sun-Shine,* 36.
55. Eliot, *A Brief Narrative of the Progress of the Gospel,* 5.
56. Samuel Eliot Morison, *Harvard in the Seventeenth Century* Vol. I (Cambridge, MA: Harvard University Press, 1936), 340–360. Jill Lepore, *The Name of War: King Philip's War and the Origins of American Identity* (New York: Knopf, 1998), 21–47.
57. Company for the Propagation of the Gospel in New England and the Parts Adjacent in America, *Some correspondence,* 10.
58. Henry Whitfield, *Strength out of Weakness Or a Glorious Manifestation of the further Progresse of the Gospel amongst the Indians in New-England; Held forth in sundry Letters from divers Ministers and others to the Corporation established by Parliament for promoting the Gospel among the Heathen in New-England....* (London: M. Simmons, 1652), 6.
59. Bowden and Ronda, eds., *John Eliot's Indian Dialogues,* 61.
60. Ibid., 65.
61. Ibid., 85.
62. Society for the Propagation of the Gospel in New England, *The New England Company,* xlviii.
63. Shepard, *The Clear Sun-Shine,* 34.
64. Gookin, *Historical Collections,* 33.
65. Letter from John Eliot to William Ashurst, October 1, 1671, in Company for the Propagation of the Gospel in New England, *Some Correspondence,* 50.
66. Mather, *The triumphs of the reformed religion, in America,* 119–120.
67. Shepard, *The Clear Sun-Shine,* 31 and Letter from John Eliot to Thomas Shepard, September 4, 1647, in ibid., 19.
68. Anonymous, *New England's First Fruits,* 4.
69. Salisbury, "Religious Encounters in a Colonial Context": 502.
70. Mayhew, *Indian Converts,* xvi.
71. John Endecott to the President of the New England Company, August 27, 1651, in Whitfield, *Strength out of Weakness,* 28–29.
72. Whitfield, *The light appearing,* 3.

73. Mather, *Magnalia Christa Americana*, 385–386.
74. John Eliot, *The Dying Speeches of several Indians* (Cambridge, MA: Samuel Green, 1685), 11.
75. Mather, *Magnalia Christa Americana*, 516. Mayhew, *Indian Converts*, 6.
76. Matthew Mayhew, *The conquests and triumphs of grace: being a brief narrative of the success which the gospel hath had among the Indians of Martha's Vineyard (and the places adjacent) in New-England . . . further explaining and confirming the account given of those matters, by Mr. Cotton Mather, in the Life of the renowned Mr. John Eliot* (London: Nath. Hiller, 1695), 20.
77. Eliot, *The Dying Speeches of Several Indians*, 3.
78. Eliot, *A Further Accompt*, 9.
79. Letter from the New England Commissioners to Robert Boyle, September 10, 1662, in Gookin, *Historical Collections*, 77.
80. Letter from the New England Commissioners to Robert Boyle, September 8, 1670, in Company for the Propagation of the Gospel in New England, *Some correspondence*, 35.
81. Letter from Eliot to Robert Boyle, June 7, 1669, in Company for the Propagation of the Gospel in New England, *Some correspondence*, 28.
82. Mayhew, *The conquests and triumphs*, 34.
83. Gookin, *Historical Collections of the Indians in New England*, 43–53.
84. Increase Mather, *A Brief History of the Warr with the Indians in New-England* (Boston: J. Foster, 1676), 11. See Lepore, The Name of War, 21–47.
85. Lepore, *The Name of War*, 183.
86. Letter from John Eliot to the Robert Boyle of the New England Company (undated), in Company for the Propagation of the Gospel in New England and the Parts Adjacent in America, *Some correspondence*, 53.
87. Daniel Gookin, *An Historical Account of the Doings and Sufferings of The Christian Indians in New England, in the Years 1675, 1676, 1677*, in American Antiquarian Society, *Archaeologia Americana: Transactions and Collections of the American Antiquarian Society* Vol. II (Worcester: The Society, 1834), 504.
88. Gookin, *An Historical Account of the Doings and Sufferings of the Christian Indians*, 475–482. Lepore, *The Name of War*, 141–143.
89. Gookin, *An Historical Account of the Doings and Sufferings of the Christian Indians*, 436.
90. Neal Salisbury, "Embracing Ambiguity: Native Peoples and Christianity in Seventeenth-Century North America," *Ethnohistory* 50 No. 2 (Spring 2003): 248. Lepore, *The Name of War*, 136–149. Hilary E. Wyss, *Writing Indians: Literacy, Christianity, and Native Community in Early America* (Amherst: University of Massachusetts Press, 2000), 41–51.
91. Gookin, *An Historical Account of the Doings and Sufferings of the Christian Indians*, 483.
92. Ibid.

93. Letter from Increase Mather to William Ashurst, 20 January 1697, in
Company for the Propagation of the Gospel in New England and the Parts
Adjacent in America, *Some correspondence*, xviii. Mayhew, *Indian
Converts*, xvii.
94. Petition of Natick Indians to John Eliot, 19 March 1683, in Company for
the Propagation of the Gospel in New England and the Parts Adjacent in
America, *Some correspondence*, 74–75.
95. William Kellaway, *The New England Company, 1649–1776: Missionary
Society to the American Indians* (New York: Barnes and Noble, Inc.,
1961), 237.
96. Letter from Cotton Mather to Sir William Ashurst, 10 October, 1712, in
"Cotton and Increase Mather Letters, 1713–1726" Massachusetts
Historical Society Manuscript Collection, 7.
97. Daniel R. Mandell, *Behind the Frontier: Indians in Eighteenth-Century
Eastern Massachusetts* (Lincoln: University of Nebraska Press, 1996), 35
and 104–105.

2. The Expansion of the Indigenous Missionary Enterprise

1. St. George Ashe, *A Sermon Preach'd before the Incorporated Society for
the Propagation of the Gospel in Foreign Parts; At Their Anniversary
Meeting in the Parish-Church of St. Mary-le-Bow; on Friday the 18th of
February, 1714* (London: J. Downing, 1715), 49.
2. A brief summary of the Prince's visit can be found in Alden T. Vaughan,
Transatlantic Encounters: American Indians in Britain, 1500–1776 (New
York: Cambridge University Press, 2006), 133–135.
3. Mary Rowlandson, *The Sovereignty and Goodness of God, Together with
the Faithfulness of His Promises Displayed. Being a Narrative of the
Captivity and Restoration of Mrs. Mary Rowlandson and Related
Documents* ed. Neal Salisbury (Boston: Bedford/St. Martin's, 1997), 98.
4. Jill Lepore, *The Name of War: King Philip's War and the Origins of
American Identity* (New York: Knopf, 1998), 52 and 173–190. Hilary E.
Wyss, *Writing Indians: Literacy, Christianity, and Native Community in
Early America* (Amherst: University of Massachusetts Press, 2000),
30–51.
5. Daniel Gookin, *Historical Collections of the Indians in New England*
(Boston: Belknap and Hall, 1792), 32 and 81.
6. Cotton Mather, *Another Tongue brought in, to Confess the Great
SAVIOUR of the World. Or, some COMMUNICATIONS of Christianity,
Put into a Tongue used among the Iroquois Indians, in America....*
(Boston: B. Green, 1707).
7. Matthew Mayhew, *A Brief Narrative of the Success which the Gospel
hath had, among the Indians, of Martha's-Vineyard (and the Places
Adjacent) in New-England ... Further Explaining [sic] and Confirming
the Account given of those matters, by Mr. Cotton Mather in the Life
of the Renowned Mr. John Eliot* (Boston: Bartholomew Green, 1694).

Experience Mayhew, *The Massachuset Psalter, or, Psalms of David: with the Gospel according to John: in columns of Indian and English: being an introduction for training up the aboriginal natives in reading and understanding the Holy Scriptures* (Boston: B. Green, 1709).

8. Neal Salisbury, "Red Puritans: The "Praying Indians" of Massachusetts Bay and John Eliot," *The William and Mary Quarterly* 31 No. 1 (January 1974): 53. Daniel R. Mandell, *Behind the Frontier: Indians in Eighteenth-Century Eastern Massachusetts* (Lincoln: University of Nebraska Press, 1996).

9. Experience Mayhew, *Indian converts, or, Some account of the lives and dying speeches of a considerable number of the Christianized Indians of Martha's Vineyard, in New-. . . .* (London: S. Gerrish, 1727).

10. Frederick L. Weis, "The New England Company of 1649 and its Missionary Enterprises," *Publications of the Colonial Society of Massachusetts* Volume XXXVII (Boston: Colonial Society of Massachusetts, 1959), 134–218. Goddard and Kathleen J. Bragdon, *Native Writings in Massachusett*, Vol. II (Philadelphia: The American Philosophical Society, 1988), 672.

11. Mayhew, *Indian Converts*, xvii. Letter from Increase Mather to Dr. John Leusden, July 12, 1687, in Cotton Mather, *Magnalia Christi Americana, or The Ecclesiastical History of New England, From its First Planting In the Year 1620, Unto the Year of the Our Lord, 1698.* Vol. I. (Hartford: Silus Andrus, 1820), 508–509.

12. David J. Silverman, "Indians, Missionaries, and Religious Translation: Creating Wampanoag Christianity in Seventeenth-Century Martha's Vineyard," *William and Mary Quarterly* 62 No. 2 (April 2005): 141–174. Silverman, *Faith and Boundaries: Colonists, Christianity, and Community Among the Wampanoag Indians of Martha's Vineyard, 1600–1871* (New York: Cambridge University Press, 2005). James P. Ronda, "Generations of Faith: The Christian Indians of Martha's Vineyard," *The William and Mary Quarterly* 38 No. 3 (July 1981): 369–394.

13. Colin G. Calloway, *The American Revolution in Indian Country: Crisis and Diversity in Native American Communities* (New York: Cambridge University Press, 1995), 9–11.

14. Rev. Experience Mayhew, *A brief Journal of my Visitation of the Pequot & Mohegin Indians, at the desire of the Honourable Commissioners for the Propagation of the Gospel among the Indians in New England* (1713), from Company for the Propagation of the Gospel in New England and the Parts Adjacent in America, *Some correspondence between the governors and treasurers of the New England Company in London and the commissioners of the United Colonies in America, the missionaries of the company, and others between the years 1657 and 1712, to which are added the journals of the Rev. Experience Mayhew in 1713 and 1714 [Edited by] John W. Ford [Governor of the New England Company]* (New York: B. Franklin, 1970), 102–103 and 126–127. "Account of an Indian Visitation, A.D. 1698." Copied for Dr. Stiles, By Rev. Mr. Hawley, Missionary at

Mashpee, From the Printed Account Published in 1698, in *Collections of the Massachusetts Historical Society, First Series, Vol. X* (Boston: The Society, 1809), 130–134. Mandell, *Behind the Frontier*, 59 and 126. Cotton Mather, *Just commemorations. The death of good men, considered; and the characters of some who have lately died in the service of the churches, exhibited. . . .* (Boston: B. Green, 1715), 53–55.

15. Mayhew, *A brief Journal of my Visitation of the Pequot & Mohegin Indians*, 97–98.

16. Mayhew, *A Brief Narrative of the Success which the Gospel hath had, among the Indians, of Martha's Vineyard*, 31.

17. Letter from Zachary Hossueit to Solomon Briant (spelled Priant), 17 January 1766, from the Watkinson Library of Trinity College, Hartford, in Goddard and Bragdon, *Native Writings in Massachusett*, Vol. I, 361. "Petition from the native assembly at Mashpee to the Commissioners of the New England Company on behalf of their minister Solomon Briant, and incidentally concerning a proposal to send an English minister to them," 22 November 1753, from the Massachusetts State Archives (32:427), in Goddard and Bragdon, *Native Writings in Massachusett*, Vol. I, 179.

18. Jack Campisi, *The Mashpee Indians: Tribe on Trial* (Syracuse, N.Y.: Syracuse University Press, 1991), 84. Goddard and Bragdon, *Native Writings in Massachusett*, Vol. I, 35–37, 81, 85, 269, 305, 333, 281, 307.

19. Petition by Martha's Vineyard Indians to the Boston Commissioners, 5 September, 1479, in Goddard and Bragdon, *Native Writings in Massachusett*, Vol. I, 173–175.

20. "Petition from the natives of Gay Head to the Commissioners of the New England Company objecting to the appointment of Elisha Amos as a local Magistrate," at the Massachusetts Historical Society, Miscellaneous Unbound Manuscripts, in Goddard and Bragdon, *Native Writings in Massachusett*, Vol. I, 225.

21. Letter from Jonathan Parsons (Lyme) to Benjamin Colman about teaching the Indians at Lyme and settling the question of their land boundaries, 26 Feb. 1734 in the Benjamin Colman Papers, 1641–1806, Massachusetts Historical Society Manuscript Collection.

22. James Ned's 1754 land deed, from "In Their Own Write: Native American documents from the collections of Pilgrim Hall Museum," www.pilgrimhall .org (accessed on 11 August 2011). Silverman, *Faith and Boundaries*, 121–156.

23. William Kellaway, *The New England Company, 1649–1776: Missionary Society to the American Indians* (New York: Barnes and Noble, Inc., 1961), 241.

24. John Eliot, *A Letter of the Reverend John Eliot of Roxbury to the Reverend Thomas Shepard of Charlestown, August 22, 1673 concerning the state of the gospel work among the Indians* (Portland, M.E.: Anthoensen Press, 1952), 3. William Scranton Simmons, *Spirit of the New England Tribes:*

History and Folklore, 1620–1984 (Hanover: University Press of New England, 1986), 21.

25. Quoted from Kellaway, *The New England Company*, 229.

26. Cotton Mather, *A letter, about the present state of Christianity, among the Christianized Indians of New-England. Written to the Honourable, Sir William Ashhurst, governour of the Corporation, for Propagating the Gospel among the Indians, in New-England, and Parts Adjacent, in America* (Boston: Timothy Green, 1705), 7–8.

27. Letter from Samuel Treat, 23 August 1693, in Mayhew, *A Brief Narrative of the Success which the Gospel hath had, among the Indians, of Martha's Vineyard*, 48. Weis, "The New England Company of 1649," 184.

28. Mather, *A Letter, About the Present State of Christianity*, 9. Mather, *Just Commemorations*, 50. Samuel Sewall Diary, 1714–1729, Massachusetts Historical Society (on Microfilm), 30.

29. Ibid.

30. James Axtell, *The Invasion Within: The Contest of Cultures in Colonial North America* (New York, Oxford University Press, 1985), 16–17.

31. Mayhew, *Indian Converts*, 49–57.

32. Transcription of an Eliot Bible from the Congregational Society Library, in Goddard and Bragdon, *Native Writings in Massachusett*, Vol. I, 387, 409, and 445.

33. Transcription of an Eliot Bible from the Congregational Society Library, in Goddard and Bragdon, *Native Writings in Massachusett*, Vol. I, 423 and 433. "Account of an Indian Visitation," 133.

34. Douglas L. Winiarski, "Native American Popular Religion in New England's Old Colony, 1670–1770," *Religion and American Culture: A Journal of Interpretation* 15 No. 2 (Summer 2005), 154.

35. Philip Bisse, *A Sermon Preach'd before the Incorporated Society for the Propagation of the Gospel in Foreign Parts; At Their Anniversary Meeting in the Parish-Church of St. Mary-le-Bow; on Friday the 21st of February, 1717* (London: Joseph Downing, 1718), 20.

36. Bisse, *A Sermon Preach'd before the Incorporated Society for the Propagation of the Gospel in Foreign Parts*, 2.

37. Cotton Mather to William Ashurst, 9 November 1710, in Company for the Propagation of the Gospel in New England and the Parts Adjacent in America, *Some correspondence between the governors and treasurers of the New England Company in London and the commissioners of the United Colonies in America*, 11. Cotton Mather to Sir William Ashurst, 1 April 1714, in "Cotton and Increase Mather Letters, 1713–1726," Massachusetts Historical Society Manuscript Collections.

38. Thomas Bray, *Apostolick Charity, Its Nature and Excellence Consider'd, in a Discourse Upon Dan. 12. 3. Preached at St. Paul's, at the Ordination of some Protestant Missionaries to be sent into the Plantations. To which is Prefixt, A General View of the English Colonies in America, with respect to Religion. . . .* (London: William Hawes, 1699), from the fifth

point of his "General View." This section of the document lacks page numbers.

39. Mayhew, *A Brief Narrative of the Success which the Gospel hath had, among the Indians, of Martha's-Vineyard,* 32.

40. Quoted from William Byrd II, in Stitt Robinson, Jr., "Indian Education and Missions in Colonial Virginia," *The Journal of Southern History* 17 (February–November 1952): 166. Axtell, *The Invasion Within,* 190–196.

41. Vaughan, *Transatlantic Encounters,* 120. Eric Hinderaker, "The 'Four Indian Kings' and the Imaginative Construction of the First British Empire" *The William and Mary Quarterly* 53 No. 3 (July 1996): 487–526.

42. Society for the Propagation of the Gospel in Foreign Parts, *An Account of the Propagation of the Gospel in Foreign Parts: What the Society Establish'd in England by Royal Charter hath done since their Incorporation, June the 16th 1701. in her Majesty's Plantations, Colonies, and Factories....* (London: J. Downing, 1704), 1–2. Indian Sachems to the SPG, undated, in Society for the Propagation of the Gospel in Foreign Parts, *Records of the Society for the Propagation of the Gospel* (East Ardsley, Yorkshire: Micro Methods, 1964) (hereafter referred to as *SPG Records*), Letter Series A, Volume 5

43. Quoted from Vaughan, *Transatlantic Encounters,* 120.

44. Daniel K. Richter, "Some of Them ... Would Always Have a Minister with Them": Mohawk Protestantism, 1683–1719," *American Indian Quarterly* 16 No. 4 (Autumn 1992): 471–484.

45. Society for the Propagation of the Gospel in Foreign Parts, *An Account of the Society for Propagating the Gospel in Foreign Parts: Established by the Royal Charter of King William III. With their Proceedings and Success, and Hopes of continual Progress under the Happy Reign of Her Most excellent Majesty Queen Anne* (London: Joseph Downing, 1706), 56–57.

46. Undated letter from the Indian Sachems to the Archbishop of Canterbury, in *SPG Records,* Letter Series A, Volume 6. Eric Hinderaker, *The Two Hendricks: Unraveling a Mohawk Mystery* (Cambridge, MA: Harvard University Press, 2010).

47. Quoted from Vaughan, *Transatlantic Encounters,* 133.

48. John G. Garrant, *The Four Indian Kings* (Ottawa: Public Archives, 1985), 139–143.

49. Vaughan, *Transatlantic Encounters,* 131. Patricia U. Bonomi, *Under the Cope of Heaven: Religion, Society, and Politics in Colonial America* (New York: Oxford University Press, 2003), xiii.

50. Church of England, *The Morning and Evening Prayer, The Litany, Church Catechism, Family Prayers, and Several Chapters of the Old and New-Testament, Translated into the Mahaque Indian Language, by Lawrence Claesse, Interpreter to William Andrews....* (New York: William Bradford, 1715), 37 and 54. Axtell, *The Invasion Within,* 16.

51. Mr. Barclay to the SPG, 26 September 1710, in *SPG Records,* Letter Series A, Volume 5.

52. Quoted from Ernest Hawkins, *Historical Notices of the Missions of the Church of England in the North American Colonies, previous to the independence of the United States: Chiefly From the MS Documents of the Society for the Propagation of the Gospel in Foreign Parts* (London: B. Fellowes, 1845), 269.

53. Daniel K. Richter, *The Ordeal of the Longhouse: The Peoples of the Iroquois in the Era of European Colonization* (Chapel Hill, NC: University of North Carolina Press, 1992), 214–236.

54. George Stanhope, *The early Conversion of Islanders a wise Expedient for propagating Christianity. A Sermon Preached before the Incorporated Society for the Propagation of the Gospel in Foreign Parts; At Their Anniversary Meeting In the Parish-Church of St. Mary-le-Bow; On Friday the 19th of February, 1713–14* (London: J. Downing, 1714), 32.

55. Frank J. Klingberg, "The Mystery of the Lost Yamasee Prince" *South Carolina Historical Magazine* 63 No. 1 (1962): 18–32.

56. Quoted in Vaughan, *Transatlantic Encounters,* 134.

57. Yamassee Prince to the SPG, 8 December 1715, quoted in Klingberg, "The Mystery of the Lost Yamassee Prince": 27.

58. Quoted in Vaughan, *Transatlantic Encounters,* 15.

59. Gideon Johnston to the SPG, 19 December 1715, quoted in Klingberg, "The Mystery of the Lost Yamassee Prince": 28.

60. Joseph Wilcocks, *A Sermon Preach'd before the Incorporated Society for the Propagation of the Gospel in Foreign Parts; At Their Anniversary Meeting in the Parish-Church of St. Mary-le-Bow; on Friday the 18th of February, 1725* (London: Joseph Downing, 1726), 36.

61. Stephen Neill, *A History of Christianity in India, 1707–1858* (New York: Cambridge University Press, 1985), 28–58.

62. George Berkeley, *A Proposal For the Better Supplying of Churches in our Foreign Plantations, and For Converting the Savage Americans to Christianity, By a College to be Erected in the Summer Islands, Otherwise Called the Isles of Bermuda* (Dublin: George Grierson, 1725), 3.

63. Edwin S. Gaustad, "George Berkeley and New World Community," *Church History* 48 No. 1 (March 1979): 5–17. A. A. Luce, "Berkeley's Bermuda Project and His Benefactions to American Universities, with Unpublished Letters and Extracts from the Egmont Papers," *Proceedings of the Royal Irish Academy* Volume 42, Section C, No. 6 (London: Williams & Norgate, 1934). Graham P. Conroy, "Berkeley and Education in America," *Journal of the History of Ideas* 21 No. 2 (April–June 1960): 211–221. Benjamin Rand, ed., *Berkeley and Percival: The Correspondence of George Berkeley Afterwards Bishop of Cloyne and Sir John Percival Afterwards Earl of Egmont* (Cambridge: Cambridge University Press, 1914), 31–46.

64. Berkeley, *A Proposal for the Better Supplying of Churches,* 4–5, 14–17.

65. Ibid., 12.

66. Sir John Percival to George Berkeley, 30 June 1723, in Rand, ed., *Berkeley and Percival,* 209.

67. Berkeley, *A Proposal for the Better Supplying of Churches,* 5.
68. Samuel Clyde McCullough, "A Plea for Further Missionary Activity in Colonial America—Dr. Thomas Bray's Missionalia" (n.p., 1946), reprinted from *Historical Magazine of the Protestant Episcopal Church* (September 1946), 10.
69. William Byrd to Sir John Percival, 10 June 1729, in Rand, ed., *Berkeley and Percival,* 244–255.
70. Journal of Sir John Percival, 27 February 1732, in Rand, ed., *Berkeley and Percival,* 282. William Byrd to Sir John Percival, 10 June 1729, in Rand, ed., *Berkeley and Percival,* 244
71. Berkeley to Sir John Percival, 4 March 1723, in Rand, ed., *Berkeley and Percival,* 206.
72. Bray, *Apostolick Charity,* the fifth point from "A General View."
73. Thomas Bray, *Missionalia: Or, A Collection of Missionary Pieces Relating to the Conversion of the Heathen; Both the African Negroes and American Indians* (London: W. Roberts, 1727), A2, 44–46, and 77–79.
74. Bishop Edmund Gibson, *Letter to the Masters and Mistresses of Families in the English Plantations abroad; Exhorting them to encourage and promote the Instruction of their Negroes in the Christian Faith,* in David Humphreys, *An Account of the Endeavours Used By The Society For the Propagation of the Gospel in Foreign Parts, To instruct the Negroe Slaves in New York. Together with Two of Bp. Gibson's Letters on that Subject. Being an Extract from Dr. Humphreys's Historical Account of the Incorporated Society for the Propagation of the Gospel in Foreign Parts, from its Foundation to the Year 1728* (London: s.n., 1730), 23.
75. The best treatment of this problem can be found in Travis Glasson, *Mastering Christianity: Missionary Anglicanism and Slavery in the Atlantic World* (New York: Oxford University Press, 2012).
76. Peter H. Wood, *Black Majority: Negroes in Colonial South Carolina From 1670 Through the Stono Rebellion* (New York: Knopf, 1974), 131–142. Annette Laing, "Heathens and Infidels"? African Christianization and Anglicanism in the South Carolina Low Country, 1700–1750," *Religion and American Culture* 12 No. 2 (Summer 2002): 197–228. Shawn Comminey, "The Society for the Propagation of the Gospel in Foreign Parts and Black Education in South Carolina, 1702–1764," *The Journal of Negro History* 84 No. 4 (Autumn 1999): 360–369.
77. John Moore, *Of the Truth & Excellency of the Gospel: A Sermon Preached before the Society for the Propagation of the Gospel in Foreign Parts, At Their Anniversary Meeting, In the Parish-Church of St. Mary-le-Bow, on Friday the 20th of February, 1712/13* (London: J. Downing, 1713), 49.
78. See, for example, Morgan Godwyn, *The Negro's [and] Indians Advocate: Suing for their Admission to the Church: or A Persuasive to the Instructing and Baptizing of the Negro's and Indians in our Plantations . . . To which is added, A brief Account of Religion in Virginia* (London: J. D., 1680).
79. Edmund Gibson, *Letter to the Masters and Mistresses of Families in the English Plantations abroad,* in Frederick Dalcho, *An historical account of*

the Protestant Episcopal Church in South-Carolina ... To which are added; the laws relating to religious worship; the journals and rules of the convention of South-Carolina; the constitution and canons of the Protestant Episcopal church, and the course of ecclesiastical studies. (Charleston, SC: E. Thayer, 1820), 109.

80. Thomas N. Ingersoll, "'Releese us out of this Cruell Bondegg': An Appeal from Virginia in 1723," *The William and Mary Quarterly,* Third Series 51 No. 4 (Oct., 1994): 782.

81. Society for the Propagation of the Gospel in Foreign Parts, *Classified Digest of the Records of the Society for the Propagation of the Gospel in Foreign Parts, 1701–1892* (London: Society for the Propagation of the Gospel in Foreign Parts, 1893), 64. George Berkeley, *A Sermon Preached before the Incorporated Society for the Propagation of the Gospel in Foreign Parts; At Their Anniversary Meeting in the Parish-Church of St. Mary-Le-Bow, on Friday the 18th of February, 1731* (London: J. Downing, 1732), 20.

82. William Fleetwood, *A Sermon Preached before the Society for the Propagation of the Gospel in Foreign Parts, At the Parish-Church of St. Mary-le-Bow, on Friday the 16th of February, 1710/11, Being the Day of their Anniversary Meeting* (London: J. Downing, 1711), 17–22.

83. Samuel Bradford, *A Sermon Preached before the Incorporated Society for the Propagation of the Gospel in Foreign Parts; At Their Anniversary Meeting In the Parish-Church of St. Mary-le-Bow; On Friday the 19th of February, 1719* (London: John Wyat, 1720), 36–37. "An Act for the Better Ordering and Governing of Negroes and Slaves," in Dalcho, *An historical account of the Protestant Episcopal Church in South-Carolina,* 94–95.

84. Fleetwood, *A Sermon Preached,* 25.

85. Moore, *Of the Truth & Excellency of the Gospel,* 41.

86. Glasson, *Mastering Christianity,* 141–170.

87. Luce, "Berkeley's Bermuda Project": 107.

3. Slave Preachers and Indian Separatism

1. Sylvia R. Frey and Betty Wood, *Come Shouting to Zion: African American Protestantism in the American South and British Caribbean to 1830* (Chapel Hill: University of North Carolina Press, 1998), 70–73. Shawn Comminey, "The Society for the Propagation of the Gospel in Foreign Parts and Black Education in South Carolina, 1702–1764," *The Journal of Negro History* 84 No. 4 (Autumn 1999): 363–365. Albert J. Raboteau, *Slave Religion: The "Invisible Institution" in the Antebellum South* (New York: Oxford University Press, 2004), 116–117.

2. Ezra Stiles to Eleazar Wheelock, 26 January 1768, in Stiles, *The Papers of Ezra Stiles at Yale University* (New Haven: Yale University Press, 1976), Microfilm Reel 2.

3. Quoted in Jane T. Merritt, *At the Crossroads: Indians and Empires on a Mid-Atlantic Frontier, 1700–1763* (Chapel Hill: University of North Carolina Press, 2003), 102.

4. Moravian missionaries previously possessed the American Philosophical Society's copies of Church of England, *The Morning and Evening Prayer, The Litany, Church Catechism, Family Prayers, and Several Chapters of the Old and New-Testament, Translated into the Mahaque Indian Language, by Lawrence Claesse, Interpreter to William Andrews, Missionary to the Indians, from the Honourable and Reverend the Society for the Propagation of the Gospel in Foreign Parts* (New York: William Bradford, 1715).

5. A Dissenting Minister in England to a Gentleman in Scotland (anonymous and undated), in Anonymous, *Copy of Three Letters, The First Written by Dr. John Nicol at New-York, to Mr. William Wardrobe, Surgeon in the Grassmarket of Edinburgh; the Second by a Dissenting Minister in England to a Gentleman in Scotland; the Third From a Minister at Boston to His Friend at Glasgow. Giving an Account of the Progress and Success of the Gospel in Foreign Parts* (Edinburgh: A. Alison, 1740), 6–7.

6. Rachel Wheeler, "Women and Christian Practice in a Mahican Village," *Religion and American Culture* 13 No. 1 (Winter 2003): 27–67.

7. Merritt, *At the Crossroads,* 105. Aaron Fogleman, *Jesus is Female: Moravians and the Challenge of Radical Religion in Early America* (Philadelphia: University of Pennsylvania Press, 2007).

8. Mark M. Smith, "Remembering Mary, Shaping Revolt: Reconsidering the Stono Rebellion," *The Journal of Southern History* 67 No. 3 (August 2001): 513–534. John K. Thornton, "African Dimensions of the Stono Rebellion," *The American Historical Review* 96 No. 4 (October 1991): 1101–1113.

9. John K. Thornton, "On the Trail of Voodoo: African Christianity in Africa and the Americas," *The Americas* 44 No. 3 (January 1988): 269–274.

10. Thornton, "On the Trail of Voodoo": 271–272.

11. C. G. A. Oldendorp, *A Caribbean Mission,* ed. Johann Jakob Bossard, trans. By Arnold R. Highfield and Vladimir Barac (Ann Arbor, M.I.: Karoma Publishers, Inc., 1987), 427, 457, and 586.

12. Oldendorp, *A Caribbean Mission,* 333 and 629.

13. Ibid., 628.

14. Frey and Wood, *Come Shouting to Zion,* 1–62. Raboteau, *Slave Religion,* 4–92.

15. Oldendorp, *A Caribbean Mission,* 420. Jon F. Sensbach, *Rebecca's Revival: Creating Black Christianity in the Atlantic World* (Cambridge, MA: Harvard University Press, 2005).

16. Oldendorp, *A Caribbean Mission,* 418–419, 470, and 487. Frey and Wood, *Come Shouting to Zion,* 85.

17. Oldendorp, *A Caribbean Mission,* 418–420.

18. Cornelius to the Catechumens at New Herrnhut, in Oldendorp, *A Caribbean Mission,* 628. For more on African Islam in the Americas, see Michael Angelo Gomez, *Exchanging Our Country Marks: The Transformation of African Identities in the Colonial and Antebellum South* (Chapel Hill: University of North Carolina Press, 1998), 59–87.

19. Oldendorp, *A Caribbean Mission*, 333.

20. Frey and Wood, *Come Shouting To Zion*, 56–59.

21. Sensbach, *Rebecca's Revival*.

22. Oldendorp, *A Caribbean Mission*, 419 and 458.

23. Sensbach, *Rebecca's Revival*, 133–161.

24. St. Thomas Negroes Congregation to the King of Denmark, 15 February 1739, in *The Christian Monthly History: Or, An Account of the Revival and Progress of Religion, Abroad, and at Home* Number IV. For February 1744 (Edinburgh: R. Fleming and A. Alison, 1743–1746), 59.

25. Oldendorp, *A Caribbean Mission*, 574.

26. Nathanael's speech to the catechumens at New Herrnhut, in Oldendorp, *A Caribbean Mission*, 627.

27. Oldendorp, *A Caribbean Mission*, 570.

28. Ibid., 8–27 and 418.

29. Mingo to the Members of Bethlehem and Nazareth, in Oldendorp, *A Caribbean Mission*, 493.

30. St. Thomas Negroes Congregation to the King of Denmark, 15 February, 1739, in *The Christian Monthly History*, 58. See also Anna Van Popo to the Queen of Denmark, in ibid., 60.

31. Oldendorp, *A Caribbean Mission*, 420.

32. Evangeline Walker Andrews and Charles McLean Andrews, eds., *Journal of a Lady of Quality; Being the Narrative of a Journey from Scotland to the West Indies, North Carolina, and Portugal, in the years 1774 to 1776* (New Haven: Yale University Press, 1939), 108–109.

33. Emilia Viotti da Costa, *Crowns of Glory, Tears of Blood: The Demerara Slave Rebellion of 1823* (New York: Oxford University Press, 1994).

34. Oldendorp, *A Caribbean Mission*, 542–543.

35. Ibid., 611.

36. Ibid., 493.

37. See Rachel M. Wheeler, *To Live Upon Hope: Mohicans and Missionaries in the Eighteenth-Century Northeast* (Ithaca: Cornell University Press, 2008), Jane T. Merritt, "Dreaming of the Savior's Blood: Moravians and the Indian Great Awakening in Pennsylvania," *The William and Mary Quarterly* 54 No. 4 (October 1997): 723–746, and Aaron Spencer Fogleman, *Jesus is Female: Moravians and the Challenge of Radical Religion in Early America* (Philadelphia: University of Pennsylvania Press, 2007).

38. Wheeler, "Women and Christian Practice in a Mahican Village": 27–67.

39. Ibid., 34.

40. *Records of the Moravian mission among the Indians of North America*, Film Number 1279 at the American Philosophical Society. Reel 34, Box 319, Item 8, Folder 2.

41. John Heckewelder, "An Account of the History, Manners, and Customs, of The Indian Nations, Who Once Inhabited Pennsylvania and the Neighbouring States," in *Transactions of the Historical & Literary Committee of the American Philosophical Society, Held at Philadelphia,*

For Promoting Useful Knowledge Vol. I (Philadelphia: Abraham Small, 1819), 129.

42. Wheeler, "Women and Christian Practice in a Mahican Village." Merritt, *At the Crossroads,* 100–121. Amy C. Schuttl, ""What Will Become of Our Young People?" Goals for Indian Children in Moravian Missions," *History of Education Quarterly* 38 No. 3 (Autumn 1998): 268–286.

43. Nicodemus, Elder of the Indian Congregation at Gnadenhutten, January of 1747, in *Records of the Moravian mission among the Indians of North America.* Film Number 1279, American Philosophical Society. Reel 34, Box 319, Item 8, Folder 3.

44. Quoted in Merritt, *At the Crossroads,* 97–98.

45. Gregory Evans Dowd, *A Spirited Resistance: The North American Indian Struggle For Unity, 1745–1815* (Baltimore, MD: Johns Hopkins University Press, 1992), 85–88.

46. George Whitefield, *An Expostulatory Letter Addressed to Count Zinzendorff, And Lord Advocate of the Unitas Fratrum* (Philadelphia: William Bradford, 1753), 4.

47. Oldendorp, *A Caribbean Mission,* 625–626. Frey and Wood, *Come Shouting to Zion,* 86–87.

48. Summary of a letter from Alexander Garden to the SPG, 10 October 1743, in Journal of the SPG, Society for the Propagation of the Gospel in Foreign Parts, *Records of the Society for the Propagation of the Gospel* (East Ardsley, Yorkshire: Micro Methods, 1964), Volume 9, 238. Another recent treatment of the school is in Travis Glasson, *Mastering Christianity: Missionary Anglicanism and Slavery in the Atlantic World* (New York: Oxford University Press, 2012), 123–129.

49. Frey and Wood, *Come Shouting to Zion,* 71.

50. Thornton, "African Dimensions of the Stono Rebellion": 1101–1113. Smith, "Remembering Mary, Shaping Revolt: Reconsidering the Stono Rebellion": 513–534.

51. Early Anglican efforts at black education can be found in Shawn Comminey, "The Society for the Propagation of the Gospel in Foreign Parts and Black Education in South Carolina, 1702–1764" *The Journal of Negro History* 84 No. 4 (Autumn 1999): 360–369, Annette Laing, "Heathens and Infidels"? African Christianization and Anglicanism in the South Carolina Low Country, 1700–1750," *Religion and American Culture* 12 No. 2 (Summer 2002): 197–228, as well as throughout Glasson, *Mastering Christianity.*

52. George Whitefield to the Inhabitants of Maryland, Virginia, North and South-Carolina 23 January 1740, in *A Collection of Papers, Lately printed in the Daily Advertiser* (London: Booksellers in Town and Country, 1740), 2, 8–10.

53. George Whitefield to a friend in London, 27 April, 1740, *A Collection of Papers, Lately printed in the Daily Advertiser,* 2.

54. "The Manner of the Childrens spending their Time at the Orphan-House

in Georgia," in *A Collection of Papers, Lately printed in the Daily Advertiser,* 43.

55. Frey and Wood, *Come Shouting to Zion,* 94.

56. Alexander Garden to the SPG, 9 April 1742, in Society for the Propagation of the Gospel in Foreign Parts, *Records of the Society for the Propagation of the Gospel* (East Ardsley, Yorkshire: Micro Methods, 1964) (hereafter referred to as *SPG Records*), Letter Series B, 48–49.

57. Alexander Garden to George Whitefield, 30 July 1740, in Alexander Garden, *Six Letters To The Rev. Mr. George Whitefield* . . . (Boston: T. Fleet, 1740), 51–53.

58. Summary of a letter from Alexander Garden to the SPG, 6 May 1740, in SPG Journal, *SPG Records,* Volume 8, 176.

59. Summary of a letter from Alexander Garden to the SPG, 6 May 1740, in SPG Journal, *SPG Records,* Volume 8, 173–176.

60. Anthony Ellys, *A Sermon Preached before the Incorporated Society for the Propagation of the Gospel in Foreign Parts; At Their Anniversary Meeting In the Parish-Church of St. Mary-le-Bow; On Friday February 23, 1759* (London: E. Owen and T. Harrison, 1759), 30–31.

61. Frey and Wood, *Come Shouting to Zion,* 72.

62. Alexander Garden to the SPG, 9 April 1742, in *SPG Records,* Letter Series B, 48–49.

63. Alexander Garden to the SPG, 10 October 1742, in *SPG Records,* Letter Series B.

64. Glasson, *Mastering Christianity,* 141–170.

65. Robert Hay Drummond, *A Sermon Preached before the Incorporated Society for the Propagation of the Gospel in Foreign Parts; At Their Anniversary Meeting In the Parish-Church of St. Mary-le-Bow; on Friday February 15, 1754* (London: E. Owen, 1754), 19.

66. Philip Bearcroft, *A Sermon Preached before the Incorporated Society for the Propagation of the Gospel in Foreign Parts; At Their Anniversary Meeting In the Parish-Church of St. Mary-le-Bow; On Friday February 15, 1744* (London: Edward Owen, 1744), 19.

67. Summary of a letter from Alexander Garden to the SPG, 6 May 1740, in SPG Journal, *SPG Records,* Volume 8, 174.

68. Alexander Garden to the SPG, 24 September 1742, in *SPG Records,* Letter Series B.

69. W. Guy to the SPG, 26 March 1744, in *SPG Records,* Letter Series B.

70. Summary of a letter from Alexander Garden to the SPG, *SPG Records,* SPG Journal, Volume 10, 11–12.

71. Summary of a letter from Alexander Garden to the SPG, *SPG Records,* SPG Journal, Volume 11, 300.

72. Alexander Garden to the SPG, 18 October 1744, *SPG Records,* Letter Series B.

73. John Thomas, *A Sermon Preach'd before the Incorporated Society for the Propagation of the Gospel in Foreign Parts; At Their Anniversary Meeting*

in the Parish-Church of St. Mary-le-Bow; on Friday February 20, 1746 (London: Edward Owen, 1747), 55–56.

74. Alexander Garden to the SPG, 4 February 1750, in *SPG Records*, Letter Series B.

75. Edward Cressett, *A Sermon Preached before the Incorporated Society for the Propagation of the Gospel in Foreign Parts; At Their Anniversary Meeting In the Parish-Church of St. Mary-le-Bow; on Friday, February 16, 1753* (London: Edward Owen, 1753), 53–54.

76. Jonathan Boucher to John Waring, 28 April 1764, in John C. Van Horne, ed., *Religious Philanthropy and Colonial Slavery: The American Correspondence of the Associates of Dr. Bray, 1717–1777* (Chicago: University of Illinois Press, 1985), 206.

77. Jonathan Boucher to John Waring, 9 March 1764, in Van Horne, ed., *Religious Philanthropy and Colonial Slavery*, 255.

78. John Barnett to John Waring, 17 August 1767, in Van Horne, ed., *Religious Philanthropy and Colonial Slavery*, 262.

79. William B. Hart, "Mohawk Schoolmasters and Catechists in Mid-Eighteenth Century Iroquoia: An Experiment in Fostering Literacy and Religious Exchange," in *The Language Encounter in the Americas, 1492–1800*, ed. Edward G. Gray and Norman Fiering (New York: Berghahn Books, 2000), 230–257.

80. Thomas Kidd, "Passing as a Pastor: Clerical Imposture in the Colonial Atlantic World," *Religion and American Culture* 14 No. 2 (Summer 2004): 149–174.

81. A Dissenting Minister in England to a Gentleman in Scotland (unauthored and undated), in Unauthored, *Copy of Three Letters*, 6.

82. Draft of a letter from Benjamin Colman to Governor Shirley, 18 June 1742, in Benjamin Colman Letters, 1728–1745, Massachusetts Historical Society Manuscript Collections.

83. "A Letter From Rev. John Devotion of Saybrook, to the Rev. Dr. Stiles, Inclosing, Mr. Occum's Account of the Montauk Indians," in *Collections of the Massachusetts Historical Society*, First Series, Vol. X (Boston: Munro, Francis, and Parker, 1809), 110.

84. See Linford D. Fisher, *The Indian Great Awakening: Religion and the Shaping of Native Cultures in Early America* (New York: Oxford University Press, 2012).

85. Richard Trevor, *A Sermon Preach'd before the Incorporated Society for the Propagation of the Gospel in Foreign Parts; At Their Anniversary Meeting in the Parish-Church of St. Mary-le-Bow; on Friday February 16, 1749* (London: E. Owen, 1750), 41.

86. John Freebairn, *A Caution Against False Teachers. A Sermon Preached before The Society in Scotland for propagating Christian Knowledge, At their Anniversary Meeting, In the High Church of Edinburgh, On Friday, June 7. 1771.* (Edinburgh: Robert Mundell, 1771).

87. Charles Chauncy, *Seasonable thoughts on the state of religion in New-England, a treatise in five parts. . . .* (Boston: Rogers and Fowle, 1743), 226.

88. Quoted in William S. Simmons and Cheryl L. Simmons, *Old Light on Separate Ways: The Narragansett Diary of Joseph Fish, 1765–1776* (Hanover, NH: University Press of New England, 1982), 39, ff1.
89. For more on Niles, see Fisher, *The Indian Great Awakening,* 113–117.
90. Simmons and Simmons, *Old Light on Separate Ways,* xxiv.
91. Harry S. Stout and Peter Onuf, "James Davenport and the Great Awakening in New London," *The Journal of American History* 70 No. 3 (December 1983): 556–578.
92. John Beach, *A Continuation of the Calm and Dispassionate Vindication of the Professors of the Church of England, Against The Abusive Misrepresentations and fallacious Argumentations of Mr. Noah Hobart, in his second Address to them. Humbly offered to the Consideration of the good People of New-England* (Boston: D. Fowle, 1751), 70.
93. Andrew Eliot to Joseph Fish, 2 January 1765, in Simmons and Simmons, *Old Light on Separate Ways,* 19 ff3.
94. Diary entry for 22 May, 1769, in Simmons and Simmons, *Old Light on Separate Ways,* 59.
95. Diary entry for 4 September 1769, in Simmons and Simmons, *Old Light on Separate Ways,* 60.
96. Joseph Fish to Andrew Oliver, 15 November 1762, in Massachusetts Historical Society Miscellaneous Bound Manuscripts.
97. Robert Clelland to Andrew Oliver, 19 September 1764, Massachusetts Historical Society Miscellaneous Bound Manuscripts.
98. William S. Simmons, "Red Yankees: Narragansett Conversion in the Great Awakening" *American Ethnologist* 10 No. 2 (May 1983): 262–264.
99. Joseph Fish to Joseph Sewall, written after 18 September 1765, in Simmons and Simmons, *Old Light on Separate Ways,* 4–5.
100. Andrew Eliot to Joseph Fish, 2 January 1765, in Simmons and Simmons, *Old Light on Separate Ways,* 11.
101. Diary entry for 8 May 1772, in Ezra Stiles, *The Literary Diary of Ezra Stiles, ed. Under the Authority of the Corporation of Yale University,* Vol. I., ed. Franklin Bowditch Dexter (New York: C. Scribner's Sons, 1901), 233.
102. Diary entry for 8 May 1772, in Stiles, *The Literary Diary of Ezra Stiles,* Vol. I, 232.
103. Joseph Fish to Joseph Sewall, 18 September 1765, in Simmons and Simmons, *Old Light on Separate Ways,* 4–6.
104. Diary entry for 8 May 1772, in Stiles, *The Literary Diary of Ezra Stiles,* Vol. I, 232.
105. Joseph Fish to Joseph Sewall, 18 September 1765, in Simmons and Simmons, *Old Light on Separate Ways,* 5.
106. Quoted in Simmons and Simmons, *Old Light on Separate Ways,* xxvi.
107. Diary entry for 4 September 1769, in Simmons and Simmons, *Old Light on Separate Ways,* 60.
108. Joseph Fish to Andrew Oliver, 15 November 1762, in Massachusetts Historical Society Miscellaneous Bound Manuscripts.

109. Diary entry for 8 November 1773, in Simmons and Simmons, *Old Light on Separate Ways*, 98.

110. James Axtell, *The Invasion Within: The Contest of Cultures in Colonial North America* (New York: Oxford University Press, 1985), 15–16.

111. Diary entry for 5 July 1773, in Simmons and Simmons, *Old Light on Separate Ways*, 93.

112. Diary entry for 8 November 1773, in Simmons and Simmons, *Old Light on Separate Ways*, 98.

113. Quoted in Simmons and Simmons, *Old Light on Separate Ways*, xxvii. Joseph Fish to Nathaniel Whitaker, 30 July 1766, in Simmons and Simmons, *Old Light on Separate Ways*, 29. Andrew Eliot to Joseph Fish, 2 January, 1765, in Simmons and Simmons, *Old Light on Separate Ways*, 11.

114. Andrew Eliot to Joseph Fish, 2 January, 1765, in Simmons and Simmons, *Old Light on Separate Ways*, 11.

115. Joseph Fish to Joseph Sewall, 18 September 1765, in Simmons and Simmons, *Old Light on Separate Ways*, 5.

116. Diary entry for 22 May 1769, in Simmons and Simmons, *Old Light on Separate Ways*, 59.

117. Diary entry for 21 November 1774, in Simmons and Simmons, *Old Light on Separate Ways*, 110.

118. For Woyboy see Joseph Fish to Andrew Oliver, 15 November 1762 in Massachusetts Historical Society Miscellaneous Bound Manuscripts. For Daniel see Joseph Fish, "Accounts of journeys and lectures, 23 October 1771," in Massachusetts Historical Society Miscellaneous Bound Manuscripts, Diary entry for 27 May 1771 in Simmons and Simmons, *Old Light on Separate Ways*, 77, and Joseph Fish to Andrew Oliver, 10 November 1773 in Simmons and Simmons, *Old Light on Separate Ways*, 99. For Shattock see Simmons and Simmons, *Old Light on Separate Ways*, 70 ff. 11 and Joseph Fish and John Shattock, Sr., to Eleazar Wheelock, 30 January 1771 in McCallum, *The Letters of Eleazar Wheelock's Indians*, 214–215. See also Joseph Fish's diary entry for 24 September, 1770 in Simmons and Simmons, *Old Light on Separate Ways*, 67.

119. Charles Chauncy, *All Nations of the Earth blessed in Christ, the Seed of Abraham. A Sermon Preached at Boston, At The Ordination of the Rev. Mr. Joseph Bowman, To The Work of the Gospel-Ministry, More Especially Among the Mohawk-Indians, on the Western Borders of New-England. August 31. 1762* (Boston: John Draper, 1762), 34–35.

120. David Brainerd, *An Abridgment of Mr. David Brainerd's Journal among the Indians. Or, the Rise and Progress of a Remarkable Work of Grace among a Number of the Indians. In the Provinces of New-Jersey and Pensylvania* (London: John Oswald, 1748), 108.

121. Merritt, *At the Crossroads*, 126–127.

122. John Heckewelder, "An Account of the History, Manners, and Customs, of The Indian Nations," 286–295. See also Dowd, *A Spirited Resistance*.

123. Henry Louis Gates, Jr., and William L. Andrews, *Pioneers of the Black Atlantic: Five Slave Narratives From the Enlightenment, 1772–1815* (Washington, D.C. Civitas, 1998), 1–29. Frank Lambert, "'I Saw the Book Talk: Slave Readings on the First Great Awakening,'" *The Journal of Negro History* 77 No. 4 (Autumn 1992): 185–198.

4. A Black among Blacks

1. Philip Quaque to Edward Bass of Newburyport, 31 July 1775, in Philip Quaque, *Letters of the Rev. Philip Quaque of West Africa* (East Ardsley, England: Micro Methods Ltd., 1980–1985), hereafter referred to as *Quaque Letters*. For the best printed edition of Quaque's letters, see Vincent Caretta and Ty M. Reese, *The Life and Letters of Philip Quaque, The First African Anglican Missionary* (Athens: University of Georgia Press, 2010). Edmund Sears Morgan, *American Slavery, American Freedom: The Ordeal of Colonial Virginia* (New York: Norton, 1975).
2. Graham Russell Hodges, *Slavery and Freedom in the Rural North: African Americans in Monmouth County, New Jersey, 1665–1865* (Madison: Madison House, 1997), 68–71.
3. Thomas Thompson, *An Account of Two Missionary Voyages By the Appointment of the Society for the Propagation of the Gospel in Foreign Parts. The One to New Jersey in North America, the Other from America to the Coast of Guiney* (London: Printed for Benj. Dod, at the Bible and Key in Ave-Mary-Lane, near St. Paul's., 1758), 86.
4. David Hume, *The Life of David Hume, Esq. The Philosopher and Historian, Written by Himself. To Which Are Added, The Travels of a Philosopher, Containing Observations on the Manners and Arts of Various Nations, in Africa and Asia* (Philadelphia: Robert Bell, 1778), 19.
5. Isaac Maddox, *A Sermon Preached before the Incorporated Society for the Propagation of the Gospel in Foreign Parts; at the Parish-Church of St. Mary-le-Bow, on Friday the 15th of February, 1733; Being the Day of their Anniversary Meeting* (London: J. Downing, 1734), 25. Maddox was citing William Bosman, *A New and Accurate Description of the Coast of Guinea, Divided into the Gold, the Slave, and the Ivory Coasts. Containing a Geographical, Political and Natural History of the Kingdoms and Countries....* (London: James Knapton and Dan. Midwinter, 1705), 117.
6. Eliga H. Gould, "Zones of Law, Zones of Violence: The Legal Geography of the British Atlantic Circa 1772," *The William and Mary Quarterly* 60 No. 3 (July 2003): 471–510.
7. Maddox, *A Sermon Preached*, 25.
8. *Thompson, An Account of Two Missionary Voyages*, 30–32.
9. Undated letter from Quaque to the SPG, likely in the fall of 1767, and Quaque to the SPG, 7 March 1767, both in *Quaque Letters*.
10. Quaque to the SPG, 17 March 1773, in *Quaque Letters*.

11. Letter from George Whitefield to Robert Keen, 12 November 1766, in Whitefield, *The Works of the Reverend George Whitefield, M.A . . . Containing All his Sermons and Tracts Which Have Been Already Published: With a Select Collection of Letters, Written to His Most Intimate Friends, and Persons of Distinction . . . from the Year 1734, to 1770 . . . Compiled from his Original Papers and Letters 6 vols* (Volume III) (London: Edward and Charles Dilly, 1771), 340.

12. Edmund Keene, *A Sermon Preach'd before the Incorporated Society for the Propagation of the Gospel in Foreign Parts; At Their Anniversary Meeting in the Parish-Church of St. Mary-le-Bow; on Friday February 18, 1757* (London: E. Owen, 1757), 59–60.

13. Bosman, *A New and Accurate Description of the Coast of Guinea,* 104–105.

14. Anthony Benezet, *A Short Account Of that Part of Africa, Inhabited by the Negroes. With Respect to the Fertility of the Country; the good Disposition of many of the Natives, and the Manner by which the Slave Trade is carried on. . . .* (Philadelphia: W. Dunlap, 1762), 15–16.

15. *Thompson, An Account of Two Missionary Voyages,* 56, 72, and 84–85.

16. John K. Thornton, "The Development of an African Catholic Church in the Kingdom of Kongo, 1483–1750," *Journal of African History* 25 No. 2 (April 1984): 147–67.

17. Margaret Priestly, "Philip Quaque of Cape Coast" in *Africa Remembered: Narratives by West Africans from the Era of the Slave Trade,* ed. Philip D. Curtin (Madison: University of Wisconsin Press, 1967), 100, ff. 3. Jon F. Sensbach, *Rebecca's Revival: Creating Black Christianity in the Atlantic World* (Cambridge, MA: Harvard University Press, 2005), 162–171. Jacobus Elisa Joannes Capitein, *The Agony of Asar: A Thesis on Slavery by the Former Slave, Jacobus Elisa Johannes Capitein, 1717–1747* trans. Grant Parker (Princeton: Markus Wiener, 2001). Francis L. Bartels, "Jacobus Eliza Johannes Capitein, 1717–1747," *Transactions of the Historical Society of Ghana* Vol. 4 Part I (1959): 3–13.

18. Travis Glasson, "Missionaries, Methodists, and a Ghost: Philip Quaque in London and Cape Coast, 1756–1816," *Journal of British Studies* 48 No. 1 (January 2009): 35.

19. Quaque to the SPG, 28 September 1766, in *Quaque Letters.*

20. Quaque to the SPG, 6 February 1771, in *Quaque Letters.*

21. Bosman, *A New and Accurate Description of the Coast of Guinea,* 109.

22. Quaque to the SPG, 26 June 1778, in *Quaque Letters.*

23. C. P. Groves, *The Planting of Christianity in Africa: Volume One to 1840* (London: Lutterworth Press, 1948), 176.

24. Quaque to the SPG, 12 June 1780, in *Quaque Letters.*

25. Society for the Propagation of the Gospel in Foreign Parts, *Records of the Society for the Propagation of the Gospel* (East Ardsley, Yorkshire: Micro Methods, 1964), (Hereafter referred to as *SPG Records*), SPG Journal, Volume 22, 165.

26. Quaque to the SPG, 19 March 1774, in *Quaque Letters.*

27. Quaque to the SPG, 7 March 1767, Quaque to the SPG, 6 August 1782, and Quaque to the SPG, 19 August 1771, all in *Quaque Letters.*

28. Quaque to the SPG, 17 January 1778, in *Quaque Letters.* Priestly, "Philip Quaque of Cape Coast,"103.

29. Quaque to the SPG, 28 September 1766, in *Quaque Letters.*

30. Undated letter from Quaque to the SPG, probably written in the fall of 1767, in *Quaque Letters.*

31. Ibid.

32. Ibid.

33. Quaque to the SPG, 12 June 1780, in *Quaque Letters.*

34. Quaque to the SPG, 8 March 1772, in *Quaque Letters.*

35. Quaque to the SPG, 15 April 1769, in *Quaque Letters.*

36. Travis Glasson, *Mastering Christianity: Missionary Anglicanism and Slavery in the Atlantic World* (New York: Oxford University Press, 2012), 181 and 188.

37. Glasson, "Missionaries, Methodists, and a Ghost": 43–46.

38. *SPG Records,* SPG Journal, Volume 18, 266.

39. Quaque to the SPG, 27 September 1770, in Carretta and Reese, eds., *The Life and Letters of Philip Quaque,* 93.

40. Quaque to the SPG, 19 August 1771, in *Quaque Letters.*

41. *SPG Records,* SPG Journal, Volume 18, 266. Quaque to the SPG, 28 September 1766, in *Quaque Letters.*

42. Quaque to the SPG, 5 September 1769, in Carretta and Reese, eds., *The Life and Letters of Philip Quaque,* 84.

43. *SPG Records,* SPG Journal, Volume 18, 337.

44. Quaque to the SPG, 27 September 1770, in *Quaque Letters.*

45. Undated letter from Quaque to the SPG, probably written in the fall of 1767, in *Quaque Letters.*

46. Quaque to the SPG, 5 September 1769, in *Quaque Letters.*

47. Quaque to the SPG, 12 April 1770, in *Quaque Letters.*

48. Quaque to the SPG, 21 July 1792, in *Quaque Letters.*

49. Undated letter from Quaque to the SPG, probably written in the fall of 1767, in *Quaque Letters.*

50. Ibid.

51. Quaque to Samuel Johnson, 26 November 1767 and 5 April 1769, both in Herbert and Carol Schneider, eds., *Samuel Johnson, President of King's College: His Career and Writings* Vol. I (New York: Columbia University Press, 1929), 425–429.

52. Glasson, "Missionaries, Methodists, and a Ghost": 41–50. Glasson, *Mastering Christianity,* 184–190.

53. Thomas Thompson, *The African Trade for Negro Slaves, Shewn to be Consistent With Principles of Humanity, and With the Laws of Revealed Religion* (Canterbury: Simmons and Kirkby, 1772). Capitein, *The Agony of Asar.*

54. Quaque to the SPG, 19 August, 1771, in *Quaque Letters.*

55. Quaque to the SPG, 6 February 1771, in *Quaque Letters.*

56. William Warburton, *A Sermon Preached before the Incorporated Society for the Propagation of the Gospel in Foreign Parts; At Their Anniversary Meeting in the Parish-Church of St. Mary-Le-Bow, on Friday February 21, 1766* (London: E. Owen, 1766), 25–26.

57. Granville Sharp, *An essay on slavery, proving from Scripture its inconsistency with humanity and religion; in answer to a late publication, entitled, "The African trade for Negro slaves shewn to be consistent with principles of humanity, and with the laws of revealed religion"* (Burlington, N.J., 1773), 22–23.

58. Quaque to the SPG, 10 April 1772, in *Quaque Letters.*

59. Quaque to the SPG, 17 March 1773, in *Quaque Letters.*

60. Quaque to the SPG, 11 September 1779, in *Quaque Letters. SPG Records,* SPG Journal, Volume 21, 31.

61. Quaque to the SPG, 15 April 1769, *Quaque Letters.*

62. Thompson, *An Account of Two Missionary Voyages,* 69.

63. *SPG Records,* SPG Journal, Volume 18, 267.

64. Quaque to the SPG, 17 March 1773, in *Quaque Letters.*

65. Ty M. Reese, "'Sheep in the Jaws of So Many Ravenous Wolves': the Slave Trade and Anglican Missionary Activity at Cape Coast Castle, 1752–1816," *Journal of Religion in Africa* 34 No. 3 (September 2004): 348–37. Reese, "Philip Quaque (1741–1816): African Anglican Missionary on the Gold Coast," in *The Human Tradition in the Black Atlantic World* ed. Beatriz G. Mamigonian and Karen Racine (New York: Roman and Littlefield Publishers, 2010).

66. Glasson, *Mastering Christianity,* 193–194.

67. Carretta and Reese, *The Life and Letters of Philip Quaque,* 1.

5. Native Evangelists in the Iroquoian Borderlands

1. Joseph Woodby (Woolley) to Samuel Kirkland, 11 February 1765, in Samuel Kirkland, *The Journals of Samuel Kirkland: 18th-century Missionary to the Iroquois, Government Agent, Father of Hamilton College,* ed. Walter Pilkington (Clinton, NY: Hamilton College, 1980) (hereafter referred to as *Kirkland Journals*), 17. E. B. O'Callaghan, ed., *The Documentary History of the State of New-York* Vol. IV (Albany: Charles Van Benthuysen, 1851), 218.

2. Kirkland to Woolley, 31 March 1765, in Kirkland, *Kirkland Journals,* 18–19. See also Alan Taylor, *The Divided Ground: Indians, Settlers and the Northern Borderland of the American Revolution* (New York: Alfred A. Knopf, 2006), 46–76.

3. Quoted in James Axtell, "Dr. Wheelock's Little Red School," in *Natives and Newcomers: The Cultural Origins of North America* (New York: Oxford University Press, 2001), 180.

4. Colin G. Calloway, *The Scratch of a Pen: 1763 and the Transformation of North America* (New York: Oxford University Press, 2006).

5. Edmund Keene, *A Sermon Preach'd before the Incorporated Society for the Propagation of the Gospel in Foreign Parts; At Their Anniversary Meeting in the Parish-Church of St. Mary-le-Bow; on Friday February 18, 1757* (London: E. Owen, 1757), 48.

6. Quoted in William DeLoss Love, *Samson Occom and the Christian Indians of New England* (Boston: The Pilgrim Press, 1899), 85

7. Eleazar Wheelock, *A Plain and Faithful Narrative of the Original Design, Rise, Progress and Present State of the Indian Charity-School at Lebanon, in Connecticut* (Boston: Richard and Samuel Draper, 1763), 23.

8. John Hume, *A Sermon Preached before the Incorporated Society for the Propagation of the Gospel in Foreign Parts; At Their Anniversary Meeting in the Parish-Church of St. Mary-Le-Bow, on Friday February 19, 1762* (London: E. Owen, 1762), 45. This quote is taken from a Mr. Beach, an Anglican missionary stationed in the colonies.

9. Journal of Samuel Kirkland, 20 June 1774, in Kirkland, *Kirkland Journals,* 94. Charles Chauncy, *All Nations of the Earth blessed in Christ, the Seed of Abraham. A Sermon Preached at Boston, At The Ordination of the Rev. Mr. Joseph Bowman, To The Work of the Gospel-Ministry, More Especially Among the Mohawk-Indians, on the Western Borders of New-England. August 31. 1762* (Boston: John Draper, 1762), 28.

10. Joseph Johnson to Eleazar Wheelock, 2 May 1768, in Johnson, *To Do Good To My Indian Brethren: The Writings of Joseph Johnson, 1751–1776,* ed. Laura J. Murray (Amherst, MA: University of Massachusetts Press, 1998) (hereafter referred to as *To Do Good*), 70–72.

11. Daniel K. Richter, "Iroquois versus Iroquois: Jesuit Missions in Village Politics, 1642–1686," *Ethnohistory* 32 No. 1 (Winter 1985): 1–16.

12. Eleazar Wheelock to Sir William Johnson, June 1761, in David McClure, *Memoirs of the Rev. Eleazar Wheelock, D.D. Founder and President of Dartmouth College and Moor's Charity School; With a Summary History of the College and School: To Which are Added, Copious Extracts from Dr. Wheelock's Correspondence* (Newburyport, M.A.: Edward Little & Co., 1811), 227.

13. Letter from Nathaniel Whitaker to Eleazar Wheelock, 16 July 1765, in Leon Burr Richardson, ed., *An Indian Preacher in England: Being Letters and Diaries Relating to the Mission of the Reverend Samson Occom and the Reverend Nathaniel Whitaker to Collect Funds in England for the Benefit of Eleazar Wheelock's Indian Charity School, From Which Grew Dartmouth College* (Hanover, N.H.: Dartmouth College Publications, 1933), 40. This quote was originally attributed to Nathaniel Ells, a minister in Stonington, Connecticut.

14. Eleazar Wheelock's Address to the Sachems and Chiefs of the Mohawk, Oneida, Tuscarora, and other Nations and tribes of Indians, in Callaghan, ed., *The Documentary History of the State of New-York,* Vol. IV., 224.

15. Eleazar Wheelock, *A Continuation of the Narrative of the State, &c. of the Indian Charity-School, at Lebanon, in Connecticut;: From Nov. 27th,*

1762, to Sept. 3d, 1765 (Boston: Richard and Samuel Draper, 1765), 19. Richardson, *An Indian Preacher in England*, 12.

16. The Society in Scotland for Propagating Christian Knowledge, *Recommendation By The Society in Scotland for propagating Christian Knowledge, In favour of the Academy established by Mr Eleazar Wheelock, of Lebanon, in Connecticut, in New England, For the education of Indian Missionaries* (Edinburgh: s.n., 1767), 2.

17. Henry Barclay to the SPG, 17 November 1742, in Society for the Propagation of the Gospel in Foreign Parts, *Records of the Society for the Propagation of the Gospel* (East Ardsley, Yorkshire: Micro Methods, 1964) (hereafter referred to as *SPG Records*), Letter Series B.

18. Henry Barclay to the SPG, 4 November 1743, in *SPG Records* Letter Series B. John Gilbert, *A Sermon Preached before the Incorporated Society for the Propagation of the Gospel in Foreign Parts; At Their Anniversary Meeting In the Parish-Church of St. Mary-le-Bow; On Friday February 17, 1743–44* (London: J. and H. Pemberton, 1744), 46. See also William B. Hart, "Mohawk Schoolmasters and Catechists in Mid-Eighteenth Century Iroquoia: An Experiment in Fostering Literacy and Religious Exchange," in *The Language Encounter in the Americas, 1492–1800*, ed. Edward G. Gray and Norman Fiering (New York: Berghahn Books, 2000), 230–257.

19. Henry Barclay to the SPG, 4 June 1744, in *SPG Records* Letter Series B.

20. Henry Barclay to the SPG, 12 March 1745, in *SPG Records*, Letter Series B.

21. Thomas Hayter, *A Sermon Preached before the Incorporated Society for the Propagation of the Gospel in Foreign Parts; At Their Anniversary Meeting in the Parish-Church of St. Mary-Le-Bow, on Friday February 21, 1755* (London: Edward Owen, 1755), 49.

22. John Ogilvie to the SPG, 27 July 1750, quoted in John Wolfe Lydekker, *The Faithful Mohawks* (New York: The MacMillan Company, 1938), 67.

23. "A Letter from Rev. Jonathan Edwards, to Hon. Thomas Hubbard, Esq. of Boston, Relating to the Indian School at Stockbridge." 31 August 1751, in *Collections of the Massachusetts Historical Society*, First Series, Vol. X (Boston: Massachusetts Historical Society, 1809), 143–151.

24. SPG Journal from 27 December 1755, quoted in Lydekker, *The Faithful Mohawks*, 83.

25. John Ogilvie to the SPG, 27 July 1750, quoted in Lydekker, *The Faithful Mohakws*, 68–69.

26. Keene, *A Sermon Preach'd*, 47 and Robert Hay Drummond, *A Sermon Preached before the Incorporated Society for the Propagation of the Gospel in Foreign Parts; At Their Anniversary Meeting In the Parish-Church of St. Mary-le-Bow; on Friday February 15, 1754* (London: E. Owen, 1754), 54.

27. "Memoir of the Rev. John Stuart, D.D. The Last Missionary to the Mohawks," in O'Callaghan, ed., *The Documentary History of the State of New-York*, 314. Church of England, *The Morning and Evening Prayer*.

The Litany, and Church Catechism. . . . (Boston: Richard and Samuel Draper, 1763).

28. Eric Hinderaker, *The Two Hendricks: Unraveling a Mohawk Mystery* (Cambridge, MA: Harvard University Press, 2010), 266 and 280–281. Daniel Claus, *A Primer for the Use of the Mohawk Children: to Acquire the Spelling and Reading of Their Own, As Well As to Get Acquainted With the English Tongue; Which for That Purpose Is Put on the Opposite Page* (London: Printed by C. Buckton, 1786).

29. Colin G. Calloway, *The American Revolution in Indian Country: Crisis and Diversity in Native American Communities* (New York: Cambridge University Press, 1995), 9–10 and 108–128.

30. "A Letter from Rev. Jonathan Edwards to Hon. Thomas Hubbard, Esq. of Boston, Relating to the Indian School at Stockbridge," 31 August 1751, in *Collections of the Massachusetts Historical Society*, First Series, Vol. X (Boston: Massachusetts Historical Society, 1809), 146. Love, *Samson Occom and the Christian Indians of New England*, 83 ff. 4.

31. Gideon Hawley to Andrew Oliver, 20 May 1761, in Gideon Hawley Letters, 1754–1807, in Mss. Collections of the Massachusetts Historical Society (typescript version).

32. Gideon Hawley to Eleazar Wheelock, 26 November 1761, in Gratz Collection, Chaplains of the French and Indian War and the Revolution, Case 8, Box 26, Mss Collections of the Historical Society of Pennsylvania.

33. Gideon Hawley to Andrew Oliver, 20 May 1761, in Gideon Hawley Letters, 1754–1807, in Mss. Collections of the Massachusetts Historical Society (typescript version).

34. Quoted in Calloway, *The American Revolution in Indian Country*, 114.

35. Gideon Hawley to Andrew Oliver, 10 October 1765, in Gideon Hawley Letters, 1754–1807, in Mss. Collections of the Massachusetts Historical Society (typescript version). See also Joseph T. Glatthaar and James Kirby Martin, *Forgotten Allies: The Oneida Indians and the American Revolution* (New York: Hill and Wang, 2006), 26–75.

36. Quoted in Glatthaar and Martin, *Forgotten Allies*, 52.

37. Journal of Ralph Wheelock for 27 Sunday March 1768, in Eleazar Wheelock, *A Continuation of the Narrative of the Indian Charity-School, in Lebanon in Connecticut, New England : Founded and Carried on by The Rev. Dr. Eleazar Wheelock ; With an Appendix, Containing the Declaration of the Trustees of That Charity; A List of the Names of the Subscribers; An Account of Monies Received and Paid; Together with Dr. Wheelock's Annual Account of his Receipts and Disbursements* (London: J. and W. Oliver, 1769), 48.

38. Journal of Samuel Kirkland for 28 March 1765, in Kirkland, *Kirkland Journals*, 3.

39. Gideon Hawley to Eleazar Wheelock, 26 November 1761, in Gratz Collection, Chaplains of the French and Indian War and the Revolution, Case 8, Box 26, Mss Collections of the Historical Society of Pennsylvania.

40. Extracts from a letter from Samuel Kirkland, 12 April 1768, in Wheelock, *A Continuation of the Narrative of the Indian Charity-School,* 56–59.
41. Glatthaar and Kirby Martin, *Forgotten Allies,* 7–99, especially 18 and 36. Calloway, *The American Revolution in Indian Country,* 12 and 124. Quotes are from Francis W. Halsey, ed., *A Tour of Four Great Rivers: The Hudson, Mohawk, Susquehanna, and Delaware in 1769, Being the Journal of Richard Smith of Burlington, New Jersey* (New York: Charles Scribner's Sons, 1906), 68 and Journal of Samuel Kirkland, 31 March 1765, in Kirkland, *Kirkland Journals,* 18.
42. David Fowler to Eleazar Wheelock, 24 June 1765, in Whitaker, *A Brief Narrative of the Indian Charity-School,* 40.
43. Quoted in Taylor, *The Divided Ground,* 53–56.
44. Isaac Dakayenensere and Adam Waonwanoron to Eleazar Wheelock, 31 July 1765, in James Dow McCallum, *The Letters of Eleazar Wheelock's Indians* (Hanover, NH: Dartmouth College Publications, 1932) (hereafter referred to as *Indian Letters*), 79–80.
45. Eleazar Wheelock to Gideon Hawley, 10 June 1761, in McCallum, *Indian Letters,* 35–36. "Recommendation of Samuel Ashpo, 29 July 1762," in McCallum, *Indian Letters,* 37–38. Hart, "Mohawk Schoolmasters and Catechists in Mid-Eighteenth Century Iroquoia": 246.
46. Quoted in Taylor, *The Divided Ground,* 55.
47. Hart, "Mohawk Schoolmasters and Catechists in Mid-Eighteenth Century Iroquoia": 233–246.
48. Johnson, *To Do Good,* 13.
49. Extracts from the letters of Samuel Kirkland, in Wheelock, *A Continuation of the Narrative of the Indian Charity-School,* 37–38.
50. Journal of Samuel Kirkland, 28 October 1769, in Kirkland, *Kirkland Journals,* 58. Glatthaar and Martin, *Forgotten Allies,* 63–65.
51. Joseph Woolley to Eleazar Wheelock, 17 September 1765, in McCallum, *Indian Letters,* 270–271.
52. List of David Fowler's Books, in McCallum, *Indian Letters,* 93.
53. Extracts of a Letter from Titus Smith, 3 August 1765, from Nathaniel Whitaker, A Brief Narrative of the Indian Charity-School in Lebanon in Connecticut, New England: Founded and Carried on by That faithful Servant of God, The Rev. Mr. Eleazar Wheelock (London: J. and W. Oliver, 1766), 45. See Margaret Szasz, Indian Education in the American Colonies, 1607–1783 (Albuquerque: University of New Mexico Press, 1988), 233–257.
54. David Fowler to Eleazar Wheelock, 29 May 1765, in McCallum, *Indian Letters,* 90–91.
55. Hezekiah Calvin to Eleazar Wheelock, 11 August 1766, in McCallum, *Indian Letters,* 49–51.
56. David Fowler to Eleazar Wheelock, 15 June 1765, in McCallum, *Indian Letters,* 93–95.
57. Hezekiah Calvin to Eleazar Wheelock, 11 August 1766, in McCallum, *Indian Letters,* 51.

58. Joseph Johnson to Eleazar Wheelock, 10 November 1767, in Johnson, *To Do Good*, 63–65.

59. Samson Occom to Eleazar Wheelock, 19 July 1762, in The American Colonial Clergy Section of the Gratz Collection, Case 8, Box 24, Mss. Collections of the Historical Society of Pennsylvania.

60. Joseph Johnson to Eleazar Wheelock, 2 May 1768, in Johnson, *To Do Good*, 70–72. Glatthaar and Martin, *Forgotten Allies*, 22–23.

61. Address to the Sachems and Chiefs of the Mohawk, Oneida, Tuscarora, and other Nations and tribes of Indians," 29 April 1765, in O'Callaghan, ed., *The Documentary History of the State of New-York* Vol. IV, 224–225.

62. David Fowler to Eleazar Wheelock, 15 and 24 June 1765 McCallum, *Indian Letters*, 94–96.

63. Journal of Samuel Kirkland, 31 March 1765, in Kirkland, *Kirkland Journals*, 19.

64. Extracts of Letters from David Fowler, 24 June 1765, in Whitaker, *A Brief Narrative of the Indian Charity-School*, 40.

65. Hezekiah Calvin to Eleazar Wheelock, 14 August 1767, in McCallum, *Indian Letters*, 58.

66. David Brainerd, *Mirabilia Dei inter Indicos, or the Rise and Progress Of a Remarkable Work of Grace Amongst a Number of the Indians In the Provinces of New-Jersey and Pennsylvania, Justly Represented in A Journal Kept by Order of the Honourable Society (in Scotland) for Propagating Christian Knowledge. With some General Remarks* (Philadelphia: William Bradford, 1746), 228.

67. Whitaker, *A Brief Narrative of the Indian Charity-School*, 7.

68. Jacob Woolley to Eleazar Wheelock, 14 December 1761, in McCallum, *Indian Letters*, 251.

69. Samson Occom, *A Sermon, Preached at the Execution of Moses Paul, an Indian; Who Was Executed at New-Haven, on the Second of September, 1772; For the Murder of Mr. Moses Cook, Late of Waterbury, on the 7th of December, 1771. Preached at the Desire of Said Paul. By Samson Occom, Minister of the Gospel, and Missionary to the Indians* (New Haven: T. and S. Green, 1772), 3.

70. New York State, *Journals of the Military Expedition of Major General John Sullivan Against the Six Nations of Indians in 1779: With Records of Centennial Celebrations* (New York: Knapp, Peck and Thomson, Printers, 1887), 459.

71. Wheelock, *A Plain and Faithful Narrative*, 39.

72. David Fowler to Eleazar Wheelock, 29 May 1765, in McCallum, *Indian Letters*, 91

73. David Fowler to Eleazar Wheelock, 21 January 1766 and 13 May 1766, in McCallum, *Indian Letters*, 100–102.

74. Lydekker, *The Faithful Mohawks*, 81. George R. Hamell, "The Iroquois and the World's Rim: Speculations on Color, Culture, and Contact," *American Indian Quarterly* 6 No. 4 (Autumn 1992): 464 ff. 7.

75. Quoted in Glatthaar and Martin, *Forgotten Allies*, 62.

76. Gideon Hawley to Eleazar Wheelock, 26 November 1761, in Chaplains of the French and Indian War and the Revolution, Gratz Collection, Case 8, Box 26, Mss. Collections of the Historical Society of Pennsylvania.

77. Joseph Johnson to Moses Paul, 29 March 1772, in Johnson, *Letter from J——h J——n, one of the Mohegan Tribe of Indians, to his Countryman, Moses Paul, under Sentence of Death, in New-Haven Goal* (New London: Timothy Green, 1772), 2–7.

78. Samuel Kirkland to Eleazar Wheelock, 9 September 1767, in Wheelock, *A Continuation of the Narrative of the Indian Charity-School*, 24–25.

79. Quoted in Johnson, *To Do Good*, 62.

80. Samuel Ashpo to Eleazar Wheelock, 22 August 1766, in McCallum, *Indian Letters*, 45. "An Account of Certain Exhortations," November 1771, Ibid., 142

81. Quoted in Richter, "Some of Them . . . Would Always Have a Minister With Them": 480.

82. "A Letter From Rev. John Devotion of Saybrook, to the Rev. Dr. Stiles, Inclosing, Mr. Occum's Account of the Montauk Indians," in *Collections of the Massachusetts Historical Society*, First Series, Vol. X (Boston: Massachusetts Historical Society, 1809), 108. Journal of Samuel Kirkland, 9 October 1773, in Kirkland, *Kirkland Journals*, 80–81. James Axtell, *The Invasion Within: The Contest of Cultures in Colonial North America* (New York, Oxford University Press, 1985), 168.

83. Charles Beatty, *The Journal of a Two Months Tour: With a View of Promoting Religion Among the Frontier Inhabitants of Pennsylvania, and of Introducing Christianity Among the Indians to the Westward of the Alegh-geny. . . .* (London: William Davenhill, 1768), 54. See also Richard Cullen Rath, *How Early America Sounded* (Ithaca: Cornell University Press, 2003), 30–38 and 151–165.

84. John Heckewelder, "An Account of the History, Manners, and Customs, of The Indian Nations, Who Once Inhabited Pennsylvania and the Neighbouring States," in *Transactions of the Historical & Literary Committee of the American Philosophical Society, Held at Philadelphia, For Promoting Useful Knowledge* Vol. I (Philadelphia: Abraham Small, 1819), 203.

85. "An Account of the Missionaries and Schoolmasters Employed Among the Remote Nations of Indians," in Whitaker, *A Brief Narrative of the Indian Charity-School*, 30.

86. Jacob Fowler to Eleazar Wheelock, 28 November 1766, in McCallum, *Indian Letters*, 117.

87. Joseph Johnson to Eleazar Wheelock, 10 February 1768, in Johnson, *To Do Good*, 66–68.

88. Samson Occom, *A Choice Collection of Hymns and Spiritual Songs: Intended for the Edification of Sincere Christians, of All Denominations* (New London: Timothy Green, 1774), 3. Joanna Brooks, "Six Hymns by Samson Occom," *Early American Literature* 38 No. 1 (2003): 67–87.

89. Papers of John Witherspoon, 1758–1783, Box 1, page 48, Mss. Collections

of the Library of Congress. Call Number MMC-2604 and Control Number: MM81046185.

90. Quoted in Glatthaar and Martin, *Forgotten Allies*, 68.

91. David Fowler's Confession, 20 November 1764, in McCallum, *Indian Letters*, 87. David Fowler to Eleazar Wheelock, 2 December 1766, in Ibid., 106.

92. Hezekiah Calvin to Eleazar Wheelock, 14 August 1767, in McCallum, *Indian Letters*, 57.

93. Extract of a Letter from Joseph Woolley, July 1765, in Whitaker, *A Brief Narrative of the Indian Charity-School*, 41.

94. Joseph Johnson to Eleazar Wheelock, 10 November 1767, in Johnson, *To Do Good*, 63–65. Samson Occom to Eleazar Wheelock, 10 February 1767, in Richardson, ed., *An Indian Preacher in England*, 221–222. Samson Occom to Eleazar Wheelock, 24 July 1771, in Occom, *The Collected Writings of Samson Occom, Mohegan: Leadership and Literature in Eighteenth-Century Native America*, ed. Joanna Brooks (New York: Oxford University Press, 2006), 98–100.

95. David Fowler to Eleazar Wheelock, 2 December 1766, in McCallum, *Indian Letters*, 106.

96. Jacob Fowler to Eleazar Wheelock, 31 January 1767, in McCallum, *Indian Letters*, 117.

97. Jacob Woolley's Confession, 25 July 1763, in McCallum, *Indian Letters*, 254.

98. Eleazar Wheelock, *A Continuation of the Narrative of the Indian Charity-School, in Lebanon, in Connecticut; From the Year 1768, to the Incorporation of it with Dartmouth-College, And Removal and Settlement of it in Hanover, In the Province of New-Hampshire, 1771* (Hartford: Ebenezer Watson, 1771), 22. Taylor, *The Divided Ground*, 49. Eleazar Wheelock to Lord Dartmouth, 22 December 1768, in McClure, *Memoirs of the Rev. Eleazar Wheelock, D.D.*, 282. Eleazar Wheelock to the Warkmans Sisters, 17 August 1768, in Ibid., 279. Whitaker, *A Brief Narrative of the Indian Charity-School* (1767), 53.

99. Eleazar Wheelock to the Earl of Dartmouth, 8 October 1767, from Ralph Wheelock's Journal for 13 September 1767, in Wheelock, *A Continuation of the Narrative of the Indian Charity-School* (1769), 32. Samuel Johnson to Eleazar Wheelock, 27 October 1766, in Ibid., 7.

100. Samson Occom to Eleazar Wheelock, 19 July 1762, in Case 8, Box 24 of the Gratz Collection (American Colonial Clergy) at the Historical Society of Pennsylvania.

101. Joseph Woolley to Eleazar Wheelock, 6 July 1765, in McCallum, *Indian Letters*, 267.

102. Hezekiah Calvin to Eleazar Wheelock, 11 August 1766, in McCallum, *Indian Letters*, 49–51.

103. David McClure to Eleazar Wheelock, 25 September 1765, in McCallum, *Indian Letters*, 76–77. Joseph Johnson to Eleazar Wheelock, 20 April 1768, in Johnson, *To Do Good*, 68–69.

104. Joseph Johnson to Eleazar Wheelock, 29 December 1767, in McCallum, *Indian Letters,* 65–66. David Fowler to Eleazar Wheelock, 24 June 1765, in McCallum, *Indian Letters,* 97.

105. Joseph Woolley to Eleazar Wheelock, 6 July 1765, in McCallum, *Indian Letters,* 268.

106. Laura M. Stevens, *The Poor Indians: British Missionaries, Native Americans, and Colonial Sensibility* (Philadelphia: University of Pennsylvania Press, 2004).

107. David Fowler to Eleazar Wheelock, 24 June 1765, in McCallum, *The Letters of Eleazar Wheelock,* 96. David Fowler to Eleazar Wheelock, 21 January 1766, in McCallum, *The Letters of Eleazar Wheelock,* 99.

108. Joseph Woolley to Eleazar Wheelock, July 1765, in Whitaker, *A Brief Narrative of the Indian Charity-School* (1766), 41.

109. Occom, *A Sermon Preached at the Execution of Moses Paul, an Indian,* 4 and 10.

110. Journal of Samson Occom, 14 June 1761, in Love, *Samson Occom and the Christian Indians of New England,* 87–88.

111. Eleazar Wheelock to George Whitefield, 25 November 1761, in Love, *Samson Occom and the Christian Indians of New England,* 92–94. Gideon Hawley to Eleazar Wheelock, 19 September 1761, in Gratz Collection, Case 8, Box 22, Mss. Collections of the Historical Society of Pennsylvania.

112. Lament for Joseph Woolley, 29 December 1765, in McCallum, *Indian Letters,* 272–273.

113. David Fowler to Eleazar Wheelock, 21 January 1766, in McCallum, *Indian Letters,* 100.

114. Suspension of Samuel Ashpo by the Connecticut Board of Correspondents, 1 July 1767, in McCallum, *Indian Letters,* 45–46. Gideon Hawley to Eleazar Wheelock, 26 November 1761, in Chaplains of the French and Indian War and the Revolution, Gratz Collection, Case 8, Box 22, Mss. Collections of the Historical Society of Pennsylvania.

115. Hezekiah Calvin to Eleazar Wheelock, 11 August 1766 and March 1768, in McCallum, *Indian Letters,* 49–51 and 62–63. Samuel Johnson to Eleazar Wheelock, 12 February 1767, in McCallum, *Indian Letters,* 52.

116. Samuel Kirkland to Eleazar Wheelock, 29 December 1768, in Johnson, *To Do Good,* 77–78.

117. Joseph Johnson to Eleazar Wheelock, 28 December 1768, in Johnson, *To Do Good,* 74–77.

118. Ibid.

119. Samuel Kirkland to Eleazar Wheelock, 29 December 1768, in Johnson, *To Do Good,* 77–78.

120. Quoted in Axtell, *The Invasion Within,* 209.

121. Quoted in Taylor, *The Divided Ground,* 59.

122. Samuel Kirkland to Eleazar Wheelock, 29 December 1768, in Johnson, *To Do Good,* 77–78.

123. David Fowler to Eleazar Wheelock, 17 March 1767, in McCallum, *Indian Letters,* 108–109.

124. Joseph Johnson to Eleazar Wheelock, 29 December 1767, in McCallum, *Indian Letters,* 65–66.

125. Samson Occom to Eleazar Wheelock, 12 May 1762, in Occom, *The Collected Writings of Samson Occom, Mohegan,* 69. Samson Occom to Eleazar Wheelock, 9 November 1762, in American Colonial Clergy, Gratz Collection, Case 8, Box 24, Mss. Collections of the Historical Society of Pennsylvania.

126. Calloway, *The American Revolution in Indian Country,* 117.

127. David Fowler to Eleazar Wheelock, 26 February 1767, in McCallum, *Indian Letters,* 107–108.

128. Eleazar Wheelock to George Whitefield, 24 April 1769, in Richardson, ed., *An Indian Preacher in England,* 353.

129. Wheelock, *A Continuation of the Narrative of the Indian Charity-School, in Lebanon, in Connecticut,* 22. See Axtell, *The Invasion Within,* 204–217. Axtell, *Natives and Newcomers,* 183–188. Axtell, "Dr. Wheelock's Little Red School," 174–188.

6. Afro-Christian Evangelism and Indian Missions

1. Diary entry for 22 November 1774 in Ezra Stiles, *The Literary Diary of Ezra Stiles, D.D., LL.D., President of Yale College,* ed. Franklin Dexter Bowditch, Vol. I (New York: Charles Scribners's Sons, 1901), 486.

2. Joseph A. Conforti, *Samuel Hopkins and the New Divinity movement: Calvinism, the Congregational Ministry, and Reform in New England Between the Great Awakenings* (Grand Rapids: Christian University Press, 1981), 142–158. James T. Campbell, *Middle Passages: African American Journeys to Africa, 1787–2005* (New York: The Penguin Press, 2006), 21–22.

3. Ezra Stiles, *To the Public* (Newport, RI: Solomon Southwick, 1776), 1. Samuel Hopkins, "A Narrative of the rise & progress of a proposal and attempt to send the gospel to guinea, by educating, and sending two negroes there to attempt to christianize their brethren," 22 March 1784, Mss. in the Gratz Collection (Eminent Clergymen), Case 8, Box 23 at the Historical Society of Pennsylvania.

4. Jay Coughtry, *The Notorious Triangle: Rhode Island and the African Slave Trade, 1700–1807* (Philadelphia: Temple University Press, 1981). Elaine Forman Crane, *A Dependent People: Newport, Rhode Island, in the Revolutionary Era* (New York: Fordham University Press, 1985), 76–83. Edward E. Andrews, "'Creatures of Mimic and Imitation': Black Elections, The Liberty Tree, and the Politicization of African Religious Space in Revolutionary Newport, Rhode Island" *Radical History Review* 99 (Fall 2007): 121–139.

5. Philip Quaque to the Society for Propagating the Gospel in Foreign Parts, 19 March 1774, in Philip Quaque, *Letters of the Rev. Philip Quaque of*

West Africa (East Ardsley, England: Micro Methods Ltd., 1980–1985) (hereafter referred to as *Quaque Letters*).

6. John K. Thornton, *Africa and Africans in the Making of the Atlantic World, 1400–1800* (New York: Cambridge University Press, 1998), 235–271.

7. Sylvia R. Frey and Betty Wood, *Come Shouting to Zion: African American Protestantism in the American South and British Caribbean to 1830* (Chapel Hill: University of North Carolina Press, 1998), 1–62. Albert J. Raboteau, *Slave Religion: The "Invisible Institution" in the Antebellum South* (New York: Oxford University Press, 2004), 4–92.

8. Diary entry for 13 April 1773, in Stiles, *The Literary Diary of Ezra Stiles,* Vol. I, 366. Peter H. Wood, *Black Majority: Negroes in Colonial South Carolina From 1670 Through the Stono Rebellion* (New York: W.W. Norton & Company, 1996), 181–186.

9. Diary entry for 13 April 1773, in Stiles, *The Literary Diary of Ezra Stiles,* Vol. I, 366.

10. Diary entry for 26 January 1772 in Stiles, *The Literary Diary of Ezra Stiles,* Vol. I, 207. Diary entry for 16 June 1776 in Ibid., Vol. II, 16. Diary entry for 3 October 1779 in Ibid., Vol. II, 376.

11. Charles E. Hambrick-Stowe, "The Spiritual Pilgrimage of Sarah Osborn (1714–1796)," *Church History* 61 No. 4. (December 1992): 408–421. Mary Beth Norton, "My Resting Reaping Times": Sarah Osborn's Defense of Her "Unfeminine" Activities, 1767," *Signs* 2 No. 2 (Winter 1976): 515–529.

12. Sarah Osborn to Joseph Fish, 21 April 1765, Sarah Osborn, *Letters, 1743–1770; 1779,* Box O, Folder 6, in Manuscript Collection at the American Antiquarian Society.

13. Sarah Osborn to Joseph Fish, 28 February–7 March, 1767, in Norton, "My Resting Reaping Times": 519–523.

14. Samuel Hopkins, Memoirs of the Life of Mrs. Sarah Osborn: Who Died at Newport, Rhode Island, on the Second Day of August, 1796, in the Eighty Third Year of Her Age (Catskill, N.Y.: N. Elliott, 1814), 76.

15. Sarah Osborn to Joseph Fish, 28 February–7 March, 1767, in Norton, "My Resting Reaping Times": 524.

16. Norton, "My Resting Reaping Times": 515–529. Barbara E. Lacey, "The Bonds of Friendship: Sarah Osborn of Newport and the Reverend Joseph Fish of Stonington, 1743–1779" *Rhode Island History* 45 No. 4 (November 1986): 127–136.

17. Diary entry for 12 October 1773 in Stiles, *The Literary Diary of Ezra Stiles,* Vol. I, 415.

18. Stiles, *To the Public,* 1. Hopkins, "A Narrative of the rise & progress," 2.

19. Vincent Carretta, *Equiano, The African: Biography of a Self-Made Man* (Athens: University of Georgia Press, 2005).

20. James Albert Ukawsaw Gronniosaw, "A Narrative of the Most Remarkable Particulars in the Life of James Albert Ukawsaw Gronniosaw, an African Prince, as Related by Himself," in Gates, Jr. and Andrews, eds., *Pioneers of the Black Atlantic,* 59.

21. Phillis Wheatley to Arbour Tanner, 19 May 1772, in John C. Shields, ed., *The Collected Works of Phillis Wheatley* (New York: Oxford University Press, 1988), 164.

22. Phillis Wheatley, *Poems on Various Subjects, Religious and Moral* (London: Printed for A. Bell, bookseller, Aldgate; and sold by Messrs. Cox and Berry, King-Street, Boston, 1773), 18.

23. Phillis Wheatley to Samuel Hopkins, 9 February 1774, in Wheatley, *The Collected Works of Phillis Wheatley,* 175–176. Stiles, *To the Public,* 5.

24. Samuel Hopkins, *A Dialogue, Concerning the Slavery of the Africans: Shewing it to be the Duty and Interest of the American Colonies to Emancipate All Their African Slaves: With an Address to the Owners of Such Slaves: Dedicated to the Honorable Continental Congress* (Norwich, C.T.: Judah P. Spooner, 1776), 13.

25. Samuel Hopkins, "Sermon Before the Providence Society for Abolishing the Slave Trade, &C., 1793" in Hopkins, *The Works of Samuel Hopkins, D.D., First Pastor of the Church in Great Barrington, Mass., Afterwards Pastor of the First Congregational Church in Newport, R.I.: With a Memoir of His Life and Character* Vol. I (Boston: Doctrinal Tract and Book Society, 1854), 144.

26. Thomas Wilson, *An Essay Towards An Instruction For The Indians; Explaining the most Essential Doctrines of Christianity. Which may be of Use To such Christians . . . Together with Directions and Prayers for The Heathen World, Missionaries, Catechumens, Private Persons, Families, of Parents, for their Children, for Sundays, &c.* (London: J. Osborn, 1740), xix.

27. Stiles, *To the Public,* 3. Hopkins, *Memoirs of the Life of Sarah Osborn,* 79.

28. Hopkins, *A Dialogue, Concerning the Slavery of the Africans.* Samuel Hopkins, *A Discourse Upon the Slave-Trade, and the Slavery of the Africans. Delivered in the Baptist Meeting-House At Providence, Before the Providence Society for Abolishing the Slave-Trade, &c. At Their Annual Meeting, on May 17, 1793. By Samuel Hopkins, D.D. Pastor of First Congregational Church in Newport, and Member of Said Society* (Providence: J. Carter, 1793). Joseph A. Conforti, "Samuel Hopkins and the New Divinity: Theology, Ethics, and Social Reform in Eighteenth-Century New England," *The William and Mary Quarterly* 34 No. 4 (October 1977): 572–589. David S. Lovejoy, "Samuel Hopkins: Religion, Slavery, and the Revolution," *The New England Quarterly* 40 No. 2 (June 1967): 227–243.

29. Crane, *A Dependent People,* 16–33. Samuel Hopkins to the Pennsylvania Abolition Society, 7 January 1789, in the Pennsylvania Abolition Society Papers, Microfilm Reel 11, Historical Society of Pennsylvania.

30. John Quamine to Moses Brown, 5 June 1776, in Mack Thompson, *Moses Brown, Reluctant Reformer* (Chapel Hill: University of North Carolina Press, 1962), 105 (the original text was at the Rhode Island Historical Society in the Moses Brown Papers, Volume II, 59).

31. Stiles, *To the Public,* 2.
32. Diary entry for 13 April 1773, in Stiles, *The Literary Diary of Ezra Stiles,* Vol. I, 366.
33. Hopkins, "A Narrative of the rise & progress," 2.
34. Stiles, *The Literary Diary of Ezra Stiles,* Vol. I, 32. First Congregational Church Marriages Baptisms, 1744–1825, Mss at the Newport Historical Society.
35. Stiles, *To the Public,* 6.
36. Philip Quaque to Samuel Hopkins, 30 September 1773, in Gratz Autograph Collection, Historical Society of Pennsylvania.
37. Philip Quaque to the SPG, 19 March 1774, in *Quaque Letters.*
38. Stiles, *To the Public,* 1. Hopkins, "A Narrative of the Rise & Progress," 1.
39. Stiles, *To the Public,* 1. Hopkins, "A Narrative of the rise & progress," 1.
40. Hopkins, "A Narrative of the rise & progress," 1.
41. Diary entry for 13 April 1773, in Stiles, *The Literary Diary of Ezra Stiles,* Vol. I, 366.
42. Edward M. Griffin, *Old Brick: Charles Chauncy of Boston, 1705–1787* (Minneapolis: University of Minnesota Press, 1980).
43. Charles Chauncy to Ezra Stiles, 1 October 1773, in Gratz Collection, Case 8, Box 21, at the Historical Society of Pennsylvania.
44. George Gibbs Channing, *Early Recollections of Newport, R.I., from the year 1793 to 1811.* (Newport: A. J. Ward, C. E. Hammet, Jr.; Boston, Mass., Nichols and Noyes, 1868), 88.
45. Charles Chauncy to Ezra Stiles, 14 November 1769 and 20 December 1769, in Ezra Stiles, *Extracts From the Itineraries and Other Miscellanies of Ezra Stiles, D.D., LL.D., 1755–1794 : With a Selection From His Correspondence,* ed. Franklin Bowditch Dexter (New Haven: Yale University Press, 1916), 450.
46. Chauncy Whittelsey to Ezra Stiles, 26 February 1770, in Stiles, *Letters and Papers of Ezra Stiles President of Yale College 1778–1795* ed. Isabel M. Calder (New Haven: Yale University Library, 1933), 25.
47. Charles Chauncy to Ezra Stiles, 1 October 1773, in Gratz Collection, Case 8, Box 21, at the Historical Society of Pennsylvania.
48. Ezra Stiles to Charles Chauncy, 8 December 1773, in Ezra Stiles, *The Papers of Ezra Stiles at Yale University* (New Haven: Yale University Press, 1976), Microfilm Reel 3.
49. Philip Quaque to Samuel Hopkins, 30 September 1773, in Gratz Autograph Collection (Philip Quaque) at the Historical Society of Pennsylvania. Philip Quaque to Samuel Hopkins, 19 May 1773, in Gratz Collection (American Clergy), Case 9, Box 16, at the Historical Society of Pennsylvania.
50. Philip Quaque to the SPG, 19 March 1774, in *Quaque Letters.*
51. Ibid.
52. Philip Quaque to Samuel Hopkins, 19 May 1773, in Gratz Collection (American Clergy), Case 9, Box 16, at the Historical Society of Pennsylvania.

53. Vincent Carretta and Philip Gould, eds., *Genius in Bondage: Literature of the Early Black Atlantic* (Lexington: University Press of Kentucky, 2001). Walt Nott, "From 'Uncultivated Barbarian' to 'Poetical Genius': The Public Presence of Phillis Wheatley," *MELUS* 18 No. 3 (Autumn 1993): 21–32.

54. Samson Occom to Susanna Wheatley, 5 March 1771, in Samson Occom, *The Collected Writings of Samson Occom, Mohegan: Leadership and Literature in Eighteenth-Century Native America,* Joanna Brooks, ed. (New York: Oxford University Press, 2006), 97.

55. Phillis Wheatley to John Thornton, 30 October 1774, in Kenneth Silverman, "Four New Letters by Phillis Wheatley," *Early American Literature* 8 No. 3 (Winter 1974): 267–268.

56. John Witherspoon, "A Description of the State of New-Jersey" in Witherspoon, *The Miscellaneous Works of the Rev. John Witherspoon, D.D. L.L.D. Late President of the College of New-Jersey* (Philadelphia: William W. Woodward, 1803), 312.

57. Thomas Bray, *Missionalia: Or, A Collection of Missionary Pieces Relating to the Conversion of the Heathen; Both the African Negroes and American Indians* (London: W. Roberts, 1727), 13 and 56.

58. Phillis Wheatley to John Thornton, 29 March 1774, in Kenneth Silverman, "Four New Letters by Phillis Wheatley," *Early American Literature,* 8 No. 3 (Winter, 1974), 266.

59. Phillis Wheatley to John Thornton, 1 December 1773, in Silverman, "Four New Letters by Phillis Wheatley": 265. Silverman, "Four New Letters by Phillis Wheatley": 259.

60. John Marrant, *A Narrative of the Lord's Wonderful Dealings with John Marrant, a Black (Now Going to Preach the Gospel in Nova-Scotia) Born in New-York, in North-America* (London: Gilbert and Plummer, 1785), 28–31. John Marrant, "A Journal of the Rev. John Marrant, from August the 18th, 1785, to the 16th of March, 1790," in Joanna Brooks and John Saillant, eds., *"Face Zion Forward": First Writers of the Black Atlantic, 1785–1798* (Boston: Northeastern University Press, 2002), 161–176.

61. Olaudah Equiano, *The Interesting Narrative of the Life of Olaudah Equiano, or Gustavus Vassa, the African. Written by Himself* (Norwich: n.a., 1794), 275. Thomas Wilson, *The Knowledge and Practice of Christianity Made Easy to the Meanest Capacities: or, an Essay Towards an Instruction for the Indians: . . . Together with Directions and Prayers* (London: J. Osborn, 1741). Lawrence Harlow, *The Conversion of an Indian, in a Letter to a Friend* (London: n.a., 1778).

62. Olaudah Equiano, *The Interesting Narrative of the Life of Olaudah Equiano, or Gustavus Vassa, The African, Written By Himself* (New York: W. Durell, 1791), 304. Carretta, *Equiano, The African,* 180–199.

63. Samuel Hopkins, *Sketches of the Life of the Late Rev. Samuel Hopkins, D.D., Pastor of the First Congregational Church in Newport, Written by Himself, Interspersed with Marginal Notes Extracted From His Private*

Diary; to Which is Added, a Dialogue, by the Same Hand, on the Nature and Extend of the Christian Submission; Also, a Serious Address to Professing Christians, Closed by Dr. Hart's Sermon at his Funeral (Hartford: Stephen West, 1805), 53–54.

64. Samuel Hopkins, *Historical memoirs, relating to the Housatunnuk Indians, or, An account of the methods used, and pains taken, for the propagation of the gospel among that heathenish-tribe, and the success thereof, under the ministry of the late Reverend Mr. John Sergeant....* (Boston: S. Kneeland, 1753).

65. Gideon Hawley to Andrew Oliver, 20 May 1761, in Gideon Hawley Letters, 1754–1807, Typescript Version, Manuscript Collections of the Massachusetts Historical Society.

66. Justus Forward to Ezra Stiles, 24 January 1792, in Stiles, *Letters and Papers of Ezra Stiles*, 111.

67. Edmund S. Morgan, *The Gentle Puritan, A Life of Ezra Stiles, 1727–1795* (New Haven and London: Yale University Press, 1962), 136–139.

68. Ezra Stiles, "An Account of Indian Churches in New-England, in a Letter Written A.D. 1673, by Rev. John Eliot, of Roxbury. Copied Under President Stiles's Inspection from the Original MS. Letter in Mr. Eliot's Own Hand Writing, in the Library of the Mathers at Boston," in *Collections of the Massachusetts Historical Society*, First Series, Vol. X (Boston: Munro, Francis, and Parker, 1809). "Account of an Indian Visitation, A.D. 1698. Copied for Dr. Stiles, By Rev. Mr. Hawley, Missionary at Mashpee, From the Printed Account Published in 1698," in *Collections of the Massachusetts Historical Society*, First Series, Vol. X.

69. Stiles, *Extracts From the Itineraries and Other Miscellanies of Ezra Stiles*, 302. Stiles, "An Account of the Potenummecut Indians. Taken by Dr. Stiles, On the Spot, June 4, 1762," in *Collections of the Massachusetts Historical Society*, First Series, Vol. X. Gideon Hawley to Ezra Stiles, 22 January 1771 in Stiles, *Extracts From the Itineraries and Other Miscellanies of Ezra Stiles*, 499.

70. Benjamin Church, *The entertaining history of King Philip's war, which began in the month of June, 1675. As also of expeditions more lately made against the common enemy, and Indian rebels, in the eastern parts of New-England: with some account of the divine providence towards Col. Benjamin Church: by Thomas Church, esq. his son* (Newport: Solomon Southwick, 1772).

71. "A Letter From Rev. John Devotion of Saybrook, to the Rev. Dr. Stiles, Inclosing, Mr. Occum's Account of the Montauk Indians," in *Collections of the Massachusetts Historical Society*, First Series, Vol. X. Eleazar Wheelock to Ezra Stiles, August 1771, in Stiles, *Letters & Papers of Ezra Stiles*. David McClure to Ezra Stiles, 11 November 1771, in Stiles, *Letters and Papers of Ezra Stiles*, 36–37. Elam Potter to Ezra Stiles, 12 September 1768, in Stiles, *Extracts From the Itineraries and Other Miscellanies of Ezra Stiles*, 552–553. Ezra Stiles, Manuscript Map of Connecticut, 25 June 1767 at the Massachusetts Historical Society.

72. Diary entry for 8 May 1772, in Stiles, *The Literary Diary of Ezra Stiles*, Vol. I, 233.

73. Ezra Stiles to John Rodgers, 25 April 1774, in Stiles, *The Papers of Ezra Stiles at Yale University*, Microfilm Reel 3.

74. Quoted in Francis Parsons, *Six Men of Yale* (Freeport, New York: Books for Libraries Press, 1939), 46.

75. Ezra Stiles to Charles Chauncy, 8 December 1773, in Stiles, *The Literary Diary of Ezra Stiles*, Vol. I, 364. Campbell, *Middle Passages*, 18.

76. Ezra Stiles to Noah Welles, 26 August 1769, in Stiles, *The Literary Diary of Ezra Stiles*, Vol. I, 20–21.

77. Ezra Stiles to John Hubbard, 26 August 1769, quoted in Morgan, *The Gentle Puritan*, 207. Ezra Stiles, *A Discourse on Saving Knowledge: Delivered at the Instalment of the Reverend Samuel Hopkins, A.M. Into the Pastoral Charge of the First Congregational Church in Newport, Rhode-Island, Wednesday, April 11, 1770* (Newport: Solomon Southwick, 1770).

78. John Sergeant to Ezra Stiles, 16 September 1773, in Stiles, *The Papers of Ezra Stiles at Yale University*, Microfilm Reel 3.

79. John Witherspoon to Samuel Hopkins, 14 December 1773, in "Signers of the Declaration of Independence Bound Manuscript Collection," Volume 2, at The Morgan Library and Museum, New York.

80. Ezra Stiles to John Sergeant, 15 July 1774, in *The Papers of Ezra Stiles at Yale University*, Microfilm Reel 3. Stiles, *To the Public*. Hopkins, "A Narrative of the rise & progress."

81. Minutes of the General Meetings of the Scottish Society for Propagating Christian Knowledge, 22 November 1753, Records of the SSPCK in Edinburgh, RG GD95/1/4. 1 January 1736–15 November 1759. See especially the minutes for 23 March 1749, 22 March 1750, and 22 November 1753.

82. Stiles, *To the Public*, 4.

83. Elihu Spencer to Eleazar Wheelock, 9 December 1772, in Gratz Collection (American Colonial Clergy), Case 8, Box 24, at the Historical Society of Pennsylvania.

84. Ezra Stiles to Eleazar Wheelock, 4 November 1767, in Stiles, *The Papers of Ezra Stiles at Yale University*, Microfilm Reel 2.

85. Diary entry for 12 October 1773, in Stiles, *The Literary Diary of Ezra Stiles*, Vol. I, 415.

86. Ruth L. Woodward and Wesley Frank Craven, *Princetonians, 1784–1790: A Biographical Dictionary* (Princeton: Princeton University Press, 1991), l.

87. Eleazar Wheelock, *A Plain and Faithful Narrative of the Original Design, Rise, Progress and Present State of the Indian Charity-School at Lebanon, in Connecticut* (Boston: Richard and Samuel Draper, 1763), 23.

88. Hopkins, "A Narrative of the rise & progress of a proposal," 3. The Society in Scotland for Propagating Christian Knowledge, *An Account of The Society in Scotland for propagating Christian Knowledge. From its commencement, in 1709. In which is included, The present state of the*

Highlands and Islands of Scotland with regard to Religion (Edinburgh: A. Murray and J. Cochrane, 1774), 18–19.

89. Diary entry for 21 March 1778, in Stiles, *The Literary Diary of Ezra Stiles,* Vol. II, 265.

90. Diary entry for 24 May 1779, in Stiles, *The Literary Diary of Ezra Stiles,* Vol. II, 338.

91. Diary entry for 8 April 1773, in Stiles, *The Literary Diary of Ezra Stiles,* Vol. I, 364.

92. Stiles, *To the Public,* 2.

93. Samuel Hopkins to Levi Hart, 7 February 1774, in Hopkins, *The Works of Samuel Hopkins,* 132.

94. John Maclean, *History of the College of New Jersey Vols. I and II* (New York: Arno Press and the New York Times, 1969), Vol. I, 372.

95. John Witherspoon, *Address to the Inhabitants of Jamaica, And Other West-India Islands, In Behalf of the College of New-Jersey* (Philadelphia: William and Thomas Bradford, 1772), 23 and 11.

96. Quoted in Maclean, *History of the College of New Jersey,* Vol. I, footnote to page 233.

97. John Witherspoon, *The absolute Necessity of Salvation through Christ, A Sermon, Preached Before the Society in Scotland for propagating Christian Knowledge, In the High Church of Edinburgh, On Monday, January 2. 1758. To which is subjoined, A short Account of the present State of the Society* (Edinburgh: W. Miller, 1758), 41.

98. Ezra Stiles to Charles Chauncy, November 1768, quoted in L. H. Butterfield, ed., *John Witherspoon Comes to America: A Documentary Account Based Largely on New Materials* (Princeton: Princeton University Press, 1953), 82. Diary entry for 24 June 1773, in Stiles, *The Literary Diary of Ezra Stiles,* Vol. I, 390.

99. Francis Alison to Ezra Stiles, 1 August 1769, in Stiles, *Extracts From the Itineraries and Other Miscellanies of Ezra Stiles,* 435.

100. Charles Chauncy, *All Nations of the Earth blessed in Christ, the Seed of Abraham. A Sermon Preached at Boston, At The Ordination of the Rev. Mr. Joseph Bowman, To The Work of the Gospel-Ministry, More Especially Among the Mohawk-Indians, on the Western Borders of New-England. August 31, 1762* (Boston: John Draper, 1762), 26.

101. Ezra Stiles to Eleazar Wheelock, 26 January 1768, in Stiles, *The Papers of Ezra Stiles at Yale University,* Microfilm Reel 2. David Cranz, *The history of Greenland: containing a description of the country, and its inhabitants: . . . By David Crantz. Translated from the High-Dutch, . . . In two volumes* (London: Printed for the Brethren's Society for the Furtherance of the Gospel among the Heathen: and sold by J. Dodsley; T. Becket and P. A. de Hondt; and T. Cadell, successor to A. Millar; W. Sandby; S. Bladon; E. and C. Dilly; and at all the Brethren's chapels, 1767).

102. Witherspoon, *Address to the Inhabitants of Jamaica,* 15–18.

103. John Witherspoon, *A Sermon on the Religious Education of Children. Preached in the Old Presbyterian Church in New-York, to a Very*

Numerous Audience, on the Evening of the Second Sabbath in May (Elizabethtown: Shepard Kollock, 1789), 10.

104. Woodward and Craven., *Princetonians*, l. Stiles, *To the Public*, 5.

105. John Erskine to Ezra Stiles, 15 June 1789, in Stiles, *Letters & Papers of Ezra Stiles*, 106.

106. Ezra Stiles to Charles Chauncy, 8 December 1773, in *The Papers of Ezra Stiles at Yale University*, Microfilm Reel 3.

107. Woodward and Craven, *Princetonians*, li.

108. Hopkins, "A Narrative of the rise & progress," 1–2.

Conclusion

1. David J. Silverman, *Red Brethren: The Brothertown and Stockbridge Indians and the Problem of Race in Early America* (Ithaca, NY: Cornell, University Press, 2010). Brad D. E. Jarvis, *The Brothertown Nation of Indians: Land Ownership and Nationalism in Early America, 1740–1840* (Lincoln: University of Nebraska Press, 2010).

2. Journal entries for 30 September 1785 (in Journal 11) and 18 October 1785 (in Journal 12) in Samson Occom, *The Collected Writings of Samson Occom, Mohegan: Leadership and Literature in Eighteenth-Century Native America*, ed. Joanna Brooks (New York: Oxford University Press, 2006), 300 and 305. Linford Fisher correctly notes that most Algonquian Indians decided to stay put in New England. See Linford D. Fisher, *The Indian Great Awakening: Religion and the Shaping of Native Cultures in Early America* (New York: Oxford University Press, 2012).

3. Richard Allen, *The Life, Experience, and Gospel Labours of the Rt. Rev. Richard Allen. To Which is Annexed The Rise and Progress of the African Methodist Episcopal Church in the United States in America. Containing a Narrative of the Yellow Fever in the Year of Our Lord 1793: With an Address to the People of Colour in the United States. Written by Himself, and Published by His Request* (Philadelphia: Martin & Boden, Printers, 1833), 16–17

4. Absalom Jones, *A Thanksgiving Sermon, Preached January 1, 1808, in St. Thomas's, or the African Episcopal Church, Philadelphia: On Account of The Abolition of the African Slave trade. On That Day, by the Congress of the United States* (Philadelphia: Fry and Kammerer, 1808). For later iterations of the Exodus narrative in black rhetoric, see Eddie S. Glaude, *Exodus! Religion, Race, and Nation in Early Nineteenth-Century Black America* (Chicago: University of Chicago Press, 2000).

5. Albert J. Raboteau, *Slave Religion: The "Invisible Institution" in the Antebellum South* (New York: Oxford University Press, 2004), 131. Sylvia R. Frey and Betty Wood, *Come Shouting to Zion: African American Protestantism in the American South and British Caribbean to 1830* (Chapel Hill: University of North Carolina Press, 1998). Albert J. Raboteau, "The Slave Church in the Era of the American Revolution," in *Slavery and Freedom in the Age of the American Revolution*, ed. Ira Berlin

and Ronald Hoffman (Charlottesville: University Press of Virginia, 1983), 193–213. Mechal Sobel, *Trabelin' On: The Slave Journey to an Afro-Baptist Faith* (Westport, CT: Greenwood Press, 1979). Michael Angelo Gomez, *Exchanging Our Country Marks: The Transformation of African Identities in the Colonial and Antebellum South* (Chapel Hill: University of North Carolina Press, 1998), 244–290.

6. Cassandra Pybus, *Epic Journeys of Freedom: Runaway Slaves of the American Revolution and Their Global Quest for Liberty* (Boston: Beacon Press, 2006). James St. G. Walker, *The Black Loyalists: The Search for a Promised Land in Nova Scotia and Sierra Leone, 1783–1870* (New York: Africana Pub. Co., 1976).

7. James Sidbury, *Becoming African in America: Race and Nation in the Early Black Atlantic* (New York: Oxford University Press, 2007), 95. Pybus, *Epic Journeys of Freedom,* 146–150.

8. Journal of Paul Cuffee for 1 December and 2 December 1811, in Sheldon H. Harris, *Paul Cuffe: Black America and the African Return* (New York: Simon and Schuster, 1972), 114–115.

9. Thomas Thurlow, *A Sermon Preached before the Incorporated Society for the Propagation of the Gospel in Foreign Parts; At Their Anniversary Meeting in the Parish-Church of St. Mary-Le-Bow, on Friday February 17, 1786* (London: T. Harrison and S. Brooke, 1786), 23.

Note on Sources

The evidentiary basis for *Native Apostles* is the trail of publications, missionary accounts, letters, sermons, and other sources that white, black, and Indian evangelical figures throughout the early modern British Atlantic world left behind. There is a surprisingly large body of sources written by native preachers themselves. Philip Quaque, the African Anglican missionary at the Cape Coast, wrote nearly 200 pages of letters over fifty years, and the Algonquian Indians who conducted missionary trips to Iroquoia composed dozens of letters, sermons, diary entries, and other sources that offer a window into their world. Letters between white missionaries, such as Gideon Hawley, Ezra Stiles, Eleazar Wheelock, Samuel Kirkland, John Eliot, and others, form another foundation. These can be found in a range of forms, including in the manuscript collections of archives or historical societies, copied onto microfilm, or published in edited collections. There are also popular missionary accounts from well known projects, including the famous Eliot tracts, Eleazar Wheelock's narrative of missionary work, and annual sermons printed by the Society for the Propagation of the Gospel in Foreign Parts. These published sources, along with missionary histories, sermons, and printed solicitations for funding, are invaluable for exploring the transatlantic debates about the role that blacks and Indians played in Christian missionary work. These three sets of sources—writings by native preachers, letters and correspondence by white participants in native missionary work, and published accounts—provide a range of views on native missionaries, from the private to the public, from the views of those funding the missions to those native preachers conducting them.

The following collection of secondary sources is in no way intended to be exhaustive, but rather representative of the scholarly problems that *Native Apostles* addresses. This book is most concerned with the intersections between religion, race, and colonialism in early America and the Atlantic world. Some of the most significant works that have addressed these issues are David J.

Silverman, *Faith and Boundaries: Colonists, Christianity, and Community Among the Wampanoag Indians of Martha's Vineyard, 1600–1871* (New York: Cambridge University Press, 2005), Linford D. Fisher, *The Indian Great Awakening: Religion and the Shaping of Native Cultures in Early America* (New York: Oxford University Press, 2012), Travis Glasson, *Mastering Christianity: Missionary Anglicanism and Slavery in the Atlantic World* (New York: Oxford University Press, 2012), Carla Gardina Pestana, *Protestant Empire: Religion and the Making of the British Atlantic World* (Philadelphia: University of Pennsylvania Press, 2011), Joel W. Martin and Mark A. Nicholas, eds., *Native Americans, Christianity and the Reshaping of the American Religious Landscape* (Chapel Hill: University of North Carolina Press, 2010), and Erik R. Seeman, *Death in the New World: Cross-Cultural Encounters, 1492–1800* (Philadelphia: University of Pennsylvania Press, 2010).

John Eliot's mission to the New England Indians in the seventeenth century has generated an incredibly rich corpus of works on seventeenth century New England Indians and their encounter with Christian evangelists. The scholarly literature on the Eliot missions is overwhelming, but a good starting point is Richard W. Cogley, *John Eliot's Mission to the Indians before King Philip's War* (Cambridge, MA: Harvard University Press, 1999). See also James Axtell's *The Invasion Within: The Contest of Cultures in Colonial North America* (New York: Oxford University Press, 1985). Two helpful, but somewhat outdated, bibliographies can be found in James P. Ronda and James Axtell, eds., *Indian Missions: A Critical Bibliography* (Bloomington: Indiana University Press, 1978) and Michael P. Clark, ed, *The Eliot Tracts: With Letters from John Eliot to Thomas Thorowgood and Richard Baxter* (Westport, CT: Praeger Publishers, 2003), 46–52. See also Neal Salisbury, "Red Puritans: The "Praying Indians" of Massachusetts Bay and John Eliot," *The William and Mary Quarterly* 31 No. 1 (January 1974): 27–54, Kenneth Morrison, "That Art of Coyning Christians": John Eliot and the Praying Indians of Massachusetts, *Ethnohistory* 21 No. 1 (Winter 1974): 77–92, Francis Jennings, *The Invasion of America: Indians, Colonialism, and the Cant of Conquest* (Chapel Hill: University of North Carolina Press, 1975), 228–281, James P. Ronda, "We Are Well As We Are: An Indian Critique of Seventeenth-Century Christian Missions," *The William and Mary Quarterly* 34 No. 1 (January 1977), 66–82, Elise M. Brenner, "To Pray or to Be Prey: That is the Question. Strategies for Cultural Autonomy of Massachusetts Praying Town Indians," *Ethnohistory* 27 No. 2 (Spring 1980): 135–152, Harold W. Van Lonkhuyzen, "A Reappraisal of the Praying Indians: Acculturation, Conversion, and Identity at Natick, Massachusetts, 1646–1730," *The New England Quarterly* 63 No. 3 (September 1990), 396–428, Constance Post, "Old World Order in the New: John Eliot and the "Praying Indians" in Cotton Mather's *Magnalia Christi Americana*," *The New England Quarterly* 46 No. 3 (September 1993): 416–433, and Joshua David Bellin, "John Eliot's Playing Indian," *Early American Literature* 42 No. 1 (January 2007): 1–31.

Recent studies by literary scholars have interrogated how English evangelical enterprises derived their sense of mission and identity from its encounter with

Indians. See Laura M. Stevens, *The Poor Indians: British Missionaries, Native Americans, and Colonial Sensibility* (Philadelphia: University of Pennsylvania Press, 2004), Kristina Bross, *Dry Bones and Indian Sermons: Praying Indians and Colonial American Identity* (Ithaca, NY: Cornell University Press, 2004), and Pestana, *Protestant Empire* (cited above).

The last few years have also witnessed an explosion in interest in Moravians, and some of the most fruitful works are Jon F. Sensbach, *A Separate Canaan: The Making of an Afro-Moravian World in North Carolina, 1763–1840* (Chapel Hill: University of North Carolina Press, 1998), Sensbach, *Rebecca's Revival: Creating Black Christianity in the Atlantic World* (Cambridge, MA: Harvard University Press, 2005), Rachel M. Wheeler, *To Live Upon Hope: Mohicans and Missionaries in the Eighteenth-Century Northeast* (Ithaca: Cornell University Press, 2008), Jane T. Merritt, "Dreaming of the Savior's Blood: Moravians and the Indian Great Awakening in Pennsylvania," *The William and Mary Quarterly* 54 No. 4 (October 1997): 723–746, Aaron Spencer Fogleman, *Jesus is Female: Moravians and the Challenge of Radical Religion in Early America* (Philadelphia: University of Pennsylvania Press, 2007), Michele Gillespie and Robert Beachy, eds., *Pious Pursuits: German Moravians in the Atlantic World* (New York: Berghahn Books, 2007), and Katherine Carté Engel, *Religion and Profit: Moravians in Early America* (Philadelphia: University of Pennsylvania Press, 2009).

Classic studies on Afro-Christianity have helped provide the intellectual foundations for our understanding of black religion. The most noteworthy examples are Albert J. Raboteau, *Slave Religion: The "Invisible Institution" in the Antebellum South* (New York: Oxford University Press, 2004), Sylvia R. Frey and Betty Wood, *Come Shouting to Zion: African American Protestantism in the American South and British Caribbean to 1830* (Chapel Hill: University of North Carolina Press, 1998), Mechal Sobel, *Trabelin' On: The Slave Journey to an Afro-Baptist Faith* (Westport, CT: Greenwood Press, 1979), Michael Angelo Gomez, *Exchanging Our Country Marks: The Transformation of African Identities in the Colonial and Antebellum South* (Chapel Hill: University of North Carolina Press, 1998), John K. Thornton, *Africa and Africans in the Making of the Atlantic World, 1400–1800* (New York: Cambridge University Press, 1998), and Thornton, "On the Trail of Voodoo: African Christianity in Africa and the Americas," *The Americas* 44 No. 3 (January 1988): 261–278.

For historical and literary analyses of the Algonquian Indians who went to Iroquoia, see William DeLoss Love, *Samson Occom and the Christian Indians of New England* (Boston: The Pilgrim Press, 1899), Margaret Szasz, *Indian Education in the American Colonies, 1607–1783* (Albuquerque: University of New Mexico Press, 1988), Szasz, "Samson Occom: Mohegan as Spiritual Intermediary," in *Between Indian and White Worlds: The Cultural Broker,* ed. Margaret Connel Szasz (Norman: University of Oklahoma Press, 1994), Laura J. Warner, "What Did Christianity Do for Joseph Johnson? A Mohegan Preacher and His Community," in *Possible Pasts: Becoming Colonial in Early America,* Robert Blair St. George (Ithaca: Cornell University Press, 2000), 160–180, Joseph Johnson, *To Do Good to My Indian Brethren: The Writings of Joseph*

Johnson, 1751–1776, ed. Laura J. Murray (Amherst, MA: University of Massachusetts Press, 1998), and Joanna Brooks, *American Lazarus: Religion and the Rise of African-American and Native American Literatures* (New York: Oxford University Press, 2003). For an excellent work on early native literacy, see Hilary E. Wyss, *Writing Indians: Literacy, Christianity, and Native Community in Early America* (Amherst: University of Massachusetts Press, 2000).

Philip Quaque has received more attention in the last few decades. The best examinations of Philip Quaque are Travis Glasson, "Missionaries, Methodists, and a Ghost: Philip Quaque in London and Cape Coast, 1756–1816," *Journal of British Studies* 48 No. 1 (January 2009): 29–50, Ty M. Reese, "'Sheep in the Jaws of So Many Ravenous Wolves': the Slave Trade and Anglican Missionary Activity at Cape Coast Castle, 1752–1816," *Journal of Religion in Africa* 34 No. 3 (September 2004): 348–372, and Margaret Priestly, "Philip Quaque of Cape Coast" in *Africa Remembered: Narratives by West Africans from the Era of the Slave Trade,* ed. Philip D. Curtin (Madison: University of Wisconsin Press, 1967). Glasson also devotes a chapter to Quaque in *Mastering Christianity* (cited above). Fortunately, Quaque's letters have recently been edited and published. See Vincent Carretta and Ty M. Reese, eds., *The Life and Letters of Philip Quaque, the First African Anglican Missionary* (Athens: University of Georgia Press, 2010).

Historians of later nineteenth century missions have produced a much larger body of influential and provocative work that explores the connections between empire, indigenous peoples, and religions. See Andrew Porter, *Religion versus Empire? British Protestant missionaries and overseas expansion, 1700–1914* (Manchester: University of Manchester Press, 2004), Norman Etherington, ed., *Missions and Empire* (The Oxford History of the British Empire) (Oxford: Oxford University Press, 2005), Jeffrey Cox, *The British Missionary Enterprise Since 1700* (New York: Routledge, 2008), Terrence Ranger, "Christianity and Indigenous Peoples: A Personal Overview." *The Journal of Religious History* 27 No. 3 (October 2003): 255–271, Lamin O. Sanneh, *Translating the Message: The Missionary Impact on Culture* (Maryknoll, NY: Orbis Books, 1989), Sanneh, *Whose Religion is Christianity: The Gospel Beyond the West* (Grand Rapids, MI: Wm. B. Eerdmans Publishing Co., 2003), Peggy Brock, *Indigenous Peoples and Religious Change* (Boston: Brill, 2005), Brock, "Two Indigenous Evangelists: Moses Tjalkabota and Arthur Wellington Clah," *The Journal of Religious History* 27 No. 3 (October 2003): 348–366, Elizabeth Elbourne, *Blood Ground: Colonialism, Missions, and the Contest for Christianity in the Cape Colony and Britain, 1799–1853* (Montreal: McGill University Press, 2002), J. D. Y. Peel, *Religious Encounter and the Making of the Yoruba* (Bloomington, IN: Indiana University Press, 2000), and Isabel Hofmeyr, *The Portable Bunyan: A Transnational History of The Pilgrim's Progress* (Princeton, NJ: Princeton University Press, 2004).

Acknowledgments

I was assisted in the colossal task of researching and writing *Native Apostles* by a multitude of individuals and institutions. I would first like to thank the Department of History at the University of New Hampshire, which granted me a two-year Atlantic History Fellowship as well as exceptional institutional support while I was beginning this project. I would also like to thank the Graduate School at the University of New Hampshire, which offered me two Summer Fellowships to jump-start this project. I want to offer sincere gratitude to the institutions which offered research fellowships that supported this project, including the American Antiquarian Society, American Philosophical Society, Boston Athenaeum, John Carter Brown Library, Library Company of Philadelphia, and the Massachusetts Historical Society. The facilities, staff, and hospitality at all of these institutions were truly extraordinary, and this book could not have been completed without the assistance of the wonderful staff and resources there. I also want to thank the interlibrary loan and microfilm reading room staff at the University of New Hampshire's Dimond Library, as well as the staff at the Newport Historical Society; the Historical Society of Pennsylvania; the Rhode Island Historical Society; the Moravian Archives in Bethlehem, Pennsylvania and Herrnhut, Germany; the Yale University Art Gallery; the Public Records Office of the Commonwealth of Massachusetts; the Hood Art Museum at Dartmouth College; and the Morgan Library in New York City. In all of these places the staff has offered priceless assistance by helping me locate sources, incorporate images for the book, and pursue fruitful research leads. Finally, I'd like to thank Providence College—Margaret Manchester and the Office of Academic Affairs in particular—for supporting my scholarship and creating an ideal environment in which to teach and pursue that scholarship.

Many individuals offered generous feedback on my work, and I would like to first express my appreciation to Eliga Gould, who guided this project during its inception and helped me see what was important about it even when I was uncertain myself. Lige has been an invaluable mentor, a careful editor, and a caring friend. Erik Seeman and an anonymous reviewer for Harvard University Press offered priceless feedback on how to sharpen the argument, add nuance, and make the book more useful for its intended audience. Erik also read and provided wonderfully insightful comments on previous iterations of my work. For comments and suggestions at different stages of the process, I thank Funso Afolayan, Bob Allison, James Allegro, Jeff Bolster, Vin Carretta, Paul Erickson, Lin Fisher, William Fowler, Jr., Travis Glasson, James Green, John Grigg, Shona Johnston, Margaretta Lovell, Dan Richter, Kyle Roberts, David Silverman, Caroline Sloat, Joshua Stein, Jennifer Thorn, Cynthia Van Zandt, Ted Widmer, Conrad Wright, and Karin Wulf. These individuals have demonstrated the importance of academic collegiality for a young scholar, and their varied expertise and interests in the project have helped me refine it in countless ways. At Harvard University Press, I want to thank Jeannette Estruth, Brian Distelberg, and especially Joyce Seltzer. Her support, critiques, and editorial suggestions have not only made this a better book, but have also made me a better scholar. I also thank Catherine Watterson and Rose Marie Kuebbing, who offered invaluable editorial feedback.

I was fortunate to present parts of my work at several conferences and seminars, including The Omohundro Institute for Early American History and Culture, The McNeil Center for Early American Studies, The American Society for Eighteenth Century Studies, The Roger Williams University Conference on Church-State Relations, The American Society for Ethnohistory, and The Colonial Society of Massachusetts. I thank everyone who commented on my work for their questions and suggestions. I also want to thank *The Journal of Church and State* for offering me a venue through which I could explore some of my ideas on Philip Quaque.

I offer my deepest gratitude to my family, including Paula and Beth Von Euw. Mom, Chris, Regina, and Isabelle, you have been an inspiration and crutch for me during the most trying of times. Will Andrews, who was born about five hours before I received the contract for this book, provided unconditional love and powerful inspiration, especially as the manuscript was being completed. Finally, I dedicate this to Mary, my wife and best friend, who means everything to me.

Index

DATE DUE